REPAIRING
and
UPGRADING
YOUR PC

**Robert Bruce Thompson
and Barbara Fritchman Thompson**

BEIJING · CAMBRIDGE · FARNHAM · KÖLN · PARIS · SEBASTOPOL · TAIPEI · TOKYO

Repairing and Upgrading Your PC

by Robert Bruce Thompson and Barbara Fritchman Thompson

Published by O'Reilly Media, Inc., 1005 Gravenstein Highway North, Sebastopol, CA 95472.

O'Reilly books may be purchased for educational, business, or sales promotional use. Online editions are also available for most titles (*safari.oreilly.com*). For more information, contact our corporate/institutional sales department: 800-998-9938 or *corporate@oreilly.com*.

Print History:

February 2006:   First Edition.

Editor:	Brian Jepson
Production Editor:	Darren Kelly
Cover Designer:	Marcia Friedman
Interior Designers:	David Futato and Melanie Wang

The O'Reilly logo is a registered trademark of O'Reilly Media, Inc. The *Projects* series designations, *Repairing and Upgrading Your PC*, and related trade dress are trademarks of O'Reilly Media, Inc.

Many of the designations used by manufacturers and sellers to distinguish their products are claimed as trademarks. Where those designations appear in this book, and O'Reilly Media, Inc. was aware of a trademark claim, the designations have been printed in caps or initial caps.

RepKover™ This book uses RepKover™, a durable and flexible lay-flat binding.

0-596-00866-X

[F]

To our parents, who taught us to love books.

✳

Contents

Foreword

Why do books have foreword sections?

I suppose one reason is to associate the foreword writer's name with the book in the hopes that it will increase sales. That's not likely in this case. The last time I did a foreword for one of Bob and Barbara Thompson's books (*Building The Perfect PC*), O'Reilly had not one word about my foreword on the front or back cover, and since the book has deservedly sold very well indeed it obviously didn't need my help. Besides, if you know who I am you probably know who Bob Thompson is, since I tend to rely on him for hardware advice. A lot.

Another reason for a foreword is to add one last dab of persuasion if you have the book in your hands and you're wondering if you should buy it. But that can't be right either. You're an intelligent person, and you already know I endorse the book and think you should buy it, or I wouldn't be in here.

Well, enough on that. This is, unsurprisingly, an endorsement, and yes, if you're thinking of upgrading your old (or even your almost new) computer, investing in this book before you start is a very good idea. Not only will the Thompsons tell you how to do just about anything a sane person would want to do to upgrade his computer, but they will tell you whether or not you ought to bother.

A few years ago I would have told you not to bother at all. For not a lot more than the cost of upgrading your old system, you could build a new one and network to the old. That's still good advice, sometimes, depending on the computers involved, and even more on what you intend to do with the machine(s). For example, if what you want is a screaming games machine, don't even think of upgrading unless you have a very late model system and you're just tweaking. If you want a screaming games machine and you don't have a pretty good one now, it's cheaper to start over. Cheaper is a relative term: if you insist on the very latest for a screaming games machine, there won't be anything cheap about it. In any event, for that you'll need Thompson's other book, *Building The Perfect PC*.

Even then, though, you may want this one. If you get a new machine and network to the old one, you may decide that disk drives are faster than tape, and the right way to backup your system is to have a big box of drives and back up to that. This book will tell you how to do enough upgrade to your old machine to make it an excellent backup system host.

And if you don't want a screaming games (or CAD) machine and you're not doing hydrodynamics simulations or something else that eats computing cycles, chances are that you have all the machine you need, and upgrading will be worth your effort. You can add USB 2.0, FireWire, Serial ATA disk drives, and a passel of other new features, and no one including you will even know you have an upgrade rather than a new machine.

This book will tell you all of that, and a lot more. It will tell you if you should upgrade, and if so, what to, depending on what you want the machine to do; and once you decide what you want to do, it will tell you how to do it. If this is not your first Thompson book, you already know that it's written in clear English, understandable, written by someone who never went to that school that teaches how to prove you've explained something even though no one has understood one word you said. Graduation from that school seems to be a requirement for employment in writing Microsoft HELP files, but the Thompsons never attended it. If this is your first Thompson book, you're in for a pleasant surprise, particularly if what you're used to is graduates of that school.

If you need this book, you need it badly; and if you're contemplating upgrading, or deciding whether to upgrade or buy a new computer, you definitely need it.

—Jerry Pournelle
Chaos Manor
Hollywood, 2005

Preface

We live in a throw-away society. Disposable this, recyclable that—few consumer products nowadays are designed to be fixable, let alone upgradable. PCs are an exception, although you wouldn't know it from reading the mainstream media. While we were writing this book, we were flabbergasted to read an article in a respected publication that seriously suggested the best cure for a spyware-infested PC was to throw it out and buy a new one!

The article did have a valid point, though. Paying someone to disinfect a spyware-laden system can easily cost hundreds of dollars. Similarly, one of our readers was quoted a price of more than $200 to replace a failed power supply in a two-year-old system. The problem, of course, is that parts are cheap but skilled labor is expensive. In most parts of the country, PC technician time is billed at $60 to $100 per hour. At that rate, it doesn't take long for the bill to add up to the cost of a new PC. Fortunately, you can bypass those high labor costs by doing the work yourself, and you needn't have special equipment or be a computer wizard to do it. If you can change the oil in your car or hook up a DVD player, you can repair or upgrade your own PC.

You won't be alone, either. If you visit a local big-box store, you'll find aisle upon aisle of PC components—motherboards, processors, drives, memory, power supplies—everything you need to repair or upgrade your current system. The trick, of course, is knowing what needs to be done and how to do it. That's what this book is about.

Organization of This Book

Each chapter of this book is devoted to one topic, and is self-contained. The first three chapters provide detailed advice on maintaining, securing, and working on your system. They describe the tools and software you'll need, explain basic procedures like installing expansion cards and first-level troubleshooting, and detail the tips and tricks we've learned during 20 years of working on PCs. These chapters include:

> Chapter 1, *Introduction*
>
> Chapter 2, *Working on PCs*
>
> Chapter 3, *System Maintenance*

The second group of chapters covers the core components of your PC—the motherboard, processor, and memory. These chapters describe in detail the important characteristics of each of these components; how to choose compatible, cost-effective replacement or upgrade components; how to install and configure them; and how to troubleshoot problems. This group includes the following chapters:

> Chapter 4, *Motherboards*
>
> Chapter 5, *Processors*
>
> Chapter 6, *Memory*

The third group of chapters covers storage devices—hard disk drives, optical drives, and removable storage such as external hard drives and USB flash drives. Storage devices are more failure-prone than most PC components, so it's important to understand how to troubleshoot and replace them. Storage devices are also popular upgrade items, so we've covered how to choose, install, and configure them in great detail. This group includes the following chapters:

> Chapter 7, *Hard Disk Drives*
>
> Chapter 8, *Optical Drives*
>
> Chapter 9, *External and Removable Storage Devices*

The fourth group of chapters covers the components that allow you to get information into and out of your PC. We describe the important characteristics of video adapters, CRT monitors and LCD displays, sound cards and speakers, and input devices—keyboards, mice, and game controllers—and explain how to choose, install, configure, and troubleshoot them. We also provide information on installing a wireless networking adapter to your PC. This group includes the following chapters:

Chapter 10, Video Adapters

Chapter 11, Displays

Chapter 12, Audio

Chapter 13, Input Devices

Chapter 14, Wireless Networking

The fifth and final group of chapters covers three components—cases, power supplies, and power protection—that receive little attention, but are important for system reliability and usability. We detail the important characteristics of each, and provide guidelines for choosing the best case, power supply, and power protection for your system. This group includes the following chapters:

Chapter 15, Cases

Chapter 16, Power Supplies and Power Protection

In our earlier PC hardware books, we recommended specific components by brand and model. The problem with doing that, of course, is that PC hardware changes in Internet time. Products that were leading-edge (or even preproduction engineering samples) when we wrote about them will be mainstream products by the time the book arrives in bookstores, and might be discontinued by the time you read it. So instead of focusing on ephemera in print, we instead concentrate here on important characteristics and guidelines, which don't change nearly as fast.

We recognize, though, that many people want specific advice by make and model—"Which motherboard/drive/display should I buy?" is one of the most common questions we get—so we maintain a web site that provides detailed recommendations, by brand name and model. Visit this site at *http://forums.hardwareguys.com.*

We base our recommendations on our own experience, not after using the product for a day or a week, but after extensive day-in-day-out use under realistic conditions. If we say that we found a particular DVD burner to be durable, that means that we used that DVD burner extensively and burned a bunch of DVDs with it. If we say that a particular motherboard is stable, that means we used it in one or more of our own systems over a period of weeks or months and found that it doesn't crash, even when performing stressful tasks like running a full benchmark suite or compiling a Linux kernel. If we say that a particular display is the best we've used, it's because we sat in front of it for many long hours while writing this book. And so on.

Acknowledgments

Repairing and Upgrading Your PC was conceived one summer day in 2005. We had finished work on one book, *Astronomy Hacks*, and were starting work on the next, the fourth edition of *PC Hardware in a Nutshell*. As we bounced ideas back and forth with our friends and colleagues—Mark Brokering and Brian Jepson with O'Reilly and our agent David Rogelberg with Studio B Productions—it became clear that we all wanted to do more than a simple revision of *PC Hardware in a Nutshell*.

Mark, Brian, and David noted that *Building the Perfect PC* was selling quite well, and that perhaps we should do a similar book—large format with lots of full-color illustrations—that focused on repairing and upgrading PCs instead of building new ones. And so *Repairing and Upgrading Your PC* was born.

In addition to Mark, Brian, David, and the O'Reilly production staff, we want to thank our technical reviewers, who did yeoman duty in finding our mistakes and in making numerous suggestions, all of which made this a better book.

> **Brian Bilbrey** has been working with computers nearly continuously since Springsteen's *Born to Run* was released. Through that span of time, he's been a Banana Slug (UCSC student), an associate engineer with a medical electronics firm, managed an electronics assembly house, and been variously an administrator, a jack-of-all-trades, and/or a consultant at a variety of small- and medium-sized businesses. Brian has written tutorials for IBM DeveloperWorks, co-authored a Linux tome that got canceled on the way to the printers, and scribbles copiously online at *http://www.orbdesigns.com*. Currently the Senior Systems Administrator for NFR Security, Inc., Brian lives in Bowie, Maryland, with his lovely wife Marcia and their two rescue dogs, Lucy and Molly.

> **Jim Cooley** built his first computer in the early 1990s to do custom stock-charting for brokers. As the Internet gradually put him out of a job, he ended up repairing them instead. After putting in a ten-year stint of computer doctoring in San Francisco, he recently moved to Athens, Ohio, where he shares a home with his partner and two attack ferrets. He continues to trade stocks, build and repair computers, and in his spare time enjoys languages, the piano, and roller-blading. His occasional grumble about this and that can be found at *http://www.alwaysthecritic.com*.

> **Francisco García Maceda** has assembled and fixed computers for a score of years on both sides of the Atlantic. He is an IT consultant and has designed, installed, and administrated enterprise networks in both the private and public sectors, from petrochemical companies to gov-

ernment agencies in Mexico. Francisco is a self-taught college dropout who has managed to earn the respect of his clients and peers by solving problems. He currently lives in Mexico City with his wife Consuelo and their newborn daughter María de los Àngeles.

Ron Morse has been an electronics hobbyist for as long as he can remember. "Probably longer, but there was that unfortunate incident as a teenager when I removed the back of a then-new color television set just to see what was going on in there." In the more than 30 years since he was released from the hospital, he has devoted every spare dollar and available credit card balance to pursuing his interests in aviation, photography, and electronics. He bought his first personal computer in 1983 and has been repairing, upgrading, and modifying them (not necessarily in that order) since.

In his spare time, Ron served as an active duty Navy officer for 26 years, retiring in 2001 with the rank of Captain. He was awarded the Bronze Star medal for his service in Bahrain and Saudi Arabia during Operation Desert Shield and Desert Storm and also holds the Defense Superior Service Medal, among others.

Since retiring from the Navy, Ron has been designing and maintaining custom computer systems for small businesses as well as serving as Director of the Rinconada Group, a strategic communications firm specializing in programs for elected officials and government agencies at the local, state, and federal levels.

He lives with his wife Deborah, three Border collies, and a Queensland Blue Heeler in Albuquerque, New Mexico.

We also want to thank our contacts at the hardware companies, who provided technical help, evaluation units, and other assistance. There are far too many to list individually, but they know who they are. Last, but by no means least, we want to thank our readers, many of whom have taken the time to offer useful suggestions for improvements to the book. Thanks, folks. We couldn't have done it without you.

We'd Like to Hear from You

We have tested and verified the information in this book to the best of our ability, but we don't doubt that some errors have crept in and remained hidden despite our best efforts and those of our editors and technical reviewers to find and eradicate them. Those errors are ours alone. If you find an error or have other comments about the book, you can contact the publisher or the authors.

How to Contact O'Reilly

Please address comments and questions concerning this book to the publisher:

O'Reilly Media, Inc.
1005 Gravenstein Highway North
Sebastopol, CA 95472
(800) 998-9938 (in the United States or Canada)
(707) 829-0515 (international or local)
(707) 829-0104 (fax)

You can also send us email. To be put on our mailing list or to request a catalog, send email to:

info@oreilly.com

For comments on the book, send email to:

bookquestions@oreilly.com

For more information about books, conferences, Resource Centers, and the O'Reilly Network, go to:

http://www.oreilly.com

How to Contact the Authors

To contact one of the authors directly, send mail to:

barbara@hardwareguys.com

robert@hardwareguys.com

We read all mail we receive from readers, but we cannot respond individually. If we did, we'd have no time to do anything else. But we do like to hear from readers.

We also maintain online forums, where you can read and post messages about PC hardware topics. You can read messages as a guest, but if you want to post messages, you must register. We keep registration information confidential, and you can choose to have your mail address hidden on any messages you post.

http://forums.hardwareguys.com

We each maintain a personal journal page, updated daily, which frequently includes references to new PC hardware we're working with, problems we've discovered, and other things we think are interesting. You can view these journal pages at:

Barbara: *http://www.fritchman.com/diaries/thisweek.html*

Robert: *http://www.ttgnet.com/thisweek.html*

Thank you for buying *Repairing and Upgrading Your PC*. We hope you enjoy reading it as much as we enjoyed writing it.

Getting Started

If you find the thought of doing your own repairs or upgrades to your PC a bit intimidating, you're not alone. Nearly everyone feels that way at the beginning, but there's really nothing to worry about. Working on a PC is no more technically challenging than changing the oil in your car or hooking up a DVD player. Compared to assembling one of those "connect Tab A to Slot B" toys for your kids, it's a breeze.

PC components connect like building blocks. Component sizes, screw threads, mounting hole positions, cable connectors, and so on are standardized, so you needn't worry about whether something will fit. There are minor exceptions, of course. For example, some small cases accept only half-height or half-length expansion cards. There are important details, certainly. If you're upgrading your processor, for example, you must verify that your current motherboard supports the new processor. But overall there are few "gotchas" involved in repairing or upgrading a PC.

Nor do you need to worry much about damaging the PC—or it damaging you. Taking simple precautions such as grounding yourself before touching static-sensitive components and verifying cable connections before you apply power are sufficient to prevent damage. Other than inside the power supply or CRT monitor—which you should *never* open—the highest voltage used inside a modern PC is 12V, which presents no shock hazard.

If you've never taken the cover off your PC before, you'll probably be amazed at how empty it is inside. Spend a few minutes comparing the photographs in this book to what you see inside the case, and you'll soon be able to identify all the important parts and what they do. From there, it's only a small step to repairing or upgrading your system by installing new parts to replace the old. Sooner than you think, you'll be an expert.

Upgrading or Repairing Versus Buying New

With entry-level PCs selling for less than $500 and fully equipped mainstream PCs selling for $1,200, you might wonder if it's even worthwhile to repair or upgrade your old system. After all, a new system comes with a warranty, all new software, and shiny new parts. The problem is—and we'll try to put this politely—a cheap new system is just that. Cheap. Year after year, consumer-grade, mass-market PCs are cost-reduced more and more. That shiny new cheap system comes with a cheap, unreliable motherboard; a small, slow hard drive; barely adequate memory; a marginal power supply; and so on. TANSTAAFL: There Ain't No Such Thing As A Free Lunch.

Is it impossible, then, to buy a good system, manufactured with high-quality components? Of course not, but don't expect to get it at a bargain price. Business-grade systems from name-brand vendors and systems targeted at gamers and other enthusiasts use high-quality components, but those systems are priced 50% to 200% higher than consumer-grade, mass-market systems. If you compare apples to apples, you'll often find that it's cheaper overall to repair or upgrade your current system than to buy an equivalent new system.

There are other good reasons to repair or upgrade your PC rather than replace it:

More choice

When you buy a PC, you get a cookie-cutter computer. You can choose such options as a larger hard drive, more memory, or a better monitor, but basically you get what the vendor decides to give you. If you want something that few people ask for, like a better power supply or quieter cooling fans or a motherboard with more features, you're out of luck. Those options aren't available.

And what you get is a matter of chance. High-volume direct vendors like Gateway and Dell often use multiple sources for components. Two supposedly identical systems ordered the same day might contain significantly different components, including such important variations as different motherboards or monitors with the same model number but made by different manufacturers. When you upgrade your PC yourself, you decide exactly what goes into it.

Optimum configuration

One of the best things about upgrading your own PC is that you can focus on what is important to you and ignore what isn't. Off-the-shelf commercial PCs are by nature jacks of all trades and masters of none. System vendors have to strike a happy medium that is adequate, if not optimum, for the mythical "average" user. Want to store your entire DVD collection on your computer? You can upgrade your system to a terabyte (1,000 GB) or more of hard disk space. Want your system to be almost silent? You can choose upgrade components with that in mind, and end up with a system that's nearly inaudible even in a quiet room. When you upgrade your existing system, you choose where to focus your efforts; when you buy a PC, you get what's being offered.

Better component quality

Most computer vendors cut costs by using cheaper OEM (original equipment manufacturer) versions of popular components if they're "visible" and no-name components if they're not. By "visible," we mean a component that people might seek out by brand name even in a pre-built PC, such as an ATI or NVIDIA video adapter. Invisible components are ones that buyers seldom ask about or notice, such as motherboards, optical and hard drives, power supplies, and so on.

OEM components may be identical to retail models, differing only in packaging. But even if the parts are the same, there are often significant differences. Component vendors usually do not support OEM versions directly, for example, instead referring you to the system vendor. If that system vendor goes out of business, you're out of luck, because the component maker provides no warranty to end users. Even if the maker does support OEM products, the warranty is usually much shorter on OEM parts—often as little as 30 to 90 days. The products themselves may also differ significantly between OEM and retail-boxed versions. Major PC vendors often use downgraded versions of popular products; for example, an OEM video adapter that has the same or a very similar name as the retail-boxed product, but runs at a lower clock rate than the retail version. This allows PC makers to pay less for components and still gain the cachet from using the name-brand product.

It's worse when it comes to "invisible" components. We've popped the lid on scores of consumer-grade PCs over the years, and it never ceases to surprise us just how cheaply they're built. Not a one of them had a power supply that we'd even consider using in one of our own systems, for example. They're packed with no-name motherboards, generic memory, the cheapest optical drives available, and so on. Even the cables are often shoddy. After all, why pay a buck more for a decent cable? In terms of reliability, we consider a consumer-grade PC a disaster waiting to happen.

Warranty

The retail-boxed components you'll use for your own PC include full manufacturer warranties that typically last for one to five years or more, depending on the component. PC makers use OEM components that often include no manufacturer warranty to the end user. If something breaks, you're at the mercy of the PC maker to repair or replace it. We've heard from readers who bought PCs from makers who went out of business shortly thereafter. When a hard drive or video card failed six months later, they contacted the maker of the item, only to find that they had OEM components that were not under manufacturer warranty.

Fewer problems

When you repair or upgrade your own computer, you know exactly what you put into it, and you're in a much better position to resolve any problems that may occur. If you buy a cheap computer, you're likely to have many problems with it, and you'll end up spending hours on hold or talking to someone abroad with an impenetrable accent. And, at the end of it all, they'll probably insist that you install the replacement parts yourself anyway.

Environmental friendliness

There is growing concern among many people about the millions of PCs that are discarded every year. By repairing or upgrading your current system to extend its life, you minimize the burden on the environment.

Before you decide whether to repair or upgrade your current system or to replace it, first weigh all of the costs and all of the advantages and disadvantages.

Popular Upgrades

The most popular upgrades fall into one or more of the following categories:

- *Feature upgrades* add capabilities to your PC, such as DVD burning, video capture, or wireless networking.

- *Reliability upgrades* are targeted at reducing the likelihood, frequency, and severity of hardware failures.

- *Performance upgrades* speed up your system.

- *Quiet upgrades* reduce the noise level of your system.

- *Convenience upgrades* make it easier to do things you want to do.

- *Data safety upgrades* reduce the likelihood that your bdata will be corrupted or lost.

Table 1-1 lists the 20 most popular PC upgrades by type, cost, and difficulty, ordered from least to most expensive. The actual cost of an upgrade obviously varies by the specific component you choose, but we've provided approximate ranges, as follows:

$:	$0 to $50
$$:	$50 to $125
$$$:	$125 to $250
$$$$:	$250+

Table 1-1. The top 20 upgrades

Action	Feature	Reliability	Performance	Quiet	Convenience	Data safety	Cost	Difficulty	Chapter
Install case fans or ducting		•		•			$	Medium	15
Install card reader	•						$	Medium	9
Replace keyboard/ mouse	•	•			•		$–$$	Easy	13
Add/replace memory			•				$–$$	Medium	6
Upgrade CPU heatsink/fan		•		•			$–$$	Medium	5
Replace the audio adapter	•		•		•		$–$$$	Easy	12
Add USB flash drive	•					•	$–$$$$	Easy	9
Install power protection		•				•	$–$$$$	Easy	16
Replace the speakers	•				•		$–$$$$	Easy	12
Replace video adapter	•		•		•		$–$$$$	Medium	10
Install external hard drive	•						$$–$$$	Easy	9
Install DVD writer	•					•	$$	Medium	8
Replace power supply		•		•			$$	Medium	16
Add/replace hard drive		•	•	•			$$–$$$	Medium	7
Install RAID		•	•			•	$$–$$$	Medium	7
Install secure wireless networking	•				•		$$–$$$	Difficult	14
Install a video capture card	•				•		$$$$$	Difficult	10
Replace motherboard	•	•	•				$$$$$	Difficult	4
Upgrade processor			•				$$–$$$$	Difficult	5
Replace the display	•		•		•		$$$–$$$$	Easy	11

Choosing Components

As much as we would like to recommend specific components by brand name and model number in this book, those recommendations would be outdated soon after the book was printed. To avoid this timeliness problem, we maintain online forums where you can always read about our current recommendations (and those of our expert forum members). Before you buy components to repair or upgrade your system, visit our forums at:

http://forums.hardwareguys.com

SEARCH BEFORE YOU ASK

It's best to search before you ask on the forums. The same questions are often asked (and answered) repeatedly, so please spend a few minutes browsing and searching the forums before you post a question. Chances are good that the search engine will locate an existing answer to your specific question among the thousands of posts. If not, post your question, but make sure to give as as much specific information as possible. The more pertinent information you provide with your question, the more likely the answers are to be fast, complete, and accurate.

Buying Components

Until the early 1990s, most computer products were bought in computer specialty stores. Retail sales still make up a significant chunk of computer product sales—although the emphasis has shifted from computer specialty stores to local "big-box" retailers like Best Buy, CompUSA, Fry's, Wal-Mart, and Costco—but online resellers now account for a large percentage of PC component sales.

Should you buy from a local brick-and-mortar retailer or an online reseller? We do both, because each has advantages and disadvantages.

Local retailers offer the inestimable advantage of instant gratification. Unless you're more patient than we are, when you want something, you want it *right now*. Buying from a local retailer puts the product in your hands instantly, instead of making you wait for FedEx to show up. You can also examine the product in person before purchase, something that's not possible if you buy from an online reseller. Local retailers also offer a big advantage if you need to return or exchange a product. If something doesn't work right, or if you simply change your mind, you can just drive back to the store rather than dealing with the hassles and cost of returning a product to an online reseller.

Online resellers have the advantage in breadth and depth of product selection. If you want the less-expensive OEM version of a product, for example, chances are that you won't find it at local retailers, most of which stock only retail-boxed products. If an online reseller stocks a particular manufacturer's products, it tends to stock the entire product line, whereas local retailers often pick and choose only the most popular items in a product line. Of course, the popular products are usually popular for good reasons. Online resellers are also more likely to stock niche products and products from smaller manufacturers. Sometimes, if you must have a particular product, the only option is to buy it online.

Online resellers usually advertise lower prices than local retailers, but it's a mistake to compare only nominal prices. When you buy from a local retailer, you pay only the advertised price plus any applicable sales tax. When you buy from an online retailer, you pay the advertised price plus shipping, which could end up costing you more than buying locally.

THERE'S NO ESCAPING DEATH AND TAXES

Ah, but you don't have to pay sales tax when you buy online, right? Well, maybe. In most jurisdictions, you're required by law to pay a *use tax* in lieu of sales tax on out-of-state purchases. Most people evade use taxes, of course, but that free ride is coming to an end. States faced with increasing budget problems—which is to say, all of them—are starting to clamp down on people who buy from online resellers and don't pay use tax. States are using data-mining techniques to coordinate with each other and with credit card companies and online retailers to uncover unpaid use taxes. If you don't pay use taxes, one day soon you're likely to hear from the audit division of your state department of revenue, asking what these credit card charges were for and why you didn't report the use taxes due on them. Count on it.

Although online resellers may have a lower overall price on a given component, it's a mistake to assume that is always the case. Local retailers frequently run sales and rebate promotions that cut the price of a component below the lowest online price. For example, we bought a spindle of 100 CD-R discs on sale from a local retailer for $19.95 with a $10 instant rebate and a $20 mail-in rebate. After the cost of the stamp to mail in the rebate form, they paid us $9.68 to carry away those 100 discs, which is a pretty tough deal for an online reseller to match. Similarly, we bought an 80 GB hard drive for $79.95 with a $15 instant rebate and a $30 mail-in rebate. Net cost? About $35 for a retail-boxed 80 GB hard drive, which no online vendor could come close to matching.

Whether you purchase your PC components from a local brick-and-mortar store or a web-based retailer, here are some guidelines to keep in mind:

- Make sure you know exactly what you're buying. For example, a hard drive might be available in two versions, each with the same or a similar model number but with an added letter or number to designate different amounts of cache. Or a hard drive maker might produce two models of the same size that differ in price and performance. Always compare using the exact manufacturer model number. Before you buy a product, research it on the manufacturer's web site and on the numerous independent web sites devoted to reviews. We usually search Google with the product name and "review" in the search string.

- Vendors vary greatly. Some we trust implicitly, and others we wouldn't order from on a bet. Some are always reliable, others always unreliable, and still others seem to vary with the phases of the moon. We check *http://www.resellerratings.com*, which maintains a database of customer-reported experiences with hundreds of vendors.

- The list price or *suggested retail price* (*SRP*) is meaningless. Most computer products sell for a fraction of SRP; others sell for near SRP; and for still others the manufacturer has no SRP, but instead publishes an *estimated selling price* (*ESP*). To do meaningful comparisons, you need to know what different vendors charge for the product. Fortunately, there are many services that list what various vendors charge. We use *http://www.pricescan.com*, *http://www.pricewatch.com*, and *http://www.pricegrabber.com*. These services sometimes list 20 or more different vendors, and the prices for a particular item can vary dramatically. We discard the top 25% and the bottom 25% and eyeball average the middle 50% to decide a reasonable price for the item.

AMIR

If you like getting good deals (and who doesn't?), check out the sites dealnews (*http://www.dealnews.com*) and SlickDeals (*http://www.slickdeals.net*), which are great for finding rebates and sales. With careful shopping, your *AMIR* (*After Manufacturer and Instant Rebates*) price can actually be zero or less.

- Many components are sold in retail-boxed and OEM forms. The core component is likely to be similar or identical in either case, but important details could vary. For example, Intel CPUs are available in retail-boxed versions that include a CPU cooler and a three-year warranty. They are also available as OEM components (also called *tray packaging* or *white box*) that do not include the CPU cooler and have only a 90-day warranty. OEM items are not intended for retail distribution, so some manufacturers provide no warranty to individual purchasers. OEM components are fine, as long as you understand the differences and do not attempt to compare prices between retail-boxed and OEM.

- The market for PCs and components is incredibly competitive and margins are razor-thin. If a vendor advertises a component for much less than other vendors, it may be a "loss leader." More likely, though, particularly if its prices on other items are similarly low, that vendor cuts corners, either by using your money to float inventory, by shipping returned products as new, by charging excessive shipping fees, or, in the ultimate case, by taking your money and not shipping the product. If you always buy from the vendor with the rock-bottom price, you'll waste a lot of time hassling with returns of defective, used, or discontinued items and dealing with your credit card company when the vendor fails to deliver at all. Ultimately, you're also likely to spend more money than you would have by buying from a reputable vendor in the first place.

- The actual price you pay may vary significantly from the advertised price. When you compare prices, include all charges—particularly shipping charges. Reputable vendors tell you exactly how much the total charges will be. Less reputable vendors might "forget" to mention shipping charges, which can be very high. Some vendors break up the full manufacturer pack into individual items. For example, if a retail-boxed hard drive includes mounting hardware, some vendors will quote a price for the bare drive without making it clear that they have removed the mounting hardware and charge separately for it. Also be careful when buying products that include a rebate from the maker. Some vendors quote the net price after rebate without making it clear that they are doing so.

WHEN EVERYONE ADVERTISES A PRODUCT AT THE SAME PRICE...

Some component makers set a *minimum advertised price* (*MAP*) for some or all of their products. Although manufacturers cannot legally set a minimum selling price, they can set minimum prices at which their dealers can advertise their products. If a product is covered by MAP, online vendors all advertise it at the same price, tell you to "call for price" rather than listing a price, or force you to add the product to your shopping basket before they'll show a price for it. Many discount resellers will actually sell you a MAP product for less (sometimes much less) than the advertised price, but you may have to ask.

- Some vendors charge more for an item ordered via their 800 number than they do for the same item ordered directly from their web site. Some others add a fixed processing fee to phone orders. These charges reflect the fact that taking orders on the web is much cheaper than doing it by phone, so this practice has become common. In fact, some of our favorite vendors, such as NewEgg.com, do not provide telephone order lines.

- It can be very expensive to ship heavy items such as CRTs, UPSs, and printers individually. This is one situation in which local big-box stores like Best Buy have a huge advantage over online vendors. The online vendor has to charge you for the cost of shipping, directly or indirectly, and that cost can amount to $50 or more for a heavy item that you need quickly. Conversely, the big-box stores receive inventory items in truckload or even railcar shipments, so the cost to them to have a single item delivered is quite small. They can pass that reduced cost on to buyers. If you're buying a heavy item, don't assume that it will be cheaper online. Check your local Best Buy or other big-box store and you may find that it actually costs less there, even after you pay sales tax. And you can carry it away with you instead of waiting for FedEx to show up with it.

- Most direct resellers that take phone orders are willing to sell for less than the price they advertise. All you need do is tell your chosen vendor that you'd really rather buy from them, but not at the price they're quoting. Use lower prices you find with the price comparison services as a wedge to get a better price. But remember that reputable vendors must charge more than the fly-by-night operations if they are to make a profit and stay in business. If we're ordering by phone, we generally try to beat down our chosen vendor a bit on price, but we don't expect them to match the rock-bottom prices that turn up on web searches. Of course, if you're ordering from a web-only vendor, dickering is not an option, which is one reason why web-only vendors generally have better prices.

- Using a credit card puts the credit card company on your side if there is a problem with your order. If the vendor ships the wrong product, defective product, or no product at all, you can invoke charge-back procedures to have the credit card company refund your money. Vendors who live and die on credit card orders cannot afford to annoy credit card companies, and so tend to resolve such problems quickly. Even your threat to request a charge-back may cause a recalcitrant vendor to see reason.

- Some vendors add a surcharge, typically 3%, to their advertised prices if you pay by credit card. Surcharges violate credit card company contracts, so some vendors instead offer a similar discount for paying cash, which amounts to the same thing. Processing credit card transactions costs money, and we're sure that some such vendors are quite reputable, but our own experience with vendors that surcharge has not been good. We always suspect that their business practices result in a high percentage of charge-back requests, and so they discourage using credit cards.

- Good vendors allow you to return a defective product for replacement or a full refund (often less shipping charges) within a stated period, typically 30 days. Buy only from such vendors. Nearly all vendors exclude some product categories, such as notebook computers, monitors, printers, and opened software, either because their contracts with the manufacturer require them to do so or because some buyers commonly abuse return periods for these items, treating them as "30-day free rentals." Beware of the phrase "all sales are final." That means exactly what it says.

- Check carefully for any mention of restocking fees. Many vendors who trumpet a "no questions asked money-back guarantee" mention only in the fine print that they won't refund all your money. They charge a restocking fee on returns, and we've seen fees as high as 30% of the

A Cunning Plan

Nearly all retailers refuse to refund your money on opened software, DVDs, and so on, but will only exchange the open product for a new, sealed copy of the same title. One of our readers tells us how he gets around that common policy. He returns the open software in exchange for a new, sealed copy of the same product, keeping his original receipt. He then returns the new, sealed copy for a refund. That's probably unethical and might even be illegal for all we know, but it does work.

purchase price. These vendors love returns, because they make a lot more money if you return the product than if you keep it. Do not buy from a vendor that charges restocking fees on exchanges (as opposed to refunds). For refunds, accept no restocking fee higher than 10% to 15%, depending on the price of the item.

THE CUSTOMER ISN'T ALWAYS RIGHT

Even some of our favorite vendors have started charging restocking fees in response to abuses by customers. (See the sidebar "Another Cunning Plan"). Yes, there are sleazy customers as well as sleazy resellers. For example, we heard from one guy who was desperate to get his hands on the latest high-end video adapter as soon as possible. No reseller had the video card in stock yet, and everyone had a waiting list. This sweetheart ordered the same card from three or four different resellers, hoping to maximize his chances of getting it quickly.

He installed the first one that arrived, and returned the others, claiming they were defective. He demanded a full refund, including shipping both ways! He even opened the boxes to "prove" he'd attempted to use them. If he'd asked for replacements, there wouldn't have been any problem, but he wanted a refund. Naturally, the victimized resellers refused to refund the shipping costs and charged him a restocking fee. He was outraged, and emailed Robert to suggest he warn his readers not to buy from those resellers. He seemed surprised that Robert had no sympathy for him. Nowadays, he'd probably auction the extra ones on eBay and make a killing.

Most of the better resellers that charge restocking fees do so to protect themselves against such abuses, and most are willing to make exceptions on a case-by-case basis. Before you buy from a reseller, verify their restocking fees and policies and determine under what conditions they are willing to make exceptions.

- If you order by phone, don't accept verbal promises. Insist that the reseller confirm your order in writing, including any special terms or conditions, before charging your credit card or shipping product. If a reseller balks at providing written confirmation of their policies, terms, and conditions, find another vendor. Most are happy to do so. If you're ordering from a vendor that uses web-based ordering exclusively, use a screen capture program or your browser's save function to grab copies of each screen as you complete the order. Most vendors send a confirming email, which we file in our "Never Delete" folder.

- File everything related to an order, including a copy of the original advertisement; emailed, faxed, or written confirmations provided by the reseller; copies of your credit card receipt; a copy of the packing list and invoice; and so on. We also jot down notes in our PIM regarding telephone conversations, including the date, time, telephone number and extension, name of person spoken to, purpose of the call, and so on. We print a copy of those to add to the folder for that order.

Another Cunning Plan

If you buy from a local retailer, open the box from the bottom rather than the top. If you need to return a non-defective item, that makes it easier for the retailer to repackage the product with the manufacturer's seals intact, which can help avoid restocking fees.

- Make it clear to the reseller that you expect them to ship the exact item you have ordered, not what they consider to be an "equivalent substitute." Require they confirm the exact items they will ship, including manufacturer part numbers. For example, if you order an ATI RADEON X800 XT Platinum Edition PCIe graphics card, make sure that the order confirmation specifies that item by name, full description, and ATI product number. Don't accept a less detailed description such as "graphics card," "ATI graphics card," or even "ATI RADEON X800 graphics card." Otherwise, you almost certainly won't get what you paid for. You might get an X800 Pro AGP model rather than the X800 XT Platinum Edition PCIe model you ordered, a plain X800 XT rather than the more expensive X800 XT Platinum Edition, an OEM card with a slower processor or less memory, or even a "Powered by ATI" card—which is a card with an ATI processor made by another manufacturer—rather than a "Built by ATI" card. Count on it.

- Verify warranty terms. Some manufacturers warrant only items purchased from authorized dealers in full retail packaging. For some items, the warranty begins when the manufacturer ships the product to the distributor, which may be long before you receive it. OEM products typically have much shorter warranties than retail-boxed products—sometimes as short as 90 days—and may be warranted only to the original distributor rather than to the final buyer. Better resellers may *endorse the manufacturer warranty* for some period on some products, often 30 to 90 days. That means that if the product fails, you can return the item to the reseller, who will ship you a replacement and take care of dealing with the manufacturer. Some resellers disclaim the manufacturer warranty, claiming that once they ship the item, dealing with warranty claims is your problem, even if the product arrives DOA. We've encountered that problem a couple of times. Usually, mentioning phrases like *merchantability and fitness for a particular purpose* and *revocation of acceptance* leads them to see reason quickly. We usually demand the reseller ship us a new replacement product immediately and include a prepaid return shipping label if they want the dead item back. We don't accept or pay for dead merchandise under any circumstances, and neither should you.

- Direct resellers are required by law to ship products within the time period they promise. But that time period may be precise ("ships within 24 hours") or vague ("ships within three to six weeks"). If the vendor cannot ship by the originally promised date, they must notify you in writing and specify another date by which the item will ship. If that occurs, you have the right to cancel your order without penalty. Make sure to make clear to the reseller that you expect the item to be delivered in a timely manner. Reputable vendors ship what they say they're going to ship when they say they're going to ship it.

Unfortunately, some vendors have a nasty habit of taking your money and shipping whenever they get around to it. In a practice that borders on fraud, some vendors routinely report items as "in stock" when in fact they are not. Make it clear to the vendor that you do not authorize them to charge your credit card until the item actually ships, and that if you do not receive the item when promised, you will cancel the order.

Recommended Sources

The question we hear more often than any other is, "What company should I buy from?" When someone asks us that question, we run away, screaming in terror. Well, not really, but we'd like to. Answering that question is a no-win proposition for us, you see. If we recommend a vendor and that vendor treats the buyer properly, well that's no more than was expected. And that's the best that can happen.

Still, we realize that many of our readers would like to know where we buy our stuff. Over the years, we've bought from scores of online vendors, and our favorites have changed. For the last few years, our favorite has been NewEgg. com (*http://www.newegg.com*). NewEgg offers an extraordinarily good combination of price, wide product selection, support, shipping, and return or replacement policies. We know of no other direct vendor that even comes close.

NewEgg's prices aren't always rock-bottom, but they generally match any other vendor we're willing to deal with. NewEgg runs daily specials that are often real bargains, so if you're willing to consider alternatives and to accumulate components over the course of a few weeks, you can save a fair amount of money. (Of course, if you do that, your warranty and return privileges on earlier orders are winding down as you wait.) NewEgg ships what they say they're going to ship, when they say they're going to ship it, and at the price they agreed to ship it for. If there's a problem, they make it right. It's hard to do better than that.

All of that said, if you buy from NewEgg and subsequently your goldfish dies and all of your teeth fall out, don't blame us. All we can say is that NewEgg treats us right. Things can change overnight in this industry, and while we don't expect NewEgg to take a sudden turn for the worse, it could happen.

As for local retailers, we buy from—in no particular order—Best Buy, CompUSA, Target, Office Depot, OfficeMax, and our local computer specialty stores, depending on what we need and who happens to have advertised the best prices and rebates in the Sunday ad supplements. Wal-Mart used to sell only assembled PCs. It has recently started stocking PC components, such as video adapters, so we'll add Wal-Mart to our list as well.

Even if you follow all of these guidelines, you could have a problem. Even the best resellers sometimes drop the ball. If that happens, don't expect the problem to go away by itself. If you encounter a problem, remain calm and notify the reseller first. Good resellers are anxious to resolve problems. Find out how the reseller wants to proceed, and follow their procedures, particularly for labeling returned merchandise with an RMA (return materials authorization) number. If things seem not to be going as they should, explain to the vendor why you are dissatisfied, and tell them that you plan to request a charge-back from your credit card company. Finally, if the reseller is entirely recalcitrant and any aspect of the transaction (including, for example, a confirmation letter you wrote) took place via U.S. Postal Service, contact your postmaster about filing charges of mail fraud. That really gets a reseller's attention, but use it as a last resort.

Troubleshooting

Your first PC repair or upgrade can be pretty intimidating. What if it doesn't work? Worse still, what if the PC goes up in flames the first time you turn it on? Set your mind at ease. This isn't rocket surgery. Any reasonably intelligent person can repair or upgrade a PC with a high degree of confidence that it will work normally afterward. If you use good components and work carefully, everything usually just works.

Still, stuff happens. So, although we provide more detailed troubleshooting suggestions for specific components throughout this book, we thought it was a good idea to summarize early in the book some basic troubleshooting steps to cover the most common problems that occur during a system repair or upgrade.

Possible problems fall into one of four categories, easy versus hard to troubleshoot and likely versus unlikely. Always check the easy/likely problems first. Otherwise, you may find yourself tearing down the system again before you notice that the power cord isn't plugged in. After you exhaust the easy/likely possibilities, check the easy/unlikely ones followed by hard/likely and, finally, hard/unlikely.

Most problems that occur during repairs and system upgrades result from one or more of the following:

Cable problems

> Disconnected, misconnected, and defective cables cause more problems than anything else. The plethora of cables inside a PC makes it very easy to overlook a disconnected data cable or to forget to connect power to a drive. It's possible to connect some cables backward. Ribbon cables are a particularly common problem, because some can be appear connected, yet be offset by a row or column of pins. And the cables

Don't Forget the Flashlight

One of our technical reviewers observes, "A good flashlight with a tight beam (I use a mini Maglite) really helps to spot offset ribbon connector problems, even if workspace lighting is otherwise adequate. I've done systems where a handheld magnifier became an indispensable tool."

themselves cannot always be trusted, even if they are new. If you have a problem that seems inexplicable, always suspect a cable problem first.

CABLES ARE COMMONPLACE

Fortunately, most problems with defective cables involve ribbon cables, and those are pretty easy to come by. For example, when we recently assembled a new PC, the motherboard came with two IDE cables and a floppy drive cable. The floppy drive came with a cable, the hard drive with another IDE cable, and the optical drive with still another IDE cable. That gave us four IDE cables and two floppy cables, so we ended up with two spare IDE cables and a spare floppy cable. Those went into our spares kit, where they'll be available if we need to swap cables to troubleshoot another system.

Configuration errors

Years ago, motherboards required a lot more manual configuration than do modern motherboards. There were many switches and jumpers, all of which had to be set correctly or the system wouldn't boot. Modern motherboards auto-configure most of their required settings, but may still require some manual configuration, either by setting physical jumpers on the motherboard or by changing settings in CMOS Setup. Motherboards use silkscreened labels near jumpers and connectors to document their purposes and to list valid configuration settings. These settings are also listed in the motherboard manual. Always check both the motherboard labels and the manual to verify configuration settings. If the motherboard maker posts updated manuals on the web, check those as well.

Incompatible components

In general, you can mix and match modern PC components without worrying much about compatibility. For example, any IDE hard drive or optical drive works with any IDE interface, and any ATX12V power supply is compatible with any ATX12V motherboard (although a cheap or older power supply may not provide adequate power, which means you need to visit Chapter 16). Most component compatibility issues are subtle. For example, you may have installed a 1 GB memory module in your system. When you power it up, the system sees only 256 MB or 512 MB because the motherboard doesn't recognize 1 GB memory modules properly. It's worth checking the detailed documentation on the manufacturers' web sites to verify compatibility.

DOA (dead-on-arrival) components

Modern PC components are extremely reliable, but if you're unlucky, one of your components may be DOA. This is the least likely cause of a problem, however. Many novices think they have a DOA component, but the true cause is almost always something else—usually a cable or configuration problem. Before you return a suspect component, go through the detailed troubleshooting steps we describe. Chances are good that the component is just fine.

THE HAPPY NOISE

A healthy PC finishes the POST (Power-On Self-Test) with one happy-sounding beep. If you hear some other beep sequence during startup, there is some sort of problem. BIOS beep codes provide useful troubleshooting information, such as identifying the particular subsystem affected. Beep codes vary, so check the motherboard documentation for a description of what each code indicates.

Here are the problems you are most likely to encounter when you repair or upgrade a system, and what to do about them:

Problem: When you apply power, nothing happens

- Verify that the power cable is connected to the PC and to the wall receptacle, and that the wall receptacle has power. Don't assume. We have seen receptacles in which one half worked and the other didn't. Use a lamp or other appliance to verify that the receptacle to which you connect the PC actually has power. If the power supply has its own power switch, make sure that switch is turned to the "on" or "1" position. If your local mains voltage is 110/115/120V, verify that the power supply voltage selector switch, if present, is not set for 220/230/240V. (If you need to move this switch, disconnect power before doing so.)

- If you are using an outlet strip or UPS, make sure that its switch (if equipped) is on and that the circuit breaker or fuse hasn't blown.

- If you installed a video adapter, pop the lid and verify that the adapter is fully seated in its slot. Even if you were sure it seated fully initially—and even if you thought it snapped into place—the adapter may still not be properly seated. Remove the card and reinstall it, making sure that it seats completely. If the motherboard has a retention mechanism, make sure the notch on the video card fully engages the retention mechanism. Ironically, one of the most common reasons for a loose video card is that the screw used to secure it to the chassis may torque the card, pulling it partially out of its slot. This problem is rare with high-quality cases and video cards, but is quite common with cheap components.

- Verify that the main ATX power cable and the ATX12V power cable are securely connected to the motherboard and that all pins are making contact. If necessary, remove the cables and reconnect them. Make sure that the latch on each cable plug snaps into place on the motherboard jack.

- Verify that the front-panel power switch cable is connected properly to the front-panel connector block. Check the silkscreen label on the motherboard and the motherboard manual to verify that you are connecting the cable to the right set of pins. Very rarely, you may encounter a defective power switch. You can eliminate this possibility by temporarily connecting the front-panel reset switch cable to the power switch pins on the front panel connector block. (Both are merely momentary on switches, so they can be used interchangeably.) Alternatively, you can carefully use a small flat-blade screwdriver to short the power switch pins on the front-panel connector block momentarily. If the system starts with either of these methods, the problem is the power switch.

- Start eliminating less likely possibilities, the most common of which is a well-concealed short circuit. Begin by disconnecting the power and data cables from the hard, optical, and floppy drives, one at a time. After you disconnect each, try starting the system. If the system starts, the drive you just disconnected is the problem. The drive itself may be defective, but it's far more likely that the cable is defective or was improperly connected. Replace the data cable, and connect the drive to a different power supply cable.

SWAPPING POWER SUPPLIES

If you have a spare power supply—or can borrow one temporarily from another system—you might as well try it, as long as you have the cables disconnected. A new power supply being DOA is fairly rare, at least among good brands, but as long as you have the original disconnected, it's not much trouble to try a different power supply.

- If you have expansion cards installed, remove them one by one. Remove all but the video adapter. If the motherboard has embedded video, temporarily connect your display to it and remove the video card as well. Attempt to start the system after you remove each card. If the system starts, the card you just removed is causing the problem. Try a different card, or install that card in a different slot.

- Remove and reseat the memory modules, examining them to make sure that they are not damaged, and then try to start the system. If you have two memory modules installed, install only one of them initially. Try it in both (or all) memory slots. If that module doesn't work in any slot, the module may be defective. Try the other module, again in every available memory slot. By using this approach, you can determine if one of the memory modules or one of the slots is defective.

Chapter 1: Getting Started

- Remove the CPU cooler and the CPU. Check the CPU to make sure that there are no bent pins. If there are, you may be able to straighten them using a credit card or a similar thin, stiff object, but in all likelihood you will have to replace the CPU. Check the CPU socket to make sure there are no blocked holes or foreign objects present.

USE NEW THERMAL GOOP EVERY TIME

Before you reinstall the CPU, always remove the old thermal compound and apply new compound. You can generally wipe off the old compound with a paper towel, or perhaps by rubbing it gently with your thumb. (Keep the processor in its socket while you remove the compound.) If the compound is difficult to remove, try heating it gently with a hair dryer. Never operate the system without the CPU cooler installed.

- Remove the motherboard and verify that no extraneous screws or other conductive objects are shorting the motherboard to the chassis. Although shaking the case usually causes such objects to rattle, a screw or other small object can become wedged so tightly between the motherboard and chassis that it will not reveal itself during a shake test.

- If the problem persists, the most likely cause is a defective motherboard.

Problem: The system seems to start normally, but the display remains black

- Verify that the display has power and the video cable is connected. If the display has a noncaptive power cable, make sure that the power cord is connected both to the display and to the wall receptacle. If you have a spare power cord, use it to connect the display.

- Verify that the brightness and contrast controls of the display are set to midrange or higher.

- Disconnect the video cable and examine it closely to make sure that no pins are bent or shorted. Note that the video cable on some analog (VGA) monitors is missing some pins and may have a short jumper wire connecting other pins, which is normal. Also check the video port on the PC to make sure that all of the holes are clear and that no foreign objects are present.

- If you are using a standalone video adapter in a motherboard that has embedded video, make sure that the video cable is connected to the proper video port. Try the other video port just to make sure. Most motherboards with embedded video automatically disable it when they sense that a video card is installed, but that is not universally true. You may have to connect the display to the embedded video, enter CMOS Setup, and reconfigure the motherboard to use the video card.

- Try using a different display, if you have one available. Alternatively, try using the problem display on another system.

- If you are using a video card, make certain it is fully seated. Many combinations of video card and motherboard make it very difficult to seat the card properly. You may think the card is seated. You may even feel it snap into place. That does not necessarily mean it really is fully seated. Look carefully at the bottom edge of the card and the video slot, and make sure the card is fully in the slot and parallel to it. Verify that installing the screw that secures the video card to the chassis did not torque the card, forcing one end up and out of the slot.

- If your video card requires a supplemental power cable, be sure to connect it and make sure it snaps into place.

- If the system has PCI or PCIe expansion cards installed, remove them one by one. (Be sure to disconnect power from the system before you remove or install a card.) Each time you remove a card, restart the system. If the system displays video after you remove a card, that card is either defective or is conflicting with the video adapter. Try installing the PCI or PCIe card in a different slot. If it still causes the video problem, the card is probably defective. Replace it.

Problem: When you connect power (or turn on the power switch on the back of the power supply), the power supply starts briefly and then shuts off

All of the following steps assume that the power supply is adequate for the system configuration. This symptom may also occur if you use a grossly underpowered power supply. Worse still, doing that may damage the power supply, motherboard, and other components.

- This may be normal behavior. When you connect power to the power supply, it senses the power and begins its startup routine. Within a fraction of a second, the power supply notices that the motherboard hasn't ordered it to start, so it shuts itself down immediately. Press the main power switch on the case and the system should start normally.

- If pressing the main power switch doesn't start the system, you have probably forgotten to connect one of the cables from the power supply or front panel to the motherboard. Verify that the power switch cable is connected to the front-panel connector block, and that the 20-pin or 24-pin main ATX power cable and the 4-pin ATX12V power cable are connected to the motherboard. Connect any cables that are not connected, press the main power switch, and the system should start normally.

- If the preceding steps don't solve the problem, the most likely cause is a defective power supply. If you have a spare power supply, or can borrow one temporarily from another system, install it temporarily in the new system. Alternatively, connect the problem power supply to another system to verify that it is bad.

- If the preceding step doesn't solve the problem, the most likely cause is a defective motherboard. Replace it.

Problem: When you apply power, the floppy drive LED lights solidly and the system fails to start

- The FDD (floppy disk drive) cable is defective or misaligned. Verify that the FDD cable is properly installed on FDD and on the motherboard FDD interface. This problem is caused by installing the FDD cable backward or by installing it offset by one row or column of pins.

- If the FDD cable is properly installed, it may be defective. Disconnect it temporarily and start the system. If the system starts normally, replace the FDD cable.

- If the FDD cable is known-good and installed properly, the FDD itself or the motherboard FDD interface may be defective. Replace the FDD. If that doesn't solve the problem and you insist on having an FDD, either replace the motherboard or disable the motherboard FDD interface and install a PCI adapter that provides an FDD interface, or, if your motherboard allows you to boot from USB devices, purchase a USB external floppy drive for the purpose.

Problem: The optical drive appears to play audio CDs, but no sound comes from the speakers

- Make sure the volume/mixer is set appropriately; that is, that the volume is up and CD Audio isn't muted. There may be multiple volume controls in a system. Check them all.

- Try a different audio CD. Some recent audio CDs are copy-protected in such a way that they refuse to play on a computer optical drive.

- If you have tried several audio CDs without success, this may still be normal behavior, depending on which player application you are using. Optical drives can deliver audio data via the analog audio-out jack on the rear of the drive or as a digital bit stream on the bus. If the player application pulls the digital bit stream from the bus, sound is delivered to your speakers normally. If the player application uses analog audio, you must connect a cable from the analog audio-out jack on the back of the drive to an audio-in connector on the motherboard or sound card.

- If you install an audio cable and still have no sound from the speakers, try connecting a headphone or amplified speakers directly to the headphone jack on the front of the optical drive (if present). If you still can't hear the audio, the drive may be defective. If you can hear audio via the front headphone jack but not through the computer speakers, it's likely the audio cable you installed is defective or installed improperly.

SPECIAL AUDIO CABLES

Few optical drives or motherboards include an analog audio cable, so you will probably have to buy a cable. In the past, audio cables were often proprietary, but modern drives and motherboards all use a standard ATAPI audio cable. However, most modern optical drives will send audio over the ATAPI data cable.

Problem: SATA drives are not recognized

- How SATA (Serial ATA) drives are detected (or not detected) depends on the particular combination of chipset, BIOS revision level, SATA interface, and the operating system you use. Failing to recognize SATA devices may be normal behavior.

- If you use a standalone PCI SATA adapter card, the system will typically not recognize the connected SATA drive(s) during startup. This is normal behavior. You will have to provide an SATA device driver when you install the operating system.

- If your motherboard uses a recent chipset—e.g., an Intel 865 or later—and has embedded SATA interfaces, it should detect SATA devices during startup and display them on the BIOS boot screen. If the drive is not recognized and if you have not already done so, update the BIOS to the latest version. Restart the system and watch the BIOS boot screen to see whether the system recognizes the SATA drive. Run BIOS Setup (usually by pressing Delete or F1 during startup) and select the menu item that allows you to configure ATA devices. If your SATA drive is not listed, you can still use it, but you'll have to provide a driver on diskette during OS installation.

- Recognition of SATA drives during operating system installation varies with the OS version and the chipset. The original release of Windows 2000 does not detect SATA drives with any chipset. To install Windows 2000 on an SATA drive, watch during the early part of Setup for the prompt to press F6 if you need to install third-party storage drivers. Press F6 when prompted and insert the SATA driver floppy. Windows XP may or may not recognize SATA drives, depending on the chipset the motherboard uses. With recent chipsets—e.g., the Intel 865 series and later—Windows XP recognizes and uses SATA drives natively. With earlier chipsets—e.g., the Intel D845 and earlier—Windows XP does not recognize the SATA drive natively, so you will have to press F6 when prompted and provide the SATA driver on floppy. Most recent Linux distributions (those based on the 2.4 kernel or later) recognize SATA drives natively.

- If the SATA drive is still not recognized, pop the lid and verify that the SATA data and power cables are connected properly. Try removing and reseating the cables and, if necessary, connecting the SATA drive to a

Why Only 128 GB or 137 GB?

If you install Windows XP from an early distribution disc, it will recognize at most 137 GB (decimal) or 128 GB (binary) of hard drive capacity, even if the drive is much larger. You can use the remaining space after Windows is installed, but only if you format it as a separate volume. If you want the entire capacity of a large hard drive to be used as a single volume by Windows XP, you'll need a more recent distribution disc that includes Service Pack 2 (SP2) or later.

different motherboard interface connector. If the drive still isn't accessible, try replacing the SATA data cable. If none of this works, the SATA drive is probably defective.

Problem: The monitor displays BIOS boot text, but the system doesn't boot and displays no error message

- This may be normal behavior. Restart the system and enter BIOS Setup. Choose the menu option to use default CMOS settings, save the changes, exit, and restart the system.

- If the system doesn't accept keyboard input and you are using a USB keyboard and mouse, temporarily swap in a PS/2 keyboard and mouse. If you are using a PS/2 keyboard and mouse, make sure you haven't connected the keyboard to the mouse port and vice versa.

- If the system still fails to boot, run BIOS Setup again and verify all settings, particularly CPU speed, FSB speed, and memory timings.

- If the system hangs with a DMI pool error message, restart the system and run BIOS Setup again. Search the menus for an option to reset the configuration data. Enable that option, save the changes, and restart the system.

- If you are using an Intel motherboard, power down the system and reset the configuration jumper from the 1-2 (Normal) position to 2-3 (Configure). Restart the system, and BIOS Setup will appear automatically. Choose the option to use default CMOS settings, save the changes, and power down the system. Move the configuration jumper back to the 1-2 position and restart the system. (Actually, we do this routinely any time we build a system around an Intel motherboard. It may not be absolutely required, but we've found that doing this minimizes problems.)

- If you are still unable to access BIOS Setup, power down the system, disconnect all of the drive data cables and restart the system. If the system displays a Hard Drive Failure or No Boot Device error message, the problem is a defective cable (more likely) or a defective drive. Replace the drive data cable and try again. If the system does not display such an error message, the problem is probably caused by a defective motherboard.

Problem: The monitor displays a Hard Drive Failure or similar error message

- This problem is almost always due to a hardware issue. Verify that the hard drive data cable is connected properly to the drive and the interface and that the drive power cable is connected.

- Use a different drive data cable and connect the drive to a different power cable.

- Connect the drive data cable to a different interface.

- If none of these steps corrects the problem, the most likely cause is a defective drive.

Problem: The monitor displays a No Boot Device, Missing Operating System, or similar error message

- This behavior is normal if you have not yet installed an operating system. Error messages like this generally mean that the drive is physically installed and accessible, but the PC cannot boot because it cannot locate the operating system. Install the operating system.

- If the drive is inaccessible, verify that all data and power cables are connected properly. If it is a parallel ATA drive, verify that master/slave jumpers are set correctly, and that the drive is connected to the primary interface.

- If you upgrade your motherboard, but keep your original hard drive (or use a utility such as Norton Ghost to clone your original), your operating system installation may not have the drivers necessary to function with your new hardware. If you're upgrading your motherboard, chances are good that enough things are different that Windows won't be able to boot. You'll need to reinstall Windows.

Problem: The system refuses to boot from the optical drive

- All modern motherboards and optical drives support the El Torito specification, which allows the system to boot from an optical disc. If your new system refuses to boot from a CD, first verify that the CD is bootable. Most, but not all, operating system distribution CDs are bootable. Some OS CDs are not bootable, but have a utility program to generate boot floppies. Check the documentation to verify that the CD is bootable, or try booting the CD in another system.

- Run CMOS Setup and locate the section where you can define boot sequence. The default sequence is often (1) floppy drive, (2) hard drive, and (3) optical drive. Sometimes, by the time the system has decided that it can't boot from the FDD or hard drive, it "gives up" before attempting to boot from the optical drive. Reset the boot sequence to (1) optical drive and (2) hard drive. We generally leave the system with that boot sequence. Most systems configured this way prompt you to "Press any key to boot from CD" or something similar. If you don't press a key, they then attempt to boot from the hard drive, so make sure to pay attention during the boot sequence and press a key when prompted.

- Some high-speed optical drives take several seconds to load a CD, spin up, and signal the system that they are ready. In the meantime, the BIOS may have given up on the optical drive and gone on to try other boot devices. If you think this has happened, try pressing the reset button to reboot the system while the optical drive is already spinning and up to speed. If you get a persistent prompt to "press any key to boot from CD," try leaving that prompt up while the optical drive comes up to speed. If that doesn't work, run CMOS Setup and reconfigure the boot sequence to put the FDD first and the optical drive second. (Make sure there's no diskette in the FDD.) You can also try putting other boot device options, such as a Zip drive, network drive, or boot PROM ahead of the optical drive in the boot sequence. The goal is to provide sufficient delay for the optical drive to spin up before the motherboard attempts to boot from it.

- If none of these steps solves the problem, verify that all data cable and power cable connections are correct, that master/slave jumpers are set correctly, and so on. If the system still fails to boot, replace the optical drive data cable.

- If the system still fails to boot, disconnect all drives except the primary hard drive and the optical drive. If they are parallel ATA devices, connect the hard drive as the master device on the primary channel and the optical drive as the master device on the secondary channel and restart the system.

- If that fails to solve the problem, connect both the hard drive and optical drive to the primary ATA interface, with the hard drive as master and the optical drive as slave.

- If the system still fails to boot, the optical drive is probably defective. Try using a different drive.

Problem: When you first apply power, you hear a continuous high-pitched screech or warble

- The most likely cause is that one of the system fans either has a defective bearing or a wire is contacting the spinning fan. Examine all of the system fans—CPU fan, power supply fan, and any supplemental fans—to make sure that they haven't been fouled by a wire. Sometimes it's difficult to determine which fan is making the noise. In that case, use a cardboard tube or rolled up piece of paper as a stethoscope to localize the noise. If the fan is fouled, clear the problem. If the fan is not fouled but still noisy, replace the fan.

- Rarely, a new hard drive may have a manufacturing defect or have been damaged in shipping. If so, the problem is usually obvious from the amount and location of the noise and possibly because the hard drive is vibrating. If necessary, use your cardboard tube stethoscope to localize the noise. If the hard drive is the source, the only alternative is to replace it.

Working on PCs

2

Popping the lid of a PC for the first time can be pretty intimidating, but there's really no need for concern. There's nothing inside that will hurt you, other than sharp edges and those devilish solder points (fortunately much reduced in recent years with increased surface mounting of electrical components). There's also nothing inside that you're likely to damage, assuming that you take the few simple precautions detailed in this chapter.

Some PCs—particularly those from big-box stores—have seals that warn you that the warranty is void if they're broken. This isn't so much to protect them against your ham-handedness as it is to ensure that you have to come back to them and pay their price for upgrades. We advise people to break such seals if they need to, do their own upgrades, and fight it out later if they have a problem that should be covered under warranty.

We've never heard of anyone being refused warranty service because of a broken seal, but there's always a first time. If you have a sealed PC that is still under warranty, the decision is yours. Note that some individual components inside, such as hard disks, are a special case. Breaking the seal on a hard disk does actually destroy it and will without question void the warranty. And, unless you are qualified to do so, don't ever open up a power supply or CRT monitor. Dangerous voltages await you inside.

Those issues aside, feel free to open your PC and tinker with it as you see fit. Far from forbidding you to work on your own PC, most online computer vendors actually expect you to do your own upgrades and repairs. As a matter of fact, most of them will try very hard to talk you into doing your own warranty repairs so that they can avoid sending a technician to do them for you. The rest of this chapter explains the fundamentals you need to understand to start upgrading and repairing your PC.

Rules to Upgrade and Repair By

We've upgraded and repaired hundreds of systems over the years, and learned a lot of lessons the hard way. Here are the rules we live by. We'll admit that we don't always take each of these steps when we're doing something simple like swapping a video card, but you won't go far wrong if you follow them until you have enough experience to know when it's safe to depart from them.

Back everything up.

Twice. Do a verify pass, if necessary, to make sure that what is on the backup matches what is on the hard drive. Better still, do at least a partial restore to a scratch directory to make sure that your backups are readable. If you're connected to a network, copy at least your data and configuration files to a network drive. If there's room on the network drive, create a temporary folder and copy the entire contents of the hard disk of the machine about to undergo surgery. If you don't have a network but you do have a CD or DVD writer, back up at least your important data and configuration files to optical discs. About 99 times in 100, all of this will be wasted effort. The hundredth time—when everything that can go wrong does go wrong—will pay you back in spades for the other 99. Be sure to check out Chapter 3, which discusses backups and other preventative maintenance in detail.

Make sure you have everything you need before you start.

Have all of the hardware, software, and tools you'll need lined up and waiting. You don't want to have to stop mid-upgrade to go off in search of a small Phillips screwdriver or to drive to the store to buy a cable. If your system can boot from the optical drive, configure it to do that and test it before proceeding. Otherwise, make sure that you have a boot disk with drivers for your optical drive, and test it before you start tearing things down. Create a new emergency repair disk immediately before you start the upgrade. Make certain that you have the distribution discs for the operating system, service packs, backup software, and any special drivers you need. If you're tearing down your only PC, download any drivers you will need and copy the unzipped or executable versions to floppies or burn them to CD *before* you take the computer apart.

DON'T WORK IN THE DARK

You can't work efficiently and effectively without adequate light. Don't try to work on a PC that's under a desk or otherwise inaccessible. Disconnect all the external cables and move the system to a well-lit working area (the kitchen table is traditional) before you begin work. The more light, the better. We often use a desk lamp or two to shed more light on a system while we're working on it. Barbara prefers to use a head-mounted light to provide hands-free lighting that points automatically in the direction she's looking.

Make sure you can get the answers you need.

Read the manual first. A quick read-through often uncovers potential problems, hints, and tips that can make the upgrade much smoother. Check the web site for any new component you are installing. You'll often find FAQs (Frequently Asked Questions), readme files, updated drivers, and other information that can make the difference between a trouble-free upgrade and a major mess. In fact, the quality of the web site that supports a component is a large factor in our purchase decision, and we suggest that you make it one in yours. Before we even consider buying a major component, we check the web site to verify that it is likely to have answers to any questions that may arise.

YOU NEED ANSWERS

Google (*http://www.google.com*) is your friend. When we encounter a problem, our usual first step is to Google for pages that describe that problem. Often, you'll find a quick solution without having to reinvent the wheel. The secret is to be specific. For example, if you're having problems getting an ATI X800XT video card to work properly in your MSI K8N Neo4-F motherboard, don't just search for "video problem". You'll get thousands or millions of hits, most of which have nothing to do with your problem. Search instead for combinations of specific terms such as "X800XT" and "K8N Neo4-F". If it exists, you'll probably find exactly the document you need on the first page of hits.

If Google doesn't help right away, use Google Groups (*http://groups.google.com*). On the surface, it may look like a clone of Yahoo Groups, but Google Groups has the added benefit of including the entire archive of articles ever posted to USENET (except that embarrassing one you wrote in sixth grade that you asked Google to remove). A dud web search on Google's site often turns to gold when you click that "Groups" link on the top of the results page.

Make the technology work for you.

You might have a choice between a slow manual way and a quick automatic way to accomplish a given task. The easy way could require spending a few bucks for a special-purpose utility program, but could also save you hours of trial and error, manual labor, and aggravation. For example, if you are replacing a hard disk, you can move the contents of the existing disk to the new disk by spending hours doing a backup and restore, or you can use a free or inexpensive utility program that does the same thing in a few minutes. (Most hard drives now come with software to migrate your data and programs automatically from the old hard drive to the new one. All you need to do is download it from the manufacturer's web site.)

Record everything.

During an upgrade, it's often important to be able to return to your starting point. If you've just spent an hour swapping components in and out and changing jumpers, it's almost impossible to remember what went where originally. So, record each change as you make it. Use a digital camera to take "before" close-up shots of each change, dictate the details of each change into a digital voice recorder, or simply make detailed written notes.

Change one thing at a time.

When replacing multiple components, change one thing at a time. If you're replacing the video card and adding more memory, leave the old video card in place until the new memory is installed and working. If you swap multiple components simultaneously, problems are harder to troubleshoot, because you're never sure which change caused the problem.

Ground yourself frequently to avoid static electricity damage.

Many PC components are vulnerable to static electricity, particularly processors and memory. The easiest way to avoid damaging components is to ground yourself frequently while working on the system. Do that by touching the metal chassis or the power supply, as shown in Figure 2-1. You needn't keep the system plugged in while you work on it; the chassis and power supply provide a sufficient "sink" to dissipate any static charge.

Figure 2-1. Ground yourself by touching the chassis or power supply

Keep track of the screws and other small parts.

Disassembling a PC yields an incredible number of screws and other small pieces. As you tear a PC down, organize these parts using an egg carton or old ice cube tray. One errant screw left on the floor can destroy a vacuum cleaner, or, if left in the case, even short out and destroy the motherboard. Make sure that all of the small parts are accounted for when you reassemble the PC.

Use force when necessary, but use it cautiously.

Many books tell you never to force anything, and that's good advice as far as goes. If doing something requires excessive force, chances are that a part is misaligned, that you have not removed a screw, or something similar. But sometimes there is no alternative to applying force judiciously. For example, drive power cables sometimes fit so tightly that the only way to get them off is to grab them with pliers and pull hard. Some combinations of expansion card and slot fit so tightly that you must press very hard to seat the card. If you encounter such a situation, verify that everything is lined up and otherwise as it should be (and that there isn't a stray wire obstructing the slot). Then use whatever force it takes to do the job, which may be substantial.

Check and recheck before you apply power.

An experienced PC technician does a quick scan of the entire PC before performing the *smoke test* by applying power to the PC. Don't skip this step, and don't underestimate its importance. Most PCs that fail the smoke test do so because this step was ignored. Until you gain experience, it may take several minutes to verify that all is as it should be—all components secure, all cables connected properly, no loose screws, no tools or other metal parts shorting anything out, and so on. Once you are comfortable working inside PCs, this step takes 15 seconds, but that can be the most important 15 seconds of the whole upgrade. (We usually pick up the case and shake it, then rotate it vertically and back gently to see if anything rattles.)

Start small for the first boot.

The moment of greatest danger comes when you power up the PC for the first time. Do what's necessary to minimize damage if the smoke test fails. If the system fails catastrophically—which sometimes happens no matter how careful you are—don't put any more of your components at risk than you have to. If you're installing a fast new video adapter and a new power supply to support its higher current draw, for example, install the new power supply first. Once you're sure it's working properly, then install your expensive new video adapter.

Don't throw the old stuff away.

Don't discard the components you pull. With new hard drives selling for $0.50 per gigabyte, an old 20 GB hard drive may not seem worth keeping. But you could be glad you have it the next time you need to troubleshoot your system. (It can also come in handy if you pop it into one of the external USB/FireWire drive enclosures described in Chapter 9.) Despite those correspondence school ads that show a technician using an oscilloscope to troubleshoot a PC, nobody really does it that way. In the real world, you troubleshoot PCs by swapping components.

Screwed Up

Some PCs use a variety of screws that look very similar but are in fact threaded differently. For example, the screws used to secure some case covers and those used to mount some disk drives appear to be identical, but swapping them could result in stripped threads. If in doubt, keep each type of screw in a separate compartment of your organizer.

Swap Meet

If you have more than one computer, use the second system as a source of parts for swap-out troubleshooting. Just make sure that the parts are compatible and of sufficient capacity. For example, if you suspect that the 500W power supply in your gaming system is the problem, swapping in a 300W power supply from a secondary system won't accomplish anything except burning out the 300W power supply.

Keeping old components you pull during upgrades is a convenient (and free) way to accumulate the swappers you'll need later on to troubleshoot problems with this or another PC. Label them "known good," date them, and put them on the shelf. Conversely, label bad stuff "BAD," even if you're going to throw it out. There's nothing more frustrating in an emergency than finding out that the unlabeled hard drive in the back of your closet is actually dead.

Leave the cover off until you're sure everything works.

Complete the upgrade or repair and test the system before you reassemble the case. Otherwise, you may find yourself repeatedly assembling and disassembling the case. The corollary to this rule is that you should always put the cover back on the case when you're finished working. Cases are designed to direct cooling air across the major heat-generating components, processors, and drives, but this engineering is useless if you run the PC uncovered. Replace the cover to avoid overheating components. The other good reason to replace the cover is that running a system without the cover releases copious amounts of RF to the surrounding environment. An uncovered system can interfere with radios, monitors, televisions, and other electronic components over a wide radius.

Hand Tools

Despite those snazzy-looking PC toolkits you see anywhere PC components are sold, you really don't need much in the way of tools to work on a standard PC. Figure 2-2 shows our standard toolkit—a #1 Phillips screwdriver, flashlight, and needlenose pliers—and we seldom need the pliers.

Figure 2-2. A basic toolkit: #1 Phillips screwdriver, flashlight, and needlenose pliers

A bottle or pen of Wite-Out and a Sharpie marker can be useful for labeling items. Depending on your system, you may also need a #0 or #2 Phillips screwdriver, although the #1 Phillips generally works fine for the screw heads used in standard PCs. If your system uses Torx fasteners, you may need a #10, #15, or #20 Torx screwdriver. There are other tools that are convenient rather than essential. If you're replacing a motherboard, for example, a 5 mm or 6 mm nut driver makes it faster to install the standoffs, and a screw starter makes it easier to insert screws in inaccessible places. But you can get along just fine with only a screwdriver or two, a flashlight, and needlenose pliers for setting jumpers. You needn't buy special "computer" tools, either.

Regular tools from the hardware store, Sears, or a home improvement center work just fine.

Software Tools

In addition to basic hand tools, you may need some software tools to diagnose and troubleshoot problems and to recover from them. The conundrum, of course, is that most diagnostic software utilities run under Windows, but quite often when you're troubleshooting it's because Windows won't load or run because it's corrupted itself or been damaged by a virus or worm.

Fortunately, there's an alternative. A "Live Linux CD" such as Knoppix (*http://www.knoppix.org*), shown in Figure 2-3, allows you to boot and run a full-featured Linux operating system directly from the CD, without altering the contents of your hard drive. Knoppix and similar Live CD distributions include a plethora of graphics-based tools that allow you to diagnose, test, and burn-in the various hardware components of your system.

Figure 2-3. The Knoppix desktop

Knoppix is priceless when you need to recover data from a corrupted or otherwise inaccessible hard drive that Windows won't touch. Figure 2-3, for example, shows Knoppix running on a system that had crapped out under Windows. Windows refused to boot, and we didn't want to risk a reinstall before we salvaged the data on the drive.

Knoppix gave us read-only access to the Windows partition, and allowed us to browse it and copy the data files to a safe location. Knoppix even recognized the Windows network we were connected to, and allowed us to save the recovered files to a shared Windows volume on another machine on the network. If the machine hadn't been connected to a network, we could have used K3b (a Linux CD/DVD burning application) to write the recovered files to a CD or DVD—all of this simply by pointing and clicking, just like Windows. You don't need to learn Linux to use Knoppix.

We don't have room here to detail all of the many capabilities of Knoppix. Download a copy for yourself (now, before you need it) and play around with it. Search Google for "Knoppix recover" or "Knoppix rescue" and you'll find dozens of documents that explain the hardware analysis, testing, and data recovery features of Knoppix. Oh, did we mention that Knoppix is free for the download? Knoppix is also available on CD for a nominal fee from online vendors like CheapBytes (*http://shop.cheapbytes.com*) and many others. For plenty of information on all that you can do with Knoppix, see *Knoppix Hacks* (O'Reilly, 2004).

When Windows is running, you might also want a general Windows-based diagnostic utility. The best diagnostic utility we know of is Everest Home Edition, from Lavalys Consulting Group, Inc. (*http://www.lavalys.com*; $30, free trial available), shown in Figure 2-4. Lavalys sells versions with additional features, but for diagnosing and repairing a home PC, the trial version should get you by.

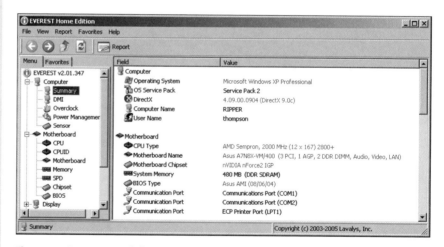

Figure 2-4. Everest general diagnostic utility

You may also find some or all of the following items useful for various tasks:

Operating system distribution discs

You need the OS distribution discs to replace a failed hard disk, but you may also need them for routine upgrades and maintenance. For example, Windows prompts for the distribution disc to load drivers for a new device, and Linux distribution discs may contain hundreds of programs that weren't loaded during the initial installation. If you've

Advice from Brian Bilbrey

Label a large manila envelope for each computer (by assigned system name) and use it to store all the docs and discs that came with the components or software that are installed. As a part of my spring and fall cleaning routine, I review the contents of those envelopes, removing stuff that's not in play any longer. This habit makes remodels and refurbishing much easier.

updated the operating system from the initial distribution version (that is, by applying a Windows Service Pack), also keep the Service Pack or update CD handy.

PUT ALL THAT SPACE TO USE

With huge hard disks costing so little, we create a separate "distribution partition" on the hard disk for most Windows systems we build. We copy the distribution CD to this partition, along with service packs, the Office CD (and any other programs the system uses), the driver CDs for installed hardware, and so on. This trick has several benefits, including faster installation, not having to locate the CD when you change options or want to install additional modules, and that you can if necessary completely rebuild the system using only a boot floppy to get started.

Backup utility

If you use a third-party backup utility, keep a copy of the distribution CD in your kit to make sure that you can restore backups after reinstalling the operating system. Few things are more frustrating than getting a failed computer up again and having a good backup, but not having the software at hand that you need to restore it. Research backup tools well. For example, one of our tech reviewers notes that Nero's BackItUp 6 ate data from a relative's network storage drive . . . the *only* place where that data was stored.

Antivirus scanner

Any time a Windows system behaves oddly, your first step should be to scan it for viruses, Trojans, and worms. In fact, it's a good idea to scan any Windows system regularly even if it's operating normally, because recent viruses and worms avoid overtly hostile behavior. Instead, they take control of the system unobtrusively and use it to relay spam, host porn files, launch DoS attacks, and so on. The most popular AV products are sold by McAfee and Symantec (Norton), but we suggest you avoid them. Our own experience and reports from our readers suggest that these bloated products cause nearly as many problems as they solve. We recommend Grisoft AVG Anti-Virus (*http://www.grisoft. com*), which is free for personal use, seems about as reliable as any of its competitors, and uses few system resources.

Malware scanner

Spyware and adware, which we refer to collectively as malware, are close cousins to viruses, Trojans, and worms. The least malicious forms of malware may simply display ads and perhaps report your web browsing activities to a central server. Malignant forms of malware may capture passwords, bank account and credit card information, and other private personal data and relay that information to criminals who use it to steal your identity and empty your bank account. Standard antivirus software doesn't detect most malware. To do that, you need a malware

Advice from Brian Jepson

When I did a clean install recently, Windows XP Service Pack 2 complained that there was no antivirus software installed. So, I decided to see what would happen if I followed the prompts from the Windows Security Center. It lead me to a page on Microsoft with trials for many products, including a one-year trial for Computer Associates' eTrust EZ Antivirus. I Googled it, and although I heard some gripes, lots of folks were swearing by it, claiming the least resource usage of any antivirus product. I'm still testing it out, so the only useful advice here is to check Microsoft's list of antivirus partners, because you might find a nice free trial:

http://www.microsoft.com/athome/ security/viruses/wsc/

scanner. We recommend AdAware (*http://www.lavasoftusa.com*) and Spybot Search & Destroy (*http://www.safer-networking.org*), both of which have versions that are free for personal use. (Use both, because each detects problems that the other does not.)

THE HEN GUARDING THE FOXHOUSE

Although it has excellent features, we do not use or recommend Microsoft AntiSpyware. In March 2005, Microsoft changed the default action for detected Claria products from "remove" or "quarantine" to "ignore." Any malware scanner that recommends ignoring Claria products is not one we trust to protect our systems.

Memory Aids

Before you conclude that memory errors are caused by defective memory or a faulty power supply, remove each memory module, polish the contacts with a new dollar bill, and reinstall the memory modules, making sure that they are fully seated and locked. Quite often, these simple steps eliminate the memory errors.

Memory testing utility

Memory errors are among the most commonly encountered hardware problems. The trouble is that such errors may be caused by defective memory or by a marginal or failing power supply. The best way to determine the cause of the errors is to use a memory testing utility such as MemTest86 (*http://www.memtest86.com*) to isolate the errors. If the errors occur reproducibly at the same physical memory addresses, the most likely cause is a defective memory module. If the errors appear at random memory addresses, it's more likely that a marginal or failing power supply is the problem. MemTest86 is available as a bootable floppy disk or a bootable ISO CD image, and can usually be run even when memory errors are so severe that Windows or Linux cannot load. (If you're running Knoppix, just type memtest and press Enter at the boot prompt to run memtest86.)

WINDOWS RECOVERY CONSOLE

Windows Recovery Console can repair all sorts of problems. Although you can run it from the Windows installation disc, Jim Cooley recommends installing it as an option on the Windows startup menu. To do so, once Windows is installed, open a command prompt and go to the root of your installation folder (usually *i386*). Type `setup32.exe /cmdcons` and Bob's your uncle.

Emergency repair disk

Recent versions of Windows and Linux allow you to create an emergency disk that contains critical system configuration data, part or all of the registry, and so on. Create or update this disk for a computer any time you make a significant change to it. Label and date the disk and store it near the computer or keep it with your toolkit. If you don't have a recent copy, do yourself a favor and make one right now. Use the following procedures and tools to create an emergency disk:

Windows 2000/XP Emergency Repair Disk (ERD)

Run Start → Programs → Accessories → System Tools → Backup. With Backup running, click the Emergency Repair Disk icon to create the disk. In the resulting dialog, check the *Also backup the registry...* box to copy key system files to the repair directory on the hard disk. The Windows 2000/XP ERD is not bootable. To repair Windows 2000/XP, you must boot either from the distribution CD or the boot floppies and initiate a repair from the boot menu. You'll be prompted to insert your repair disk at some point in the procedure.

The Windows 2000/XP ERD does not contain any registry files. Creating the ERD copies the registry files to the *%SystemRoot%\ Repair* folder, where they may be lost if the hard disk crashes. To be safe, before you create or update the ERD, copy the entire contents of that folder to another hard disk, network volume, or optical disc. (The repair folder will be empty if you've never run Ntbackup.)

Linux

Use the mkbootdisk command to produce an emergency boot floppy disk. This disk is specific to your system configuration, and should be updated any time you make significant hardware or configuration changes.

GETTING ORGANIZED

Nowadays, most motherboards, video cards, and other components come with a driver CD. Just keeping them all straight is hard enough, let alone making sure that you have the correct and most recent driver for a particular component. When we buy or build a computer, we create a folder for it on a network drive. When we buy a component that comes with a floppy diskette or CD with drivers, we copy the contents of that disk to a subfolder of that folder. If you have a CD or DVD burner, use it to make a customized CD or DVD disc for each computer. Collect all the drivers and other miscellany in a folder and copy them to one optical disc for that system. Include a change log in the root directory. When you replace a component, note that in the change log and burn a new disc with the updated and new drivers. If there's room on the disc, also include the operating system, diagnostic tools, and so forth.

Putting the Boot In

You can find various boot disks and other utilities at *http:// www.bootdisk.com.* Although we are not lawyers and haven't looked into the legality of all these utilities, many of them appear to be quite useful.

General Procedures

With the hand tools and utilities described in the preceding sections, you have everything you need to upgrade or repair a PC except for the new components. Before you start, take a few minutes to read through the following sections, which describe the common procedures and general knowledge you need to work on PCs. These sections describe the common tasks involved in working on a PC—things like opening the case, setting jumpers, manipulating cables, and adding or removing expansion cards. Instructions for specific tasks like replacing a motherboard, disk drive, or power supply are given in the relevant chapter.

Before you open the case

Although you may be raring to get in there and fix something, taking the time to prepare properly before you jump in pays big dividends later. When your system has problems, do the following before you open the case:

Make sure it's not a cable problem.
> Weird things can happen with cables. Disconnect all unessential cables, leaving only the mouse, keyboard, and display attached. Unplug the printer, USB hub, and any other attached peripherals to give them a chance to reset themselves. Turn your computer off, then restart it. If the problem is gone, try reattaching the cables one at a time to see if it comes back.

Make sure it's not a software problem.
> The old saying that "if all you have is a hammer, everything looks like a nail" is nowhere more true than with PC repairs. Before you assume that it's a hardware problem, make sure that the problem isn't caused by an application, by Windows, or by a virus. Use Knoppix and your virus/malware scanners *before* you assume the hardware is at fault and start disconnecting things. If the system boots and runs Knoppix successfully, defective hardware is very unlikely to be the problem.

Make sure it's not a power problem.
> The reliability of electrical power varies by where you live, which individual circuit you are connected to, and even from moment to moment as other loads on the circuit kick in and out. Sporadic problems such as spontaneous reboots are often caused by poor-quality power. Before you start tearing your system down, make sure the problem isn't caused by bad electrical power. At a minimum, use a surge protector to smooth incoming power. Better still, connect the system to a *UPS* (*Uninterruptible Power Supply*). If you don't have a UPS, connect the system to a power receptacle on a different circuit.

Wallets Aren't Just for Money Anymore

The best way we've found to organize and protect CDs and DVDs is to lose the jewel cases and store them—or, better still, copies of them—in one of those zippered vinyl or Cordura disc wallets you can buy for a few dollars at Wal-Mart or Best Buy. These wallets use plastic or Tyvek sleeves to protect the discs, hold from half a dozen to several dozen discs, and make it easy to find the one you want. If the disc has a serial number or activation key on the original jewel case, make sure to record it on the CD, using a soft permanent marker on the *label* side. It's also a good idea to record the serial number or initialization (init) key on the disc sleeve or a small card so that the number is accessible when the disc is already in the drive.

We stock one of these wallets with essential discs—Windows and Linux distribution CDs, applications, various diagnostics, and so on—and always have it at hand. We also buy a disc wallet for each PC we buy or build. New PCs usually arrive with several discs, as do individual components. Storing these discs in one place, organized by the system they belong to, makes it much easier to locate the one you need.

Make sure it's not an overheating problem.

Modern systems—particularly 'high-performance models—run very hot. Sporadic problems, or those that occur only after a system has been running for some time, are often caused by excessive heat. Most modern motherboards include built-in temperature sensors—generally one embedded in the processor socket to report CPU temperature and one or more others near the memory, chipset, and other critical components.

Most motherboard manufacturers supply utility programs that report and log temperature readings, as well as such other critical information as the speeds of the CPU and other system fans, the voltages on specific voltage rails, and so on. If no such utility is available for your operating system, simply reboot the computer, run BIOS Setup, and navigate the Setup menus until you find the option for Hardware Monitoring or something similar. Because the built-in temperature, voltage, and fan-speed sensors report their readings to the BIOS, you can read and record those values directly from the BIOS Setup screen. It's best to reboot and take the reading after the computer's been up and running for a while, and preferably just after it's exhibited the problems you are trying to resolve.

It's useful to establish baseline values for temperature readings, because "normal" temperatures vary significantly depending on the type and speed of the processor, the type of heatsink/fan unit used, the number and type of supplementary case fans, ambient temperature, degree of system load, and so on. For example, a processor that normally idles at 35°C may reach 60°C or higher when it runs a CPU-intensive program. The idle and loaded temperatures are both important. An increase in idle temperature probably indicates a cooling problem, such as clogged air inlets or a failing CPU fan, while very high loaded temperatures may result in system errors, processor slow-downs due to "thermal clamping," or, in the worst case, actual damage to the processor.

MONITOR YOUR MOTHERBOARD

To protect your system against thermal problems, we recommend installing and activating the monitoring utility supplied with the motherboard. Most such utilities allow you to set user-defined "tripwire" values that produce an alarm if the temperature becomes too high, the voltages are out of tolerance, or the fans are running too slowly. Most of these utilities can also shut down the system to prevent damage if the readings exceed the limits you've set. To determine the proper range of settings, refer to the documentation included with your system, motherboard, or processor.

Think things through.

Inexperienced technicians dive in willy-nilly without thinking things through first. Experienced ones first decide what is the most likely cause of the problem, what can be done to resolve it, in what order they should approach the repair, and what they'll need to complete it. Medical students have a saying, "when you hear thundering hooves, don't think about zebras." In other words, most of the time it'll be horses, and you can waste a lot of time looking for nonexistent zebras. Determine the most likely causes of the problem in approximate ranked order, decide which are easy to check for, and then eliminate the easy ones first. In order, check easy/likely, easy/unlikely, hard/likely, and finally hard/unlikely. Otherwise, you may find yourself tearing down your PC and removing the video card before you notice that someone unplugged the monitor.

Back up the hard drive(s).

We'll say it again: before you start upgrading or repairing a system, back up the important data on its hard drive. Every time you pop the cover of a PC, there's a small but ever-present risk that something that used to work won't work when you put everything together again. One of the wires in a cable may be hanging by a thread, or the hard drive may be teetering on the edge of failure. Just opening the case may cause a marginal component to fail irreversibly. So, before you even think of doing PC surgery, make sure that the hard drive is backed up.

Disconnect external cables.

It may seem obvious, but you need to disconnect all external cables before you can move the PC itself to the operating room. Many PCs are under desks or somewhere that otherwise makes it difficult to see the rear panel. If necessary, get down on the floor and crawl behind the PC with a flashlight to make sure it isn't still tethered to something. We've dragged modems, keyboards, and mice off desks because we weren't paying attention, and we once came within inches of pulling a $2,000 monitor onto the floor. Check the cables or pay the price.

Set the display safely aside.

CRT displays are not only fragile, but can cause serious injuries if the tube implodes. Flat-panel LCD displays aren't dangerous in that respect, but it's easy to do a lot of expensive damage very quickly if you don't take care. A display on the floor is an accident waiting to happen. If you're not moving the display to the work area, keep it on the desk out of harm's way. If you must put it on the floor, at least turn the screen toward the wall.

Take antistatic precautions.

You can eliminate most of the risk of damaging components by static electricity simply by making it a habit to touch the case chassis or power supply to ground yourself before touching the processor, memory modules, or other static-sensitive components. It's also a good idea to avoid rubber-soled shoes and synthetic clothing and to work in an uncarpeted area.

MISTER SAFETY

If the air is particularly dry, use one of those spray/mister bottles that you can buy at any hardware store or supermarket. Fill it with water and add a few drops of dishwashing liquid or fabric softener. Before you begin work, mist the work area liberally, both air and surfaces. The goal isn't to get anything wet. Just the added humidity is enough to all but eliminate static electricity.

Removing and replacing the case cover

It sounds stupid, but it's not always immediately obvious how to get the cover off the chassis. We've worked on hundreds of different PCs from scores of manufacturers over the years, and we're still sometimes stumped. Manufacturers use an endless variety of fiendish ways to secure the cover to the chassis. Some were intended to allow tool-free access, others to prevent novice users from opening the case, and still others were apparently designed just to prove that there was yet one more way to do it.

We've seen novice upgraders throw up their hands in despair, figuring that if they couldn't even get the case open they weren't destined to become PC technicians. Nothing could be further from the truth. It just sometimes takes a while to figure it out.

The most evil example we ever encountered was a mini-tower case that had no screws visible except those that secured the power supply. The cover appeared seamless and monolithic. The only clue was a two-inch long piece of silver "warranty void if removed" tape that wrapped from the top of the cover to one side, making it clear that the separation point was there. We tried everything we could think of to get that cover off. We pulled gently on the front of the case, thinking that perhaps it would pop off and reveal screws underneath. We pressed in gently on the side panels, thinking that perhaps they were secured by a spring latch or friction fit. Nothing worked.

Finally, we turned the thing upside down and examined the bottom. The bottom of computer cases is almost always unfinished metal, but this one was finished beige material that looked just like the other parts of the cover. That seemed odd, so we examined the four rubber feet closely. They had what appeared to be center inserts, so we pried gently on one of these with our small screwdriver. Sure enough, it popped off and revealed a concealed screw within the rubber foot. Once we removed those four screws, the cover slid off easily, bottom first.

The moral is that what one person can assemble, another person can disassemble. It sometimes just takes determination, so keep trying. Your first resort should be the manual or, lacking that, the web site of the system or case manufacturer. Fortunately, most cases don't use such convoluted methods, so opening the case is usually straightforward.

Managing Internal Cables and Connectors

When you pop the cover of a PC, the first thing you'll notice is cables all over the place. These cables carry power and signals between various subsystems and components of the PC. Making sure they're routed and connected properly is no small part of working on PCs.

The cables used in PCs terminate in a variety of connectors. By convention, every connector is considered either male or female. Many male connectors, also called *plugs* or *headers*, have protruding pins, each of which maps to an individual wire in the cable. The corresponding female connector, also called a *jack*, has holes that match the pins on the mating male connector. Matching male and female connectors are joined to form the connection.

Some cables use unsheathed wires joined to a connector. Three cables of this sort are common in PCs—those used to supply power to the motherboard and drives; those that connect front-panel LEDs, switches, and (sometimes) USB, FireWire, and audio ports to the motherboard; and those that connect audio-out on an optical drive to a sound card or motherboard audio connector. Figure 2-5 shows the front-panel power LED cable already connected to the motherboard, and the female jack of the front-panel reset switch cable being seated against the male motherboard header-pin connector for that cable.

Oddball Cables

Rather than using pins and holes, the connectors used on some cables—for example, modular telephone cables and 10/100/1000BaseT Ethernet cables—use other methods to establish the connection. The connector that terminates a cable may mate with a connector on the end of another cable, or it may mate with a connector that is permanently affixed to a device, such as a hard disk or a circuit board. Such a permanently affixed connector is called a *socket*, and may be male or female.

Figure 2-5. Typical unsheathed cables

Some PC cables contain many individual wires packaged as a *ribbon cable*, so called because individually insulated conductors are arranged side-by-side in a flat array that resembles a ribbon. Ribbon cables provide a way to organize the wires required to connect devices like drives and controllers, whose interfaces require many conductors. Ribbon cables are used primarily for low-voltage signals, although they are also used to conduct low voltage/low current power in some applications. Ribbon cables are normally used only inside the case, because their electrical characteristics cause them to generate considerable RF emissions, which can interfere with nearby electronic components.

Square Peg, Round Hole

System designers attempt to avoid two potential dangers with regard to PC cables. Most important is to prevent connecting a cable to the wrong device. For example, connecting 12-volt power to a device that expects only 5 volts might have a catastrophic result. This goal is achieved by using unique connectors that physically prevent the cable from connecting to a device not designed to receive it. The second potential error is connecting a cable upside-down or backward. Most PC cables prevent this by using unsymmetrical connectors that physically fit only if oriented correctly, a process called *keying*.

Two keying methods are commonly used for PC cables, either individually or in conjunction. The first uses mating connectors whose bodies connect only one way, and is used for all power cables and some ribbon cables. The second, used by some ribbon cables, blocks one or more holes on the female connector and leaves out the corresponding pin on the male connector. Such a ribbon cable can be installed only when oriented so that missing pins correspond to blocked holes.

Ideal PC cables use unambiguous keyed connectors. You can't connect these cables to the wrong thing because the connector only fits the right thing; you can't connect them backwards, because the connector only fits the right way. Fortunately, most of the dangerous cables in PCs—the ones that could damage a component or the PC itself if they were misconnected—are of this sort. Power cables for disk drives and ATX motherboards, for example, fit only the correct devices and cannot be connected backwards.

Some PC cables, on the other hand, require careful attention. Their connectors may physically fit a component that they're not intended to connect to, and/or they may not be keyed, which means you can easily connect them backwards if you're not paying attention. Connecting one of these cables wrong usually won't damage anything, but the system may not work properly, either. The cables that link front-panel switches and indicator LEDs to the motherboard are of this variety.

Figure 2-6 shows a 40-wire ATA ribbon cable connected to the secondary ATA interface on an ASUS K8N-E Deluxe motherboard. The 40 individual wires are visible as raised ridges in the ribbon cable assembly. ASUS has provided a pull tab on the motherboard end of the cable to make it easier to remove, and has labeled the pull tab to recommend using it with optical drives. (Hard drives use the 80-wire version of the cable, shown later in Figure 2-7.)

Figure 2-6. A 40-wire ATA cable connected to the secondary motherboard ATA interface

All ribbon cables appear similar. They're often light gray, although some newer motherboards targeted at gamers and other enthusiasts include cables that are black, a bright primary color, or rainbow-colored. All of them use a contrasting colored stripe to indicate pin 1—red on standard gray cables; white on the cable shown here; brown on rainbow cables. But there are the following differences among ribbon cables:

Number of pins

Common ribbon cable connectors range from the 10-pin connectors on the cables that are often used to extend serial, USB, FireWire, and audio ports from the motherboard header-pin connector to the front or back panel, through 34-pin floppy drive connectors, 40-pin ATA (IDE) drive connectors, to 50-, 68-, and 80-pin SCSI connectors.

Number of connectors

Some ribbon cables have only two connectors, one at either end. ATA cables, used to connect hard drives and optical drives, have three connectors, a motherboard connector at one end, a connector for the master drive at the other end, and a connector for the slave drive in the middle (but located nearer the master drive connector). SCSI cables, used in servers and high-end workstations, may have five or more drive connectors.

Two for One

With one exception, the number of wires in a cable matches the number of pins on the connector, or very nearly so. The exception is Ultra-ATA hard drive cables, which use 40-pin connectors with 80-wire cables. The "extra" 40 wires are ground wires that are placed between the signal wires to reduce interference. Although the physical connectors are identical, if you connect an Ultra-ATA hard drive with a 40-wire ATA cable drive, performance will be significantly slower than if you use the proper 80-wire cable.

Cable-select cables

Some ATA drive cables, called *cable-select* or *CS* cables, cut one conductor between the two device connectors. That is, while all 40 signal wires connect to the drive connector in the middle of the cable, only 39 of those signal wires are routed to the drive connector on the end of the cable. This missing conductor allows the position of the device on the cable to determine whether that device functions as a master or slave device, without requiring jumpers to be set.

FLAT VERSUS ROUND

So-called "round" ribbon cables have recently become popular, particularly with makers who cater to gamers and other enthusiasts. A round ribbon cable is simply a standard cable that has been sliced longitudinally into smaller groups of wires. For example, a standard flat 40-wire IDE ribbon cable might be sliced into ten 4-wire segments, which are then bound with cable ties or otherwise secured into a more or less round package. The advantage to round ribbon cables is that they reduce clutter inside the case and improve air flow. The disadvantage is that doing this reduces signal integrity on the individual wires because signal-bearing wires are put into closer proximity than intended. We recommend you avoid round ribbon cables, and replace any you find in any of your systems with flat ribbon cables. Note, however, that some round cables, such as Serial ATA cables, are designed to be round, and need not be replaced.

All ribbon cables used in current and recent systems use a *header-pin connector* similar to the ones shown in Figures 2-6 and 2-7. (Very old systems—those from the days of 5.25" floppy drives—used another type of connector called a card-edge connector, but that connector has not been used in new systems for more than a decade.) Header-pin connectors are used on cables for hard drives, optical drives, tape drives, and similar components, as well as for connecting embedded motherboard ports to external front or rear panel jacks.

The female header-pin connector on the cable has two parallel rows of holes that mate to a matching array of pins on the male connector on the motherboard or peripheral. On all but the least-expensive drives and other peripherals, these pins are enclosed in a plastic socket designed to accept the female connector. On inexpensive motherboards and adapter cards, the male connector may be just a naked set of pins. Even high-quality motherboards and adapter cards often use naked pins for secondary connectors (like USB ports or feature connectors).

Figure 2-7 shows an Ultra-ATA hard drive cable—compare the 80-wire cable shown here with the 40-wire cable shown in the preceding image—and two ATA interfaces on the motherboard. This cable uses two keying methods. The raised tab visible at the top of the cable connector mates to the slot visible on the lower edge of the connector shroud of the blue primary ATA interface on the motherboard. The blocked hole in the lower row of holes on the cable connector matches the missing pin visible in the top row of pins on the motherboard connector. Although there are 80 conductors, there are still only 40 pins. The 80-conductor cables have a grounded wire running between each pair of signal wires, which reduces electrical crosstalk, thus permitting higher data rates with greater reliability.

Figure 2-7. An 80-wire Ultra-ATA cable and two motherboard interfaces, showing keying

Also note the keying arrangements for the black secondary ATA motherboard connector. Like the primary motherboard connector, the secondary connector is keyed with a missing pin. But the secondary connector lacks the cut-out slot present in the primary motherboard connector, which means that this cable cannot be inserted into the secondary connector. That's by design. Although the 80-wire cable would function properly with the secondary connector, ASUS has chosen to key this Ultra-ATA cable to ensure that it can be connected only to the primary motherboard ATA interface connector, which is typically used to connect a hard drive. The secondary motherboard ATA connector, which is usually used to connect an optical drive, requires a cable that doesn't have the keying tab, such as the one shown in Figure 2-6.

Some header-pin connectors, male and female, are not keyed. Others use connector body keying, pin/hole keying, or both. This diversity means that it is quite possible to find that you cannot use a particular header-pin cable for its intended purpose. For example, we once attempted to use the ATA cable supplied with a drive to connect that drive to the secondary ATA header pin connector on the motherboard. The motherboard end of that cable was keyed by a blocked hole, but the header-pin connector on the motherboard had all pins present, which prevented the cable from seating. Fortunately, the cable that came with the motherboard fit both the motherboard and the drive connectors properly, allowing us to complete the installation.

If you run into such a keying problem, there are three possible solutions:

Use an unkeyed cable.
> The IDE and other header-pin cables that most computer stores sell use connectors that use neither connector body nor pin/hole keying. You can use one of these cables of the proper size to connect any device, but the absence of all keying means that you must be especially careful not to connect it backwards.

Remove the key from the cable.

If you don't have an unkeyed cable available, you may be able to remove the key from the existing cable. Most keyed cables use a small bit of plastic to block one of the holes. You may be able to use a needle to pry the block out far enough that you can extract it with your needlenose pliers. Alternatively, try pushing a pin into the block at an angle, then bending the top of the pin over and pulling both bent pin and block out with your pliers. If the key is a solid, integral part of the cable (which is rarely the case), you may be able to use a heated needle or pin to melt the key out of the hole far enough for the pin to seat.

Unblock the offending hole.

Heat a needle with a pair of pliers over a flame and carefully insert to a depth of 3/8" to bore open the offending plug.

Remove the offending pin.

Sometimes you have no choice. If the stores are closed, the only cable you have uses pin/hole keying with a solid block that you can't get out, and you must connect that cable to a header-pin connector that has all pins present, you have to go with what you have. You can use diagonal cutters to nip off the pin that prevents you from connecting the cable. Obviously, this is drastic. If you nip the wrong pin, you'll destroy the motherboard or expansion card, or at least render that interface unusable. Before you cut, see if you can swap cables within the PC to come up with an unkeyed cable for the problem connector. If not, you can sometimes bend the offending pin *slightly*—enough to allow the female connector to partially seat. This may be good enough to use as a temporary connection until you can replace the cable. If all else fails and you need to cut the pin, before doing so, align the keyed female connector with the pin array and verify just which pin needs to be cut. Also, check the manual for a detailed list of signal/pin assignments on that interface. The pin you are about to remove should be labeled No Connection or N/C in that list. Use the old carpenter's maxim here—measure twice and cut once.

Connector and keying issues aside, the most common mishap with header-pin connectors occurs when you install the cable offset by a column or a row. The shrouded male connectors used on most drives make this impossible to do, but the male connectors used on some cheap motherboards are an unshrouded double row of pins, making it very easy to install the connector with the pins and holes misaligned. Working in a dark PC, it's very easy to slide a connector onto a set of header pins and end up with an unconnected pair of pins at one end and an unconnected pair of holes at the other. It's just as easy to misalign the connector the other way, and end up with an entire row of pins and holes unconnected. One of our reviewers did this and fried a client's hard drive. If you need reading glasses, this isn't the time to find out the hard way.

Locating Pin 1

If you upgrade your system and it fails to boot or the new device doesn't work, chances are that you connected a ribbon cable backwards. This can't happen if all connectors and cables are keyed, but many systems have at least some unkeyed connectors. The good news is that connecting ribbon cables backwards almost never damages anything. We're tempted to say "never" without qualification, but there's a first time for everything. If your system doesn't boot after an upgrade, go back and verify the connections for each cable. Better yet, verify them before you restart the system.

To avoid connecting a ribbon cable backwards, locate pin 1 on each device and then make sure that pin 1 on one device connects to pin 1 on the other. This step is sometimes easier said than done. Nearly all ribbon cables use a colored stripe to indicate pin 1, so there's little chance of confusion there. However, not all devices label pin 1. Those that do usually use a silk-screened numeral 1 on the circuit board itself. If pin 1 is not labeled numerically, you can sometimes determine which is pin 1 in one of the following ways:

- Instead of a numeral, some manufacturers print a small arrow or triangle to indicate pin 1.

- The layout of some circuit boards allows no space for a label near pin 1. On these boards, the manufacturer may instead number the last pin. For example, rather than pin 1 being labeled on an ATA connector, pin 40 may be labeled on the other side of the connector.

- If there is no indication of pin 1 on the front of the board, turn it over (this is tough for an installed motherboard) and examine the reverse side. Some manufacturers use round solder connections for all pins other than 1, and a square solder connection for pin 1.

- If all else fails, you can make an educated guess. Many disk drives place pin 1 closest to the power supply connector. On a motherboard, pin 1 is often the one closest to the memory or processor. We freely admit that we use this method on occasion to avoid having to remove a disk drive or motherboard to locate pin 1 with certainty. We've never damaged a component using this quick-and-dirty method, but we use it only for ATA drives, rear-panel port connectors, and other cables that do not carry power. Don't try this with SCSI—particularly differential SCSI.

Once you locate an unmarked or unclearly marked pin 1, use nail polish or some other permanent means to mark it so that you won't have to repeat the process the next time. Wite-Out is really handy for this. Make a single stripe across both cable connector and plug and you'll have a visual confirmation that they align correctly.

For many years, most PCs used only the types of cables we've already described. In 2003, motherboards and drives began shipping that used a new standard called *Serial ATA* (often abbreviated *S-ATA* or *SATA*). For clarity, old-style ATA drives are now sometimes called *Parallel ATA* (*P-ATA* or *PATA*), although the formal name of the older standard has not changed.

The obvious difference between ATA devices and SATA devices is that they use different cables and connectors for power and data. Rather than the familiar wide 40-pin data connector and large 4-pin Molex power connector used by ATA devices (shown in Figure 2-8), SATA uses a 7-pin thin, flat data connector and a similar 15-pin power connector (shown in Figure 2-9).

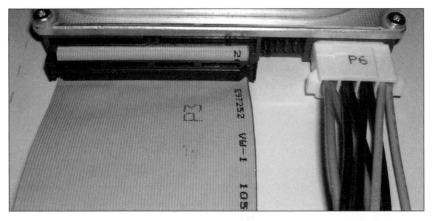

Figure 2-8. PATA data connector (left) and power connector

Figure 2-9. SATA power connector (left) and data connector

Missing Voltages

The SATA power cable shown in Figure 2-9 supplies only +5V on the red wire and +12V on the yellow wire, with two black ground wires. A fully compliant SATA power connector adds an orange +3.3V wire.

Perhaps coincidentally, the 15-pin SATA power connector is exactly the same width as the 4-pin Molex PATA power connector, although the SATA power connector is considerably thinner. At 8 mm wide, the 7-pin SATA data connector is much narrower than the 40-pin PATA data connector. This reduced overall width and thickness made SATA a natural for 2.5" notebook hard drives, which are becoming increasingly common in desktop systems as well.

FRAGILE CONNECTORS

Be very careful when you install or remove SATA data and power cables. The thinness of SATA connectors means they are fragile, although recent SATA connectors seem more robust than early models. Do not twist or torque the connector as you install or remove it. Install a connector by aligning the cable connector with the device connector and pressing straight inward until the connector seats. Remove a connector by pulling it straight outward, without putting any sideways force on it. Otherwise, you may snap off the connector.

The relatively large number of pins in the SATA power connector accommodates two SATA design goals. First, additional connectors are required to support hot-plugging—installing or removing drives without turning off the system—which is a part of the SATA standard. Second, SATA power connectors are designed to provide voltages of +3.3V, +5V, and +12V, rather than just the +5V and +12V provided by the PATA power connector. The lower +3.3V voltage is a forward-looking provision for smaller, quieter, cooler-running drives that will be introduced over the coming years.

Although all PATA power connectors are keyed, the same cannot be said for PATA data connectors. One of the design goals of SATA was to use unambiguous keying. SATA uses L-shaped contact bodies, as shown in Figure 2-10, which prevent a cable from being installed upside-down or backward. (While there's no Pin 1 to worry about, you may find it handy to use a Wite-Out pen to label the UP position of the SATA cable and the connector, or to run a stripe across both.)

Figure 2-10. A group of four SATA data connectors on a motherboard, showing the L-shaped keying

SATA differs from PATA in two other respects. First, PATA allows two devices to be connected to each interface, one jumpered as master and the other as slave. An SATA interface supports only one device, eliminating the need for configuring the device as master or slave. In effect, all SATA devices are master devices. Second, PATA limits the length of data cables to 18" (45.7 cm), while SATA allows data cables as long as 1 meter (39.4"). The thinness and additional length of SATA data cables makes it much easier to route and dress the cables in the case—particularly in a full-tower case—and contributes to improved air flow.

Working with expansion cards

Expansion cards are circuit boards that you install in a PC to provide functions that the PC motherboard itself does not provide. Figure 2-11 shows an ATI All-In-Wonder 9800 Pro AGP graphics adapter and video capture card, a typical expansion card.

Figure 2-11. ATI All-In-Wonder 9800 Pro, a typical expansion card

Years ago, most PCs had several expansion cards installed. A typical vintage-2000 PC might have had a video card, a sound card, a LAN adapter, an internal modem, and perhaps a communications adapter of some sort or a SCSI host adapter. It wasn't uncommon for PCs back then to have all of their expansion slots filled.

Things are different nowadays. Nearly all recent motherboards include embedded audio and LAN adapters. Many include embedded video, and some include less common features such as embedded FireWire, modems, SCSI host adapters, and other devices. Because so many features are routinely incorporated in modern motherboards, it's not unusual for a relatively new PC to have no expansion cards installed at all.

Still, installing an expansion card is an easy, inexpensive way to upgrade an older system. You might, for example, install an AGP graphics card to upgrade the on-board video, a video capture card to turn your PC into a digital video recorder, an SATA controller to add support for SATA drives, a USB adapter to add more USB 2.0 ports, or an 802.11g card to add wireless networking.

Don't Leave Holes in Your Case

Cheap cases sometimes have slot covers that must be twisted off to be removed and are destroyed in the process. If you need to cover an open slot in such a case and don't have a spare slot cover, ask your local computer store, which probably has a stack of them in back. Or just use duct tape to cover the gap. (Put it on the outside of the case, where it won't goop up a slot that you may need to use later.) If you're worried about RF leakage, 3M makes some metal tapes that are conductive through the adhesive, but you'd have to put them inside the case, of course, to take advantage of that.

Each expansion card plugs into an *expansion slot* located on the motherboard or on a *riser card* that attaches to the motherboard. The rear panel of the PC chassis includes a cutout for each expansion slot, which provides external access to the card. The cutouts for vacant expansion slots are covered by thin metal *slot covers* that are secured to the chassis. These covers prevent dust from entering through the cutout and also preserve the cooling air flow provided by the power supply fan and any auxiliary fans installed in the system.

To install an expansion card, remove the slot cover, which may be secured by a small screw or may simply be die-stamped into the surrounding metal. In the latter case, carefully twist off the slot cover using a screwdriver or your needlenose pliers. (Be careful! The edges can be quite sharp.) If you need to replace the slot cover later, secure it to the chassis using a small screw that fits a notch in the top portion of the slot cover. The back of the expansion card forms a bracket that resembles a slot cover and is secured to the chassis in the same way. Depending on the purpose of the card, this bracket may contain connectors that allow you to connect external cables to the card.

There is frequently a need to install and remove expansion cards when you work on a PC. Even if you are not working on a particular expansion card, you must sometimes remove it to provide access to the section of the PC that you do need to work on. Installing and removing expansion cards can be hard or easy, depending on the quality of the case, the motherboard, and the expansion card itself. High-quality cases, motherboards, and expansion cards are built to tight tolerances, making expansion cards easy to insert and remove. Cheap cases, motherboards, and expansion cards have such loose tolerances that you must sometimes literally bend sheet metal to force them to fit.

People often ask whether it matters which card goes into which slot. Beyond the obvious—there are different kinds of expansion slots, and a card can be installed only in a slot of the same type—there are four considerations that determine the answer to this question:

Physical restrictions

> Depending on the size of the card and the design of the motherboard and case, a given card may not physically fit a particular slot. For example, the case design may prevent a particular slot from accepting a full-length card. If this occurs, you may have to juggle expansion cards, moving a shorter card from a full-length slot to a short slot and then using the freed-up full-length slot for the new expansion card. Also, even if a card physically fits a particular slot, a connector protruding from that card may interfere with another card, or there may not be enough room to route a cable to it.

Technical restrictions

> There are several variables, including slot type, card type, BIOS, and operating system, that determine whether a card is position sensitive.

For this reason, although it may not always be possible, it's good general practice to reinstall a card into the same slot that you removed it from. If you do install the card in a different slot, don't be surprised if Windows forces you to reinstall the drivers. If you're really lucky, you might even have the pleasure of going through Product Activation again.

ON THE GRIPPING HAND . . .

Although interrupt conflicts are rare with PCI motherboards and modern operating systems, they can occur. In particular, PCI motherboards with more than four PCI slots share interrupts between slots, so installing two PCI cards that require the same resource in two PCI slots that share that interrupt may cause a conflict. If that occurs, you can eliminate the conflict by relocating one of the conflicting expansion cards to another slot. Even in a system with all PC slots occupied, we have frequently eliminated a conflict just by swapping the cards around. See your motherboard manual for details.

Two's a Crowd

Rather than installing two expansion cards in adjacent slots, try to space them out as far as possible to improve air flow and cooling and to make any connectors or jumpers on the cards as accessible as possible.

Electrical considerations

Although it is relatively uncommon nowadays, some combinations of motherboard and power supply can provide adequate power for power-hungry expansion cards like internal modems only if those cards are installed in the slots nearest the power supply. This was a common problem years ago, when power supplies were less robust and cards required more power than they do now, but you are unlikely to experience this problem with modern equipment. One exception to this is AGP video cards. Many recent motherboards support only AGP 2.0 1.5V video cards and/or AGP 3.0 0.8V video cards, which means that old 3.3V AGP cards are incompatible with that slot.

Interference considerations

Another problem that is much less common with recent equipment is that some expansion cards generate enough RF to interfere with cards in adjacent slots. Years ago, the manuals for some cards (notably some disk controllers, modems, and network adapters) described this problem, and suggested that their card be installed as far as possible from other cards. We haven't seen this sort of warning on a new card in years, but you may still encounter it if your system includes older cards.

To install an expansion card, proceed as follows:

1. Read the instructions that come with the card. In particular, read carefully any instructions about installing software drivers for the card. For some cards, you must install the driver before you install the card; for other cards, you must install the card first and then the driver.

2. Remove the cover from the chassis and examine the motherboard to determine which expansion slots are free. Locate a free expansion slot of the type required by the expansion card. Recent PCs may have

several types of expansion slots available, including 32- and 64-bit PCI general-purpose expansion slots, an AGP video card slot, one or two PCI Express x16 video card slots, and one or more PCI Express x1 feature slots. If more than one slot of the proper type is free, you can reduce the likelihood of heat-related problems by choosing one that maintains spacing between the expansion cards rather than one that clusters the cards. Figure 2-12 shows a standard arrangement of slots for an AGP motherboard, with five white 32-bit PCI slots at the upper left and one dark brown AGP slot below and to the right of the PCI slots. Figure 2-13 shows a standard arrangement of slots for a PCI Express motherboard, with, from left to right, two white 32-bit PCI slots; two short, black PCI Express X1 slots; two more white PCI slots; and one long, black PCI Express X16 slot for a video adapter.

Figure 2-12. Five white PCI slots and a dark brown AGP slot

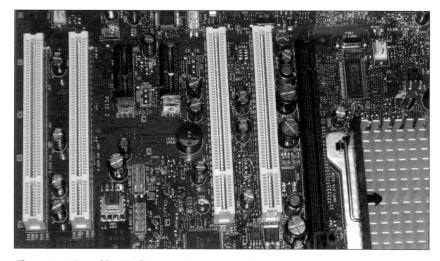

Figure 2-13. Two white PCI slots, two PCI Express X1 slots, two more white PCI slots, and a black PCI Express X16 video card slot

3. An access hole for each expansion slot is present on the rear of the chassis. For unoccupied slots, this hole is blocked by a thin metal slot cover secured by a screw that threads downward into the chassis. Determine which slot cover corresponds to the slot you chose. This may not be as easy as it sounds. Some types of expansion slots are offset, and the slot cover that appears to line up with that slot may not be the right one. You can verify which slot cover corresponds to a slot by aligning the expansion card itself with the slot and seeing which slot cover the card bracket matches to.

4. Remove the screw that secures the slot cover, slide the slot cover out, and place it and the screw aside.

5. If an internal cable blocks access to the slot, gently move it aside or disconnect it temporarily, noting the proper connections so that you will know where to reconnect it.

6. Guide the expansion card gently into position, but do not yet seat it. Verify visually that the tongue on the bottom of the expansion card bracket will slide into the matching gap in the chassis and that the expansion card bus connector section aligns properly with the expansion slot. With a high-quality case, everything should align properly with no effort. With a cheap case, you may have to use pliers to bend the card bracket slightly to make the card, chassis, and slot all line up. Rather than doing that, we prefer to replace the case.

7. When you are sure that everything is properly aligned, position your thumbs on the top edge of the card, with one thumb at each end of the expansion slot below the card, and press gently straight down on the top of the card until it seats in the slot, as shown in Figure 2-14. Apply pressure centered on the expansion slot beneath the card, and avoid twisting or torquing the card. Some cards seat easily with little tactile feedback. Others require quite a bit of pressure and you can feel them snap into place. Once you complete this step, the expansion card bracket should align properly with the screw hole in the chassis.

Figure 2-14. Seat the expansion card by pressing down evenly

8. Replace the screw that secures the expansion card bracket, and replace any cables that you temporarily disconnected while installing the card. Connect any external cables required by the new card—don't tighten the thumbscrews quite yet—and give the system a quick once-over to make sure you haven't forgotten to do anything.

9. Turn on the PC and verify that the new card is recognized and that it functions as expected. Once you have done so, power the system down, replace the cover, and reconnect everything. Store the unused slot cover with your spares.

To remove an expansion card, proceed as follows:

1. Remove the system cover and locate the expansion card to be removed. It's surprising how easy it is to remove the wrong card if you're not careful. No wonder surgeons occasionally get it wrong.

2. Once you're sure you've located the right card, disconnect any external cables connected to it. If the card has internal cables connected, disconnect those as well. You may also need to disconnect or reroute other unrelated cables temporarily to gain access to the card. If so, label those you disconnect.

3. Remove the screw that secures the card bracket, and place it safely aside.

4. Grasp the card firmly near both ends and pull straight up with moderate force. If the card will not release, *gently* rock it from front to back (parallel to the slot connector) to break the connection. Be careful when grasping the card. Some cards have sharp solder points that can cut you badly if you don't take precautions. If there's no safe place to grasp the card and you don't have a pair of heavy gloves handy, try using heavy corrugated cardboard between the card and your skin.

5. If you plan to save the card, place it in an antistatic bag for storage. It's a good idea to label the bag with the date and the make and model of the card for future reference. If you have a driver disk, throw that in the bag as well. If you are not installing a new expansion card in the vacated slot, install a slot cover to ensure proper air flow and replace the screw that secures the slot cover.

If you're removing an AGP or PCI Express video card, take particular care. Many motherboards include a video card retention mechanism, shown in Figure 2-16, that physically latches the card into place. When you remove a a video card, release the latch and pull gently upward on the card until it comes free. If you attempt to force it, you could damage the video card and/or the motherboard.

Figure 2-15. Barbara pulls a recalcitrant expansion card the safe way

Figure 2-16. The AGP retention bracket physically locks an AGP card into the slot

Danger, Will Robinson!

You may someday encounter an expansion card that's seated so tightly that it appears to be welded to the motherboard. When this happens, it's tempting to gain some leverage by pressing upwards with your thumb on a connector on the back of the card bracket. Don't do it. The edges of the chassis against which the bracket seats may be razor sharp, and you may cut yourself badly when the card finally gives. Instead, loop two pieces of cord around the card to the front and rear of the slot itself, and use them to "walk" the card out of its slot, as shown in Figure 2-15. Your shoelaces will work if nothing else is at hand. For a card that's well and truly stuck, you may need a second pair of hands to apply downward pressure on the motherboard itself to prevent it from flexing too much and possibly cracking as you pull the card from the slot.

Setting jumpers

Jumpers are sometimes used to set hardware options on PCs and peripherals. Jumpers allow you to make or break a single electrical connection, which is used to configure one aspect of a component. Jumper or switch settings specify such things as the front-side bus speed of the processor, whether a PATA drive functions as a master or slave device, whether a particular function on an expansion card is enabled or disabled, and so on.

Older motherboards and expansion cards may use dozens of jumpers to set most or all configuration options. Recent motherboards use fewer jumpers, and instead use the BIOS setup program to configure components. In fact, most current motherboards have only one or a few jumpers. You use these jumpers when you install the motherboard to configure static options such as processor speed or to enable infrequent actions such as updating the BIOS.

More properly called a *jumper block*, a *jumper* is a small plastic block with embedded metal contacts that can bridge two pins to form an electrical connection. When a jumper block bridges two pins, that connection is called *on*, *closed*, *shorted*, or *enabled*. When the jumper block is removed, that connection is called *off*, *open*, or *disabled*. The pins themselves are also called a jumper, usually abbreviated JPx, where x is a number that identifies the jumper.

Jumpers with more than two pins may be used to select among more than two states. One common arrangement, shown in Figure 2-17, is a jumper

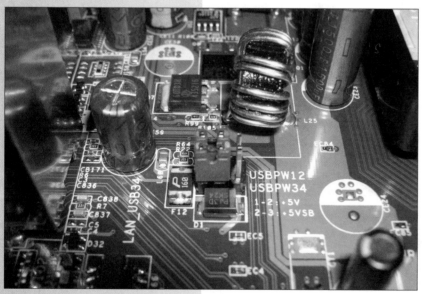

Figure 2-17. Two jumpers shorting the 1–2 pins of 3-pin jumper blocks

that contains a row of three pins, numbered 1, 2, and 3. You can select among three states by shorting pins 1 and 2, pins 2 and 3, or by removing the jumper block entirely. Note that you cannot jumper pins 1 and 3 because a jumper can be used to close only an adjacent pair of pins. In this example, the USBPW12 and USBPW34 jumpers allow you to set the Wake-on-USB configuration for the four USB ports numbered 1 through 4. These jumpers are shown shorting pins 1 and 2, which configures the motherboard to use +5V for Wake-on-USB. If we moved those jumpers to the 2–3 position, Wake-on-USB would use +5Vsb.

You can often use your fingers to install and remove isolated jumpers, but needlenose pliers are usually the best tool. However, jumpers are sometimes clustered so tightly that even needlenose pliers may be too large to grab just the jumper you want to work on. When this happens, use a hemostat or mosquito forceps (available from any drugstore). When you need to set a jumper open, don't remove the jumper block entirely. Instead, install it on just one pin. This leaves the connection open, but ensures that a jumper block will be handy if you later need to close that connection.

Jumper blocks come in at least two sizes that are not interchangeable:

- Standard blocks are the larger and the more commonly used size, and are often dark blue or black. (The jumpers shown in Figure 2-17 are the standard size.)

- Mini jumper blocks are used on some disk drives and boards that use surface-mount components, and are often white or light blue.

New components always come with enough jumper blocks to configure them. If you remove one when configuring a device, tape it to a convenient flat area on the device for possible future use. It's also a good idea to keep a few spares on hand, just in case you need to reconfigure a component from which someone has removed all the "surplus" jumper blocks. Any time you discard a board or disk drive, strip the jumper blocks from it first and store them in your parts tube. (If you don't have an official parts tube, do what we do: use an old aspirin bottle with a snap-on lid.)

Installing drives

We planned to write an overview section here to describe how to install and configure drives. Unfortunately, we found it impossible to condense that information to an overview level. Physical installation procedures vary significantly, and configuration procedures even more, depending on numerous factors, including:

- Drive type

- Physical drive size: both height and width, and (sometimes) depth

- Internal (hard drives) versus externally accessible (floppy, optical, and tape drives)

- Mounting arrangements provided by the particular case

- Drive interface (ATA versus Serial ATA)

For specific information about installing and configuring various drive types, including illustrations and examples, refer to the chapter that covers that type of device.

System Maintenance 3

Airlines, trucking companies, and other large organizations devote much more time, money, and effort to cleaning and preventative maintenance than they do to repairs. That's because cleaning and regular system maintenance repay their costs many times over by reducing the frequency and cost of repairs. It's almost always cheaper to prevent something from breaking than it is to fix it after it's broken. The same is true for PCs.

System Cleaning

Dirt is the main enemy of PCs. Dirt blocks air flow, causing the system to run hotter and less reliably. Dirt acts as thermal insulation, causing components to overheat and thereby shortening their service lives. Dirt causes fans to run faster (and louder) as they attempt to keep the system cool. Dirt worms its way into connectors, increasing electrical resistance and reducing reliability. Dirt corrodes contact surfaces. Dirt is nasty stuff.

Computers become dirty as a natural part of running. Fans suck dust, pet hair, and other contaminants into the case, where they rest on every surface. Even in clean rooms, operating theaters, and other very clean environments, a PC will eventually become dirty. If there's any dust in the air at all, the system fans will suck it in and deposit it inside the case, where it will become a problem sooner or later.

The severity of the problem depends on the environment. Industrial environments are often filthy, so much so that standard PCs are unusable. In a shop-floor environment, we have seen standard PCs become so clogged with dirt—literally in one day—that they stopped running because of overheating. Typical home and office environments are much better, but still surprisingly bad. Pets, carpeting, cigarette smoking, gas or oil heat—all of these contribute to dirty PCs.

Routine weekly vacuuming of the case exterior helps, but is not sufficient. Figure 3-1 shows the back I/O panel of a PC that was left running 24 hours a day for 6 months in a typical residential environment—which happens to be our home—without being cleaned other than casual vacuuming of the accessible areas of the case. (Barbara asked Robert to point out that she vacuums thoroughly and dusts every week, but that Robert specifically asked her to make no special effort to clean this system so that he could use it as an illustration.)

KEEP IT OFF THE FLOOR

Jim Cooley notes that after hundreds of house calls, he's found that systems kept off the floor are generally much cleaner. He thinks it's because dust hovers at ground level.

Figure 3-1. Rear I/O panel of a PC that has gone uncleaned for six months

Figure 3-2. Front panel of a PC that has gone uncleaned for six months

Six months without a thorough cleaning has left this system totally clogged with dust and pet hair. The purple LPT port at the upper right is stuffed with dust, as are the USB ports at the left.

The front of the system is no better, as Figure 3-2 shows. Dust and dog hair has collected at every small gap through which air is drawn into the case. And yet, this system—which happens to be Robert's den system—did not appear particularly dirty at first glance. The rear of the system was inaccessible and completely out of view. All of the dust and dog hair shown in Figure 3-2 was also invisible, concealed by a hinged door that closes over the drive bays and power switch area.

Pulling the front bezel from the case reveals the built-in air filter shown in Figure 3-3. At first glance, it doesn't appear too bad. There's some dust accumulation, but the filter appears mostly clear. That's because the filter had accumulated so much dust that when we removed the front bezel the dust fell off in a pile, partially visible at the bottom of Figure 3-3.

Routine vacuuming of the case exterior helps keep the dust down, but it's not a complete solution. Every few weeks to every few months—depending on how dirty your environment is—you'll need to do a more thorough job. To begin, vacuum the exterior surfaces of the case, if you haven't done so already, and if necessary use Windex, Fantastic, Formula 409, or a similar household cleaning solution to remove grease and other accumulations from the case exterior.

Although you can get by with just a standard vacuum cleaner and a brush or two, it's easier to do the job properly if you have the right tools. Most computer stores sell vacuum attachments intended for use with PCs. These attachments are small enough to get in all the cracks and crevices, and the adapter that you use to connect them to your home vacuum is often designed to cut down the air flow to a level more appropriate for cleaning a PC. (We've used some vacuum cleaners that we actually feared might suck components off the motherboard.)

Cleaning the exterior with a standard vacuum cleaner probably missed some dirt, so to begin the deep cleaning, connect your PC cleaning attachments and go to work. Begin with the rear of the system. Figure 3-4 shows one of these PC vacuum attachments, a small brush, being used to clean the rear I/O panel. (Don't be tempted to use a gas station air hose. The air from these hoses often contains water or oil from the compressor.)

Figure 3-3. Built-in air filter

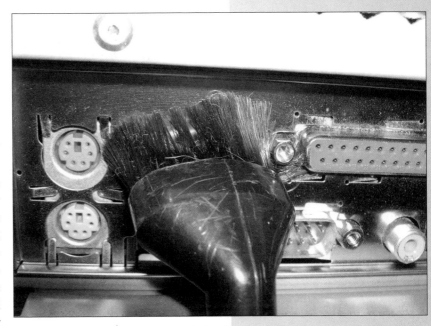

Figure 3-4. Using a vacuum attachment designed for cleaning PCs

---

Chapter 3: System Maintenance

Chances are good that the power supply fan blades are filthy. Depending on the power supply, you may or may not be able to remove the grill that protects the fan blades. If you can remove the grill, do so. Otherwise, use a screwdriver or similar implement to hold the fan blades in place as you vacuum them, as shown in Figure 3-5. (If left free, the fan blades will simply spin in the air flow of the vacuum, making them impossible to clean.)

If the vacuum isn't doing the job, use a brush with long bristles to knock the dust and grime off the fan blades and vacuum it up later. While you're cleaning the fan blades, try to position the system so that the gunk falls outward rather than into the body of the power supply. If there are areas of the fan blades you can't reach with the brush, try using "canned air" or zero-residue cleaner.

Figure 3-5. Cleaning the power supply fan

To clean a particularly filthy power supply, we sometimes remove it from the case and use an air compressor to blow it out. If you do that, make certain to prevent the fan blades from moving while the high-pressure air is striking them.

ELECTROCUTION ISN'T FUN

Although it's safe to remove the power supply from the system when it needs a thorough cleaning, *never* open the case of the power supply itself. Power supplies contain large capacitors, which may hold voltage long after the power supply is disconnected from power receptacles.

When you finish cleaning the back of the system, remove the side panel(s) from the case to expose the interior. Use the vacuum cleaner to remove the bulk of the dust from the floor of the case and other easily accessible areas. Use a brush to remove any large clumps of dust that are visible. (You'll need to revacuum these areas later, but removing most of the dust first makes it a lot more pleasant to work inside the case.)

Most mini-tower and similar cases have a removable front bezel. Some front bezels attach to the chassis with screws, but most use plastic locking tabs. Many cases have a wire mesh air filter behind the front bezel that accumulates huge amounts of dust. Even if your case has no air filter, the area between the front bezel and the front of the chassis is a dust magnet, because that's where most of the air is drawn into the case. Pull the front bezel and use your vacuum cleaner to remove the dust, hair, and other grunge, as shown in Figure 3-6.

Open the Door

While you're working on the case exterior, clean the floppy drive, tape drive, and similar drives inside and out. Access is pretty limited with such drives, but you may be able to hold the drive door open with the tip of a pen or other small instrument while you use the vacuum to suck out dust. If the drive is really filthy, use a can of compressed air to free the dust before you vacuum. Tray-based optical drives are a different matter, because the interior of the drive is blocked whether the tray is open or closed. Such drives are usually well protected against dust, so we simply do the best we can on the exterior of the drive and let it go at that.

Figure 3-6. Vacuuming the front panel area

With the bulk of the dirt removed, you can begin cleaning the inside of the case. Work from the top down, so that any dust you dislodge falls onto areas you haven't yet cleaned. Assuming that you have the case lying flat on its side, motherboard at the bottom, the next step is to clean any supplemental case fans, as shown in Figure 3-7.

Use a brush or the brush attachment of your vacuum to remove the dust and grime adhering to the fan blades, hub, and grill. Use your finger to prevent the fan blades from rotating as you clean them, and make sure to clean both sides of the fan blades and the hub. If necessary, remove the four screws that attach the fan to the case, and remove the entire fan for thorough cleaning.

Fan Mounting Connectors

Some case fans, including the one shown in Figure 3-7, are secured to the case with flexible plastic snap-in connectors rather than screws. If your case fan uses these, you'll have to cut the connectors to remove the fan. Make sure that you have replacement connectors on hand before you remove the fan. You can substitute screws if necessary, but the soft plastic pull-through connectors reduce noise and vibration by isolating the fan assembly from the case.

Figure 3-7. Cleaning a supplemental case fan

The power supply's internal grill, shown in Figure 3-8, is another area that accumulates a great deal of dirt. Nearly all modern power supplies use exhaust fans rather than intake fans, which means that air is drawn through the case and power supply before being exhausted from the rear of the power supply.

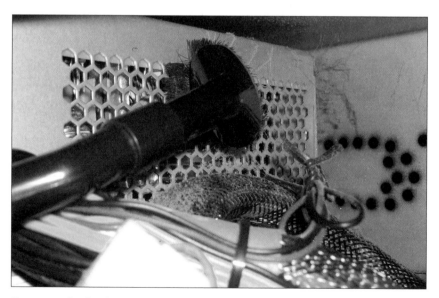

Figure 3-8. Cleaning the power supply's internal grill

It's very important to keep this area clean, because blockage of the grill not only reduces general system cooling significantly, but may cause the power supply to run quite hot. That reduces the amount of amperage the power supply can provide, and may cause fluctuations in voltage regulation, both of which reduce system stability.

Continue working your way down within the case. Clean the hard drive bays, as shown in Figure 3-9, the optical drive bays, any expansion cards, and the other areas of the case above the motherboard.

Figure 3-9. Cleaning the hard drive bay area

At this point, you have cleaned the system down to the motherboard level. There're probably some clumps of dust lying on the motherboard, so vacuum them up before proceeding.

The next step is to clean the CPU cooling fan and heatsink. This is both the most important step in system cleaning and one of the most difficult. The heatsink/fan area accumulates dust readily because the fan moves a lot of dust-laden air through the closely spaced heatsink fins. As dust accumulates, it covers the blades of the heatsink, insulating them and thereby reducing their ability to radiate the heat produced by the processor. To compensate, the CPU cooling fan spins faster (and makes more noise) as it tries to draw enough air through the heatsink to cool the processor. Eventually, the air channels in the heatsink become completely clogged and the heatsink loses its ability to cool the processor. The processor begins running very hot, which can cause data corruption, system lock-ups, and even damage to the processor itself.

To avoid such problems, it's important to keep the CPU cooler clean. To begin cleaning the CPU cooler, use a brush or vacuum cleaner to remove the muck from the top of the cooling fan, as shown in Figure 3-10. If necessary, use your finger or a small tool to prevent the fan blades from spinning as you clean them.

Figure 3-10. Vacuuming the CPU cooling fan blades

After the first pass with the vacuum cleaner or brush, the top of the cooling fan should be relatively clean. Looking through the fan blades, examine the heatsink carefully. You'll probably see a great deal of dirt clogging up the fins of the heatsink, as Figure 3-11 shows. If so, you're not finished yet. You have to get most (ideally, all) of that dust out from between the fins.

Figure 3-11. Dust clogging the heatsink fins

The quick, easy way to clean the heatsink fins is to use a can of compressed air, as shown in Figure 3-12, which you can also use to remove dirt from the underside of the fan blades.

Figure 3-12. Using canned air to clean the heatsink fins

Unfortunately, canned air often isn't enough to do the job, particularly if the heatsink fins are completely clogged with dirt. If your heatsink is clogged badly, the only alternative may be to remove the fan from the heatsink so that you can get at the dirt. Some CPU coolers, including the one shown in Figure 3-13, allow you to remove the fan simply by removing the four screws that secure it to the heatsink body. If your CPU cooler has such a design, remove the screws, disconnect the fan power cable from the fan power header on the motherboard, and lift the fan away from the heatsink.

Figure 3-13. Removing the screws that secure the CPU fan to the heatsink

Why That Can of "Air" Sloshes

If you don't have a can of zero-residue cleaner, use your canned air instead. Canned air actually contains a liquid propellant that vaporizes at low temperatures. The "air" that comes out of the tube is actually the propellant in its vapor form. If you invert the can while spraying, liquid propellant comes out of the tube. This liquid propellant is a good solvent for the greasy film on the heatsink (and on fans and elsewhere). To clean the heatsink, simply invert the can and drench the heatsink with the liquid propellant. It will dissolve the film and rinse it down to the base of the heatsink. The liquid vaporizes in a few seconds, leaving the heatsink clean.

If the design of your CPU cooler doesn't have accessible screws, the only solution is to remove the entire CPU cooler for cleaning. Depending on the arrangement of your case, motherboard, and the clamping mechanism that secures the CPU cooler to the processor socket, you may have to remove the motherboard from the case in order to remove the CPU cooler without damaging anything. If so, refer to Chapter 4.

With the CPU fan removed, all or most of the heatsink body should be visible, as shown in Figure 3-14. Use a brush with long bristles to remove as much dust as possible—not just from the top of the heatsink, but from between its fins. You'll probably scatter clumps of dust around while doing this. Vacuum them up before proceeding.

Figure 3-14. Use a brush to remove most of the dust from the heatsink

Once you've removed as much dust as possible with the brush and vacuum, used canned air to blow out the remaining dust and any bristles that came off the brush. If you smoke, or if you heat with gas or oil, you'll probably find that the heatsink fins are covered with a brown, greasy film. This film attracts and holds dust, so leaving it in place just means that your heatsink will clog up again that much faster. Remove the film by spraying zero-residue cleaner directly on the heatsink to dissolve and wash away the film.

Figure 3-15 shows the heatsink after partial cleaning. The bright reddish areas are the naked copper of the heatsink after being flooded with propellant from the canned air. The darker brownish areas are still covered by the greasy film.

Once you have the heatsink body thoroughly clean, clean the CPU fan itself and then reassemble the CPU cooler. (Make sure to install the fan right-side up, and don't forget to reconnect the CPU fan power cable to the CPU fan power header on the motherboard.)

If you want to do a complete job, remove all of the expansion cards and memory modules and vacuum out their slots thoroughly. Many expansion cards and memory modules use gold contacts, which do not oxidize. Some use contacts made of tin or other metals, however. Those are subject to oxidation, which can degrade the quality of the electrical connection.

There's not much you can do to clean the inaccessible contacts in the slots other than drenching them down with contact cleaner, but you can at least clean the contacts on the expansion cards and memory modules directly. Some people use a soft, clean rubber eraser for cleaning contacts, but we think the best tool for that purpose is a fresh dollar bill, which has just the right abrasiveness to clean the contacts without damaging them. Simply rub the dollar bill briskly against the contacts, as shown in Figure 3-16.

Do a final check to make sure that no dust remains inside the case. Check all of the cables to make sure you haven't left anything disconnected, and verify that all expansion cards and memory modules are fully seated. Once everything looks right, connect the keyboard, mouse, and monitor, and power up the system. If the system boots normally and all fans are running properly, reinstall all the panels.

Depending on the dustiness of your environment, the system shouldn't require another thorough cleaning

Figure 3-15. A partially cleaned heatsink, showing film accumulation

Figure 3-16. Polishing the contacts on an expansion card using a dollar bill

for another three to six months. If you have hardwood floors, don't smoke, heat with electricity or another clean fuel, and don't have pets, weekly vacuuming of the system exterior may suffice for another year or more.

STRIPPING DOWN

Before you reassemble the system, look at each component and decide if any are unneeded. For example, if you've recently started using broadband service and converted your home network to wireless, your internal modem and Ethernet card may no longer be needed. Removing unused components (and their drivers) frees up resources, improves system stability, reduces the amount of heat generated by the system, and improves ventilation.

Preventative Maintenance

The best way to deal with problems is to stop them from happening in the first place. That's where preventative maintenance comes in.

A good preventative maintenance program incorporates a comprehensive backup plan, measures to secure the system against malicious exploits, periodic hardware and software maintenance, and steps to maintain general system tidiness. The goals of preventative maintenance are to reduce the likelihood of hardware failures, extend the useful life of the system, minimize system crashes caused by outdated drivers and other software problems, secure the system against viruses and other malware, and prevent data loss.

The following sections outline a basic preventative maintenance program that you can use as a basis for developing a program that fits your own and your system's needs.

Backing up the system

Maintaining a good set of backups is a critical part of preventative maintenance.

The availability of inexpensive hard drives and motherboards that support RAID 1 mirroring had led many people to depend solely on RAID 1 to protect their data. That's a very bad idea. RAID 1 protects only against the failure of a hard drive, which is partial protection at best. RAID 1 does nothing to protect against:

- Data being corrupted by viruses or hardware problems
- Accidentally deleting, overwriting, or modifying important files
- Catastrophic data loss, such as fire or theft of your equipment

To protect against those and other threats, the only reliable solution is to make backup copies of your data periodically to some form of removable media, such as tapes, optical discs, or removable hard drives.

Backup hardware

In the past, there weren't any really good hardware choices for backing up home and SOHO systems. Tape drives were expensive, complex to install and configure, used fragile and expensive media, and were painfully slow. CD writers, although reasonably fast and inexpensive, stored such a small amount of data that many people who used them for backing up were reminded of the Bad Olde Days of swapping floppy disks. External hard drives were expensive and of dubious reliability.

Things have changed. Consumer-grade tape drives are still expensive and slow, although it's easier to install a modern ATAPI tape drive than it was in the days when tape drives used SCSI or proprietary interfaces. CD writers are still reasonably fast and inexpensive, and are a good solution if your data fits on one or two CDs. The most significant change in consumer-grade backup hardware has been the introduction of inexpensive DVD writers and external or removable hard drives. Table 3-1 lists the important characteristics of the types of backup hardware used for home and SOHO backups.

Table 3-1. Important characteristics of backup hardware

Method	Capacity	Transfer rate	Drive cost	Media cost/GB	Media cost/unit	Reliability
CD writer	0.65 to 1 GB	Medium	$20 to $50	$0.10 to $0.40	$0.10 to $0.25	Low
Internal DVD writer	4.4 to 8.5 GB	Medium to fast	$40 to $150	$0.05 to $0.50	$0.50 to $4.00	Low
External DVD writer	4.4 to 8.5 GB	Medium to fast	$125 to $250	$0.05 to $0.50	$0.50 to $4.00	Low
External hard drive	80 to 500 GB	Very fast	N/A	$0.50 to $1.00	$100 to $500	Medium
Removable hard drive	80 to 500 GB	Very fast	$75 to $150	$0.40 to $0.80	$75 to $400	Medium
Tape drive	10 to 100 GB	Slow to medium	$200 to $2,000	$0.30 to $5.00	$5 to $150	High

In addition to cost considerations, you face two issues in choosing backup hardware: capacity and speed. Ideally, the hardware you choose should be capacious enough to store the entire contents of your hard drive—or at least all of your user data—on one disc or tape. Just as important, the backup hardware should be fast enough to complete a full backup and verify in whatever time you have available for backups. It's easy to meet both those requirements if you have an unlimited budget, but most of us have to compromise one or the other to avoid breaking the bank.

For most home and SOHO users, a DVD writer is the best compromise. For $100 or less (possibly much less), you can buy an internal DVD writer and a supply of discs sufficient to implement a comprehensive backup plan. If you have multiple non-networked systems or notebooks to back up, you can use an external USB/FireWire DVD writer to back them all up individually.

The capacity of a writable DVD—4.4 GB for single layer and 8.5 GB for dual-layer—suffices for many systems (we'll explain why shortly). Writing and verifying a full disc takes only a few minutes, which makes it practical to back up frequently, even several times during a work day. The only downside to writable DVD is that optical discs have much less robust error correction than tapes, which means there's a small chance that a file won't be recoverable from a backup DVD. That's an easy problem to solve, though. Simply back up more frequently and keep your older backup discs. If you can't recover the file from the current disc, you'll be able to recover it from the one immediately preceding.

DISC VERSUS TAPE

We're belt-and-suspenders types when it comes to protecting our data. Before affordable DVD writers became available, we backed up our own systems every day with Travan and DDS tape drives. And we admit that the less robust error correction of optical discs initially gave us pause. But we converted a couple years ago to using DVD+R and DVD+RW for backups, and we haven't looked back. We use top-quality discs (Verbatim premium) and have never had a problem recovering a file. Tape still has its place in corporate data centers, but as far as we're concerned, it's obsolete for home and SOHO users.

If DVD isn't capacious enough, consider using external or removable hard drives, which store from 80 GB to 500+ GB. In either case, think of the hard drive as the media rather than as a drive. In other words, an external or removable hard drive is really just a funny-looking tape or disc, which you treat just as you would any other removable backup medium. Just as you need several discs or tapes for a good backup rotation, you'll also need several external or removable hard drives. In terms of reliability, hard drives are intermediate between tapes and optical discs. Hard drives have more robust error detection and correction than optical discs, but less robust than tape. Once again, this needn't be of concern if you back up to multiple external/removable hard drives. If you can't recover a file from one, you'll be able to recover it from another.

ADVICE FROM RON MORSE ABOUT BACKUPS

Make sure your latest hardware and software upgrades don't leave your archived data behind. At one time I did most of my backing up to an external CDC SCSI hard drive. At 80 MB, it wouldn't hold the system or application files (I had the original installation media for that) but it was big enough to hold my personal data until things got to the point where it wasn't. The drive got demoted to archive status and fell out of regular service. Didn't think about it too much.

One day I built myself a new machine that didn't have an SCSI adapter because the new machine didn't have any SCSI devices. The old machine got sold to some unsuspecting party. Then one day I needed to access the archive. I *really* needed to access the archive. Duh. Expensive lesson. This applies to software, too. If you have a lot of important data in a proprietary file format, possession of the files themselves is only half the challenge. You need to be able to read them, too. (Insert commercial for open file standards here.)

Organizing your data directory structure

If you back up to hard drives, you can back up your entire drive every time. If you use a DVD writer, you'll probably do full backups infrequently, with routine backups only of your data files. In that case, it's important to organize your data directories to make it as easy as possible to back up only your data while making sure that you back up all of your data. The trick here is to segregate your data into groups that can be backed up with different frequencies.

For example, our data, excluding audio and video files, totals about 30 GB. Obviously, it's impractical to back that much data up to DVDs routinely. Fortunately, it's not necessary to back it all up every time. Much of that data is historical stuff—books we wrote years ago (and that we may update sometime), old email, and so on. That all needs to be backed up, but it's not necessary to back it up every day or even every month. So we segregate our data into subdirectories of three top-level directories:

data

> This top-level directory contains our current working data—email, current book projects, recent digital camera images, and so on. This directory is backed up every day to DVD, and frequently throughout the day to mirror directories on other systems on our network. We never allow this directory to grow larger than will fit on one DVD.

archive

> This top-level directory contains all of our old data: files that we may not need from one month to the next, or even from one year to the next. This directory is backed up to multiple redundant sets of DVDs, two of

---

which are stored off-site. Each backup set currently requires six DVDs. Every time we add data to the archive directories, which doesn't happen often, we burn several new sets of backup DVDs. (We keep the old discs, too, but then we're packrats.)

holding

This top-level directory is intermediate between our working data directories and our archive directories. When the size of our working data directories approaches what will fit on one DVD, usually every two or three months, we sweep older files to the holding directory and burn new copies of the holding directory to DVD. By doing this, we can keep our working data directory at a manageable size, but not have to redo the archive directory backups very often. We also keep the size of this directory to what will fit on one DVD. When it approaches that size, we sweep everything in the holding directory to the archive directory and burn a new set of archive DVDs.

When you plan your data directory structure, it's also important to consider these aspects:

- The importance of the data
- How difficult it would be to reconstruct the data
- How often the data changes

In combination, these three factors determine how often data needs to be backed up, how many generations of backup copies you'll want to retain, and therefore where the data belongs in your directory structure. For example, your financial records and digital photographs are probably critically important to you, difficult or impossible to reconstruct if lost, and change frequently. Those files need to be backed up frequently, and you'll probably want to maintain several generations of backup copies. Those files belong in your working data directories.

Conversely, if you've ripped your CD collection to MP3s, those files are neither important nor difficult to reconstruct because you can simply re-rip the CDs if necessary. Although these files might reasonably be classified as data, chances are you'll categorize them as data that never needs to be backed up and therefore locate them somewhere in your directory structure outside the directories that are routinely backed up.

Developing a backup rotation scheme

Whatever backup hardware you use, it's important to develop an appropriate backup rotation scheme. A good rotation scheme requires half a dozen or more discs, tapes, or drives, and allows you to:

- Recover a recent copy of any file easily and quickly
- Recover multiple generations of a file

- Maintain multiple copies of your data for redundancy and historical granularity

- Store at least one copy of your data off-site to protect against catastrophic data loss

The most popular backup rotation scheme, and the one most suitable for backups to DVD+RW discs, is called *Grandfather-Father-Son* (GFS). To use this backup rotation, label the following discs:

- Five (or six) daily discs, labeled Monday through Friday (or Saturday).

- Five weekly discs, labeled Week 1 through Week 5.

- Twelve monthly discs, labeled January through December.

Back up each working day to the appropriate daily disc. On Sunday, back up to whichever numbered weekly disc corresponds to the number of that Sunday in the month. The first (or last) of each month, back up to the monthly disc. This method gives you daily granularity for the preceding week, weekly granularity for the preceding month, and monthly granularity for the preceding year. For most home and SOHO users, that scheme is more than sufficient.

You can, of course, modify the standard GFS rotation in whatever way is suitable to your needs. For example, rather than writing your weekly or monthly backups to a DVD+RW disc that will eventually be overwritten, you can write those backups to DVD+R (write-once) discs and archive them. Similarly, there's nothing to prevent you from making a second backup disc every week or every month and archiving it off-site.

If you're backing up to external or removable hard drives, you probably won't want to use the standard GFS rotation, which would require 22 hard drives. Fortunately, you can use fewer drives without significantly compromising the reliability of your backup system. Most removable hard drives have room for at least two or three full backups, if you back up your entire hard drive, or a dozen or more data-only backups.

You still don't want to keep all your eggs in one basket, but it's reasonable to limit the number of baskets to as few as two or three. The trick is to make sure that you alternate the use of the drives so that you don't end up with all of your recent backups on one drive and only older backups on another. For example, if you decide to use only two external or removable hard drives for backup, label one of them M-W-F and the other Tu-Th-S, and alternate your daily backups between the two drives. Similarly, label one of the drives 1-3-5 and the other 2-4 for your weekly backups, and one drive J-M-M-J-S-N and the other F-A-J-A-O-D for your monthly backups.

Choosing backup software

There are four broad categories of software that can be used for backing up. Each has advantages and drawbacks, and which is best for you depends on your needs and preferences.

System utilities

System utilities such as xcopy are free, flexible, easy to use, can be scripted, and create backups that are directly readable without a restore operation. They do not, however, typically provide compression or any easy means of doing a binary compare on each file that has been copied, and they can write only to a mounted device that's visible to the operating system as a drive. (In other words, you can't use them to write to an optical disc unless you're running packet-writing software that causes that disc to appear to the operating system as a drive.)

CD/DVD burning applications

CD/DVD burning applications, such as Nero Burning ROM (*http:// www.nero.com*) and K3b (*http://www.k3b.org*) are fast, can create directly readable backup copies, and generally offer robust binary verify features, but may not offer compression. Most also have little or no ability to filter by file selection criteria, such as, "back up only files that have changed today." Of course, CD/DVD burning applications have other uses, such as duplicating audio CDs and video DVDs, and chances are that you already have a burning application installed. If so, and if the burning application suits your requirements, you can use it rather than buying another application just for backing up.

Traditional backup applications

Traditional backup applications such as BackUp MyPC (*http:// www.stompsoft.com*) do only one thing, but they do it very well. They are fast, flexible, have robust compression and verification options, support nearly any type of backup media, and allow you to define standard backup procedures using scripting, detailed file selection criteria, and saved backup sets. If your needs are simple, the bundled Windows backup applet, which is a stripped-down version of Veritas Backup Exec (since sold and renamed BackUp MyPC) may suffice. Otherwise, we think the commercial BackUp MyPC is the best option for Windows users.

Disk imaging applications

Disk imaging applications, such as Acronis True Image (*http:// www.acronis.com*) produce a compressed image of your hard drive, which can be written to a hard drive, optical disc, or tape. Although they are less flexible than a traditional backup application, disk imaging applications have the inestimable advantage of providing disaster recovery features. For example, if your hard drive fails and you have a current disk image, you needn't reinstall Windows and all your applications (including the backup application) and then restore your data. Instead, you simply boot the disaster recovery disc and let 'er rip. Your system will be back to its original state in minutes rather than hours.

We use three of these four software types on our own network. Several times a day, we do what we call "xcopy backups"—even though we now run Linux instead of Windows—to make quick copies of our current working data to other systems on the network. We use a CD/DVD burning application, K3b for Linux in our case, to run our routine backups to DVDs. And, when we're about to tear a system down to repair or upgrade it, we run an image backup with Acronis True Image, just in case the worst happens.

YOU CAN NEVER BE TOO WELL BACKED UP

Whatever backup means and methods you use, keep the following in mind and you won't go far wrong:

- Back up frequently, particularly data that is important or hard to reconstruct

- Verify backups to ensure that they are readable and that you can recover the data from them

- Maintain multiple backup sets, for redundancy and to permit recovering older versions of files

- Consider using a data-rated firesafe or media safe for on-site storage

- Store a recent backup set off-site, and rotate it regularly

Although online backup services (including using Google's Gmail for ad hoc backup storage) are reasonable choices for supplemental backups, we suggest that you not use them as your primary form of backup. There are too many things that can go wrong, from your (or their) Internet connection being down to server problems at the hosting company, to the company going out of business with no notice. When you need your backups, you need them *right now*. Keep your primary backups within easy reach.

Securing the system

The most important step that you can take to secure your system against worms and other malicious intruders is to install a hardware router/firewall between your system and the Internet. A properly configured router/firewall blocks malicious scans and probes, and makes your system effectively invisible to the millions of infected systems on the public Internet that are constantly trying to infect it. Hardware router/firewall devices typically sell for only $30 to $50, so they are cheap insurance against your system being compromised by malicious intruders.

We much prefer cable/DSL routers made by D-Link, such as the DI-604 (wired only) or the DI-624 (wired/wireless), but similar broadband routers

Software Security Isn't

Although many people depend on software firewalls, such as ZoneAlarm (*http://www.zonealarm.com*) or Norton Internet Security (*http://www.symantec.com*), we think that's a mistake. Among security experts, it's a truism that software cannot protect the system that is running it. Any software firewall may be compromised by exploits that target it directly or the underlying operating system. In our opinion, a software firewall is better than nothing, but not much better.

made by NETGEAR and Linksys are also popular. All current models we are familiar with use default settings that provide adequate security, but it's still worth taking a few minutes to study the manual to make sure that your router is configured to provide a level of security that is acceptable to you.

After you install and configure your firewall/router, visit the Gibson Research Corporation web site (*http://www.grc.com*) and use their Shields UP! service to test your security. Shields UP! probes your system and reports on the status of the ports most commonly attacked by worms and other malicious exploits. Figure 3-17 shows the results of running Shields UP! against one of our Windows XP testbed systems.

WEP Security Isn't

If you install a wireless router and enable wireless networking, be sure to secure it properly. The standard used by early 802.11 wireless devices, called WEP (Wired Equivalent Privacy) is now hopelessly insecure. WEP can be cracked in literally minutes—or even seconds—using utilities that anyone can download. The newer WPA (Wi-Fi Protected Access) standard, when configured properly, is secure against all but the most sophisticated attacks. If your current wireless adapters and access points support only WEP, replace all of them immediately with devices that support WPA. Otherwise, you might as well run your wireless network with no security at all.

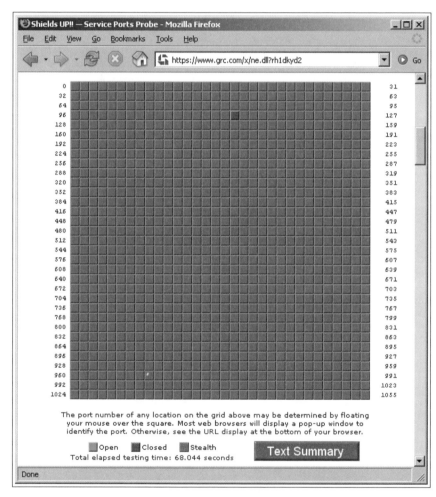

Figure 3-17. Gibson Research Shields UP! showing an (almost) fully stealthed system

Shields UP! flags open ports (very bad news) in red. Closed ports—those that do not accept connections but when probed do acknowledge being present—are flagged in blue. Stealthed ports—those that do not respond at all to probes—are flagged in green. Ideally, we'd like all our ports to be flagged green, because that in effect makes our system invisible to intruders. But for practical reasons, we've stealthed all ports except port 113 (ident), which responds to probes as being closed.

USE nmap FOR SERIOUS TESTING

For more rigorous testing, try using nmap (*http://www.insecure.org/nmap/*). Because you can run it within your network, you can use it to test individual systems, rather than just your network as a whole. It's useful to test both your router and your computers so that you know what vulnerabilities exist. You might be surprised to learn that you somehow managed to enable a web server that you never use, or that you have an unpatched version of SQL Server (the vector for the well-publicized Slammer/Sapphire worm) running that got installed along with some other software package.

Here are some other steps you should take to secure your Windows systems:

Install Firefox.

One of the most important steps you can take is to secure a Windows system is to replace the buggy, insecure Internet Explorer with a different default browser. The most popular alternative browser is Firefox (*http://www.mozilla.org*). We suggest that you install Firefox immediately and begin using it as your default browser. Ignore the Microsoft-inspired FUD that argues that Internet Explorer is just as secure as Firefox. It isn't. Firefox is an order of magnitude more secure.

Install ad-blocking software.

Although most banner ads and pop-ups are not malicious, they are annoying. And some ads contain links to malicious sites where merely clicking on a link or even simply viewing the page may install malware on your system via a "drive-by download." Using ad-blocking software minimizes the problem. We use Ad Block (*http://extensionroom. mozdev.org*), but there are many alternatives, including Privoxy (*http:// www.privoxy.org*), WebWasher (*http://www.cyberguard.com*), and AdSubtract (*http://www.intermute.com*).

Secure Internet Explorer.

Unfortunately, it's impossible to remove Internet Explorer completely from a Windows system. And IE is dangerous just sitting there on your hard drive, even if you never run it. You can minimize the danger by configuring IE to be as secure as possible. To do so, run IE, choose Tools → Options → Security tab. Select each security zones, click the Custom Level button, choose "High security" from the drop-down list, and click the Reset button. Repeat the process for each security zone. Once you have done that, Internet Explorer is pretty much unusable, but it is at least as secure as it's possible for it to be.

What Is Port 113?

Port 113 is used for ident requests, which allow remote servers to discover the user name associated with a given connection. The information discovered via ident is rarely useful, and not trustworthy. However, when a remote server tries to connect back to your computer and issue an ident response, a closed port tells it: "Sorry, I'm not running ident". A stealthed port, on the other hand, may lead the remote server to conclude that your computer doesn't exist. A remote server is more likely to permit your connection (such as FTP, HTTP, or TELNET) if it believes that you are really there.

Most hardware routers by default stealth all ports except 113, which they configure as closed. A few routers stealth port 113 as well. That's usually a bad idea, because it can cause slow response—or no response at all—from some servers. If Shields UP! reports that port 113 is stealthed, we suggest using the router's configuration utility to change port 113 to closed rather than stealthed.

Disable Windows Scripting Host.

Even if you secure Internet Explorer, *Windows Scripting Host* (WSH) remains installed and dangerous. For best security against VBS viruses, we recommend removing WSH entirely, although doing so means that Windows can no longer run any .vbs script. Depending on the version of Windows you run, you may be able to remove WSH by using the Add or Remove Programs applet in Control Panel.

If there is no option to remove WSH from Control Panel, you can remove WSH manually by deleting the files *cscript.exe* and *wscript.exe*, but you must do so in the proper sequence. Windows stores two copies of these files, the active copies in *WINDOWS\system32*, and backup copies in *WINDOWS\system32\dllcache*. Delete the backup copies first, and then the active copies. If you delete the active copies first, Windows immediately detects their absence and restores them automatically from the backup copies. After you delete both copies, Windows pops up a warning dialog that you can simply dismiss.

DE-WSHING THE EASY WAY

You can also use Noscript.exe from Symantec (*http://www.symantec.com/avcenter/noscript.exe*), which removes WSH automatically.

Replace Outlook.

Although recent versions are more secure than older versions, Outlook is still a virus magnet. If possible, we recommend replacing it with Mozilla Thunderbird or another alternative mail client.

The measures we've described thus far protect your system against being infected by worms and other exploits that do not require user intervention. Unfortunately, such automated exploits are not the only security dangers. Your system is also at risk from exploits that require your active (if unknowing) participation. The two major threats are viruses, which ordinarily arrive as attachments to email messages, and spyware, which often piggybacks on "free" software, such as P2P clients, that you install voluntarily.

New viruses are constantly written and released into the wild, so it's important to run a virus scanner regularly and keep it updated with the latest virus signatures. Although Norton AntiVirus (*http://www.symantec.com*) and McAfee VirusScan (*http://www.mcafee.com*) are two of the most popular antivirus scanners; we don't use either. Instead, we recommend installing Grisoft AVG Anti-Virus (*http://www.grisoft.com*), shown in Figure 3-18. AVG is as effective as any competing product we've used, places few demands on system resources, and is free for personal use.

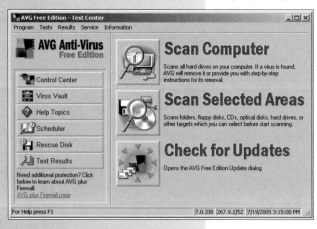

Figure 3-18. Grisoft AVG Anti-Virus Free Edition

Until a few years ago, viruses were the major security threat. Nowadays, malware is at least as great a threat. The least malicious form of malware is adware, which displays pop-up ads during browsing sessions, and may report your web browsing habits back to a central server—usually anonymously and without reporting personal information that identifies you individually—to help the adware display ads it thinks will be of interest to you. More malicious forms of adware, generally called spyware, collect and report information about you that may be of use to identity thieves and other malefactors. The most malicious forms of spyware go much further, using keystroke loggers and similar techniques to collect passwords, credit card and bank account numbers, and other critically sensitive information.

Even if you never install software that doesn't come from a trusted source, you may be victimized by spyware. Sometimes, all it takes is visiting a malicious web page that invisibly downloads and installs spyware on your system. The only way to protect yourself against such malicious software is to install a malware scanner, keep it updated, and run it regularly. There are numerous malware scanners available, many at no cost. Unfortunately, some of them are actually spyware Trojans. If you install one of those, it will indeed scan your system and report on any "foreign" malware it detects. It may even be kind enough to remove that malware, leaving your system free to run the spyware that it installs itself.

Fortunately, there are two trustworthy malware scanners we can recommend, both of which are free for personal use. Spybot Search & Destroy (*http://www.safer-networking.org*), shown in Figure 3-19, is donation-ware. Spybot is fast and extremely effective, and we use it as our first line of defense. (If you install it, please send the guy a few bucks; software this good should be encouraged.) We run Spybot daily on our Windows systems. As good as it is, even Spybot sometimes misses something. As a backup, we run AdAware (*http://www.lavasoftusa.com*) weekly. What Spybot doesn't catch, AdAware does. (The paid version of AdAware includes a real-time ad-blocking and pop-up blocking application that works well.)

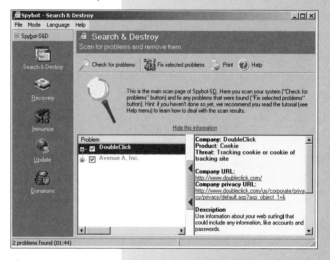

Figure 3-19. Use SpyBot Search & Destroy to detect and remove malware

By default, Windows runs many unnecessary background services. Disabling unneeded services has the dual benefit of reducing system resource consumption and eliminating potential entry points for security exploits. You can configure the startup behavior of Windows XP services using the services policy editor. To do so, click Start → Run, type **services.msc /s** in the run dialog box, and press Enter. The Services policy editor appears, as shown in Figure 3-20.

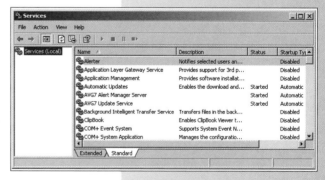

Figure 3-20. Windows XP Services policy editor

Double-click the name of any service to display the property sheet for that service, as shown in Figure 3-21. Use the "Startup type" drop-down list to set the startup type to Automatic, Manual, or Disabled, as appropriate. If the service is currently running, click the Stop button to stop it. If other services depend on that service, Windows displays a warning dialog to tell you that stopping that service will also stop dependent services. Once you have reconfigured the startup settings for all services, restart the system to put your changes into effect.

For a typical Windows XP system used routinely in a residential or SOHO environment, we recommend enabling the following Microsoft services:

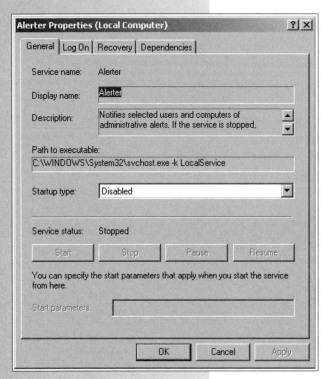

Figure 3-21. Property sheet for the Alerter service

- Automatic Updates
- Cryptographic Services
- DHCP Client
- Event Log
- Help and Support
- HID Input Service
- Plug and Play
- Print Spooler
- Protected Storage
- Remote Access Auto Connection Manager
- Remote Access Connection Manager
- Remote Procedure Call (RPC)
- Remote Procedure Call (RPC) Locator
- Script Blocking Service
- Security Center
- Shell Hardware Detection
- Windows Audio
- Windows Image Acquisition (WIA)
- Windows Installer
- Windows Management Instrumentation
- Windows Management Instrumentation Driver Extensions
- Workstation

Disable all other Microsoft services, except possibly those listed in Table 3-2. Some of these services, particularly System Restore Service and Themes, use significant system resources, and are best disabled unless you require the functionality they provide.

Table 3-2. Recommended Windows XP Services startup settings

Windows XP Service	Recommended startup setting
IMAPI CD Burning COM Service	Automatic if you use Windows CD burning applet; otherwise, disable
Network Connections	Automatic if the system is connected to a network; otherwise, disable
NT LM Security Support Provider	Automatic if you use Message Queuing or a Telnet server; otherwise, disable
Removable Storage	Automatic if you use a tape drive or similar device; otherwise, disable
Security Accounts Manager	Automatic if you run IIS Admin; otherwise, disable
Server	Automatic if your computer shares files or printers; otherwise, disable
Smart Card	Automatic if you use a Smart Card for authentication; otherwise, disable
Smart Card Helper	Automatic if you use a Smart Card for authentication; otherwise, disable
System Restore Service	Automatic if you require restore points; otherwise, disable
Telephony	Automatic if you use a dial-up modem; otherwise, disable
Themes	Automatic if you insist on XP "eye candy"; otherwise, disable
Windows Time	Automatic if you have a full-time Internet connection; otherwise, disable

In addition to the scores of services that Microsoft includes with Windows XP, many systems run third-party services. Determining which services are non-Microsoft is difficult with the Services policy editor. Fortunately, there's another alternative called the System Configuration Utility. To run it, click Start → Run, type **msconfig** in the Run dialog box, and press Enter. Click the Services tab to display installed services. Mark the Hide All Microsoft Services checkbox to show only non-Microsoft services, as shown in Figure 3-22.

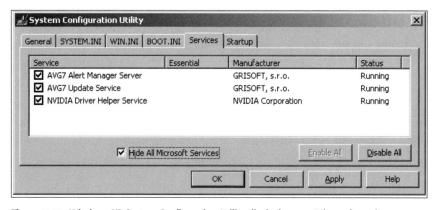

Figure 3-22. Windows XP System Configuration Utility displaying non-Microsoft services

In Figure 3-22, three non-Microsoft services are running. Two of them are a part of the AVG antivirus software we run on this system, and one is used by the NVIDIA video adapter. None of these are suspicious, so no action is needed. However, there are many other third-party services that may be malicious, including those installed by spyware. If you see a third-party service running and don't recognize its purpose, investigate further. If in doubt, clear the checkbox to disable the service and test the system to see whether disabling that service breaks anything.

You can also view the System Configuration Utility Startup page to list the executable programs that Windows runs at startup, as shown in Figure 3-23.

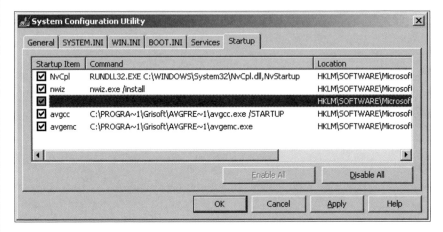

Figure 3-23. Windows XP System Configuration Utility displaying programs run at startup

In this case, four of the five executable programs that Windows runs at startup on this system are clearly innocuous. NvCpl is the NVIDIA control panel utility. nwiz is the executable for WhizFolders Organizer Pro, a file management program we use. avgcc and avgemc are the two executables for our AVG Anti-Virus software. But the highlighted item in the middle of the list concerned us because no executable program name is shown for it. That's suspicious in itself—behavior one might expect from a startup executable installed by a virus, worm, or spyware—so it's worth taking a closer look.

To do so, fire up the Registry Editor by clicking Start → Run, typing **regedt32** (or **regedit**, if you prefer a simpler editor) in the dialog, and pressing Enter. Navigate through the registry structure to view the key:

HKEY_LOCAL_MACHINE\SOFTWARE\Microsoft\Windows\CurrentVersion\Run

where startup executables are listed. Figure 3-24 shows the contents of that key, which was obviously installed by the program Registry Mechanic, and is no cause for concern. If the startup executable is clearly a malicious program, simply delete it with Registry Editor. If you're unsure about it, use Google to search for the executable name rather than simply deleting it.

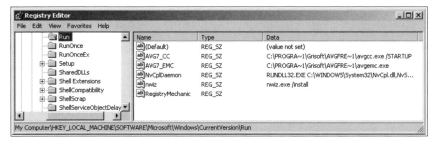

Figure 3-24. Viewing startup programs in the Registry Editor

IT'S OKAY TO PLAY

Don't hesitate to experiment with your startup configuration. There's nothing you can disable here that will harm the system. At worst, a program may not work properly with a startup executable disabled. Unless you're sure you need a particular startup program to be running—such as your antivirus and malware scanners and your PIM—go ahead and disable it. Reboot the system and see if anything is broken. If so, re-enable whatever it was you disabled, and play around some more.

Finally, we recommend periodically running a registry cleaner, such as CleanMyPC (*http://www.registry-cleaner.net*) or Registry Mechanic (*http://www.pctools.com*), shown in Figure 3-25. We include registry maintenance as an element of securing the system, because registry exploits are becoming increasingly common. Even if your system is never infected by any malicious software, though, it's still worth pruning and compacting the registry periodically to increase performance and reliability of the system.

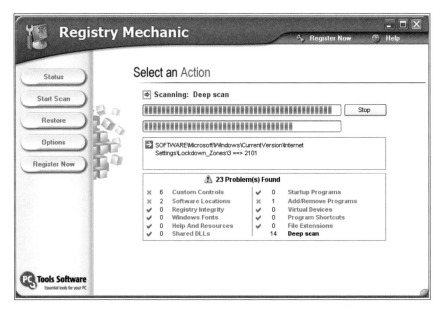

Figure 3-25. Use Registry Mechanic or a similar product to scan and clean the registry

---

There are numerous registry tools available. Most are commercial or shareware products, although many are available as crippled demos for free downloading. Some perform only one aspect of registry maintenance, such as enhanced registry editing, removing unused entries, or defragging the registry heaps. Others combine many registry-related functions into one product. We suggest you download and try one or both of the two products we mention first. If neither suffices, a Google search for "registry cleaner" turns up dozens of other possibilities.

Hard drive housekeeping

As we started to write this section, we checked one of our hard drives. It had 185,503 files in 11,607 folders. It's anyone's guess as to what they all are. Some are programs and system files, of course. We know there are hundreds of documents and spreadsheets, and thousands of audio files, images, and so on. But the majority of those 185,503 files are probably temporary and backup files, duplicates and older versions of current datafiles, browser cache files, and similar gubbage. All they do is clutter up the hard drive, wasting space and harming disk performance. They need to be pruned from time to time, if only to keep them from eating you out of house and home.

ORGANIZING YOUR TEMP(ORARY) FILES

You can set a few environment variables to cause TEMP files to be stored in one location rather than be buried in a hidden folder under your Documents and Settings directory. To do so, create the folder *C:\TEMP* and then do the following:

1. Right-click on My Computer → Properties → Advanced tab.

2. Click the Environment Variable button and change the TEMP and TMP values to *C:\TEMP* by highlighting them, choosing the Edit button, and replacing the ridiculously long path to *C:\TEMP*.

3. Use the New button to add another value called TMPDIR and set its path to *C:\TEMP* as well.

4. Do the same thing in the System variable in the box below the User variable, again adding a variable called TMPDIR and setting its value to *C:\TEMP*.

No matter what you've set these environment variables to, you can navigate quickly to any of them by opening Windows Explorer, typing the name surrounded by percent signs (such as *%TEMP%*) into the Address field, and pressing Enter or Return. You should periodically visit this directory and delete any files and folders that are more than a few weeks old. Windows installer programs are notoriously bad about leaving large temporary files behind.

Clearing your browser's cache is a good first step. After doing that, you may find that your file count has dropped by thousands of files, and, depending on the size of your browser cache, you may recover a gigabyte or more of disk space. You might then go to a command prompt and issue commands like:

```
del *.bak /s
del *.bk! /s
del *.tmp /s
```

and so on. This brute-force approach might eliminate thousands of unneeded files and recover gigabytes of disk space, but it's an imperfect solution at best. First, you'll probably leave a lot of unneeded files on the drive because you didn't think to look for every extension. Second, you may end up deleting some files you'd really rather have kept, and you may not even be aware that you've done so until you find yourself searching fruitlessly for them later. Third, if you're not paying attention, a slip of the finger can have disastrous results.

It's better to use a utility designed for file pruning. Microsoft includes an applet for this purpose, but, as is usually true of Microsoft applets, it's feature-poor. The Windows Disk Cleanup applet, shown in Figure 3-26, does nothing you can't do manually yourself in about 30 seconds flat.

Fortunately, there are better alternatives available as commercial utilities. Our favorite is ShowSize (*http://www.showsize.com*), shown in Figure 3-27, which provides all of the tools you need to keep your hard drive clean and organized.

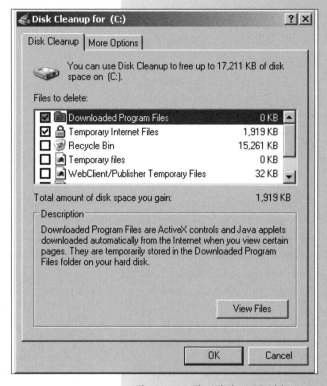

Figure 3-26. The Windows XP Disk Cleanup utility

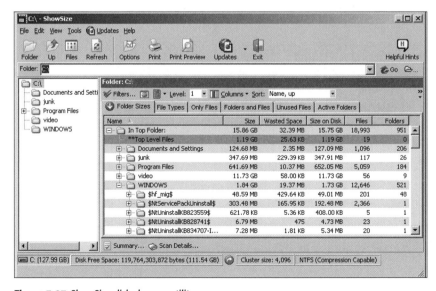

Figure 3-27. ShowSize disk cleanup utility

Once you've pruned unneeded files from your hard drive, it's time to run a disk defragger. As you write, modify, and delete files on your hard drive, Windows attempts to keep every file stored contiguously on the drive. Unfortunately, Windows isn't very good at that task, so pieces of various files end up scattered here, there, and everywhere about the drive, a phenomenon known as *file fragmentation* or *disk fragmentation*.

NTFS and Fragmentation

For years, Microsoft claimed that NTFS was not subject to fragmentation. As Figure 3-28 shows, that's not true, even on a sparsely populated drive. With only 13% of this drive in use, Windows has still fragmented the majority of the occupied space. Even after the Windows Disk Defragmenter utility has finished running, some fragmentation remains. The thin green bars are system files—the Master File Table and the paging file—that are always open when Windows is running, and so cannot be defragged by the bundled Windows utility. As to the blue bar that remains out in the middle of nowhere after defragging: we have no idea why Windows does this, but it always seems to leave at least a few files on their own rather than consolidating all of the files.

Fragmentation has several undesirable effects. Because the drive heads must constantly be repositioned to read and write files, hard disk performance suffers. Read and write performance on a badly fragmented drive is much slower than on a freshly defragmented drive, particularly if the drive is nearly full. That extra head movement also contributes to higher noise levels, and may cause the drive to fail sooner than it otherwise would. Finally, when a drive does fail, it is much easier (and less costly) to recover data if that drive had been defragmented recently.

The solution to disk fragmentation is to run a defragging utility periodically. A defragging utility reads each file and rewrites it contiguously, making file access much faster. The Disk Defragmenter utility bundled with Windows, shown in Figure 3-28, is slow, inefficient, and feature-poor. But, hey, it's free, and it's (usually) good enough to do the job.

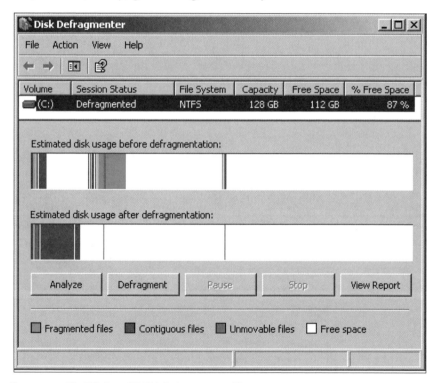

Figure 3-28. The Windows XP Disk Defragmenter utility

If you need a defragger with more features and better performance, consider buying a commercial defragging utility. The two best known commercial defraggers are Vopt (*http://www.vopt.com*) and Diskeeper (*http://www. diskeeper.com*). We've used both for years, and have never had a problem with either of them.

One major failing of the Windows XP Disk Defragmenter utility is that it cannot defrag the paging file, at least unless you're willing to go through hoops to do so. Windows uses the paging file to store applications and data for which there is no room in main memory. If you run many applications simultaneously or use large data sets, main memory inevitably becomes full. When that occurs, Windows temporarily swaps out inactive applications and data to the paging file. Because the paging file undergoes a lot of "churn," it invariably becomes heavily fragmented, which in turn causes increased fragmentation of user programs and data.

Unfortunately, the design of Windows makes it impossible to defragment the paging file while Windows is running. But there are two ways to defrag the paging file. First, use a commercial defragger like Diskeeper or the free pagedefrag (*http://www.sysinternals.com/Utilities/ PageDefrag.html*) that provides a boot-time defragging utility that runs before Windows loads. Alternatively, you can use the Windows XP Disk Defragmenter utility to defrag the paging file by taking the following steps:

1. Right-click My Computer and choose Properties to display the System Properties dialog.

2. Click the Advanced tab.

3. In the Performance pane, click the Settings button to display the Performance Options dialog.

4. Click the Advanced tab.

5. In the Virtual memory pane, click the Change button to display the Virtual Memory dialog, shown in Figure 3-29.

6. Write down or memorize the current paging file size, which you'll use later when you restore the paging file.

7. Mark the "No paging file" radio button, and click the Set button to change the paging file system to zero.

8. Restart the computer, which will now operate without a paging file.

9. Run the Windows XP Disk Defragmenter utility to defrag the hard drive.

10. When defragging completes, repeat steps 1 through 5 to display the Virtual Memory dialog.

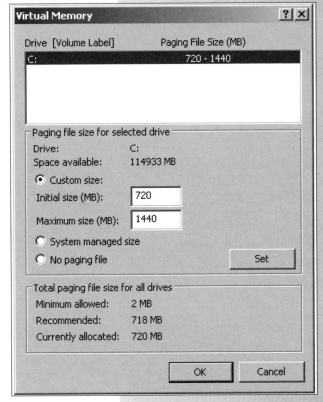

Figure 3-29. The Windows XP Virtual Memory dialog

11. Reset the paging file size to the original value.

12. Restart the system, which will now operate with a defragged paging file of the original size.

Keeping your system updated

Hardware and software companies periodically release updated software, device drivers, and firmware. These updates may be security related, or they may add support for new features or compatibility with new devices. We recommend that you keep yourself informed about such updates, but the Golden Rule when it comes to installing updates is, "If it ain't broke, don't fix it."

Evaluate each update before you install it. Most updates include release notes or a similar document that describes exactly what the update does and what problems it fixes. If a particular update solves a problem you're experiencing or adds support for something you need, install the update. Otherwise, be very leery. More than once, we've installed an update for no good reason and found that the update broke something that used to work. It's often possible to recover from a failed update by uninstalling the update and reverting to the original version, but sometimes the only solution is to format the drive and reinstall everything from scratch.

Operating system and application software updates

Operating system and application software updates are one exception to our general rule of caution. Windows in particular is under constant attack from worms and other malicious software, so it's generally a good idea to apply critical Windows patches as soon as possible.

Microsoft provides the Microsoft Update service (*http://update.microsoft.com/microsoftupdate*) to automate the process of keeping Windows and Office patched. To configure Microsoft Update to download and install patches automatically, display Control Panel and choose Security Center. At the bottom of the Security Center dialog, in the "Manage security settings for:" pane, click the Automatic Updates link to display the Automatic Updates dialog, shown in Figure 3-30.

Security Through Insecurity

Ironically, to use Microsoft's automatic update services, you must use Internet Explorer–the least secure browser on the planet.

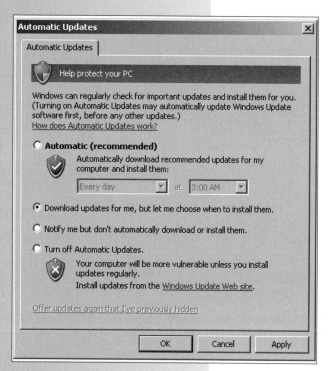

Figure 3-30. The Windows XP Automatic Updates configuration dialog

The recommended (and default) setting is Automatic, which causes Windows to download and install updates without user intervention. That's a bit too trusting for our taste. We've been burned many times by Microsoft patches that in retrospect we wish we'd never installed. We recommend choosing the second option, which causes updates to be downloaded automatically in the background, but not to be installed until you approve them, or the third option, which merely notifies you when updates are available.

Managing applications software is more problematic, because, for Windows at least, there is no central location where you can check for available updates. (Linux is far superior in this regard. Most modern Linux distributions can automatically check one central repository for available updates for the operating system and most or all installed applications.) With Windows, you have to search out updates for each application yourself.

Fortunately, most major applications nowadays, and many minor ones, automatically check periodically for updates, or at least prompt you to do so. We recommend keeping a close eye on applications that use the Internet heavily; for example, browsers, email clients, and P2P packages. Exploits against such applications are relatively common and have potentially severe consequences. Other applications, while not risk-free, don't require such close supervision. It's less likely, for example, that your CD burning application or a file viewer will suffer a severe security hole. (It's not unheard of, though; Adobe's Acrobat Reader has been patched several times to fix serious security holes.)

Device driver updates

Windows, Linux, and all other modern operating systems use an extensible architecture that allows loadable device drivers to add support for devices that are not supported directly by the OS kernel. Your system uses device drivers to support your video adapter, sound adapter, network adapter, and other peripheral devices.

Other than BIOS and other firmware code, device driver code is the most carefully debugged software running on your PC, so even old drivers are unlikely to have significant bugs. It's still a good idea to keep an eye out for updated device drivers, though, because updated drivers may improve performance, add support for additional features, and so on. In general, we recommend updating your device drivers any time you install new hardware.

Video adapter drivers (and, to some extent, audio adapter drivers) are a special case, particularly if you play 3D games on your PC. Video adapter makers update their drivers frequently to add support for new games and to tweak performance for existing games. In many cases, the performance improvements can be substantial, even if you're using an older model video adapter. If you game, check for video adapter updates every month. Otherwise, every three to six months is sufficient.

Firmware updates

Firmware is halfway between hardware and software. Firmware is software that is semi-permanently stored on nonvolatile memory chips inside your PC. The main system BIOS, for example, is firmware. But the main system BIOS is by no means the only firmware on your system. Nearly every peripheral, from video and audio adapters to network cards to RAID controllers to hard drives and optical drives, has its own firmware.

We recommend keeping an eye out for updates to your motherboard BIOS and other firmware, but use caution in deciding whether to apply those updates. Again, in general: if it ain't broke, don't fix it. To some extent, the decision depends on how old the device is. It's quite common for newly introduced components to have several firmware updates made available early in their life cycles. As time passes, firmware updates typically become less frequent, and tend to be minor fixes or feature additions rather than significant updates.

The major exception is optical writers. The firmware in CD and DVD burners includes write schema that allow the drive to use the optimum write strategies for different brands and types of media. As new brands of media are introduced, optical drive makers update their firmware to support the new types of media. We recommend checking for firmware updates for your optical writer every time you buy a new batch of discs.

BURNING YOUR BRIDGES

It's usually easy to recover from a bad firmware update. If you update the firmware in your DVD writer, for example, and it stops working properly, you can usually just update the drive again using the older firmware revision and be back to where you started. When you update your motherboard BIOS, it's a different story. A failed BIOS upgrade may render the board unusable, necessitating returning it to the factory for repair. The most frequent cause of failed motherboard BIOS upgrades is a power failure during the update process. If at all possible, connect your system to a UPS before you update the motherboard BIOS.

Better motherboards avoid this problem in one of two ways. Some have two BIOSs installed. If you bork one during a failed update, you can start the system using the backup BIOS and then recover the primary BIOS. Intel uses a different but equally effective method. If the BIOS update process fails on an Intel motherboard, you simply set a jumper to the BIOS recovery position. Even after a failed update, an Intel BIOS has enough smarts to attempt to boot from the floppy drive. You can simply copy the BIOS datafile to a floppy disk, set the jumper to the recover position, reboot the system, and allow the BIOS update to install automatically.

Curing Windows Rot

Microsoft made two very bad design decisions for Windows. Well, actually, they made a lot more than two bad decisions, but two are of primary concern.

The concept of using *DLLs* (*dynamically linked libraries* or *dynamic link libraries*) was flawed from the start, as millions of Windows users can attest. Old and new versions of the same DLL with the same name can co-exist on a system, and Windows provides no rigorous management of these diverse versions. A newer version of an application often doesn't work with an older version of a DLL it requires, which is bad enough, but older versions of an application may not work with newer versions of the DLL. That means that something as simple as installing an update for one program may break another. Welcome to *DLL Hell*.

The *Windows Registry*, apparently patterned after the bindery used in antique versions of Novell NetWare, is the second part of the double whammy. With the introduction of Windows NT, Microsoft abandoned the use of simple, plain-text configuration files for the dubious benefits of a central registry. Although the registry concept might have worked had it been implemented properly, with rigorous controls and powerful management tools, Microsoft did none of that. Instead, the registry is a gigantic heap of spaghetti that even experts have trouble deciphering. The registry on a typical Windows box grows like Topsy, with obsolete data left cluttering up the place and new data added willy-nilly without consideration for conflicts or backward compatibility. Microsoft provides only the most basic tools for maintaining the registry, and even the best commercial registry maintenance software can do only so much to eliminate the mess.

The upshot is that any Windows system contains the seeds of its own destruction. Over the months and years, as new software is installed and old software deleted, Windows gradually becomes more and more unstable. DLL conflicts become increasingly common, and performance slows. This phenomenon is universally known as *Windows Rot*. Careful installation practices and periodic registry cleaning can slow Windows Rot, but in our experience nothing can stop it completely.

Microsoft claims that Vista will solve the Windows Rot problem, this time for sure. They may even be right, but we doubt it. Unfortunately, the only sure cure we know of for Windows Rot, short of Microsoft rewriting Windows from the ground up or you switching to another operating system, is to strip the hard drive down to bare metal, reinstall Windows and all applications, and restore your data. Most power users do this every six months to a year, but even casual users will probably benefit from doing a fresh install every year or two.

One sure indication that it's time for a clean install is that your system begins behaving strangely in ways that aren't attributable to a virus or a hardware problem, particularly if that occurs immediately after you've installed new software, updated drivers, or made other significant changes to your system. But Windows Rot can manifest in much more subtle ways. If you've been using your Windows system for a year or two without a reinstall and it seems much slower than it used to be, that's probably not your imagination. Besides slow performance, Windows Rot can cause a variety of problems, from severe memory leaks to random reboots.

Because it's so difficult to pin down the particulars of Windows Rot, or even to know the extent to which a particular system suffers from it, we recommend simply doing a fresh install once a year, whether you think you need it or not.

A periodic maintenance checklist

Table 3-3 summarizes the procedures we recommend for periodic maintenance.

Table 3-3. Periodic maintenance checklist

Task	Every Day	Week	Month	3 months	6 months	Year
Back up working data sets and configuration data	•					
Run Microsoft Update (critical updates)	•					
Update antivirus scanner signatures	•					
Run antivirus scan	•					
Update malware scanner signatures	•	•				
Run malware scanner	•	•				
Vacuum the system exterior		•				
Scan/clean/compact registry		•				
Defrag hard drive		•				
Run scandisk on your drives		•	•			
Delete backup, temporary, and duplicate files		•	•			
Run Windows Update and Office Update (recommended updates)		•	•			
Check for updates to non-Microsoft applications		•	•			
Full system backup		•	•			
Remove unused, expired, and demo software			•	•		
Check for optical drive firmware updates			•	•		
Check for video adapter updates			•	•		
Check for firmware updates for hard drive, audio, network, other				•	•	
Refresh archive backups				•	•	
Check for motherboard BIOS updates (install only if needed)				•	•	
Clean system thoroughly, inside and out				•	•	•
Remove unused hardware and associated drivers					•	•
Format drive and reinstall Windows					•	•

Motherboards 4

The *motherboard* is Control Central for a computer. Every other component —processor, memory, drives, expansion cards, and even the power supply—connects to and is controlled by the motherboard. The motherboard defines the computer.

Replacing the motherboard is the most complicated and time-consuming upgrade you can make to a computer, simply because so many things connect to it. But there are many good reasons to replace a motherboard, including:

- The original motherboard has failed.
- You want additional features—such as Serial ATA, USB 2.0, FireWire, support for hard drives larger than 128 GB, or a PCI Express video slot—that your original motherboard does not provide.
- You want to upgrade your processor, but the original motherboard does not support the type or speed of processor you want to install.
- You want to install additional memory, but the type of memory used by your motherboard is no longer available or is very expensive.
- Your motherboard is one of the millions made with defective capacitors, and so may fail without warning. Figure 4-1 shows a row of six healthy capacitors on an ASUS K8N-E Deluxe motherboard. If those on your motherboard appear swollen, popped, or are leaking fluid, that motherboard will soon fail.

Figure 4-1. Healthy capacitors show no signs of bulging or leakage

If your motherboard fails, there are no options but to replace it or discard the computer. If your goal is simply to repair the system as inexpensively as possible, you can probably find a suitable motherboard for $50 to $75 that will accept your current processor and memory, unless the system is elderly.

But even if the current motherboard is operating perfectly, there are many good reasons to consider replacing it with a newer model. Installing a new motherboard in effect gives you an entirely new system, with a new BIOS and chipset that support all of the most recent standards. Even if you decide to replace the processor and memory at the same time, you can spend as little as $150 to $200 and end up with computer that compares favorably in performance and features to new systems that cost much more.

In this chapter, we'll tell you everything you need to know to choose, install, and configure a replacement motherboard.

Everything You Always Wanted to Know About Motherboards

Two fundamental characteristics determine whether a motherboard is suitable for upgrading a particular system:

Form factor

> The *form factor* of a motherboard defines its physical size, mounting hole locations, and other factors that determine whether the motherboard fits a particular case. The vast majority of computers made since 1995 use either the *ATX form factor*, also called *full ATX*, or the *microATX form factor*, also called μATX. A microATX motherboard fits a microATX case or an ATX case; an ATX motherboard fits only an ATX case. Figure 4-2 shows a typical microATX motherboard on the left, with a larger ATX motherboard on the right.

> If your current case accepts ATX or microATX motherboards and has a compatible power supply, upgrading the motherboard is a simple matter of removing the old motherboard and replacing it with the new one. Alas, some systems—primarily cheap, mass-market units—use nonstandard proprietary motherboards and/or power supplies. If the motherboard in such a system fails, that system is good for little more than the scrap heap. You may be able to salvage the processor, memory, drives, and other peripherals, but the case and motherboard are useless.

Figure 4-2. Typical microATX (left) and ATX motherboards

IF A IS GOOD, B MUST BE BETTER

In 2004, Intel began shipping motherboards based on a new form factor, called *BTX (Balanced Technology eXtended)*. Although BTX is a derivative of ATX, BTX cases and motherboards are physically incompatible with ATX components. Intel had hoped that BTX would take the market by storm, but as of early 2006 BTX had made only minimal inroads in the PC market.

BTX may be a solution in search of a problem. The original goal of BTX was to improve cooling at a reduced noise level: a necessary improvement, given the very high heat production of Intel Pentium 4 processors, some of which consume 130W. Now that Intel is shifting processor production to low-power cores that consume as little as 20W, there is no longer a real need for BTX.

Processor socket type

    Modern processors connect to the motherboard via a *processor socket*. The processor has an array of hundreds of pins that fit into matching holes on the processor socket. Figure 4-3 shows an mPGA478 socket, which accepts an Intel Pentium 4 or Celeron processor, a typical processor socket. Sockets designed to accept other types of processors are similar in appearance, but with a different number and arrangement of holes.

More Trouble than They're Worth

For all practical purposes, a processor that is designed to fit one socket cannot be installed in another type of socket. Socket adapters are available to shoehorn one type of processor into another type of socket—e.g., a Socket 479 Pentium M processor into a Socket 478 motherboard—but such adapters often have compatibility issues. We recommend you avoid socket adapters.

Figure 4-3. A typical processor socket

Most current processor sockets use a *ZIF lever* (*Zero Insertion Force lever*) to secure the processor in the socket. This lever, visible on the right edge of the socket, is raised to install the processor. Raising the lever removes the clamping force inside the socket, and allows the processor to be dropped into place without applying pressure. After the processor is seated in the socket, lowering the ZIF lever clamps the processor into place and ensures good electrical contact between the processor pins and the socket contacts.

MALE SOCKET, FEMALE PROCESSOR

Intel Socket 775 is the exception among modern processor sockets. Socket 775 reverses the usual arrangement of male processor and female socket by putting the pins in the socket and the holes in the processor. Socket 775 also dispenses with the ZIF lever, using a different clamping arrangement to secure the processor in the socket.

Table 4-1 lists the processor sockets that have been used on recent systems. Systems based on processor sockets listed as obsolete—Slot A, Slot 1, and Socket 423—are not practically upgradable, because motherboards and/or processors are no longer readily available with those sockets. By that, we mean that it isn't practical to upgrade the motherboard and processor unless you replace both; it's still feasible to install more memory, replace the drives, and make other upgrades to such systems.

Identify Your Socket

You can identify the socket type used by your current motherboard by checking the documentation, by looking up the motherboard model number on the Internet, or by running a diagnostic utility such as Everest (*http://www.lavalys.com*) or SiSoft Sandra (*http://www.sisoftware.net*). You can also identify the socket type unambiguously by examining the socket itself, although that will require removing the processor cooler and perhaps the processor itself.

Table 4-1. Processor socket types

Socket type	Manufacturer	Status	Processor types
Slot A	AMD	Obsolete	Athlon
Slot 1	Intel	Obsolete	Pentium II, Pentium III, Celeron
Socket 370	Intel	Obsolete	Pentium III, Celeron
Socket 423	Intel	Obsolete	Pentium 4, Celeron
Socket A (462)	AMD	Obsolescent	Athlon, Athlon XP, Duron, Sempron
Socket 478	Intel	Obsolescent	Pentium 4, Celeron D
Socket 754	AMD	Obsolescent	Athlon 64, Sempron
Socket 775	Intel	Current	Pentium 4, Pentium D, Celeron D
Socket 939	AMD	Current	Athlon 64, Athlon 64/ X2, Sempron

Systems that use one of the sockets we list as obsolescent—Sockets A, 478, and 754—are reasonably good upgrade candidates. Although processors and motherboards are no longer under active development for obsolescent processor sockets, motherboards that use those sockets are readily available and likely to remain so for some time, as are processors to fit those sockets.

WHEN SOCKET TYPE DOESN'T MATTER

Of course, if you plan to replace not just the motherboard, but the processor and perhaps memory as well, the type of socket used by the current motherboard and processor is immaterial. You can simply choose the best processor and compatible motherboard to fit your needs and budget.

Choosing a motherboard

Because the motherboard controls the system, it pays to select one carefully. The motherboard you choose determines which processors are supported, how much and what type of memory the system can use, what type of video adapters can be installed, the speed of the communication ports, and many other key system characteristics. In addition to choosing the correct form factor and processor socket, which are essential, use the following guidelines when choosing a motherboard:

Choose the right chipset.

The *chipset* acts like an administrative assistant to the processor. It handles what goes in and what comes out and takes care of all the ancillary functions that make it possible for the processor to compute.

New Lamps for Old

Installing an older processor in a newer motherboard seldom presents any problems, although you should always verify that your old processor is explicitly listed as supported by the new motherboard (taking into account the motherboard revision level). Installing a newer processor in an older motherboard may be problematic, because the newer, faster processor may draw more current than the motherboard is designed to supply.

The chipset determines which processors and types of memory are supported, as well as which of the two video adapter standards, AGP or PCI Express, the motherboard supports. The chipset also determines which embedded features—such as USB 2.0, Serial ATA, FireWire, video, audio, and networking—are available. Chipsets vary widely in performance, features, compatibility, and stability. Table 4-2 lists the chipsets we recommend by socket type.

Table 4-2. Recommended chipsets by socket type

Socket type	Recommended chipsets	Memory support	Video adapter support
Socket A (462)	NVIDIA nForce2 series	DDR	AGP
Socket 478	Intel 8XX series	DDR	AGP
Socket 754	NVIDIA nForce3 series	DDR	AGP
Socket 775	Intel 9XX series	DDR and/or DDR2	AGP/PCI Express
Socket 939	NVIDIA nForce3 series	DDR	AGP
Socket 939	NVIDIA nForce4 series	DDR	PCI Express

- If you are replacing a failed motherboard and plan to use your current processor, choose a motherboard that has the correct socket type and uses one of the recommended chipsets. If your current memory and/or video adapter are worth salvaging, also take into account their compatibility with the replacement motherboards you are considering.

- If you are buying a new AMD processor, choose a Socket 939 nForce3 motherboard (for AGP video) or nForce4 motherboard (for PCI Express video).

- If you are buying a new Intel processor, choose a Socket 775 motherboard that uses an Intel 945- or 955-series chipset that supports the type of video card you plan to install.

Chipsets for AMD and Intel processors are made by several other companies, such as VIA and SiS, but we have found that the performance and compatibility of these alternative chipsets leaves something to be desired. Motherboards based on Intel and NVIDIA chipsets are a bit more expensive than those based on alternative chipsets, but the small additional cost is well worth it.

Bad Cooks Ruin Good Ingredients

Although it is impossible to build a good motherboard with a poor chipset, it is quite possible to build a poor motherboard with a good chipset. We use and recommend Intel or ASUS motherboards for Intel processors and ASUS motherboards for AMD processors.

Make sure the motherboard supports the exact processor you plan to use.

Just because a motherboard claims to support a particular processor doesn't mean it supports all members of that processor family. For example, some motherboards support the Pentium 4 processor, but only slower models. Other motherboards support fast Pentium 4s, but not slower Pentium 4s or Celerons. Similarly, some motherboards support the Athlon with a 200, 266, or 333 MHz FSB, but not the 400 MHz FSB.

CLOSE ENOUGH ISN'T

Make sure the motherboard supports the *exact* processor you plan to use, before you buy it. To do so, visit the motherboard manufacturer's web site and look for the "supported processors" page for the exact motherboard you plan to use. Note that motherboard makers often "slipstream" revised models with the same model number, and the list of supported processors almost always assumes you are using the current motherboard revision. Quite often, an earlier revision does not support all of the processor models or speeds supported by a later revision. When you buy a motherboard, make sure to get the latest available revision.

Choose a board with flexible host bus speeds.

Choose a motherboard that supports at least the settings you need now and that you expect to need for the life of the board. For example, even if you are installing an existing 400 MHz FSB Socket 478 Celeron initially, choose a motherboard that also supports Pentium 4 processors using the 533 and 800 MHz FSB speeds. Similarly, even if you are installing an old 266 MHz FSB Athlon at first, choose a motherboard that supports the full range of Athlon FSB speeds—200, 266, 333, and 400 MHz. Boards that offer a full range of host bus speeds, ideally in small increments, give you the most flexibility if you later decide to upgrade the processor.

Make sure the board supports the type and amount of memory you need.

Any motherboard you buy should support current memory modules; that is, PC3200 DDR-SDRAM or DDR2 DIMMs. Do not make assumptions about how much memory a motherboard supports. A motherboard has a certain number of memory slots and the literature may state that it accepts memory modules up to a specific size, but that doesn't mean you can necessarily install the largest supported module in all of the memory slots. For example, a motherboard may have four memory slots and accept 512 MB DIMMs, but you may find that you can use all four slots only if you install 256 MB DIMMs. Memory speed may also

Advice from Ron Morse

There's an even better reason to demand the latest motherboard revision level: subtle engineering changes to the components used, board layout, or other engineering factors may be "slipstreamed" into production based upon reported problems from early production runs. These are usually subtle things. You notice them when you repeatedly beat up customer support over a recurring problem, they suddenly agree to RMA the unit, and you find the new one works flawlessly in what is otherwise the same system. I'm convinced this happens a lot. ATI RADEON 9700 Pro video cards are a prime example, and Tyan 1840 series motherboards another.

Unused Versus Unusable

Don't assume that you can use all available memory slots. For example, many early Socket 754 Athlon 64 motherboards provided three or even four DIMM slots, but could actually support only two memory modules reliably, regardless of the size or speed of those modules. Nor do all motherboards necessarily support the full amount of memory that the chipset itself supports, even if there are sufficient memory sockets to do so. Always determine exactly what combinations of memory sizes, types, and speeds are supported by a particular motherboard.

come into play. For example, a particular motherboard may support three or four PC2700 modules, but only two PC3200 modules.

For a general-purpose system, support for 1 GB of RAM is acceptable. For a system that will be used for memory-intensive tasks, such as professional graphics, database management, or complex scientific calculations, make sure the motherboard supports at least 2 GB of RAM.

DON'T BE PENNY WISE AND POUND FOOLISH

Although you may be able to find a new motherboard that allows you to migrate existing memory from your old motherboard, it's usually not a good idea to do so unless that older memory is current—i.e., PC3200 DDR-SDRAM or DDR2-SDRAM. Memory is cheap, and it makes little sense to base a new motherboard purchase decision on the ability to salvage a relatively small amount of old, slow, cheap memory.

Make sure the motherboard supports the type of video you need.

Motherboards differ in the provisions they make for video. Some motherboards provide an embedded video adapter and make no provision for installing a separate video adapter card. Other motherboards provide embedded video, but also provide a special expansion slot that accepts a standalone AGP or PCI Express video adapter card. Still other motherboards do not provide embedded video, but only an AGP or PCI Express slot that accepts a separate video adapter card. We recommend avoiding the first type of motherboard, even if you think embedded video is sufficient for your needs.

Check documentation, support, and updates.

Before you choose a motherboard, check the documentation and support that's available for it, as well as the BIOS and driver updates available. Some people think that a motherboard that has many patches and updates available must be a bad motherboard. Not true. Frequent patch and update releases indicate that the manufacturer takes support seriously. We recommend to friends and clients that they give great weight to—and perhaps even base their buying decisions on—the quality of the web site that supports the motherboard. For examples of good motherboard support sites, visit Intel (*http://www.intel.com/design/ motherbd/*) or ASUS (*http://support.asus.com*).

Choose the right manufacturer.

Manufacturers differ greatly in the quality of the motherboards they produce. Some manufacturers, such as Intel and ASUS, produce only first-rate motherboards. (For that reason, we strongly prefer to use Intel or ASUS motherboards for Intel processors, and ASUS motherboards for AMD processors.) Other manufacturers produce motherboards of varying quality; some good and some not so good. Still other manufacturers produce only junk.

The preceding issues are always important in choosing a motherboard. But there are many other motherboard characteristics to keep in mind. Some of them may be critical for some users and of little concern to others. These characteristics include:

Number and type of expansion slots

Any motherboard provides expansion slots, but motherboards differ in how many slots they provide, and of what types:

PCI slots

PCI (*Peripheral Component Interconnect*) slots have been the standard type of expansion slot for more than a decade. PCI slots accept expansion cards—such as LAN adapters, sound cards, and so on—that add various features to a system. PCI slots are available in 32-bit and 64-bit versions, although 64-bit PCI slots are commonly found only on server motherboards.

Video slot

A motherboard may have zero, one, or two dedicated video card slots. If a video slot is present, it may be AGP or *PCI Express* (*PCIe*), which are incompatible but serve the same purpose. The type of video slot determines the type of video card you can install. AGP video adapters are still popular and widely available, but PCI Express is fast becoming the dominant video adapter slot standard. Buy an AGP motherboard only if you have an AGP adapter that is worth saving. Otherwise, buy a motherboard, with or without embedded video, that provides a PCI Express x16 video slot. Do not buy any motherboard that provides embedded video but no separate video slot.

PCI Express slots

Many motherboards with a PCI Express x16 video slot also provide one or more PCI Express x1 general-purpose expansion slots, usually in place of one or two of the PCI expansion slots, but sometimes in addition to them. For the immediate future, PCI Express x1 slots are relatively useless, because there are few expansion cards that fit them. However, as PCI Express x16 video cards increasingly dominate AGP, it's likely that PCI will also gradually fade away and that PCI Express x1 expansion cards will become more common.

ATX AGP motherboards typically provide five or six PCI slots. ATX PCIe motherboards typically substitute one or two PCIe x1 slots for one or two of the PCI slots. A microATX motherboard of either type typically provides two or three fewer slots than a full ATX motherboard. Years ago, many PCs had all or nearly all of their slots occupied. Nowadays, with so many functions integrated on motherboards, it's common to see PCs with at most one or two slots occupied, so the number of slots available is much less important than it used to be. It's still important to get the types of slots you want, though.

OEM versus retail-boxed packaging

The same motherboard is often available as an *OEM product* and a *retail-boxed product*. (In fact, both forms of packaging are sold in retail channels.) The motherboard is identical or closely similar in either case, but there are differences. For example, the OEM version might have only a one-year warranty, while the retail-boxed version of the same motherboard has a three-year warranty. Also, the retail-boxed version often includes cables, adapters, a case label, a setup CD, and similar small parts that are not included with the OEM product. We generally recommend buying the retail-boxed version if it costs no more than $10 extra. Otherwise, buy the OEM version. You can download the setup CD and other software that isn't included with the OEM version.

VARIATIONS ON A THEME

There may be variations in the actual product between OEM and retail-boxed motherboards. For example, Intel often manufactures three to six variants of a motherboard, which may differ in minor ways (such as board color) and in more significant ways, such as the speed of the embedded network adapter, whether FireWire support is included, and so on. Some of these variants are available in both OEM and retail-boxed forms, and others in only one form or the other. Some variants aren't available to individual buyers. They're sold only in what Intel calls "bulk packaging," which means that the minimum order is a pallet load. Only large system makers buy bulk Intel motherboards.

Warranty

It may seem strange to minimize the importance of warranty, but the truth is that warranty should not usually be a major consideration. Motherboards generally work or they don't. If a motherboard is going to fail, it will likely do so right out of the box or within a few days of use. In practical terms, the vendor's return policy is likely to be more important than the manufacturer's warranty policy. Look for a vendor who replaces DOA motherboards quickly, preferably by cross-shipping the replacement.

Ports and connectors

At a minimum, the motherboard should provide four or more USB 2.0 ports—six or eight is better—and a dual ATA/100 or faster hard disk interface. Ideally the motherboard should also provide at least two Serial ATA connectors, and four is better. (Some motherboards with four SATA connectors include only one parallel ATA interface, which is acceptable.) We also like to have a serial port, an EPP/ECP parallel port, a PS/2 keyboard port, a PS/2 mouse port, and an FDD interface, but those "legacy" ports are fast disappearing, replaced by USB.

Embedded sound, video, and LAN

Some motherboards include embedded sound, video, and/or LAN adapters as standard or optional equipment. In the past, such motherboards were often designed for low-end systems, and used inexpensive and relatively incapable audio and video components. But nowadays many motherboards include very capable audio, video, and LAN adapters, and cost little or no more than similar motherboards without the embedded peripherals. If you buy such a motherboard, make sure that the embedded devices can be disabled if you later want to replace the embedded adapters with better components.

A Motherboard Tour

A motherboard is so complex and has so many components and connections that it can be overwhelming to someone who is not used to working inside PCs. As is true of many things, though, the easiest way to understand the working of the whole is to understand the working of the individual parts. So let's take the $2 tour of a modern motherboard, where you'll learn the functions of each important component and how to identify those components visually.

To begin, let's examine a block diagram of a chipset. Figure 4-4 shows the major components and functions of the Intel 925XE chipset. (Other modern chipsets are similar.) The 925XE chipset uses two physical chips. The *north bridge* chip, which Intel calls the *MCH (Memory Controller Hub)*, is the blue box labeled 82925X MCH. The MCH arbitrates and coordinates communications between the processor, memory, and the PCI Express video adapter. The MCH provides very high bandwidth channels: 6.4 GB/s between the MCH and processor; 8.0 GB/s between the MCH and the video adapter; and 8.5 GB/s between the MCH and memory.

The *south bridge* chip, which Intel calls the *ICH (I/O Controller Hub)*, is the blue box labeled ICH6RW. The ICH handles input/output functions, which work at much lower data rates than the processor, memory, and video channels. These channels include four 150 MB/s Serial ATA ports, six PCI slots with a cumulative 133 MB/s bandwidth, eight USB 2.0 ports with 60 MB/s bandwidth each, and four 500 MB/s PCI

Be Wary of Integrated Gigabit Ethernet

Embedded adapters often use the main CPU, which can reduce performance by a few percent. The speed of current processors means this is seldom an issue. However, if processor performance is critical, you might wish to use a motherboard that has few or no embedded functions.

Embedded Gigabit Ethernet is a particular concern. If you buy a motherboard with embedded Gigabit Ethernet, make sure it uses a dedicated communications channel, such as the Communications Streaming Architecture (CSA) channel used by Intel chipsets or a PCIe channel. Some inexpensive motherboards have embedded Gigabit Ethernet adapters that connect via the PCI bus. That's a problem because Gigabit Ethernet is fast enough to saturate the PCI bus and noticeably degrade system performance.

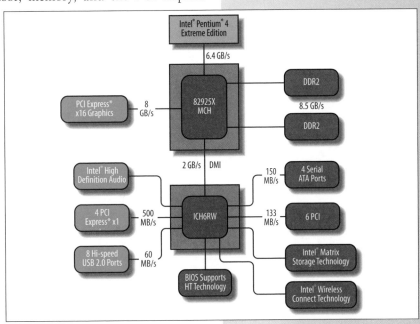

Figure 4-4. Block diagram of the Intel 925X chipset (image courtesy of Intel Corporation)

Express x1 slots. The ICH also handles such functions as embedded audio, the interface with the system BIOS, and wireless networking.

Figure 4-5 maps these chipset features to the component layout on a real-world motherboard. For illustrative purposes, we've used an Intel D925XECV2 motherboard, but any recent motherboard has similar features and layout. Not all of the components shown are present on all motherboards, and the exact positioning of some components may differ, but the essentials remain the same.

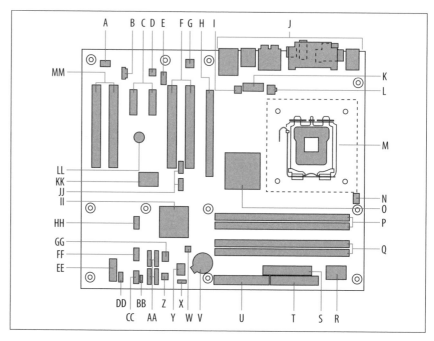

Figure 4-5. Component layout on a typical motherboard (image courtesy of Intel Corporation)

A Auxiliary rear fan connector
B ATAPI CD-ROM audio connector
C PCI Express x1 expansion slots
D Audio codec
E Front-panel audio connector
F PCI expansion slots
G Gigabit Ethernet PCI Express controller chip
H PCI Express x16 video adapter slot
I Rear case fan connector
J Back-panel I/O connectors
K Alternate power connector
L ATX12V power connector
M Processor socket
N CPU fan connector
O MCH (north bridge)
P Channel A memory slots
Q Channel B memory slots
R Supplemental I/O controller chip
S ATX main power connector
T Diskette drive interface connector

U ATA (IDE) interface connector
V Battery
W Chassis intrusion connector
X BIOS Setup configuration jumper block
Y Firmware Hub (FWH)
Z Front-case fan connector
AA Serial ATA interface connectors
BB Auxiliary front-panel power LED connector
CC Front-panel connector
DD SCSI hard disk activity indicator LED
EE Auxiliary power output connector
FF Front-panel USB interface connector
GG Trusted Platform Module (TPM) chip
HH Front-panel USB interface connector
II ICH6R (south bridge)
JJ Front-panel IEEE-1394a (FireWire) interface connectors
KK IEEE-1394a (FireWire) controller chip
LL Speaker
MM PCI expansion slots

The left rear quadrant of the motherboard, shown in Figure 4-6, is dominated by expansion slots—two pairs of white PCI slots bracketing a pair of PCI Express x1 slots, with a black PCI Express x16 video adapter slot at the far right. The white auxiliary rear fan connector is visible centered above the left pair of PCI slots. The yellow connector at top center is the front-panel audio connector, with the audio codec chip to its upper left. The Gigabit Ethernet controller chip is visible centered between the two mounting holes on the upper right. The round object below the PCI Express x1 slots is the system speaker. The large chip at bottom center is the FireWire controller, and the two blue header-pin connectors to its right are the front-panel FireWire interface connectors.

The right rear quadrant of the motherboard, shown in Figure 4-7, is dominated by the processor socket (lower right), the heatsink for the north bridge chip (bottom left), and a top view of the rear I/O panel (top). The group of three white connectors at the upper left are, from left to right, the rear case fan connector, the alternate power connector—used to provide additional current to the motherboard if the power supply has a 20-pin main power connector rather than a 24-pin connector—and the ATX12V power connector. The CPU fan connector is visible at the lower-right corner of the image.

Figure 4-8 shows the rear I/O panel connectors. Legacy PS/2 mouse (top) and keyboard connectors are visible at the far left. The second group of

Figure 4-6. Left rear quadrant of the D925XECV2 motherboard (image courtesy of Intel Corporation)

Figure 4-7. Right rear quadrant of the D925XECV2 motherboard (image courtesy of Intel Corporation)

connectors includes a parallel (LPT) port at the top and a 9-pin serial port at the lower left. At the bottom left of this group are coax (round) and optical (square) digital audio-out ports. The third group of connectors are all audio connectors, which can be configured for various functions. The fourth group of connectors has a FireWire connector at the top, with two USB 2.0 connectors beneath it. The fifth group of connectors has a Gigabit Ethernet connector at the top, with two more USB 2.0 connectors beneath it.

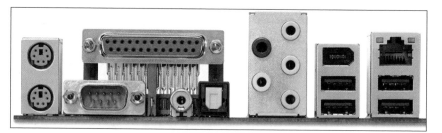

Figure 4-8. Rear I/O panel connectors (image courtesy of Intel Corporation)

I/O Connector Color Codes

It took longer than it should have, but the I/O connectors on many motherboards now use a more or less standardized color code, shown in Table 4-3. Obviously, manufacturers make some case-by-case exceptions. The coax digital audio-out connector on this motherboard, for example, is orange, which should make it a speaker-out/subwoofer. Similarly, one of the audio connectors is bright yellow, which should make it a video-out connector. Oh, well.

Table 4-3. I/O connector color codes

Connector	Color	Connector	Color
Analog VGA	Blue	PS/2-compatible keyboard	Purple
Audio line-in	Light blue	PS/2-compatible mouse	Green
Audio line-out	Lime	Serial	Teal/Turquoise
Digital monitor/flat panel	White	Speaker-out/subwoofer	Orange
IEEE 1394	Gray	Right-to-left speaker	Brown
Microphone	Pink	USB	Black
MIDI/gameport	Gold	Video-out	Yellow
Parallel	Burgundy	SCSI, LAN, telephone, etc.	Not defined

The left front quadrant of the motherboard is shown in Figure 4-9. The round object at the lower right is the battery. The large chip immediately to its left is the Firmware Hub (FWH), with the orange BIOS Setup Configuration jumper block below it. The white object to the left of the jumper block is the front case fan power connector. Above that power connector is the Trusted Platform Module (TPM) chip, and a group of four Serial ATA interface connectors appears to the left of the TPM chip and power connector. The large silver object at right center is the heatsink for the ICH6 south bridge chip. The black header pin connector to the left of the south bridge heatsink is one front-panel USB connector, with a second identical connector below it. The multicolored jumper block at the center bottom edge of the motherboard is the front-panel connector.

Figure 4-10 shows the right front quadrant of the motherboard, with the two Channel A memory slots at the top and two Channel B memory slots beneath them. The large chip at the lower right is the supplemental I/O controller chip, with the white ATX main power connector to its left. The black ATA interface connector is at the bottom left edge of this image, with the floppy drive interface connector immediately to its right.

Figure 4-9. Left front quadrant of the D925XECV2 motherboard (image courtesy of Intel Corporation)

Figure 4-10. Right front quadrant of the D925XECV2 motherboard (image courtesy of Intel Corporation)

Identifying a Motherboard

When you upgrade other system components, it's sometimes important to know the details of the motherboard and chipset you're using. The motherboard's manual and manufacturer's web site are authoritative sources of information, of course, but at times you won't be certain which motherboard is installed in the system. The easiest way to identify the motherboard and chipset is to run a diagnostic utility such as Everest Home Edition. Figure 4-11 shows Everest Home Edition identifying a motherboard as an ASUS A7N8X-VM/400, with BIOS version 1003, dated 08/06/2004. Figure 4-12 identifies the chipset in this motherboard as an NVIDIA nForce2 IGP north bridge with an NVIDIA MCP2 south bridge.

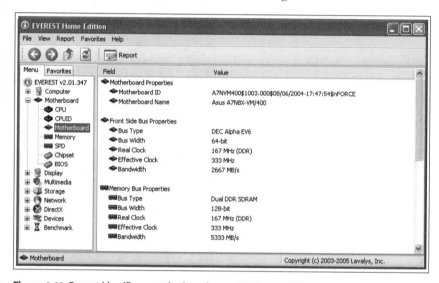

Figure 4-11. Everest identifies a motherboard as an ASUS A7N8X-VM/400

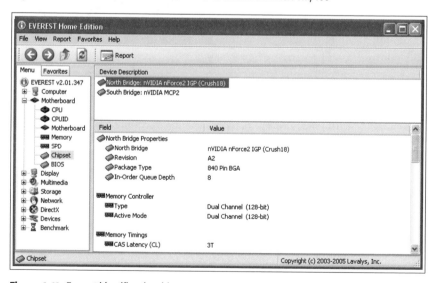

Figure 4-12. Everest identifies the chipset as an NVIDIA nForce2

Alas, it's not always possible to take the easy way out. Sometimes you have to pop the cover and actually examine the motherboard to get the information you need, because motherboard makers make slipstream revisions to their products without changing the model number. For example, an earlier revision of a motherboard may use *voltage regulator modules* (*VRMs*) that are rated to provide enough current only for processors that run at 2.8 GHz or slower. A later revision of that board, with the identical model number, may use VRMs that are rated for processors up to 3.8 GHz.

The revision number of a motherboard is ordinarily silk-screened on the board or printed on a paper label that is stuck to the board somewhere near the silkscreened model number. Most motherboard makers call their revisions by that name. Intel instead refers to its revision levels as *AA numbers* (*Altered Assembly numbers*). Figure 4-13 shows the label area of an Intel D865GLC motherboard, with an AA number of C28906-403.

Figure 4-13. Intel D865GLC motherboard with an AA number of C28906-403

Figure 4-14 shows a portion of the Intel CPU compatibility page for the D865GLC motherboard, which shows the minimum BIOS versions and AA numbers required for compatibility with various processors. Examining AA numbers tells us, for example, that our D865GLC motherboard, with an AA number of C28906-403, does not support Pentium 4 Extreme Edition processors, which require a minimum C28906 AA level of -405. You can find CPU compatibility pages on the motherboard manufacturer's web site (if the manufacturer *doesn't* provide this information, then you can add that manufacturer to the list of companies to avoid). The information you find online will generally be more up-to-date than what you find in the manual that came with your motherboard.

If an early BIOS version is the only bar to upgrading a processor, you

Processor family	Processor number	Processor speed	System bus frequency	L2 cache size	BIOS version	Notes
Intel® Pentium® 4 Extreme Edition		3.40 GHz	800 MHz	512 KB 2 MB (L3)	p11 or greater	The following board revisions (AA numbers) support these processors:
		3.20 GHz	800 MHz	512 KB 2 MB (L3)	p11 or greater	C27498-406 or later C27499-406 or later C27500-406 or later C28903-405 or later C28906-405 or later C28909-406 or later C32156-405 or later C31110-404 or later
		3.40E GHz	800 MHz	1 MB	p13 or greater	
		3.20E GHz	800 MHz	1 MB	p13 or greater	
		3E GHz	800 MHz	1 MB	p13 or greater	
		2.80E GHz	800 MHz	1 MB	p13 or greater	
		2.80A GHz	533 MHz	1 MB	p13 or greater	See the board revision note, below for an explanation
		2.40A GHz	533 MHz	1 MB	p13 or greater	

Figure 4-14. Part of an Intel CPU compatibility page

can simply update the BIOS to a later version. But if the board revision level is too low to support a particular processor, the only option is to use a different processor that is supported by the board revision level you have.

YOU CAN'T GET THERE FROM HERE

If you are upgrading to a faster processor (on a motherboard that supports it!) that requires a later BIOS version than you currently have installed, update the BIOS before you install the new processor. Otherwise, you'll find yourself in a "can't get there from here" situation, because the system won't boot with the new processor.

Unsupported Means Unsupported

Never install an unsupported processor in the hopes that it may work. The good news is that it probably will. The bad news is that it won't for long. Faster processors draw more current, and it's likely that the fast new processor that appears to work fine is pulling more current than the motherboard was designed to provide. Sooner or later, probably sooner, that excessive current draw will damage or destroy the motherboard, and possibly the processor as well.

Replacing a Motherboard

The exact steps required to replace a motherboard depend on the specifics of the motherboard and case, the peripheral components to be connected, and so on. In general terms, the process is quite simple, if time-consuming:

- Disconnect all cables and remove all expansion cards from the current motherboard.

- Remove the screws that secure the old motherboard and remove the motherboard.

- If you are reusing the CPU and/or memory, remove them from the old motherboard and install them on the new one.

- Replace the old back-panel I/O template with the template supplied with the new motherboard.

- Remove and install motherboard mounting posts as necessary to match the mounting holes on the new motherboard.

- Install the new motherboard and secure it with screws in all mounting hole positions.

- Reinstall all of the expansion cards and reconnect the cables.

The devil is in the details. In the rest of this section, we'll illustrate the process of installing the motherboard and making all the connections properly.

FIRST THINGS FIRST

In this sequence, we'll assume that you have already populated the motherboard by installing the processor and CPU cooler (Chapter 5) and the memory (Chapter 6). With very few exceptions, it's easier and safer to install the processor and memory before you install the motherboard in the case.

Getting started

Before you start tearing things apart, make sure you have at least one good backup of all your important data. You needn't worry about backing up Windows and applications—although you should, if possible, back up the configuration information for your mail client, browser, and so on—because unless you're replacing an old motherboard with an identical new motherboard, you may need to reinstall Windows and all applications from scratch.

Disconnect all cables and external peripherals from the system, and move it to a flat, well-lighted work area—the kitchen table is traditional, as we mentioned earlier. If you haven't cleaned the system recently, give it a thorough cleaning before you begin work.

HE GOT UP, GOT DRESSED, AND SHOWERED

Although by necessity we describe a particular sequence for installing the motherboard, you don't need to follow that sequence if it makes sense to depart from it. Some steps, such as installing expansion cards after you install the motherboard in the case, must be taken in the order we describe, because completing one step is a prerequisite for completing another. But the exact sequence doesn't matter for most steps. As you install the motherboard, it will be obvious when sequence matters.

Remove the access panel(s) from the case, disconnect all of the cables from the motherboard, and remove all of the screws that secure the motherboard to the case. Ground yourself by touching the power supply. Slide the motherboard slightly toward the front of the case, lift it straight out, and place it aside on the table top or another nonconductive surface.

Preparing the case

Removing the motherboard may expose more dirt. If so, use a brush and vacuum cleaner to remove that dirt before you proceed further.

Every motherboard comes with a back-panel I/O template. Unless the current template matches the port layout on the new motherboard, you'll need to remove the old template. The best way to remove an I/O template without damaging it (or the case) is to use a screwdriver handle to press gently against the template from outside the case, while using your fingers to support the template from inside the case until the template snaps out. If the old motherboard is still good, put the old template with it for possible use later.

Compare the new I/O template with the back-panel I/O ports on the new motherboard to make sure they correspond. Then press the new template into place. Working from inside the case, align the bottom, right, and left edges of the I/O template with the matching case cutout. When the I/O template is positioned properly, press gently along the edges to seat it in the cutout, as shown in Figure 4-15. It should snap into place, although getting it to seat properly sometimes requires several attempts. It's often helpful to press gently against the edge of the template with the handle of a screwdriver or nut driver.

A Little Flexibility May Be a Bad Thing

Be careful not to bend the I/O template while seating it. The template holes need to line up with the external port connectors on the motherboard I/O panel. If the template is even slightly bent, it may be difficult to seat the motherboard properly.

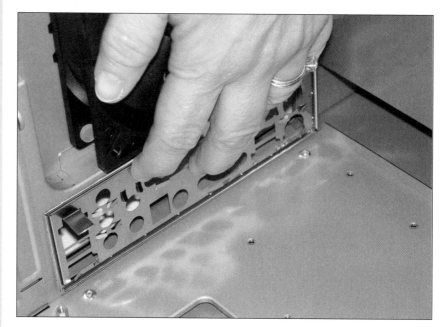

Figure 4-15. Press the new I/O template into place

After you install the I/O template, carefully slide the motherboard into place, making sure that the back-panel connectors on the motherboard are firmly in contact with the corresponding holes on the I/O template. Compare the positions of the motherboard mounting holes with the standoff mounting positions in the case. One easy method is to place the motherboard in position and insert a felt-tip pen through each motherboard mounting hole to mark the corresponding standoff position beneath it.

DON'T MISS ANY HOLES

If you simply look at the motherboard, it's easy to miss one of the mounting holes in all the clutter. We generally hold the motherboard up to a light, which makes the mounting holes stand out distinctly.

Remove any unneeded brass standoffs and install additional standoffs until each motherboard mounting hole has a corresponding standoff. Although you can screw in the standoffs using your fingers or needlenose pliers, it's much easier and faster to use a 5 mm nut driver, as shown in Figure 4-16. Tighten the standoffs finger-tight, but do not overtighten them. It's easy to strip the threads by applying too much torque with a nutdriver.

Figure 4-16. Install a brass standoff in each mounting position

Once you've installed all the standoffs, do a final check to verify that each motherboard mounting hole has a corresponding standoff, and that no standoffs are installed that don't correspond to a motherboard mounting hole. As a final check, we usually hold the motherboard in position above the case, as shown in Figure 4-17, and look down through each motherboard mounting hole to make sure there's a standoff installed below it.

Figure 4-17. Verify that a standoff is installed for each motherboard mounting hole and that no extra standoffs are installed

Don't Miss Any Standoffs

Make absolutely certain that each standoff matches a motherboard mounting hole. If you find one that doesn't, remove it. Leaving an "extra" standoff in place might cause a short circuit that could damage the motherboard and/or other components.

Pen and Ink

You can also verify that all standoffs are properly installed by placing the motherboard flat on a large piece of paper and using a felt-tip pen to mark all motherboard mounting holes on the paper. Then line one of the marks up with the corresponding standoff and press down until the standoff punctures the paper. Do the same with a second standoff to align the paper, and then press the paper flat around each standoff. If you've installed the standoffs properly, every mark will be punctured, and there will be no punctures where there are no marks.

Seating and securing the motherboard

If you have not already installed the processor and memory on the motherboard, do so before proceeding. See Chapters 5 and 6 for detailed instructions.

Slide the motherboard into the case, as shown in Figure 4-18. Carefully align the back-panel I/O connectors with the corresponding holes in the I/O template, and slide the motherboard toward the rear of the case until the motherboard mounting holes line up with the standoffs you installed earlier. You may need to tilt the motherboard slightly down towards the I/O template to slip the back-panel connectors easily under their corresponding grounding tabs without damage. Make absolutely certain that none of the grounding tabs intrude into the jacks on the I/O panel. USB ports are particularly prone to this problem, and a USB port with a grounding tab stuck into it might short out the motherboard and prevent the system from booting.

Figure 4-18. Slide the motherboard into position

Before you secure the motherboard, verify that the back-panel I/O connectors mate properly with the I/O template, as shown in Figure 4-19. The I/O template has metal tabs that ground the back-panel I/O connectors. Make sure that none of these tabs intrude into a port connector. An errant tab at best blocks the port, rendering it unusable, and at worst might short out the motherboard.

After you position the motherboard and verify that the back-panel I/O connectors mate cleanly with the I/O template, insert a screw through one mounting hole into the corresponding standoff, as shown in Figure 4-20.

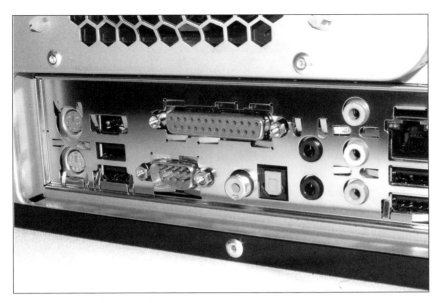

Figure 4-19. Verify that the back panel connectors mate cleanly with the I/O template

You may need to apply pressure to keep the motherboard positioned properly until you have inserted two or three screws.

If you have trouble getting all the holes and standoffs aligned, insert two screws at opposite corners but don't tighten them completely. Use one hand to press the motherboard into alignment, with all holes matching the standoffs. Then insert one or two more screws and tighten them completely. Finish mounting the motherboard by inserting screws into all standoffs and tightening them.

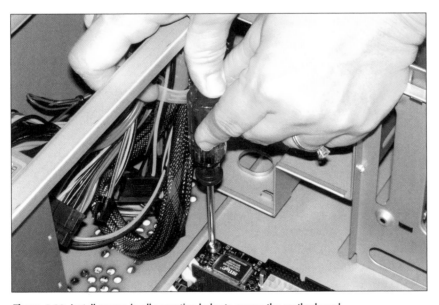

Figure 4-20. Install screws in all mounting holes to secure the motherboard

Dealing with Misalignment

With top-quality motherboards and cases, all the holes line up perfectly. With cheap products, that's not always true. At times, we've been forced to use only a few screws to secure the motherboard. We prefer to use all of them, both to physically support the motherboard and to make sure all of the grounding points are in fact grounded, but if you simply can't get all of the holes lined up, just install as many screws as you can.

Connecting front-panel switch and indicator cables

Once the motherboard is secured, the next step is to connect the front-panel switch and indicator cables to the motherboard. Before you begin connecting front-panel cables, examine the cables. Each connector should be labeled descriptively—for example, "Power," "Reset," and "HDD LED." (If not, you'll have to trace each wire back to the front of the case to determine which switch or indicator it connects to.) Match those descriptions with the front-panel connector pins on the motherboard to make sure you connect the correct cable to the appropriate pins. Figure 4-21 shows typical pinouts for the Power Switch, Reset Switch, Power LED, and Hard Drive Activity LED connectors.

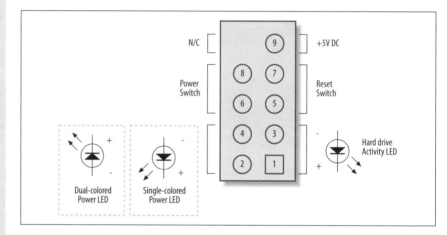

Figure 4-21. Typical front panel connector pinouts (image courtesy of Intel Corporation)

GO YOUR OWN WAY

These sample pinouts are for a specific motherboard: the Intel D865PERL. Your motherboard might use different pinouts, so make sure to verify the correct pinouts before you connect the cables.

- The Power Switch and Reset Switch connectors are not polarized, and can be connected in either orientation.

- The Hard Drive Activity LED is polarized, and should be connected with the ground (usually black) wire on Pin 3 and the signal (usually red or white) wire on Pin 1.

- Many motherboards provide two Power LED connectors, one that accepts a 2-position Power LED cable and another that accepts a 3-position Power LED cable with wires in positions 1 and 3. Use whichever is appropriate. The Power LED connectors are usually dual-polarized, and can support a single-color (usually green) Power LED or a dual-color (usually green/yellow) LED.

THE NICE THING ABOUT STANDARDS IS THAT
THERE ARE SO MANY OF THEM

Although Intel has defined a standard front-panel connector block and uses that standard for its own motherboards, few other motherboard makers adhere to that standard. Accordingly, rather than provide an Intel-standard monolithic connector block that would be useless for motherboards that do not follow the Intel standard, most case makers provide individual 1-, 2-, or 3-pin connectors for each switch and indicator.

Once you determine the proper orientation for each cable, connect the Power Switch, Reset Switch, Power LED, and Hard Drive Activity LED, as shown in Figure 4-22. Not all cases have cables for every connector on the motherboard, and not all motherboards have connectors for all cables provided by the case. For example, the case might provide a speaker cable, but the motherboard might have a built-in speaker and no connection for an external speaker. Conversely, the motherboard might provide connectors for features, such as a Chassis Intrusion Connector, for which no corresponding cable exists on the case; those connectors go unused.

Figure 4-22. Connect the front-panel switch and indicator cables

When you're connecting front-panel cables, try to get it right the first time, but don't worry too much about getting it wrong. Other than the power switch cable, which must be connected properly for the system to start, none of the other front-panel switch and indicator cables is essential, and connecting them wrong won't damage the system. Switch cables—power and reset—are not polarized. You can connect them in either orientation,

Three into Two Won't Go

Sometimes you'll encounter a situation where a 2-wire cable has a 3-pin connector, with the wires connected to pins 1 and 3. If the motherboard has a similar connector, there's no problem, but sometimes that cable needs to connect to a motherboard connector with two adjacent pins. Some motherboards provide an alternative 3-pin connector, but many do not. In that case, the best solution is to use a sharp knife or shears to cut the 3-pin connector in half, leaving you with two wires with individual connectors.

without worrying about which pin is signal and which ground. If you connect an LED cable backwards, the worst that happens is that the LED won't light. Most cases use a common wire color, usually black, for ground, and a colored wire for signal.

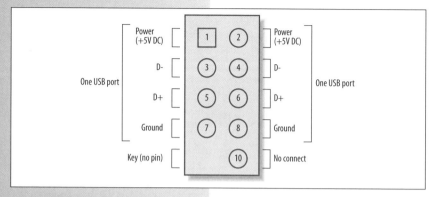

Figure 4-23. Typical front-panel USB connector pinouts (image courtesy of Intel Corporation)

Connecting front-panel ports

Most cases provide one or two front-panel USB 2.0 ports, and most motherboards provide corresponding internal USB connectors. To route USB to the front panel, you must connect a cable from each front-panel USB port to the corresponding internal connector. Figure 4-23 shows the standard Intel pinouts for the internal front-panel USB connectors, which are also used by most other motherboard makers.

Some cases provide a monolithic 10-pin USB connector that mates to motherboard USB header pins that use the standard Intel layout. With such a case, connecting the front-panel USB ports is a simple matter of plugging that monolithic connector into the header pins on the motherboard. Unfortunately, some cases instead provide eight individual wires, each with a single connector. Figure 4-24 shows Robert (finally) getting all eight of the individual wires connected to the proper pins.

Manual Dexterity

Yes, we know it looks as though Robert is sliding a single 4-pin connector onto the header pins, but trust us, those are four individual wires. Arrghh. The best way Robert found to get all the wires connected properly was to clamp the four wires between his fingers aligned as a single connector and then slide the group of connectors onto the header pins. And the second group of four is much harder to get onto the pins than the first set. Several of our tech reviewers (are we the only ones who didn't think of this?) suggested aligning the individual pins correctly, holding them in your fingers, and using a cable tie snugged down to hold them in place—thereby making a monolithic connector block out of the original individual connectors.

Figure 4-24. Connect the front-panel USB cables

If your motherboard and case make provision for front-panel FireWire and/or audio connectors, install them the same way, making sure that the pinouts of the connectors and cables correspond.

What About the Optical Disc Audio Cable?

Years ago, connecting an audio cable from the optical drive to the motherboard audio connector or sound card was an essential step, because systems used the analog audio delivered from the optical drive by that cable. If you didn't connect that cable, you didn't get audio from the drive. All recent optical drives and motherboards support digital audio, which is delivered across the bus rather than via a dedicated audio cable. Few optical drives or motherboards include an analog audio cable nowadays, because one is seldom needed.

To verify the setting for digital audio, which is ordinarily enabled by default, use the Windows 2000/XP Device Manager to display the Device Properties sheet for the optical drive. The "Enable digital CD audio . . . " checkbox should be marked. If it is not, mark the checkbox to enable digital audio. If the checkbox is grayed out, does not appear, or refuses to stay checked after a reboot, your optical drive and/or your motherboard do not support digital audio. In that case, you'll need to use an MPC analog audio cable to connect the drive to the CD-ROM audio connector on the motherboard or your sound card. Also, some older audio applications do not support digital audio, and so require an analog audio cable to be installed even if the system supports digital audio.

Many modern optical drives provide two audio connectors, a 4-pin MPC analog audio connector and a 2-pin digital audio connector that you can connect to a Sony Philips Digital Interface (SP/DIF) audio connector or a Digital-in audio connector on your motherboard or sound card. We suggest that you install an audio cable only if needed. Otherwise, you can do without.

Reconnect the drive data cables

The next step is to reconnect the drive data cables to the motherboard interfaces, as shown in Figure 4-25 and Figure 4-26. Make sure to connect each data cable to the proper interface. See Chapters 7 and 8 for details.

Figure 4-25. Connect the Serial ATA data cable(s) to the motherboard interface(s)

Neatness Counts

After you connect the drive data cables, don't just leave them flopping around loose. That not only looks amateurish, but can impede air flow and cause overheating. Tuck the cables neatly out of the way, using tape, cable ties, or tie-wraps to secure them to the case. If necessary, temporarily disconnect the cables to route them around other cables and obstructions, and reconnect them once you have them positioned properly.

Figure 4-26. Connect the ATA data cable(s) to the motherboard interface(s)

Reconnect the ATX Power Connectors

The next step is to reconnect the power connectors from the power supply to the motherboard. The Main ATX Power Connector is a 20-pin or 24-pin connector, usually located near the right front edge of the motherboard. Locate the corresponding cable coming from the power supply, verify that the cable is aligned properly with the connector, and press the cable firmly until it seats fully, as shown in Figure 4-27. The locking tab on the side of the connector should snap into place over the corresponding nub on the socket.

Figure 4-27. Connect the Main ATX Power Connector

Please Be Seated

Make absolutely certain that the Main ATX Power Connector seats fully. A partially seated connector may cause subtle problems that are very difficult to troubleshoot.

ADVICE FROM FRANCISCO GARCÍA MACEDA

Some power supplies are currently shipping with a combination 20-/24-pin connector, in which the regular 20-pin connector has on one end a couple of locking tabs or sliding grooves. The power supply also has a 4-pin connector very similar to the ATX12V connector with matching tabs or rails that you can snap or slide into the 20-pin connector, thus converting it to a 24-pin connector. I've seen people reject this kind of power supply because they don't understand how it works: either they need a 24-pin power supply and the 4-pin connector is unlatched or they need a 20-pin power supply and the 4-pin connector is latched. In either case, they don't figure out the combination mechanism, and so think the power supply is incompatible with their motherboard.

20-pin Versus 24-pin Motherboards and Power Supplies

Many recent motherboards are designed to accept the newer 24-pin ATX Main Power Connector rather than the original 20-pin version of that connector. If the new motherboard is 20-pin and your power supply is 24-pin, you may be able to connect the 24-pin cable to the 20-pin motherboard, leaving the extra four pins unused. If the motherboard has components too near the connector, the 24-pin cable may not seat. In that case, buy an adapter cable that adapts the 24-pin cable to fit the 20-pin motherboard connector.

Conversely, if the motherboard is 24-pin and your power supply 20-pin, the motherboard may require more current than the 20-pin cable can provide. In that case, the motherboard will have a standard Molex (hard drive) power connector. After you connect the 20-pin ATX Main Power Connector cable to the 24-pin socket on the motherboard, connect one of the Molex hard drive power connectors from the power supply to the auxiliary power connector socket on the motherboard. Failing to do this may cause boot failures or other problems.

Pentium 4 systems require more power to the motherboard than the standard ATX Main Power Connector supplies. Intel developed a supplementary connector, called the ATX12V Connector, that routes additional +12V current directly to the VRM (Voltage Regulator Module) that powers the processor. On most Pentium 4 motherboards, the ATX12V connector is located near the processor socket. The ATX12V connector is keyed. Orient the cable connector properly relative to the motherboard connector, and press the cable connector into place until the plastic tab locks, as shown in Figure 4-28.

Figure 4-28. Connect the ATX12V Power Connector

LIFE WITHOUT CABLE

Failing to connect the ATX12V connector is one of the most common causes of initial boot failures on newly built Pentium 4 systems. If nothing happens the first time you power up the system, chances are it's because you forgot to connect the ATX12V connector.

Reinstalling the video adapter

The next step is to reinstall the video adapter and/or any other expansion cards you removed. To do so, align each adapter with the corresponding motherboard slot. Make sure that any external connectors on the card bracket clear the edges of the slot. Carefully align the card with the slot and use both thumbs to press down firmly until it snaps into the slot, as shown in Figure 4-29.

Figure 4-29. Align the video adapter and press firmly to seat it

After you are certain that the video adapter is fully seated, secure it by inserting a screw through the bracket into the chassis, as shown in Figure 4-30. If the video card has an externally powered fan or requires an external power connection, make sure to connect a power cable to the video adapter before you move on to another task. Install any other expansion cards in the same manner, making sure to connect any power or data cables they require before you start another step.

Figure 4-30. Secure the video adapter bracket with a screw

Please Be Seated II

When a newly built system fails to boot, the most common cause is that the video adapter is not fully seated. Some combinations of adapter, case, and motherboard make it devilishly hard to install the adapter properly. It may seem that the adapter is fully seated. You may even hear it snap into place. That's no guarantee. Always verify that the card contacts have fully penetrated the slot, and that the base of the adapter is parallel to the slot and in full contact with it. Many motherboards have a retaining bracket, visible in Figure 4-29 as two brown tabs to the lower right of the heatsink. This bracket mates with a corresponding notch on the video adapter, snapping into place as the adapter is seated. If you need to remove the adapter later, remember to press those tabs to unlock the retaining bracket before you attempt to pull the card.

Finishing up the installation

At this point, the motherboard upgrade is nearly complete. Take a few minutes to double-check everything. Verify that all of the cables are connected properly and that there's nothing loose inside the case. We usually pick up the system and tilt it gently from side to side and then front to back to make sure there are no loose screws or other items that could cause a short. Use the following checklist:

- Power supply set to proper input voltage (see Chapter 16)
- No loose tools or screws (shake the case gently)
- Heatsink/fan unit properly mounted; CPU fan connected (see Chapter 5)
- Memory modules full seated and latched (see Chapter 6)
- Front-panel switch and indicator cables connected properly
- Front-panel I/O, USB, and other internal cables connected properly
- Hard drive data cable (see Chapter 7) connected to drive and motherboard
- Hard drive power cable connected
- Optical drive data cable (see Chapter 8) connected to drive and motherboard
- Optical drive power cable connected
- Optical drive audio cable(s) connected, if applicable
- Floppy drive data and power cables connected (if applicable)
- All drives secured to drive bay or chassis, as applicable
- Expansion cards fully seated and secured to the chassis
- Main ATX power cable connected
- ATX12V and/or auxiliary power cables connected (if applicable)
- Front and rear case fans installed and connected (if applicable)
- All cables dressed and tucked

Once you're certain that all is as it should be, it's time for the smoke test. Leave the cover off for now. Connect the power cable to the wall receptacle and then to the system unit. If your power supply has a separate rocker switch on the back that controls power to the power supply, turn that switch to the "1" or "on" position. Press the main power button on the front of the case, and the system should start up. Check to make sure that the power supply fan, CPU fan, and case fan are spinning. You should also hear the hard drive spin up and the happy beep that tells you the system is starting normally. At that point, everything should be working properly.

Turn off the system, disconnect the power cord, reinstall the access panels, and move the system back to its original location. Reconnect the display, keyboard, mouse, and any other external peripherals, and power the system up.

Only the Good Die Young

When you turn on the rear power switch, the system will come to life momentarily and then die. That's perfectly normal behavior. When the power supply receives power, it begins to start up. It quickly notices that the motherboard hasn't told it to start, and so it shuts down again. All you need to do is press the front-panel power switch and the system will start normally.

Saving Windows

When you replace the motherboard, unless the replacement is the same model as the original, the existing Windows XP installation is horribly misconfigured for the new motherboard. Although you can strip the hard drive down to bare metal and reinstall everything from scratch, there is an easier way.

1. Make sure that the system is configured to boot first from the optical drive.

2. Boot the Windows XP distribution disc. When you're prompted, press Enter to install Windows. (Do not choose the "R" option for Repair Console.) At the license screen, press F8 to accept the license.

3. Windows Setup detects the existing Windows installation, and gives you the option to install a fresh copy or repair the existing copy. This time, make sure the existing Windows installation is highlighted and press R to choose the Repair option.

4. Complete Windows Setup and restart the system. (You will probably have to reactivate Windows.)

5. Install the video, audio, network, and other drivers for the new motherboard.

For additional information, see the Microsoft Knowledge Base Article 315341, "How to perform an in-place upgrade (reinstallation) of Windows XP" (search the Knowledge Base at *http://support.microsoft.com*).

Troubleshooting and Maintaining Motherboards

The motherboard *is* the computer, so the usual symptom of a failed motherboard is a completely dead system. Fans, drives, and other peripherals may spin up if the motherboard is dead, but more often nothing at all happens when you turn on the power. No beeps, no lights, no fans, nothing.

If you think you have a dead motherboard, think again. The most likely cause of a dead system is a blown fuse or breaker at the wall receptacle. If you're certain the system is getting power and you have just installed the motherboard, it's much more likely that you've neglected to connect a cable or made some other basic error than that the motherboard itself is bad, assuming of course that the problem motherboard is a high-quality product.

When Bad Motherboards Turn Good

Many online vendors have stopped accepting returns of "bad" motherboards for just this reason. As it turns out, about 19 of 20 motherboards returned as defective are perfectly good. The buyer simply didn't install the motherboard correctly. Even so, many upgraders choose to buy their motherboards from a big-box store or other local source, because of their generally better return policies. In fact, some people troubleshoot their systems by buying a motherboard locally and then returning it if the motherboard turns out not to be the problem. We think that's unethical, but as any vendor will tell you, it's common practice.

What's in a Name?

Most name-brand motherboards, particularly those made by Intel and ASUS, are of very high quality; cheap motherboards, including those used in most consumer-grade mass-market systems, are of very poor quality. We've used Intel and ASUS motherboards for years. In a shipment of 100 motherboards, it's unusual to find even 1 DOA. In a shipment of 100 cheap motherboards, it's not uncommon to find half or more DOA, and many of the remainder failing soon after they're installed.

In a working system, it's very uncommon for a high-quality motherboard to fail other than from lightning damage (see Chapter 16) or other severe abuse. In particular, it's nearly unheard of for a motherboard to fail while it is running, as opposed to when you start the system. A dead system is more often caused by a dead power supply than a dead motherboard, so the first step to troubleshoot an apparently dead motherboard is to swap in a known-good power supply. If the system remains completely dead with a known-good power supply, it's likely that the motherboard is defective and must be replaced.

It's not uncommon for a motherboard to fail partially. For example, an ATA interface or the embedded video, audio, or LAN may stop working, while the rest of the motherboard functions appear to work normally. It's possible to work around such partial failures; for example, by disabling the failed function in BIOS Setup and installing an expansion card to replace the failed embedded function. We recommend against this practice, however, because a partial motherboard failure is often soon followed by a complete failure.

Configuring CMOS

Each time a system boots, the BIOS boot screen appears momentarily. While this screen is being displayed, pressing a designated key runs the CMOS Setup program, which resides in firmware. CMOS Setup is used to configure BIOS and chipset settings ranging from those as obvious as the Date and Time to those as obscure as memory timings and bus settings.

BEAUTY IS ONLY SKIN DEEP

Some motherboards replace the standard BIOS boot screen with a logo splash screen. Display the standard BIOS boot screen on such systems by pressing the Escape key while the logo is visible.

To invoke CMOS Setup, you normally press F1 (AMI), Del (Award), or F2 (Phoenix). Other BIOS manufacturers use different keys, and some system and motherboard manufacturers modify a standard BIOS to use another key. The key that invokes CMOS Setup nearly always appears on the BIOS boot screen, but if your BIOS boot screen isn't displayed or doesn't show that key, try Esc, Del, F1, F2, F10, Ctrl-Alt-S, or refer to the documentation.

The exact appearance of CMOS Setup and the available options depend on the chipset, the BIOS make and version, and changes made to the BIOS and CMOS Setup programs by manufacturers. For example, two motherboards may use the same chipset and BIOS, but one may give users complete freedom to configure chipset options, and the other allows users access to only some of the settings and uses hard-wired values for other settings.

All BIOSs default to a reasonable set of settings, one that allows the system to boot and function normally. Beyond that, it's up to you to choose settings to configure the system as you want it and to optimize its performance. Some BIOS settings are obvious—things like time and date, power management, boot sequence, and so on. Others, particularly those segregated as advanced settings and chipset settings, are anything but obvious. The brief help descriptions provided with them are usually not much help unless you already understand the issue. The primary rule here is *if you don't understand what a setting is for, don't change it*.

That's easy to say, but it ignores the fact that accepting default settings for obscure options can result in a PC that performs significantly below its potential. PC and motherboard manufacturers differ in how "aggressive" they are in choosing default settings, particularly those for such things as memory timing. Those that tend toward slower, more conservative default settings say, with some justification, that they cannot predict what components—particularly what speed and quality of memory—a user will install. Choosing conservative settings allows them to be sure that the motherboard will at least work, if not optimally. Those who are more aggressive—often PC makers who control the specific memory and other components that are installed—and who assume that users want the highest possible performance level and use components that support those aggressive settings.

The first place to look for detailed CMOS Setup instructions is in the manual that came with the computer or motherboard, or on the web page that supports that product. Some manufacturers provide detailed explanations of general CMOS Setup and Chipset Setup options, but many cover only basic BIOS settings and ignore chipset settings entirely. If that's the case with your manual, the best sources of information about advanced BIOS settings are Wim's BIOS (*http://www.wimsbios.com*) and Phil Croucher's *The BIOS Companion* (*http://www.electrocution.com/biosc.htm*).

Updating the BIOS

When you upgrade a system without replacing the motherboard, the BIOS version it uses can be a critical consideration. Some system features—e.g., support for faster or more recent processors, large hard disks, high-speed transfer modes, and AGP—are BIOS-dependent, so an in-place upgrade often requires a BIOS upgrade as well. Fortunately, recent systems use a flash BIOS, which can be upgraded simply by downloading a later version of the BIOS to replace the existing BIOS.

The exact method required to update the BIOS varies by motherboard manufacturer and model. Some motherboards are updated simply by copying the updated BIOS file to a floppy disk or CD and booting from it. Other motherboards use a DOS-based "flasher" program that runs from floppy disk and installs the BIOS file when it executes. Intel motherboards

Don't Take Chances

Be extraordinarily careful when upgrading the system BIOS. Make *absolutely* sure that the BIOS upgrade patch you apply is the *exact* one required for the current BIOS. Applying the wrong BIOS update may make the motherboard unusable, short of returning it to the factory for repair.

support Intel Express BIOS Update, which allows updating the BIOS from within Windows simply by double-clicking an executable file. (Fortunately, Intel also provides floppy disk–based BIOS update routines that those of us who run Linux or other non-Windows operating systems can use to update our BIOSs.)

Although updating the BIOS is a pretty intimidating operation the first time you try it—or the tenth time, for that matter—BIOS updates usually complete successfully if you do everything by the numbers. But if you accidentally apply the wrong patch or if the update process fails through no error of your own, the PC can end up nonbootable. If this happens, there may not be an easy way to recover. Depending on the BIOS, one of the following methods to recover from a failed BIOS update may be usable:

- A few motherboards have dual BIOS chips. If you corrupt one BIOS during an update, you can boot the system from the other BIOS and reflash the corrupted BIOS.

- Intel motherboards have a jumper that configures the motherboard for one of three modes of operation: Normal, BIOS Update, and Recovery. To update the BIOS, you must set that jumper to update mode. If the update fails for any reason, you can reset the jumper to the Recovery position, which gives the motherboard just enough smarts to access the floppy drive at boot time and attempt to load a BIOS update from the floppy drive.

BELT AND SUSPENDERS

Because a failed BIOS update can have such dire results, never update a BIOS without first connecting the system to a UPS, if only temporarily while doing the update. The one time we violated that rule, sure enough, the lights flickered about five seconds after we started the update. Hoping against hope that the PC hadn't crashed—this update was one where the screen stays blank until the update is complete—we sat staring at the blank screen for another half hour before we admitted to ourselves that we'd probably just killed the motherboard. With our fingers crossed, we powered the system down and back up again, but, as expected, it was deader than King Tut. Unless your luck is better than ours, always use a UPS when flashing a BIOS.

Processors 5

The *processor*, also called the *CPU* (*Central Processing Unit*), is the engine that drives the system. Replacing the processor requires some careful research to ensure that the new processor is compatible with the current motherboard and other system components, but a processor swap, properly done, can be one of the highest bang-for-the-buck upgrades you can make. In some cases, you can double or even triple overall system performance by spending $50 to $100 on a new processor. In this chapter, we tell you everything you need to know to choose and install a replacement processor.

The Truth About Processor Performance

Processor companies do nothing to discourage longstanding myths about processor performance. It's true that in the early days of microprocessors, a new model was often two or even three times faster than the model it replaced and sold for little or no more. In those halcyon days, the fastest available processors were sometimes 10 times faster than less expensive models that were still being sold.

There was also a favorable bang-for-the-buck ratio. If you paid twice as much for a processor, it was probably considerably more than twice as fast. We remember testing our 4.77 MHz IBM PC/XT against a 16 MHz 286 PC/AT when both were still being sold. The latter system cost two or three times as much, but was something like 10 times faster.

Those days are long past. Nowadays, processor performance increases incrementally, the accompanying price differences are large, the performance gap between the slowest and fastest current models has narrowed substantially, there are many, many more intermediate models available with minor performance differences, and the bang-for-the-buck ratio for the fastest processors has dropped well below 1:1. AMD and Intel have both learned to "work the market," maximizing their revenue in a very competitive market.

Price and performance

Here's a dirty little secret that AMD and Intel would rather you not know. At any given time, the actual performance differences between their slowest and least expensive "economy" processors and their fastest and most expensive "performance" processors is relatively small. A $750 processor you can buy today will probably be at most 2.5 to 3 times faster than the $50 processor sitting next to it on the store shelf.

Doubling or tripling performance may sound like a huge improvement, but human perception is not linear. A processor must be 30% to 50% faster than another processor before most people perceive any noticeable difference in routine use. Doubling processor speed results in an obvious difference in performance, but not a knock-your-socks-off change. Tripling processor speed provides a very noticeable performance boost, but at a very high price.

And most of that performance increase comes at the lower end of the price continuum. Paying more for a processor yields rapidly diminishing returns. For example, a $175 processor may be twice as fast as a $50 model, or nearly so. Doubling the price to $350 may buy you only a 25% faster processor, and doubling the price again to $700 less than a 10% bump in speed.

ADVICE FROM RON MORSE

Remember, processor speed is only one of the things that determines perceived system performance. Memory speed, bus speed, hard disk performance, and video performance all play a role, albeit to a lesser degree. Still, the fastest processor won't much help a system that's I/O-bound or has a slow video adapter.

But all this is true only for a particular moment in time. As AMD and Intel discontinue older processor models and introduce new ones, the whole continuum of processor performance shifts upward in lockstep. A midrange processor today is faster than the fastest performance processor of a year or 18 months previous, and even today's inexpensive "economy" processor is faster than the fastest processor of 2 to 3 years ago. That's good news, because it means it's often possible to upgrade an older system to today's level of performance at a reasonable low cost.

SOMETIMES EXPENSIVE COSTS LESS

None of this is to say that there's no place for very expensive processors. For programmers who spend their days doing iterative compiles and links, saving just a few seconds on each iteration may well be worth the higher cost of a premium processor. The same is true for highly paid executives, for whom lost seconds translate to lost dollars; for commodity traders, for whom seconds may mean the difference between a huge profit and an equally huge loss; and for serious gamers, who need every advantage they can get (not to mention bragging rights).

AMD versus Intel

Fanboys and brand zealots argue that AMD is faster than Intel, or that Intel is faster than AMD. They're both wrong, and both right. The truth is that at any given price point, Intel and AMD processors are remarkably closely matched in overall performance. That's not to say that their performance is identical for every application. AMD processors, for example, typically have better gaming performance than similarly priced Intel models, and Intel processors typically have better multimedia performance than similarly priced AMD models.

THE PROCESSOR TUG-OF-WAR

For a time, Intel processors badly beat AMD processors by most performance measures. AMD countered this fact by improving their own price/performance ratio, increasing the speed and cache size of their processors, and reducing their prices until they were again competitive with Intel processors that sold for similar prices. Then, for a time, AMD processors badly beat Intel processors by most performance measures. Intel countered this by improving their own price/performance ratio, increasing the speed and cache size of their processors, and reducing their prices until they were again competitive with AMD processors that sold for similar prices. Each time a gap in price/performance occurs, Intel or AMD adjusts processor pricing and/or performance levels to eliminate that gap. Both companies are smart enough to keep the playing field level while not leaving money on the table.

Benchmarks lie

Benchmarks are supposed to provide neutral measures of the performance of processors, both overall and in terms of specific types of tasks. But modern processors are very complex devices, with numerous strengths and weaknesses relative to competing processor models. A benchmark test that happens to play to a strength of a given processor will make that processor look (unjustifiably) very, very good. Conversely, a benchmark that gives heavy weight to a function that happens to be a weak point of a particular processor will make that processor look very, very bad, again unjustifiably.

If you allow us to choose the benchmark tests, for example, we can "prove" that a $150 AMD processor is faster than a $1,000 Intel processor. But by choosing different benchmark tests, we can just as easily "prove" that a $150 Intel processor is faster than a $1,000 AMD processor.

Broadly speaking, there are two types of benchmarks. *Synthetic benchmarks* are designed to test individual aspects of a processor's performance, such as cache efficiency, memory throughput, or floating-point performance. *Application benchmarks*, also called *natural benchmarks*, incorporate several common applications—such as MS Word, Adobe Photoshop, LightWave, and so on—with predefined suites of tasks to be performed.

The knock on synthetic benchmarks has always been that they are "meaningless" because they don't measure real-world task performance. We think that's wrong-headed. For example, if we want to decide which processor is likely to be fastest for applications that are bound by memory performance, we can use synthetic benchmarks to test the memory throughput of different processors. The results of those synthetic benchmarks will in fact give us a very good idea of the likely relative performance characteristics of different processors.

Conversely, using application benchmarks provides useful information only if we happen to be running the same applications used in the benchmark suite, in the same way, and with the same relative weighting. Two processors might achieve very similar overall results in an application benchmark, and yet one processor might be a better choice for running one of the suite applications, while the other processor might have the edge for running another.

Optimizing price/performance ratio

Dollar for dollar, AMD and Intel processors typically have very similar overall performance. We follow a few simple rules when we choose a processor, and suggest you do the same:

- At the low end, $50 to $125, AMD processors dollar for dollar provide noticeably better performance than Intel processors across the board. Intel has always paid lip service to the low-end market, but it really has no interest in competing here. It costs Intel about $40 to make a processor—any processor—so it prefers to devote its efforts to market segments with higher profit margins. On the other hand, the low-end market has until recently been AMD's bread and butter, so they devote a lot of attention to this segment.

- Choose a low-end processor unless you have a good reason for spending more. For most older systems, the most cost-effective upgrade is a processor that sells for $50 to $75, whether your motherboard is AMD- or Intel-compatible. Low-end processors are perfectly suitable for most computing tasks, including productivity applications, web browsing, email, watching videos, and so on.

- In the mainstream range, $125 to $250, Intel and AMD processors are pretty evenly matched dollar for dollar overall. Profit margins are much higher here than in the low-end segment, and unit volumes are huge, so the competition between AMD and Intel here is fierce.

- If you put heavier demands on a processor, such as casual video editing or 3D gaming, spending an extra $75 to $125 on your processor upgrade can provide major benefits. Processors in this price range are typically noticeably faster than low-end models, and for some applications that additional performance matters.

- At the high end, $250 to $1,000, Intel processors are generally somewhat faster dollar for dollar than AMD processors overall, particularly dual-core models. Although AMD produces the fastest processors in this segment, they set very high prices for those processors compared to Intel models that are only marginally slower, so Intel wins the bang-for-the-buck competition. Profit margins here are very high, but unit volumes are very low, so the actual dollars at stake are much less important than those in the mainstream segment. AMD and Intel compete here mainly for prestige and bragging rights.

- Unless the current system is very recent—a year old or less—it almost never makes sense to upgrade to a high-end processor. The potential incremental performance benefits of a high-end processor, limited as they are under optimum conditions, are even further limited by the low performance of other components in an older system. Furthermore, it's probable that installing a high-end processor would also require that the motherboard, power supply, and possibly the memory be replaced, which amounts to building an entirely new system. The one exception here is devoted gamers, some of whom think nothing of installing a new $1,000 processor every six months (not to mention a new $700 video card, or two.)

Processor Characteristics

Here are the important characteristics of processors:

Processor make and model
  The primary defining characteristic of a processor is its make—AMD or Intel—and its model. Although competing models from the two companies have similar features and performance, you cannot install an AMD processor in an Intel-compatible motherboard or vice versa.

Socket type
  Another defining characteristic of a processor is the socket that it is designed to fit. If you are replacing the processor in a Socket 478 motherboard, for example, you must choose a replacement processor that is designed to fit that socket. Table 5-1 describes upgradability issues by processor socket.

Table 5-1. Upgradability by processor socket type

Socket	Upgradability	Original processor	Upgrade processors	Considerations
Slot 1	None	Pentium II/III, Celeron	None	Slot 1 systems are not economically upgradable.
Slot A	None	Athlon	None	Slot A systems are not economically upgradable.
370	Poor	Celeron, Pentium III, VIA	Celeron, Pentium III	Limited availability of new Socket 370 processors. Relatively high cost for limited improvement.
423	None	Pentium 4	None	Socket 423 processors are no longer available new. A motherboard upgrade is the best choice for a Socket 423 system.
462	Moderate	Athlon, Athlon XP, Sempron	Sempron	Limited processor choices. A BIOS upgrade may be needed, and the memory may need to be replaced. Old Socket 462 (A) motherboards may not support Sempron processors.
478	Moderate	Celeron, Celeron D, Pentium 4	Celeron D, Pentium 4	Limited processor choices. Socket 478 processors and motherboards are becoming harder to find, and may be expensive. A BIOS upgrade may be needed, and the memory may need to be replaced. Old motherboards may not provide sufficient power to run the fastest current processors.
754	Good	Sempron, Athlon 64	Sempron, Athlon 64	Limited processor choices. A BIOS upgrade may be needed, and the memory may need to be replaced.
775	Excellent	Celeron D, Pentium 4	Celeron D, Pentium 4, Pentium D	Few issues. A BIOS upgrade may be needed. Upgrading to Pentium D dual-core requires motherboard replacement.
939	Excellent	Athlon 64, Athlon 64/FX	Athlon 64, Athlon 64/FX, Athlon 64 X2	Few issues. A BIOS upgrade may be needed.
940	Excellent	Athlon 64 FX, Opteron	Athlon 64 FX, Opteron	Few issues. A BIOS upgrade may be needed.

Clock speed

The clock speed of a processor, which is specified in megahertz (MHz) or gigahertz (GHz), determines its performance, but clock speeds are meaningless across processor lines. For example, a 3.2 GHz Prescott-core Pentium 4 is about 6.7% faster than a 3.0 GHz Prescott-core Pentium 4, as the relative clock speeds would suggest. However, a 3.0 GHz Celeron processor is slower than a 2.8 GHz Pentium 4, primarily because the Celeron has a smaller L2 cache and uses a slower host-bus speed. Similarly, when the Pentium 4 was introduced at 1.3 GHz, its performance was actually lower than that of the 1 GHz Pentium III processor that it was intended to replace. That was true because the Pentium 4 architecture is less efficient clock-for-clock than the earlier Pentium III architecture.

Clock speed is useless for comparing AMD and Intel processors. AMD processors run at much lower clock speeds than Intel processors, but do about 50% more work per clock tick. Broadly speaking, an AMD Athlon 64 running at 2.0 GHz has about the same overall performance as an Intel Pentium 4 running at 3.0 GHz.

MODEL NUMBERS VERSUS CLOCK SPEEDS

Because AMD is always at a clock speed disadvantage versus Intel, AMD uses model numbers rather than clock speeds to designate their processors. For example, an AMD Athlon 64 processor that runs at 2.0 GHz may have the model number 3000+, which indicates that the processor has roughly the same performance as a 3.0 GHz Intel model. (AMD fiercely denies that their model numbers are intended to be compared to Intel clock speeds, but knowledgeable observers ignore those denials.)

Intel formerly used letter designations to differentiate between processors running at the same speed, but with a different host-bus speed, core, or other characteristics. For example, 2.8 GHz Northwood-core Pentium 4 processors were made in three variants: the Pentium 4/2.8 used a 400 MHz FSB, the Pentium 4/2.8B the 533 MHz FSB, and the Pentium 4/2.8C the 800 MHz FSB. When Intel introduced a 2.8 GHz Pentium 4 based on their new Prescott core, they designated it the Pentium 4/2.8E.

Interestingly, Intel has also abandoned clock speed as a designator. With the exception of a few older models, all Intel processors are now designated by model number as well. Unlike AMD, whose model numbers retain a vestigial hint at clock speed, Intel model numbers are completely dissociated from clock speeds. For example, the Pentium 4 540 designates a particular processor model that happens to run at 3.2 GHz. The models of that processor that run at 3.4, 3.6, and 3.8 GHz are designated 550, 560, and 570 respectively.

Host-bus speed

The *host-bus speed*, also called the *front-side bus speed*, *FSB speed*, or simply *FSB*, specifies the data transfer rate between the processor and the chipset. A faster host-bus speed contributes to higher processor performance, even for processors running at the same clock speed. AMD and Intel implement the path between memory and cache differently, but essentially FSB is a number that reflects the maximum possible quantity of data block transfers per second. Given an actual host-bus clock rate of 100 MHz, if data can be transferred four times per clock cycle (thus "quad-pumped"), the effective FSB speed is 400 MHz.

For example, Intel has produced Pentium 4 processors that use host-bus speeds of 400, 533, 800, or 1066 MHz. A 2.8 GHz Pentium 4 with a host-bus speed of 800 MHz is marginally faster than a Pentium 4/2.8 with a 533 MHz host-bus speed, which in turn is marginally faster than a Pentium 4/2.8 with a 400 MHz host-bus speed. One measure that Intel uses to differentiate their lower-priced Celeron processors is a reduced host-bus speed relative to current Pentium 4 models. Celeron models use 400 MHz and 533 MHz host-bus speeds.

All Socket 754 and Socket 939 AMD processors use an 800 MHz host-bus speed. (Actually, like Intel, AMD runs the host bus at 200 MHz, but quad-pumps it to an effective 800 MHz.) Socket A Sempron processors use a 166 MHz host bus, double-pumped to an effective 333 MHz host-bus speed.

Cache size

Processors use two types of cache memory to improve performance by buffering transfers between the processor and relatively slow main memory. The size of *Layer 1 cache* (*L1 cache*, also called *Level 1 cache*), is a feature of the processor architecture that cannot be changed without redesigning the processor. *Layer 2 cache* (*Level 2 cache* or *L2 cache*), though, is external to the processor core, which means that processor makers can produce the same processor with different L2 cache sizes. For example, various models of Pentium 4 processors are available with 512 KB, 1 MB, or 2 MB of L2 cache, and various AMD Sempron models are available with 128 KB, 256 KB, or 512 KB of L2 cache.

For some applications—particularly those that operate on small data sets—a larger L2 cache noticeably increases processor performance, particularly for Intel models. (AMD processors have a built-in memory controller, which to some extent masks the benefits of a larger L2 cache.) For applications that operate on large data sets, a larger L2 cache provides only marginal benefit.

Process size

Process size, also called *fab(rication) size*, is specified in nanometers (nm), and defines the size of the smallest individual elements on a processor die. AMD and Intel continually attempt to reduce process size (called a *die shrink*) to get more processors from each silicon wafer, thereby reducing their costs to produce each processor. Pentium II and early Athlon processors used a 350 or 250 nm process. Pentium III and some Athlon processors used a 180 nm process. Recent AMD and Intel processors use a 130 or 90 nm process, and forthcoming processors will use a 65 nm process.

Process size matters because, all other things being equal, a processor that uses a smaller process size can run faster, use lower voltage, consume less power, and produce less heat. Processors available at any given time often use different fab sizes. For example, at one time Intel sold Pentium 4 processors that used the 180, 130, and 90 nm process sizes, and AMD has simultaneously sold Athlon processors that used the 250, 180, and 130 nm fab sizes. When you choose an upgrade processor, give preference to a processor with a smaller fab size.

Prescott, the Sad Exception

It came as a shock to everyone—not the least, Intel—to learn when it migrated its Pentium 4 processors from the older 130 nm Northwood core to the newer 90 nm Prescott core that power consumption and heat production skyrocketed. This occurred because Prescott was not a simple die shrink of Northwood. Instead, Intel completely redesigned the Northwood core, adding features such as SSE3 and making huge changes to the basic architecture. (At the time, we thought those changes were sufficient to merit naming the Prescott-core processor Pentium 5, which Intel did not.) Unfortunately, those dramatic changes in architecture resulted in equally dramatic increases in power consumption and heat production, overwhelming the benefit expected from the reduction in process size.

Special features

Different processor models support different feature sets, some of which may be important to you and others of no concern. Here are five potentially important features that are available with some, but not all, current processors. All of these features are supported by recent versions of Windows and Linux:

SSE3

SSE3 (*Streaming Single-Instruction-Multiple-Data* (*SIMD*) *Extensions 3*), developed by Intel and now available on most Intel processors and some AMD processors, is an extended instruction set designed to expedite processing of certain types of data commonly encountered in video processing and other multimedia applications. An application that supports SSE3 can run from 10% or 15% to 100% faster on a processor that also supports SSE3 than on one that does not.

64-bit support

Until recently, PC processors all operated with 32-bit internal data paths. In 2004, AMD introduced *64-bit support* with their Athlon 64 processors. Officially, AMD calls this feature *x86-64*, but most people call it *AMD64*. Critically, AMD64 processors are backward-compatible with 32-bit software, and run that software as efficiently as they run 64-bit software. Intel, who had been championing their own 64-bit architecture, which had only limited 32-bit compatibility, was forced to introduce its own version of x86-64, which it calls *EM64T* (*Extended Memory 64-bit Technology*). For now, 64-bit support is unimportant for most people. Microsoft offers a 64-bit version of Windows XP, and most Linux distributions support 64-bit processors, but until 64-bit applications become more common there is little real-world benefit to running a 64-bit processor on a desktop computer. That may change when Microsoft (finally) ships Windows Vista, which will take advantage of 64-bit support, and is likely to spawn many 64-bit applications.

Protected execution

With the Athlon 64, AMD introduced the *NX* (*No eXecute*) technology, and Intel soon followed with its *XDB* (*eXecute Disable Bit*) technology. NX and XDB serve the same purpose, allowing the processor to determine which memory address ranges are executable and which are non-executable. If code, such as a buffer-overrun exploit, attempts to run in non-executable memory space, the processor returns an error to the operating system. NX and XDB have great potential to reduce the damage caused by viruses, worms, Trojans, and similar exploits, but require an operating system that supports protected execution, such as Windows XP with Service Pack 2.

Power reduction technology

AMD and Intel both offer power reduction technology in some of their processor models. In both cases, technology used in mobile processors has been migrated to desktop processors, whose power consumption and heat production has become problematic. Essentially, these technologies work by reducing the processor speed (and thereby power consumption and heat production) when the processor is idle or lightly loaded. Intel refers to their power reduction technology as *EIST* (*Enhanced Intel Speedstep Technology*). The AMD version is called *Cool'n'Quiet*. Either can make minor but useful reductions in power consumption, heat production, and system noise level.

Dual-core support

By 2005, AMD and Intel were both reaching the practical limits of what was possible with a single processor core. The obvious solution was to put two processor cores in one processor package. Again, AMD led the way with its elegant *Athlon 64 X2* series processors, which feature two tightly integrated Athlon 64 cores on one chip. Once again forced to play catch-up, Intel gritted its teeth and slapped together a dual-core processor that it calls *Pentium D*. The engineered AMD solution has several benefits, including high performance and compatibility with nearly any older Socket 939 motherboard. The slapdash Intel solution, which basically amounted to sticking two Pentium 4 cores on one chip without integrating them, resulted in two compromises. First, Intel dual-core processors are not backward-compatible with earlier motherboards, and so require a new chipset and a new series of motherboards. Second, because Intel more or less simply glued two of their existing cores onto one processor package, power consumption and heat production are extremely high, which means that Intel had to reduce the clock speed of Pentium D processors relative to the fastest single-core Pentium 4 models.

All of that said, the Athlon 64 X2 is by no means a hands-down winner, because Intel was smart enough to price the Pentium D attractively. The least expensive Athlon X2 processors sell for more than twice as much as the least expensive Pentium D processors. Although prices will undoubtedly fall, we don't expect the pricing differential to change much. Intel has production capacity to spare, while AMD is quite limited in its ability to make processors, so it's likely that AMD dual-core processors will be premium priced for the foreseeable future. Unfortunately, that means that dual-core processors are not a reasonable upgrade option for most people. Intel dual-core processors are reasonably priced but require a motherboard replacement. AMD dual-core processors can use an existing Socket 939 motherboard, but the processors themselves are too expensive to be viable candidates for most upgraders.

HYPER-THREADING VERSUS DUAL CORE

Some Intel processors support *Hyper-Threading Technology* (*HTT*), which allows those processors to execute two program threads simultaneously. Programs that are designed to use HTT may run 10% to 30% faster on an HTT-enabled processor than on a similar non-HTT model. (It's also true that some programs run slower with HTT enabled than with it disabled.) Don't confuse HTT with dual core. An HTT processor has one core that can sometimes run multiple threads; a dual-core processor has two cores, which can always run multiple threads.

Core names and core steppings

The *processor core* defines the basic processor architecture. A processor sold under a particular name may use any of several cores. For example, the first Intel Pentium 4 processors used the *Willamette core*. Later Pentium 4 variants have used the *Northwood core*, *Prescott core*, *Gallatin core*, *Prestonia core*, and *Prescott 2M core*. Similarly, various Athlon 64 models have been produced using the *Clawhammer core*, *Sledgehammer core*, *Newcastle core*, *Winchester core*, *Venice core*, *San Diego core*, *Manchester core*, and *Toledo core*.

Using a core name is a convenient shorthand way to specify numerous processor characteristics briefly. For example, the Clawhammer core uses the 130 nm process, a 1,024 KB L2 cache, and supports the NX and X86-64 features, but not SSE3 or dual-core operation. Conversely, the Manchester core uses the 90 nm process, a 512 KB L2 cache, and supports the SSE3, X86-64, NX, and dual-core features.

You can think of the processor core name as being similar to a major version number of a software program. Just as software companies frequently release minor updates without changing the major version number, AMD and Intel frequently make minor updates to their cores without changing the core name. These minor changes are called *core steppings*. It's important to understand the basics of core names, because the core a processor uses may determine its backward compatibility with your motherboard. Steppings are usually less significant, although they're also worth paying attention to. For example, a particular core may be available in B2 and C0 steppings. The later C0 stepping may have bug fixes, run cooler, or provide other benefits relative to the earlier stepping. Core stepping is also critical if you install a second processor on a dual-processor motherboard. (That is, a motherboard with two processor sockets, as opposed to a dual-core processor on a single-socket motherboard.) Never, ever mix cores or steppings on a dual processor motherboard—that way lies madness (or perhaps just disaster).

Processor Types

A few years ago, choosing a processor was pretty straightforward. AMD and Intel each produced two series of processors, a mainstream line and a budget line. Each company used only one processor socket, and there was a limited range of processor speeds available. If you wanted an Intel processor, you might have a dozen mainstream models and a half-dozen budget models to choose among. The same was true of AMD.

Nowadays, choosing a processor isn't as simple. AMD and Intel now make literally scores of different processor models. Each company now offers several lines of processors, which differ in clock speed, L2 cache, socket type, host-bus speed, special features supported, and other characteristics. Even the model names are confusing. AMD, for example, has offered at least five different processor models under the same name—Athlon 64 3200+. An Intel Celeron model number that ends in J fits Socket 775, and the same model number without the J designates the same processor for Socket 478. A Pentium 4 processor model number that ends in J says nothing about the socket type it is designed for, but indicates that the processor supports the execute-disable bit feature. And so on.

AMD and Intel each offer the three categories of processors described in the following sections.

Budget processors

Budget processors give up a bit of performance in exchange for a lower price. At any given time, AMD or Intel's fastest available budget processor is likely to have about 85% of the performance of their slowest mainstream model. Budget processors are more than sufficient for routine computing tasks. (After all, today's budget processor was yesterday's mainstream processor and last week's performance processor.) Budget processors are often the best choice for a system upgrade, because their lower clock speeds and power consumption make it more likely that they'll be compatible with an older motherboard.

AMD Sempron

The various models of the *AMD Sempron processor* sell in the $50 to $125 range, and are targeted at the budget through low-end mainstream segment. The Sempron replaced the discontinued Socket A Duron processor in 2004, and the obsolescent Socket A Athlon XP processor in 2005. Various Sempron models are available in the obsolescent Socket A and in the same Socket 754 used by some Athlon 64 models.

AMD actually packages two different processors under the Sempron name. A Socket A Sempron, also called a *K7 Sempron*, is in fact a re-badged Athlon XP processor. A Socket 754 Sempron, shown in Figure 5-1, is also called a

OEM Versus Retail-Boxed

To further confuse matters, most AMD and Intel processors are available in two types of packaging, called OEM and retail-boxed. OEM processor packages include only the bare processor and usually provide only a 90-day warranty. Retail-boxed processors include the processor, a compatible CPU cooler, and a longer warranty, typically three years.

A retail-boxed processor is usually the better deal. It typically costs only a few dollars more than the OEM version of the same processor, and the bundled CPU cooler is usually worth more than the price difference. But if you plan to install an after-market CPU cooler—for example, because you are upgrading your system to be as quiet as possible—it may make sense to buy the OEM processor.

K8 Sempron, and is really a cut-down Athlon 64 model running at a lower clock speed with a smaller L2 cache and a single-channel memory controller rather than the dual-channel memory controller of the Athlon 64. Early Sempron models had no support for 64-bit processing. Recent Sempron models include 64-bit support, although the practicality of running 64-bit software on a Sempron is questionable. Still, like the Athlon 64, the Sempron also runs 32-bit software very efficiently, so you can think of the 64-bit support as future-proofing.

Figure 5-1. AMD Sempron processor (image courtesy of AMD, Inc.)

If you have a Socket 462 (A) or Socket 754 motherboard in your system, the Sempron offers an excellent upgrade path. You'll need to verify compatibility of your motherboard with the specific Sempron you intend to install, and you may need to upgrade the BIOS to recognize the Sempron.

For more information about Sempron processor models, visit *http://www. amd.com/sempron*.

Intel Celeron

For many years, the *Intel Celeron processor* was the poor stepsister, offering too little performance at too high a price. Cynical observers believed that the only reason Intel sold any Celeron processors at all was that system makers wanted the Intel name on their boxes without having to pay the higher price for an Intel mainstream processor.

That all changed when Intel introduced their Celeron D models, which are now available for Socket 478 and Socket 775 motherboards. While Celeron D models are still slower than Semprons dollar-for-dollar, the disparity is nowhere near as large as in years past. Celeron D processors, which sell in the $60 to $125 range, are very credible upgrade processors for anyone who owns a Socket 478 or Socket 775 motherboard. Like the Sempron, Celeron models are available with 64-bit support, although again the practicality of running 64-bit software on an entry-level processor is questionable. Once again, it's important to verify the compatibility of your motherboard with the specific Celeron you intend to install, and you may need to upgrade the BIOS to recognize the Celeron.

AVOID NON-D CELERON PROCESSORS

Celeron processors (without the "D") are based on the Northwood core and have only 128 KB of L2 cache. These processors have very poor performance, and unfortunately remain available for sale. The Celeron D models are based on the Prescott core, and have 256 KB of L2 cache.

For more information about Celeron processor models, visit *http://www. intel.com/celeron*.

Mainstream processors

Mainstream processors typically cost $125 to $250—although the fastest models sell for $500 or more—and offer anything up to about twice the overall performance of the slowest budget processors. A mainstream processor may be a good upgrade choice if you need more performance than a budget processor offers and are willing to pay the additional cost.

However, depending on your motherboard, a mainstream processor may not be an option even if you are willing to pay the extra cost. Mainstream processors consume considerably more power than most budget processors, often too much to be used on older motherboards. Also, mainstream processors often use more recent cores, larger L2 caches, and other features that may or may not be compatible with an older motherboard. An older power supply may not provide enough power for a current mainstream processor, and the new processor may require faster memory than is currently installed. If you intend to upgrade to a mainstream processor, carefully verify compatibility of the processor, motherboard, power supply, and memory before you buy the processor.

AMD Athlon 64

The *AMD Athlon 64 processor*, shown in Figure 5-2, is available in Socket 754 and Socket 939 variants. As its name indicates, the Athlon 64 supports 64-bit software, although only a tiny percentage of Athlon 64 owners run 64-bit software. Fortunately, the Athlon 64 is equally at home running the 32-bit operating systems and applications software that most of us use.

Figure 5-2. AMD Athlon 64 processor (image courtesy of AMD, Inc.)

Like the Sempron, the Athlon 64 has a memory controller built onto the processor die, rather than depending on a memory controller that's part of the chipset. The upside of this design decision is that Athlon 64 memory performance is excellent. The downside is that supporting a new type of memory, such as DDR2, requires a processor redesign. Socket 754 models have a single-channel PC3200 DDR-SDRAM memory controller versus the dual-channel controller in Socket 939 models, so Socket 939 models running at the same clock speed and with the same size L2 cache offer somewhat higher performance. For example, AMD designates a Socket 754 Newcastle-core Athlon 64 with 512 KB of L2 cache running at 2.2 GHz a 3200+ model, while the same processor in Socket 939 is designated an Athlon 64 3400+.

NUMBERS LIE

The model numbers of Athlon 64 and Sempron processors are scaled differently. For example, the Socket 754 Sempron 3100+ runs at 1800 MHz and has 256 KB of cache, and the Socket 754 Athlon 64 2800+ runs at the same clock speed and has twice as much cache. Despite the lower model number, the Athlon 64 2800+ is somewhat faster than the Sempron 3100+. Although AMD hotly denies it, most industry observers believe that AMD intends Athlon 64 model numbers to be compared with Pentium 4 clock speeds and Sempron model numbers with Celeron clock speeds. Of course, Intel also designates their recent processors by model number rather than clock speed, confusing matters even further.

For more information about Athlon 64 processor models, visit *http://www.amd.com/athlon64*.

Intel Pentium 4

The Pentium 4, shown in Figure 5-3, is Intel's flagship processor, and is available in Socket 478 and Socket 775. Unlike AMD—which sometimes uses the same Athlon 64 model number to designate four or more different processors with different clock speeds, L2 cache sizes, and sockets—Intel uses a numbering scheme that identifies each model unambiguously.

Older Pentium 4 models, which are available only in Socket 478, are identified by clock speed and sometimes a supplemental letter to indicate FSB speed and/or core type. For example, a Socket 478 Northwood-core Pentium 4 processor operating at a core speed of 2.8 GHz with the 400 MHz FSB is designated a Pentium 4/2.8. The same processor with the 533 MHz FSB is designated a Pentium 4/2.8B, and with the 800 MHz FSB it's designated a Pentium 4/2.8C. A 2.8 GHz Prescott-core Pentium 4 processor is designated a Pentium 4/2.8E.

Figure 5-3. Intel Pentium 4 600 series processor (image courtesy of Intel Corporation)

Socket 775 Pentium 4 models belong to one of two series. All 500-series processors use the Prescott core and have 1 MB of L2 cache. All 600-series processors use the Prescott 2M core and have 2 MB of L2 cache. Intel uses the second number of the model number to indicate relative clock speed. For example, a Pentium 4/530 has a clock speed of 3 GHz, as does a Pentium 4/630. The 540/640 models run at 3.2 GHz, the 550/650 models at 3.4 GHz, the 560/660 models at 3.6 GHz, and so on. A "J" following a 500-series model number (for example, 560J) indicates that the processor supports the XDB feature, but not EM64T 64-bit support. If a 500-series model number ends in 1 (for example, 571) that model supports both the XDB feature and EM64T 64-bit processing. All 600-series processors support both XDB and EM64T.

For more information about Pentium 4 processor models, visit *http:// www.intel.com/pentium4.*

Extreme Processors

We classify the fastest, most expensive mainstream processors—those that sell in the $400 to $500 range—as performance processors, but AMD and Intel reserve that category for their top-of-the-line models, which sell for $800 to $1,200. These processors—the *AMD Athlon 64 FX*, the *Intel Pentium 4 Extreme Edition*, and the *Intel Pentium Extreme Edition*—are targeted at the gaming and enthusiast market, and offer at best marginally faster performance than the fastest mainstream models.

In fact, the performance bump is generally so small that we think anyone who buys one of these processors has more dollars than sense. If you're considering buying one of these outrageously expensive processors, do yourself a favor. Buy a $400 or $500 high-end mainstream processor instead, and use part of the extra money for more memory, a better video card, a better display, better speakers, or some other component that will actually provide a noticeable benefit. Either that, or keep the extra money in the bank.

Dual-core processors

By early 2005, AMD and Intel had both pushed their processor cores to about the fastest possible speeds, and it had become clear that the only practical way to increase processor performance significantly was to use two processors. Although it's possible to build systems with two physical processors, doing that introduces many complexities, not least a doubling of the already-high power consumption and heat production. AMD, later followed by Intel, chose to go dual-core.

Combining two cores in one processor isn't exactly the same thing as doubling the speed of one processor. For one thing, there is overhead involved in managing the two cores that doesn't exist for a single processor. Also, in a single-tasking environment, a program thread runs no faster on a dual-core processor than it would on a single-core processor, so doubling the number of cores by no means doubles application performance. But in a multitasking environment, where many programs and their threads are competing for processor time, the availability of a second processor core means that one thread can run on one core while a second thread runs on the second core.

The upshot is that a dual-core processor typically provides 25% to 75% higher performance than a similar single-core processor if you multitask heavily. Dual-core performance for a single application is essentially unchanged unless the application is designed to support threading, which many processor-intensive applications are. (For example, a web browser uses threading to keep the user interface responsive even when it's performing a network operation.) Even if you were running only unthreaded applications, though, you'd see some performance benefit from a dual-core processor. This is true because an operating system, such as Windows XP, that supports dual-core processors automatically allocates different processes to each core.

AMD Athlon 64 X2

The *AMD Athlon 64 X2*, shown in Figure 5-4, has several things going for it, including high performance, relatively low power requirements and heat production, and compatibility with most existing Socket 939 motherboards. Alas, while Intel has priced its least expensive dual-core processors in the sub-$250 range, the least expensive AMD dual-core models initially sold in the $800 range, which is out of the question for most upgraders. Fortunately, by late 2005 AMD had begun to ship more reasonably priced dual-core models, although availability is limited.

Figure 5-4. AMD Athlon 64 X2 processor (image courtesy of AMD, Inc.)

For more information about Athlon 64 X2 processor models, visit *http://www.amd.com/athlon64*.

Intel Pentium D

The announcement of AMD's Athlon 64 X2 dual-core processor caught Intel unprepared. Under the gun, Intel took a cruder approach to making a dual-core processor. Rather than build an integrated dual-core processor as AMD had with its Athlon 64 X2 processors, Intel essentially slapped two slower Pentium 4 cores on one substrate and called it the *Pentium D* dual-core processor.

The 800-series 90 nm Smithfield-core Pentium D, shown in Figure 5-5, is a stop-gap kludge for Intel, designed to counter the AMD Athlon 64 X2 until Intel can bring to market its real answer, the dual-core 65 nm Presler-core processor, which is likely to be designated the 900-series Pentium D. The Presler-based dual-core processors will be fully integrated, compatible with existing dual-core Intel-compatible motherboards, and feature reduced power consumption, lower heat output, twice as much L2 cache, and considerably higher performance.

Figure 5-5. Intel Pentium D dual-core processor (image courtesy of Intel Corporation)

Reading the foregoing, you might think we had only contempt for the 800-series Pentium D processors. In fact, nothing could be further from the truth. They're a kludge, yes, but they're a reasonably cheap, very effective kludge, assuming that you have a motherboard that supports them. We extensively tested an early sample of the least expensive 800-series Pentium D, the 820. The 820 runs at 2.8 GHz, and under light, mostly single-tasking use, the 820 "feels" pretty much like a 2.8 GHz Prescott-core Pentium 4. As we added more and more processes, the difference became clear. Instead of bogging down, as the single-core Prescott would have done, the Pentium D provided snappy response to the foreground process.

For more information about Pentium D processor models, visit *http://www. intel.com/products/processor/pentium_d*.

AMD and Intel processor summaries

Table 5-2 lists the important characteristics of current AMD processors, including the special features they support.

Table 5-2. AMD processor summary

Processor	Socket	Core	L2 cache	Process	AMD64	SSE3	Cool'n' Quiet	NX	Dual-core
Athlon XP/Sempron	462 (A)	Thoroughbred	256 KB	130 nm					
Athlon XP/Sempron	462 (A)	Thorton	256 KB	130 nm					
Athlon XP/Sempron	462 (A)	Barton	512 KB	130 nm					
Sempron	754	Paris	256 KB	130 nm			•	•	
Sempron	754	Oakville	128 KB, 256 KB	90 nm			•	•	
Sempron	754	Oakville	256 KB	90 nm	•		•	•	
Sempron	754	Palermo	128 KB, 256 KB	90 nm		•	•	•	
Sempron	754	Palermo	256 KB	90 nm	•	•	•	•	
Athlon 64	754	Clawhammer	1024 KB	130 nm	•		•		
Athlon 64	754	Newcastle	512 KB	130 nm	•		•		
Athlon 64	939	Newcastle	512 KB	130 nm	•		•		
Athlon 64	939	Winchester	512 KB	90 nm	•		•		
Athlon 64	939	Venice	512 KB	90 nm	•	•	•		
Athlon 64/FX	939	Sledgehammer	1024 KB	130 nm	•		•		
Athlon 64/FX	939	San Diego	1024 KB	90 nm	•	•	•		
Athlon 64 X2	939	Manchester	512 KB × 2	90 nm	•	•	•		•
Athlon 64 X2	939	Toledo	1024 KB × 2	90 nm	•	•	•	•	•

Table 5-3 lists the important characteristics of current Intel processors, including the special features they support.

Table 5-3. Intel processor summary

Processor	Socket	Core	L2 cache	Process	EM64T	SSE3	EIST	XDB	Dual-core
Celeron	478	Northwood	128 KB	130 nm					
Pentium 4	478	Northwood	512 KB	130 nm					
Celeron D	478	Prescott	256 KB	90 nm		•			
Pentium 4	478	Prescott	1024 KB	90 nm		•			
Celeron D	775	Prescott	256 KB	90 nm	•	•		•	
Pentium 4 (5XX)	775	Prescott	1024 KB	90 nm	•	•		•	
Pentium 4 (6XX)	775	Irwindale	2048 KB	90 nm	•	•	•	•	
Pentium 4 (6XX)	775	Cedar Mill	2048 KB	65 nm	•	•	•	•	
Pentium D (8XX)	775	Smithfield	1024 KB × 2	90 nm	•	•	•	•	•
Pentium D (9XX)	775	Presler	2048 KB × 2	65 nm	•	•	•	•	•

Special features are not always implemented across an entire line of processors. For example, we list the Pentium D 8XX-series processors as supporting EM64T, SSE3, EIST, and dual core. At the time we wrote this, three Pentium D 8XX models were available: the 2.8 GHz 820, the 3.0 GHz 830, and the 3.2 GHz 840. The 830 and 840 models support all of the special features listed. The 820 model supports EM64T, SSE3, and dual-core operation, but not EIST. If a special feature listed as being supported by a particular line of processors is important to you, verify that it is supported in the exact processor model you intend to buy.

CPU Coolers

Modern CPUs consume a lot of power—as much as 130W. That power ends up as waste heat. In effect, a modern system has the equivalent of a 50W to 130W incandescent lightbulb burning constantly inside the case. That analogy understates the problem—a lightbulb dissipates its heat from the relatively large surface of the bulb. A processor must dissipate the same amount of heat over the much smaller surface area of the processor die, typically about 0.25 square inch. Without an effective heatsink to draw away this heat, the processor might literally burn itself to a crisp almost instantly.

Nearly all systems deal with this heat problem by placing a massive metal heatsink in close contact with the processor die (or integrated heat spreader) and using a small fan to draw or push air through the heatsink fins. This device is called a *heatsink/fan (HSF)* or *CPU cooler.* As the power consumption of processors has continued growing, so too has the size and mass of the heatsinks they use. Even the stock coolers packaged with retail-boxed processors nowadays are often quite large and heavy. For example, Figure 5-6 shows a stock Intel Pentium 4 CPU cooler on the left and a Thermalright XP-120 aftermarket CPU cooler on the right, with a pair of AA batteries shown for scale.

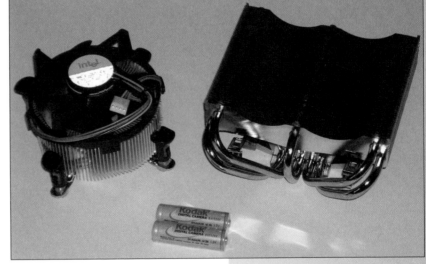

Figure 5-6. Intel stock CPU cooler (left) and Thermalright XP-120 CPU cooler, with AA batteries shown for scale

CPU Cooler Plumbing

Those things that look like pipes on the Thermalright XP-120 cooler *are* pipes. Heat pipes, to be exact. Some high-end CPU coolers, including this model, use heat pipes to increase cooling efficiency. Heat pipes operate much like your refrigerator. The heat generated by the processor vaporizes a fluid. The resulting gas rises by convection up the heat pipe to the radiator section at the top of the cooler, where it condenses, giving up its heat to the radiator.

Unlike stock coolers, some aftermarket coolers—including this Thermalright model—do not include a bundled fan. That's because such coolers tend to be used by performance- and silent-PC enthusiasts, who prefer to choose a fan with particular airflow and noise characteristics. This Thermalright cooler can use a large (120 mm) fan, which because of its size can run relatively slowly (and silently) while still providing a sufficient volume of air flow to cool the processor effectively. In fact, because of their large surface area and high efficiency, some high-performance aftermarket coolers, including the XP-120, can cool all but the fastest, hottest processors without using a CPU fan. The airflow from a case fan suffices to remove waste heat from the cooler.

JUST BECAUSE IT FITS . . .

Do not assume that merely because a heatsink fits a processor, it is sufficient to cool that processor. Faster processors are physically identical to slower models, but produce more heat. Heatsinks are rated by processor speed. For example, a heatsink rated for a 2.4 GHz Pentium 4 can physically be installed on a 3.8 GHz Pentium 4, but is grossly inadequate to cool it. Nor can you judge solely by processor speed. For example, Intel has produced 2.8 GHz Pentium 4 processors using the earlier, cooler-running Northwood core and the later, hotter-running Prescott core. A heatsink rated for use with a 2.8 GHz Northwood-core Pentium 4 is not good enough for a 2.8 GHz Prescott-core Pentium 4. Make sure that the heatsink/fan unit you choose is rated for the specific processor you use it with.

Heatsinks are constructed with different materials, according to their prices and intended uses. An inexpensive heatsink, or one intended for use with a slower processor, is likely to be of all-aluminum construction. Aluminum is inexpensive and relatively efficient in transferring heat. Copper is much more expensive than aluminum, but is also much more efficient in transferring heat. Accordingly, a more expensive heatsink, or one intended for a faster processor, might be constructed primarily of aluminum, but with copper surfaces where the processor contacts the heatsink. The most expensive heatsinks, and those intended for use with the fastest processors, are constructed of pure copper.

Heatsink/fan units also differ in the type and size of fan they use, and how fast that fan runs. Fan speed is an issue, because all other things being equal, a faster-running fan produces more noise. For equal air flow, a larger, slower fan produces less noise than a smaller, faster fan. Fan sizes have increased as processor speeds have increased, to provide the high air flow volume needed to cool the heatsink while keeping fan speed (and noise) at a reasonable level. For example, heatsinks for Pentium II processors used 30 mm fans. Heatsinks for early Pentium 4 and Athlon 64 processors typically used 60 mm or 70 mm fans. Some third-party "performance" heatsinks targeted at overclockers use 80 mm, 92 mm, or 120 mm fans. Some even use multiple fans.

In general, we recommend using the CPU coolers that are bundled with retail-boxed processors. The bundled coolers are generally midrange in terms of performance and noise level—neither as efficient nor as quiet as good aftermarket coolers, but less costly.

However, if you are concerned about PC noise, a third-party CPU cooler is the way to go. You can spend anything from about $15 to more than $100 on a quiet CPU cooler, depending on the processor you're using and just how quiet and efficient you require the cooler to be. Arctic Cooling (*http://www.arctic-cooling.com*) makes several models in the $15 to $30 range that are reasonably quiet and efficient. If you're willing to spend a bit more, look at Zalman 7000- and 7700-series coolers (*http://www.zalmanusa.com*), which are in the $30 to $45 range, and are extremely quiet and so efficient that some models can be run fanless (and therefore completely silent) with some processors. Finally, if only the best will do and you're willing to pay $60 or more for a CPU cooler, choose a Thermalright (*http://www.thermalright. com*) model and add one of the fans recommended by Thermalright.

USE WHAT IT CAME WITH

We generally use the thermal compound or phase-change medium that is provided with the cooler. (AMD in particular is very specific about which thermal transfer media are acceptable for its processors.) When we reinstall a cooler, we generally use Antec Silver Thermal Compound (*http://www.antec.com*), which is inexpensive and as good as or better than anything else we've used.

The Wrong CPU Cooler Can Kill Your Motherboard

Choosing the best aftermarket HSF is not trivial. Verifying that the cooler is rated for your processor is just the first step. Specialty coolers—those that provide high cooling efficiency or low noise levels, or both—are typically large and heavy (and expensive).

Size is important because the space around the processor socket is often cluttered with capacitors and other components that may prevent a large cooler from being seated properly. More than one system builder has learned to his dismay that a cooler that appears to fit may—upon being clamped down—bend, damage, or short out nearby components. We have never understood why most third-party CPU cooler makers don't provide motherboard compatibility lists (Zalman, for one, does). In the absence of such lists, the best way to avoid damaging your motherboard is to verify visually that all components will clear the cooler before you clamp it into place. If it doesn't fit—well, that's another good argument for buying from vendors that have good return policies.

Weight is important because Intel and AMD specify maximum heatsink weights for which the retaining brackets for their various processors are rated. Many specialty CPU coolers exceed the maximum allowable weight—sometimes by large margins—which introduces the ugly possibility of the cooler breaking free from its mount and rattling around loose inside the case. This is an issue with any tower system or other PC that mounts the motherboard vertically, and is a particular danger with portable systems, such as LAN party PCs. AMD Socket A systems are particularly prone to this problem, because the cooler clamps to the CPU socket directly rather than to a retaining bracket that is secured to the motherboard.

The best solution, if you must use such a heavy cooler, is to choose one that comes with a custom retaining bracket rather than depending on the standard motherboard bracket. It's also a good idea to transport such systems in a motherboard horizontal orientation to reduce the risk of breakage during transit.

Thermal Compound Is Critical

The best heatsink/fan can't cool a processor properly unless thermal compound is used at the processor/heatsink interface. The processor and heatsink base are both flat and polished, but even when they are pressed into close contact, a thin layer of air separates them. Air insulates well, which is the last thing you want, so thermal compound is used to displace the air.

When you install a heatsink, and each time you remove and replace it, use fresh thermal compound to ensure proper heat transfer. Thermal compound is available in the form of viscous thermal "goop" and as phase-change thermal pads, which melt as the processor heats up and solidify as it cools down. Make sure that the thermal compound you use is approved by the processor maker. For example, AMD specifies particular phase-change thermal pads for certain of its processors, and warns that using any other thermal compound voids the warranty.

Processor Upgrade Considerations

Replacing the processor with a faster model is one of the most effective and cost-efficient upgrades you can make on an older system. In some cases, you can double or triple CPU performance at a relatively small cost. Unfortunately, not all systems are good candidates for a processor upgrade. You'll have to do a bit of research to determine whether your system is suitable for a processor upgrade. Here are the factors to consider:

Processor socket type

The first consideration is the socket type provided by the motherboard. Motherboards that use a current socket—Socket 775 for Intel or Socket 939 for AMD—are the best upgrade candidates. Motherboards that use older sockets—Sockets 462 (A) or 754 for AMD or Socket 478 for Intel—offer fewer processor choices, but are still reasonable upgrade candidates. Motherboards that use very old sockets, such as Intel Socket 370, are poor upgrade candidates, because few processors are still available for them. Motherboards that use obsolete sockets—Socket 7 and earlier, Slot A, or Slot 1—are not realistically upgradable. Even if you can find the components you need to upgrade these obsolete systems, the price will be high, and even after the upgrade, the system will be too slow to be useful.

What About Socket Adapters?

Evergreen Technologies and other companies manufacture adapters that allow you to install a processor that uses a different socket than the motherboard, such as a Socket 478 processor in a Socket 423 motherboard. Such adapters have been around for years. For example, in the late 90s, "slocket" adapters allowed Socket 370 Pentium III processors to be installed in Slot 1 motherboards.

These adapters have never been very satisfactory. Sometimes they work, more or less, but they introduce many compatibility issues. They are also generally quite costly. You can usually replace the motherboard for about the same total cost. Replacing the motherboard gives you a newer chipset and BIOS, and, of course, a new motherboard rather than one that's several years old. We suggest you avoid such socket adapters.

Motherboard model and revision level

Just because a motherboard has the proper socket doesn't mean it can necessarily accept any processor that uses that socket. Before you begin an upgrade, verify the compatibility of your motherboard with the upgrade processor you are considering. (See Chapter 4.)

BIOS

Quite often, a motherboard can support a much faster processor than is currently installed, but requires a BIOS update to do so. Before you start an upgrade, check the web site for the motherboard to find the latest BIOS update available for that motherboard. Check the BIOS release notes to determine whether that BIOS version supports the processor you plan to install.

YOU CAN'T GET THERE FROM HERE

Install the BIOS update *before* you remove the old processor. Otherwise, you may not be able to install the BIOS update because the new processor won't boot with the older BIOS.

CPU cooler

Installing a new processor usually requires installing a new CPU cooler. The old cooler may fit the new processor, but chances are good that it's not good enough to cool the faster new processor. Buy a retail-boxed processor, which comes with a stock CPU cooler, or choose an appropriate aftermarket CPU cooler, as described in the preceding section.

Memory

If you have current PC3200 or DDR2 memory installed, the new processor will probably operate properly with it. If you have slower memory installed, such as PC1600, PC2100, or PC2700 DDR-SDRAM, you may need to replace the memory as well as the processor. Some motherboards support asynchronous memory operation, which is to say that they can run memory at a slower speed than the processor memory bus. Even if you have such a motherboard, though, using slower memory than the processor was designed to use reduces processor performance, which was the whole reason for upgrading the processor.

Power supply

The power supply in many older systems—particularly mass-market, consumer-grade systems—is barely adequate to run the components that were originally installed. Faster processors usually consume more power, so it's quite possible that installing a faster processor will also require installing a higher-capacity power supply. Whether to replace the power supply as a part of the upgrade is a judgment call. If the current power supply is a good brand and of reasonably high capacity, and if the new processor doesn't consume much more wattage than the original, it's probably safe to continue using the old power supply. On the other hand, if the system refuses to boot or crashes frequently after the processor upgrade, that's a good sign that the power supply needs to be replaced.

Upgrading Consumer-Grade PCs

Mass-market, consumer-grade PCs sold online and in big-box stores are generally poor candidates for processor upgrades. That's no accident. Mass-market PC vendors don't want you to upgrade your PC. They want you to buy a new one.

Accordingly, they take steps to make it difficult or impossible to upgrade the systems they build. One common practice is to use a modified BIOS that supports only a limited range of processor speeds or bus speeds, even if the motherboard itself is capable of using faster processors. Another is to conceal the actual manufacturer and model number of the motherboard, and to refuse to provide the technical documentation needed by upgraders.

Quite often, the only way to upgrade the processor in a mass-market, consumer-grade system is to replace the motherboard at the same time. In fact, some manufacturers have gone to extremes to prevent users from upgrading their systems. Dell for a time used nonstandard power supplies, which meant that the Dell power supply would destroy a standard motherboard and a standard power supply would destroy a Dell motherboard. Fortunately, most of those systems are now so old that they're not economically upgradable anyway, but it's still a good idea to keep an eye out for intentional incompatibilities. Once again, Google is your friend. Before you upgrade a PC, search Google to learn about any possible gotchas.

Identifying the current processor

It's sometimes important to identify an unknown CPU, or at least one for which you don't know all the details. If the CPU is not installed, you can identify it unambiguously by examining the markings on its surface and comparing those markings to identification information published on the manufacturer's web site. For example, Figure 5-7 shows the processor markings that Intel uses to identify Socket 775 Pentium D and Pentium Extreme Edition processors. AMD uses similar markings and publishes them on its web site.

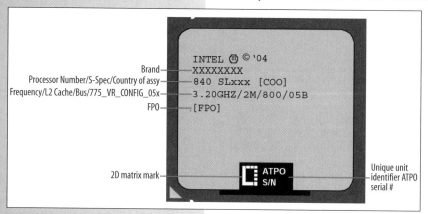

INTEL (m) © '04
Brand ——— XXXXXXXX
Processor Number/S-Spec/Country of assy —— 840 SLxxx [COO]
Frequency/L2 Cache/Bus/775_VR_CONFIG_05x —— 3.20GHZ/2M/800/05B
FPO ——— [FPO]

2D matrix mark ——— [ATPO S/N]

Unique unit identifier ATPO serial #

Figure 5-7. Intel Pentium D processor markings (image courtesy of Intel Corporation)

More often, you'll need to identify an installed processor. The easiest way to do that is to use Everest Home Edition, SiSoft Sandra, or a similar general diagnostics utility. Figure 5-8 shows Everest Home Edition identifying an installed processor as an AMD Sempron 2800+. In addition to the processor name and model, these utilities provide other potentially important information, such as the CPU core name and stepping, the cache size, and the package type.

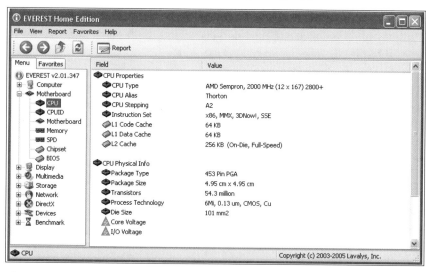

Figure 5-8. Everest Home Edition identifies an installed processor as an AMD Sempron

Choosing a replacement processor

Socket type, motherboard compatibility, and other factors limit the range of suitable upgrade processors. Even with those limitations, though, you'll likely have at least several and possibly dozens of processors to choose among. Use the following guidelines to make the best choice:

Consider total cost versus system value.

If you can simply drop a $50 processor into an old system without any other upgrades, that's one thing. If you'll also need to upgrade the memory, power supply, and/or other system components, you may be better off simply retiring the old system to less-demanding duties and building an entirely new system. (See our book *Building the Perfect PC*, O'Reilly 2004.) Conversely, if you're upgrading a more recent system, it may make sense to spend more money on the upgrade to bring that system up to current performance levels.

Consider bang for the buck.

For example, you may have a choice of several Sempron or Celeron models ranging in price from $60 to $130. If even the slowest and least expensive of those processors represents a significant performance upgrade over the original processor, it probably makes little sense to buy anything more than the slowest upgrade model. Paying more will buy you little additional performance.

Consider power consumption.

The smaller the differential between the power consumption of the old and new processors, the easier the upgrade. For example, if you're upgrading a Socket 754 motherboard, you may have a choice between a 62W Sempron and a 110W Athlon 64. As attractive as the higher performance of the Athlon 64 is, using it may introduce cooling and power supply issues.

Replacing the Processor

The exact steps required to replace a processor depend on many factors, including the type of processor, CPU cooler, motherboard, and case you are using. In the following sections, we illustrate the procedure for replacing a Socket 478 processor. Most other processors, including Socket 462 (A), Socket 754, and Socket 939 models, require similar steps. Socket 775 processors differ significantly, so we illustrate the installation of a Socket 775 processor separately.

Removing the old processor

The first step in replacing the processor is to remove the old processor. To do so, take the following steps:

1. Disconnect the power cord, monitor, keyboard, mouse, and other external peripherals, and move the system to a well-lit work area. Again, the kitchen table is traditional. Remove the cover from the case and clean the system thoroughly, inside and out. There are few things less pleasant than working on a filthy system.

Cleanliness Is Next to Goodliness

One of our tech reviewers suggests precleaning the system in a less dirt-sensitive location, such as a garage workbench, prior to moving the computer onto the kitchen table for the balance of the process. This precaution enhances domestic bliss and increases the possibility of budget increases when it comes time for the next upgrade.

2. Examine the system to decide whether to remove the motherboard before proceeding or to install the new processor with the motherboard in place. That decision depends on many factors, including your level of experience in replacing processors, the amount of working room available inside the case, the type of clamping mechanism used to secure the CPU cooler, and so on. If in doubt, remove the motherboard.

3. If you elect to remove the motherboard, record the locations of every cable that connects to it. Many people use a digital camera for that purpose. Disconnect all of the cables and remove the screws that secure the motherboard to the case. Ground yourself by touching the case structure or the power supply, lift the motherboard out of the case, and place it on a flat, nonconductive surface.

A NASTY CRACK

If you decide to install the processor with the motherboard in place, be very careful about how much pressure you apply when installing the new CPU cooler. Applying too much pressure when you install the CPU cooler can crack the motherboard.

---

4. If you haven't done so already, remove the cable that connects the CPU cooler fan to the motherboard power header. Release the clamp or clamps that secure the CPU cooler to the motherboard, and attempt to lift the CPU cooler away from the motherboard, using very gentle pressure. If necessary, you can slide the CPU cooler back and forth *very* gently in the horizontal plane, keeping its base parallel to the motherboard.

GENTLE PERSUASION

If the CPU cooler doesn't break loose with gentle persuasion, don't yank it. The thermal compound between the CPU cooler and the CPU sometimes sets up like glue. Pulling too hard can pull the CPU right out of the socket, damaging the old CPU and possibly the socket. If that happens, you may have to replace the motherboard.

If you're working with the motherboard in situ, turn the computer on and let it run for a few minutes to warm the processor, which melts the thermal compound and makes it easier to break the bond. If you've removed the motherboard, point a hair dryer at the CPU cooler and CPU and let it run for several minutes, until the CPU cooler becomes warm to the touch. At that point, the CPU cooler should separate easily from the CPU.

---

5. Set the original CPU cooler aside. If you plan to salvage it and the original processor (why not?), remove the remnants of the thermal compound from the base of the cooler. You can often do so just by rubbing

the base with your thumb to remove the compound, which usually has the consistency of rubber cement. If the thermal compound is too persistent, try using the edge of a credit card or a knife to scrape off the compound. Be careful to avoid scratching the surface of the cooler. Goof-Off or a similar solvent may also be helpful. Some people even use fine steel wool, but if you do that, make sure that no small pieces remain on the cooler. If you use the cooler later, even a tiny piece of steel wool can short out the processor or the motherboard, causing all sorts of problems.

6. With the CPU cooler removed, the processor is visible in its socket. If you intend to salvage the processor for later use, it's a good idea to remove the remnants of the thermal compound while the CPU is still seated in the socket, where it is well grounded and protected from injury. You can do so by rubbing gently with your thumb or by using the edge of a credit card as a scraper. Once again, use a hair dryer to warm the processor if you have difficulty removing the thermal compound.

7. Once the processor is clean, lift the ZIF lever to release the clamping pressure on the socket and then lift the processor from the socket. It should separate from the socket without any resistance at all. If it does not, you can apply gentle pressure to separate it, but be very careful not to bend (or snap off) any of the fragile processor pins. Even if you don't plan to reuse the processor, a snapped-off pin may render the motherboard useless.

8. For the time being, place the processor pins-up on a flat, nonconductive surface such as the tabletop. Later on, you can use the packaging from the new processor to store the old processor.

Installing the new processor (Sockets 462/A, 478, 754, 939)

The exact procedure needed to install a processor varies slightly for different processors and CPU coolers, but the general procedure is similar. In this section, we illustrate the procedure for installing a Socket 478 Pentium 4 processor, but the procedure is identical for a Celeron, and nearly so for Socket 462 (A), Socket 754, and Socket 939 Athlon 64 and Sempron processors. The only real difference is how the CPU cooler is secured, and that should be obvious to you when you examine your particular CPU cooler.

SOMEONE ALWAYS HAS TO BE DIFFERENT

Socket 775 Intel processors use a slightly different procedure. Rather than being secured with a ZIF lever that clamps the processor pins, Socket 775 processors seat loosely in the socket and are secured by clamping the processor body with a retaining mechanism that is part of the socket. See the following section for details.

We chose a retail-boxed processor to illustrate this section. One advantage of a retail-boxed processor is that it comes with a competent CPU cooler that is guaranteed to be compatible with the processor, and typically costs only a few dollars more than the bare OEM processor. The CPU coolers that Intel and AMD currently bundle with their retail-boxed processors are quite good, especially considering the low incremental cost of buying the bundle. The bundled coolers aren't quite as efficient or as quiet as the best aftermarket CPU coolers, but they suffice for most purposes.

Our retail-boxed Pentium 4 processor, shown in Figure 5-9, includes the processor itself and a large Intel-branded CPU cooler. The plastic packaging Intel uses is treacherous. We eventually got the package open using scissors, but for a time we thought we'd have to resort to a chain saw.

Figure 5-9. The retail-boxed Intel Pentium 4 processor and heatsink/fan

---

OPEN SESAME

Don't try to pry the package open using just your fingers. Robert did that once with an Intel retail-boxed processor. When the package finally popped, the heatsink/fan unit went sailing across the room and the processor landed in his lap. (Thank goodness it wasn't the converse. . . .) AMD packaging is also obnoxious, but not as bad as Intel packaging.

The first step is to lift the arm of the ZIF (zero insertion force) socket, as shown in Figure 5-10, until it is vertical. With the arm vertical, there is no clamping force on the socket holes, which allows the processor to drop into place without requiring any pressure.

Zero Means Zero

Never apply pressure to seat the processor. You'll bend the pins and destroy the processor. Note that closing the ZIF lever may cause the processor to rise up slightly from the socket. If this happens, raise the lever again and reseat the processor. After the processor is fully seated, it's safe to apply gentle pressure with your finger to keep it in place as you close the ZIF lever.

Figure 5-10. Lift the socket lever to prepare the socket to receive the processor

Correct orientation is indicated on the processor and socket by some obvious means. For Socket 478, the processor has a trimmed corner and the socket a small triangle, both visible in Figure 5-11 near the ZIF socket lever. With the socket lever vertical, align the processor with the socket and drop the processor into place, as shown in Figure 5-11. The processor should seat flush with the socket just from the force of gravity, or with at most a tiny push. If the processor doesn't simply drop into place, something is misaligned. Remove the processor and verify that it is aligned properly and that the pattern of pins on the processor corresponds to the pattern of holes on the socket.

Figure 5-11. Align the processor with the socket and drop it into place

Cleanliness Counts

If the processor has previously been used, clean off any remaining thermal compound or the remnants of the thermal pad before you install the heatsink/fan unit. You can remove old thermal compound using Goof-Off or isopropyl alcohol on a cloth, or by polishing the processor gently with 0000 steel wool. If you use steel wool, which is conductive, make absolutely sure that no stray bits of it remain after you finish polishing the processor. Even a tiny piece of steel wool can short out the processor or another motherboard component, with disastrous results. Better yet, use steel wool only when the processor is away from the motherboard, prior to installation.

With the processor in place and seated flush with the socket, press the lever arm down and snap it into place, as shown in Figure 5-12. You may have to press the lever arm slightly away from the socket to allow it to snap into a locked position.

Figure 5-12. Snap the ZIF socket lever into place to lock the processor into the socket

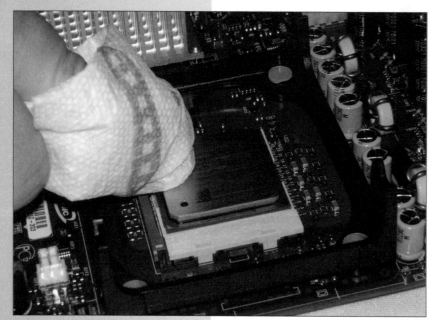

Figure 5-13. Polish the processor with a paper towel before installing the CPU cooler

To install the CPU cooler, begin by polishing the top of the processor with a paper towel or soft cloth, as shown in Figure 5-13. (Our editor, Brian Jepson, notes that he's become fond of coffee filters, as they are abrasive enough to polish, and so far haven't scratched anything. Plus, they don't seem to leave any debris.) Remove any grease, grit, or other material that might prevent the heatsink from making intimate contact with the processor surface.

Next, check the contact surface of the heatsink, shown in Figure 5-14. If the heatsink base is bare, that means it's intended to be used with thermal compound, usually called "thermal goop." In that case, also polish the heatsink base.

Some heatsinks have a square or rectangular pad made of a phase-change medium, which is a fancy term for a material that melts as the CPU heats and solidifies as the CPU cools. This liquid/solid cycle ensures that the processor die maintains good thermal contact with the heatsink. If your heatsink includes such a pad, you needn't polish the base of the heatsink. (Heatsinks use either a thermal pad or thermal goop, not both.)

ALUMINUM VERSUS COPPER

The heatsink shown in Figure 5-14 is a so-called "AlCu" hybrid unit, for the chemical symbols for aluminum and copper. The body of the heatsink is made from aluminum, and the contact surface for the processor from copper. Copper has better thermal properties, but is much more costly than aluminum.

Inexpensive heatsinks and those designed for slower, cooler-running processors use aluminum exclusively. Heatsinks designed for fast, hot-running processors (and for overclockers) use copper exclusively. Hybrid heatsinks balance cost and performance by using copper only where heat transfer properties are critical.

Figure 5-14. The base of the Intel heatsink, showing the circular copper area that contacts the processor

Intel never uses a cheap method when a better solution is available, and the packaging for their thermal compound is no exception. Rather than the usual single-serving plastic packet of thermal goop, Intel provides thermal goop in a syringe with a premeasured dose. To apply the thermal goop, put the syringe tip near the center of the processor and squeeze the entire contents of the syringe onto the processor surface, as shown in Figure 5-15.

Different Goops

Don't worry if your heatsink or thermal compound differs from those in the illustrations. The type of heatsink and thermal compound supplied with retail-boxed processors varies from model to model and may also vary within a model line.

When we replace a heatsink, we use Antec Silver Thermal Compound, which is widely available, inexpensive, and works well. Don't pay extra for "premium" brand names like Arctic Silver. They cost more than the Antec product and our testing shows little or no difference in cooling efficiency.

Too Much Is as Bad as Too Little

Incidentally, the premeasured thermal goop syringe shown here illustrates the proper amount of goop for any modern AMD or Intel processor. If you're applying goop from a bulk syringe, squeeze out only the amount shown here, about 0.1 milliliter (mL), which may also be referred to as 0.1 cubic centimeter (CC). Most people tend to use too much. (Some older processors, such as the AMD Athlon XP, have smaller heat spreaders and so require a correspondingly smaller amount of goop.)

If you apply too much thermal goop, the excess squooshes out from between the heatsink base and the CPU surface when you put the heatsink in place. Good practice suggests removing excess goop from around the socket, but that may be impossible with a large heatsink, because the heatsink blocks access to the socket area. Standard silicone thermal goop does not conduct electricity, so there is no danger of excess goop shorting anything out.

If you're a neatnik, use your finger (covered with a latex glove or plastic bag) to spread thin layers of goop on the processor surface and heatsink base before you install the HSF. We do that with silver-based thermal compounds, which we don't trust to be electrically nonconductive, despite manufacturers' claims to the contrary.

Figure 5-15. Apply thermal compound

The next step is to orient the CPU cooler above the processor, as shown in Figure 5-16, keeping it as close to horizontal as possible. Slide the CPU cooler down into the retaining bracket, making sure that the lock tabs on each of the four corners of the CPU cooler assembly are aligned with the matching slots in the CPU cooler retaining bracket on the motherboard. Press down gently and use a small circular motion to spread the thermal goop evenly over the surface of the processor.

Figure 5-16. Align the CPU cooler over the processor, making sure the locking tabs on the CPU cooler align with the corresponding slots on the retaining bracket

Make sure that both of the white plastic cam levers (one is visible near Barbara's thumb in Figure 5-16) are in the open position, not applying any pressure to the CPU cooler mechanism. With the CPU cooler aligned properly, press down firmly, as shown in Figure 5-17, until all four locking tabs snap into place in the corresponding slots on the retaining bracket. This step requires applying significant pressure evenly to the top of the CPU cooler mechanism. It's generally easier to do that using your full hand rather than just your fingers or thumbs. With some CPU coolers, it may be easier to get two opposite corners snapped in first and then do the remaining corners.

Figure 5-17. With the CPU cooler aligned, press down firmly until it snaps into place

With the CPU cooler snapped into the retaining bracket, the next step is to clamp the heatsink tightly against the processor to ensure good thermal transfer between the CPU and heatsink. To do so, pivot the white plastic cam levers from their unlocked position to the locked position, as shown in Figure 5-18.

EASY DOES IT

The first lever is easy to lock into position, because there is not yet any pressure on the mechanism. With the first lever cammed into its locked position, though, locking the second lever requires significant pressure. So significant, in fact, that the first time we tried to lock the second lever, we actually popped it out of the bracket. If that happens to you, unlock the first camming lever and snap the second one back into position. You may need to squeeze the pivot point with one hand to keep that lever from popping out of place again while you lock the lever with the other hand.

Figure 5-18. Clamp the CPU cooler into place

The thermal mass of the heatsink draws heat away from the CPU, but the heat must be dissipated to prevent the CPU from eventually overheating as the heatsink warms up. To dispose of excess heat as it is transferred to the heatsink, most CPU coolers use a muffin fan to draw air continuously through the fins of the heatsink.

YOUR MILEAGE MAY VARY

Different CPU coolers use different retention mechanisms. The CPU coolers bundled with retail-boxed CPUs are designed to be secured using the standard socket or bracket arrangement for the socket type in question. Some third-party CPU coolers use custom mounting arrangements. If you are installing such a CPU cooler, follow the directions included with the CPU cooler.

Some CPU fans attach to a drive power connector, but most (including this Intel unit) attach to a dedicated CPU fan connector on the motherboard. Using a motherboard fan power connector allows the motherboard to control the CPU fan, reducing speed for quieter operation when the processor is running under light load and not generating much heat, and increasing fan speed when the processor is running under heavy load and generating more heat. The motherboard can also monitor fan speed, which allows it to send an alert to the user if the fan fails or begins running sporadically.

To connect the CPU fan, locate the 3-pin header connector on the motherboard labeled "CPU fan," and plug the keyed cable from the CPU fan into that connector, as shown in Figure 5-19.

Figure 5-19. Connect the CPU fan cable to the CPU fan connector

Installing the new processor (Socket 775)

Intel's current *Socket 775* (also called *Socket T*) processors require slightly different installation steps than processors that use Socket 462 (A), 478, 754, or 939. This section illustrates those differences.

The fundamental difference between Socket 775 and other current processor sockets is that Socket 775 places the pins in the socket and the matching holes on the processor body rather than the converse. That means the pins are vulnerable, so Socket 775 motherboards use a plastic shield to protect the socket until the processor is installed. To begin installing a Socket 775 processor, simply snap out the socket shield, shown in Figure 5-20.

Figure 5-20. The gray plastic Socket 775 socket shield

WASTE NOT, WANT NOT

Save the socket shield for future use, or install it on the old motherboard to protect its socket.

With the socket shield removed, the socket itself is visible, as shown in Figure 5-21. The metal bracket that surrounds the socket is the processor retaining bracket, which is locked in place by the hook-shaped lever visible to the left of the socket. Release that lever and swing it vertically to unlatch the processor retaining bracket.

Figure 5-21. The processor socket is visible after you remove the socket shield

Figure 5-22. Release the latching lever and swing the processor retaining bracket upward

Figure 5-23. Align the processor and drop it into the socket

With the lever unlatched, swing the processor retaining bracket upward to make the socket accessible, as shown in Figure 5-22.

Figure 5-23 shows the two keying mechanisms used by Socket 775. A triangle is visible at the lower-right corner of the processor, pointing to the one beveled corner of the socket. Also visible near the lower-left and -right corners of the processor are two keying notches, which mate with two protrusions in the socket body. Make sure that the processor is aligned properly with the socket, and then simply drop it into place.

After you drop the processor into the socket, lower the processor retaining bracket, as shown in Figure 5-24. The retaining bracket is secured by the cammed portion of the latching lever against the lip visible at the bottom of the bracket. Make sure that the latching lever is raised far enough for the cammed portion to clear the lip on the bracket, and use finger pressure to close the retaining bracket until it seats.

With the bracket lip and latching lever aligned, press down firmly on the latching lever until it snaps into place under the latch, as shown in Figure 5-25. Use a paper towel or soft cloth to polish the top of the processor, as described in the previous section.

Figure 5-24. Verify that the latching lever clears the lip on the retaining bracket

Figure 5-25. Clamp the latching lever into place, securing the processor in the socket

Magic Marker?

In case you're wondering, the processor shown is a Pentium D 820 engineering sample, hand-labeled by Intel before they sent it to us.

Figure 5-26. A standard Socket 775 CPU cooler, with mounting posts visible at each corner

Socket 775 uses a different mechanism to secure the CPU cooler. Rather than using a plastic bracket surrounding the socket, like Socket 478, Socket 775 uses four mounting holes arrayed at the corners of the socket. Figure 5-26 shows a typical Socket 775 CPU cooler, in this case a stock Intel unit. The white square visible at the center of the copper heatsink base is a phase-change thermal pad. If your heatsink has such a pad, you needn't apply thermal compound. If your heatsink lacks a thermal pad, apply thermal compound to the top of the processor before proceeding.

To mount the CPU cooler, align it so that each of its four posts matches one of the motherboard mounting holes. Those holes form a square, so you can align the CPU cooler in any of four positions. Locate the CPU fan power connector on the motherboard and orient the CPU cooler so that the fan power cable is located near the power connector. Make sure the four posts are aligned with the mounting holes, as shown in Figure 5-27, and then seat the CPU cooler.

Strip Before Using

Some thermal pads that are pre-installed on CPU coolers include a paper or thin plastic protective sheet that must be removed before the CPU cooler is installed. Examine the thermal pad carefully and, if necessary, strip off the protective sheet before you install the CPU cooler.

Figure 5-27. Align the CPU cooler so that each mounting post enters one of the mounting holes

The CPU cooler is now connected to the motherboard but not yet locked into place. Press down on the top of each of the mounting posts, as shown in Figure 5-28, to expand the tips of the mounting posts and secure the CPU cooler in position. (If you need to remove the CPU cooler later, simply lift up each of the four posts to unlock the connectors. The CPU cooler can then be lifted off without resistance.)

Connect the CPU fan cable to the CPU fan connector to complete the processor installation.

Figure 5-28. With the HSF aligned, press down firmly until it snaps into place

Troubleshooting Processors

In one sense, there's not much troubleshooting to be done for a processor. A properly installed processor simply works. If it stops working, it's dead and needs to be replaced. That seldom happens—we're tempted to say "never"—unless the processor incurs lightning damage, is the victim of a catastrophic motherboard failure, or overheats severely (usually from misguided attempts at *overclocking*, or running the processor faster than its design speed). A processor in a system with a high-quality motherboard and power supply that is protected by a UPS or a good surge protector is likely to outlast the useful life of the system.

OLD PROCESSORS NEVER DIE . . .

In our more than 20 years' experience with many hundreds of systems, we can count on one finger the number of processors that have failed other than as a result of power spikes, overheating, or other abuse. And we suspect that one was killed by a power glitch.

In recognition of the primary danger, modern processors incorporate *thermal protection*, which slows down the processor or stops it completely if the temperature rises too high. Even if the processor isn't throttling throughput, operating it at a high temperature can reduce its life. Accordingly, it's important to monitor processor temperature, at least periodically, and if necessary, to take steps to improve processor cooling. If your system slows down for no apparent reason or hangs completely, particularly in a warm environment or when the processor is working hard, it's quite possible that overheating is responsible. Here are the most important steps you can take to avoid overheating:

Keep an eye on processor temperature.

Use the motherboard monitoring program, or reboot the system, run BIOS Setup, and view the temperature and fan speed section. Take these measurements when the system has been idle as well as when it has been running under heavy load. It's important to do this initially to establish a "baseline" temperature for the processor when it is idle and under load. You can't recognize abnormally high temperatures if you don't know what the normal temperature should be. If you run the motherboard monitoring program, set reasonable tripwire values for temperatures and configure the program to notify you when those temperatures are exceeded.

HOW COOL IS COOL ENOUGH?

As our editor pointed out, if you've installed the CPU cooler or thermal compound improperly, the baseline temperature you measure may be much too high and you may not realize that. It's impossible to say what a "normal" temperature is, because so much depends on the particular processor and CPU cooler, the case and cooling fans you use, the ambient room temperature, and so on. As a rule of thumb, with the processor at idle in a standard mini-tower case, we consider a processor temperature under 35° C to be good; the 35° C to 40° C range to be acceptable; and anything over 40° C to be good reason to improve the cooling by using a better CPU cooler and/or better case fans. If you're using a small form factor case or a hot-running processor, such as a Prescott-core Pentium 4, normal idle temperatures may be 5° C to 10° C warmer. Under heavy load, the processor temperature may increase 20° C or more. We consider anything up to 60° C normal. At 65° C we are concerned. At 70° C, we shut the system down and determine what's causing the high temperatures. Some serious gamers routinely run their processors at 80° C or even 85° C, but doing that may shorten processor lifetime dramatically.

Keep the system clean.

Blocked air vents can increase processor temperature by 20° C (36° F) or more. Clean the system as often as is necessary to maintain free air flow. If your case has an inlet air filter, check that filter frequently and clean it as often as necessary.

Use a good CPU cooler.

CPU coolers vary greatly in efficiency (and noise level). Although the CPU cooler bundled with a retail-boxed processor is reasonably efficient, replacing it with a good aftermarket CPU cooler can reduce CPU temperature by 5° to 10° C (9° to 18° F). Make sure that the processor surface is clean before you install the CPU cooler, use the right amount of a good thermal compound, and make sure that the heatsink is clamped tightly against the processor.

Install supplemental case fans.

In particular, if you've upgraded the processor or installed a high-performance video adapter, it's possible that you've added more heat load than the case was designed to handle. Adding a supplemental fan, or replacing an existing fan with one that provides higher air flow, can reduce interior case temperatures dramatically, which in turn reduces processor temperature.

TAKE YOUR SYSTEM'S TEMPERATURE

You can use an ordinary thermometer to test the adequacy of your system fans. Measure the ambient room temperature first. Then put the thermometer close to the outputs of the power supply fan and the supplemental case fan(s). If the temperature difference is 5° C (9° F) or less, adding or upgrading fans probably won't help.

Upgrade the case.

In most systems, the processor is the major heat source. A *TAC* (*Thermally Advantaged Chassis*) case provides a duct (and sometimes a dedicated fan) to route waste CPU heat directly to the outside of the case, rather than exhausting it inside the case. In our testing, using a TAC-compliant case routinely lowered CPU temperatures by 5° to 10° C (41° to 50° F) relative to running that CPU in a non-TAC case.

You can buy a TAC case, or, if you're handy with tools, turn your old case into a TAC case. To do so, simply use a 2" to 3" hole saw to cut a hole in the case side panel directly over the CPU. Make a duct of the appropriate length using cardboard or plastic tubing, and secure the duct to the case with screws or adhesive. If you want to be fancy, you can install a standard case fan between the interior panel wall and the duct.

Position the system properly.

As amazing as it sounds, changing the position of the case by only a few inches, and in some pretty non-obvious ways, can make a major difference in system and processor temperature. For example, Robert's main office system sits on the floor next to his desk, directly in front of a heating vent. During the summer, when the air conditioning is running, that processor routinely operates 5° C cooler than during the winter months, when Robert closes the vent to prevent hot air from blowing on the system. That might seem reasonable, until you realize that the cool air from the vent is blowing on the *back* of the system, which has only exhaust fans. The ambient room temperature is actually lower during winter months—and the ambient air is what's being drawn into the system—so we'd have expected the system temperature also to be lower in winter.

INCHES MATTER

During the writing of this chapter, Barbara commented to Robert that his den system was much louder than usual. Sure enough, it was. That system sits between one side of a love seat and the side of a corner table. It had somehow been moved, slid back by only four inches or so, but that was enough to reduce the air flow significantly. The CPU fan was screaming–running at about 5,700 RPM–and the CPU temperature was 52° C with the system idling. Robert slid the system out a few inches, and within minutes the CPU fan speed had dropped to about 1,800 RPM–becoming nearly silent–and the idle CPU temperature had fallen to 38° C. Inches can make a huge difference.

Despite the odds, processors do sometimes fail. If you are reasonably certain that your processor has failed, the only practical way to troubleshoot it is to install the problem processor in another system or to install a known-good processor in the problem system. The former is the safer choice. We have never heard of a failed processor harming a good motherboard, but a catastrophically failed motherboard that has killed one processor could easily kill another. For that reason, if we're convinced that a processor is bad, we always pull it and test it in another system.

Memory 6

Computers use *memory*, also called *main memory* or *RAM* (*Random Access Memory*), to store active programs—including antivirus scanners and other background services—and the data the system is using at the moment. Data can be written to and read from RAM extremely quickly—roughly a million times faster than a hard drive—but data in RAM is retained only while the system is running. RAM costs hundreds of times more than hard disk storage, byte for byte, so RAM is not an economically practical substitute for hard disk storage.

The characteristics of RAM and hard disk storage are complementary. The hard drive stores programs and data that are not currently being used, for which large capacity and permanence are important but speed is not. RAM stores active programs and data, for which access speed is important but smaller capacity and transience are not.

That's not to say that the amount of RAM you have installed in your computer is unimportant. Far from it. If your computer has insufficient RAM to hold all of your active programs and data, it slows down—sometimes dramatically. This problem occurs when the operating system must swap out active programs and data from memory to the hard drive to make room for other programs and data. In extreme cases, such as running Windows XP with several active programs in a system with only 128 MB of RAM, performance may drop to literally 10% of what it would be on a system with sufficient RAM.

Unfortunately, many commercial systems—particularly inexpensive consumer-grade models from big-box stores and online vendors such as Dell and Gateway—are sold with insufficient RAM. We checked the Sunday supplements as we started this chapter, and found that many Windows XP systems were being offered with only 256 MB of RAM and some with only 128 MB. That's a sick joke. Windows XP requires a minimum of 256 MB of RAM to load and run just one or two programs with top performance, and it really wants much more. We recommend the following amounts of RAM for a Windows XP system:

- For a lightly used budget system, 256 MB to 512 MB (some would argue for 384 MB as a dead minimum)

- For a mainstream system with typical usage, 512 MB to 1 GB

- For a performance or gaming system, 1 GB to 2 GB

Regard these as baseline figures, and increase them if you run a memory-intensive application or if you run many apps simultaneously. For example, we'd equip even a budget system that was to run Photoshop with at least 1 GB of RAM.

VISTA NEEDS MORE

For a Windows Vista system, install at least 1 GB of RAM (for 32-bit Vista) or 2 GB (for 64-bit Vista).

Robert recently experimented with the amount of memory in his main working desktop system, which uses one of the fastest processors available. That system often has many windows open—a dozen or more instances of the Mozilla browser, several StarOffice documents, his mail client, a PIM, and so on. (Robert runs Linux, which manages memory more efficiently than Windows, but the principle is the same.)

With 512 MB of RAM, performance was acceptable (as well it should be on a system with a $1,000 processor). But boosting the RAM to 1 GB paid immediate dividends. Programs loaded noticeably faster, and the lags in switching between programs disappeared. Everything became a lot snappier. Figure 6-1 shows why. At the moment this screenshot was captured, just the top three memory-consuming processes were using about 317 MB, 149 MB, and 136 MB of RAM—about 90 MB more than the 512 MB of RAM that was originally installed on this system. About 83 MB of physical RAM remains available, and only 368 *KB* of the swap file is in use. This system is running happily, with essentially all of the active programs using RAM exclusively.

Boosting the memory in this system to 1.5 GB had little beneficial effect. Most of the physical memory was still being used—Windows and Linux both use all the RAM they can get—and the swap file usage was near zero, but there was no perceptible performance difference between 1.5 GB versus 1 GB. That might change with a different mix of applications, but for Robert's system as he typically uses it, 1 GB of RAM is the sweet spot.

Your system also has a sweet spot, and chances are that the sweet spot is higher than the amount of memory you currently have installed. Installing more memory is one of the easiest, cheapest, and most effective upgrades you can make to an older system, or even to a new model that has insufficient memory. In the rest of this chapter, we'll tell you what you need to know to upgrade your memory and to troubleshoot memory problems.

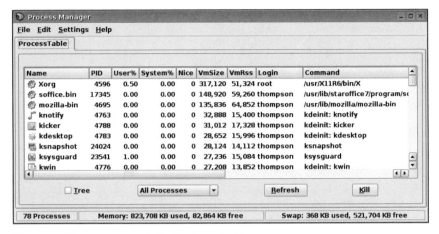

Figure 6-1. Memory usage on Robert's primary desktop system

Understanding Memory

This chapter focuses on general-purpose memory, where PCs store programs and data that are currently in use, the pipeline that supplies data to and receives results from the processor. General-purpose memory, called *read-write memory* or *Random Access Memory* (RAM), must be readable-from and writable-to. Two types of RAM are used on modern PCs:

Dynamic RAM

> *Dynamic RAM* (*DRAM*) stores data for only a tiny fraction of a second before losing it. To maintain stored data, the system must constantly *refresh* DRAM, which exacts a performance penalty and limits its speed. Typical DRAM provides 60 ns (nanosecond) access, but is inexpensive and consumes relatively little power.

Static RAM

> *Static RAM* (*SRAM*) automatically maintains its contents as long as power is applied to it, without requiring refresh. SRAM provides access times an order of magnitude faster than DRAM, but is expensive and power-hungry.

PCs use a tiered memory architecture that takes advantage of these characteristics:

Main memory

> The bulk of a PC's memory uses DRAM (modern systems use a variant called *SDRAM*, described in the next section) and is called *main memory*. It is large—typically 256 MB to 1 GB or more—but too slow

to keep up with a modern CPU. Main memory is where the CPU stores programs and data that it will soon need. Main memory functions as a buffer between the CPU and disk.

Cache memory

Cache memory is a small amount of fast SRAM that buffers access between the CPU and main memory.

Modern PCs have two layers of cache memory:

Primary cache memory

Primary cache memory, also called *Level 1 cache* or *L1 cache*, is typically 16 to 128 KB of very fast memory on the same chip as the CPU itself. L1 cache size and efficiency are major factors in CPU performance. The amount and type of L1 cache is determined by the CPU you use, and cannot be upgraded.

Secondary cache memory

L1 cache is not large enough to eliminate the speed disparity between processors and main memory. *Secondary cache memory*, also called *Level 2 cache* or *L2 cache*, bridges that gap with a reasonable compromise between cost and performance. L2 cache is a part of the CPU package (or of the CPU substrate itself) on all modern processors, including the Intel Pentium 4 and Celeron, and the AMD Athlon 64 and Sempron. Modern processors have L2 cache memory sizes ranging from 128 KB to 2 MB.

TAKE THE CACHE AND RUN

The amount of cache memory present on a processor can have a dramatic impact on performance, particularly if you work on small data sets. For example, when we tested the SETI@Home (*http://setiathome.ssl.berkeley.edu/*) client on two nearly identical processors, one with 512 KB of L2 cache and the other with 1 MB, the second processor completed work units in less than half the time required by the first. That was true because the entire work unit fit within the 1 MB L2 cache, but not within the 512 KB L2 cache. Running a similar distributed processing application that used data sets too large to fit in the 1 MB L2 cache, the processor with the larger L2 cache was only marginally faster. If you are choosing between two similar processors, always choose the one with the larger L2 cache.

Memory types

Recent systems use main memory of one of the following types:

Synchronous DRAM

Synchronous DRAM, also called *SDRAM*, began shipping in 1996 and was commonly used on PCs until 2001. Unlike older and now obsolete asynchronous forms of memory, SDRAM shares a common clock reference with the CPU. The CPU and memory are slaved together, allowing the CPU to transfer data to and from memory whenever it wishes to do so, rather than requiring the CPU to await an arbitrary window. SDRAM speeds are specified in MHz rather than in nanoseconds, as was true of earlier forms of memory. Synchronous DRAM takes one of the following forms:

JEDEC SDRAM
> *JEDEC SDRAM* or *PC66 SDRAM* is so-called to differentiate it from the later *PC100 SDRAM* and *PC133 SDRAM*.

PC100 SDRAM
> *PC100 SDRAM* is rated for use with Pentium II and Pentium III processors that use the 100 MHz FSB.

PC133 SDRAM
> *PC133 SDRAM* is rated for use on a 133 MHz FSB. Note that you cannot safely assume that PC133 memory can be used to upgrade a system that has PC66 or PC100 memory installed. Some systems, particularly those based on the Intel 440BX and 810-series chipsets require PC100 memory and will not function properly with PC133 memory installed.

In general, although PC66, PC100, and PC133 SDRAM modules are still available (although in limited distribution), any system that uses SDRAM is a poor upgrade candidate. The latest SDRAM systems are now more than five years old, and reaching the end of their service life. The fastest SDRAM systems, such as 1+ GHz Pentium III models, are still fast enough to serve in secondary roles, but the very high cost per megabyte of SDRAM makes it uneconomic to upgrade them other than by salvaging SDRAM memory from other old systems.

DDR-SDRAM
> Relative to standard SDRAM, *Double Data Rate SDRAM* (*DDR-SDRAM*) doubles the amount of data transferred per clock cycle, and thereby effectively doubles peak memory bandwidth. DDR-SDRAM is an evolutionary improvement of standard SDRAM, which is now sometimes called *Single Data Rate SDRAM* or *SDR-SDRAM* to differentiate it. Because DDR-SDRAM costs essentially the same to produce as SDR-SDRAM, it quickly obsoleted SDR-SDRAM.

> The chips used to produce a DDR-SDRAM memory module, called a DIMM (Dual In-line Memory Module) are named for their operating speed. For example, 100 MHz chips are double-pumped to 200 MHz, and so are called DDR200 chips. Similarly, chips that operate at 133 MHz are called DDR266 chips, those that operate at 166 MHz are called DDR333 chips, and those that operate at 200 MHz are called DDR400 chips.

> Unlike SDR-SDRAM DIMMs, which are designated by their chip speeds, DDR-SDRAM DIMMs are designated by their bandwidth.

Faster Isn't Necessarily Better

High-performance memory modules targeted at gamers, overclockers, and other enthusiasts are available with ratings of PC3500, PC4000, PC4200, and higher. These premium-price modules provide no benefit unless you are overclocking a system beyond its rated speed.

Their data path is 64 bits (8 bytes) wide. So, for example, a DDR-SDRAM DIMM that uses DDR200 chips transfers 8 bytes 200 million times per second, for a total bandwidth of 1,600 million bytes/second and is called a PC1600 DIMM. Similarly, DDR-SDRAM DIMMs that use DDR266 chips are labeled PC2100, those that use DDR333 chips are labeled PC2700, and those that use DDR400 chips are labeled PC3200.

The falling price of PC3200 DDR-SDRAM modules quickly obsoleted slower forms of DDR-SDRAM, although PC2700 modules remain in limited distribution. The limited availability of PC2100 and slower forms of DDR-SDRAM is not an issue for systems that use those slower variants, because PC3200 memory is backward-compatible with slower variants.

DON'T MIX AND MATCH

Mixing faster modules with slower modules causes the faster memory to run at the speed of the slowest module installed. Also, some motherboards don't deal well with memory of mixed speeds. If you are upgrading a system that has a limited amount of slower DDR-SDRAM and the processor can take advantage of the higher speed of PC3200 DDR-SDRAM, it often makes sense to replace the slower modules rather than simply adding the PC3200 modules.

Any system that uses DDR-SDRAM is a good upgrade candidate. If it is not labeled, you can identify the speed and other characteristics of an DDR-SDRAM DIMM by checking the item number on the module on the manufacturer web site. DDR-SDRAM DIMMs use 184 pins and can be discriminated from 168-pin SDR-SDRAM and 240-pin DDR2-SDRAM memory modules by noting the number of pins and the position of the single keying notch. Figure 6-2 shows a DDR-SDRAM DIMM.

Figure 6-2. A DDR-SDRAM DIMM

DDR2 SDRAM

By early 2003, the original DDR-SDRAM technology was fast approaching its limits. As AMD and Intel transitioned to higher FSB speeds, DDR-SDRAM has been hard pressed to keep pace. Mainstream DDR-SDRAM tops out at PC3200. Dual-channel DDR chipsets (which combine the bandwidth of paired memory modules) using PC3200 memory limit peak bandwidth to 6,400 MB/s. That matches the bandwidth requirements of a processor with a 64-bit (8-byte) wide memory channel operating with an 800 MHz FSB, such as mainstream Pentium 4 models, but as new processors are introduced, even dual-channel DDR-SDRAM will be unable to keep up with increases in processor bandwidth.

The long-term solution is *DDR2 SDRAM*. DDR2 incorporates a series of evolutionary improvements on standard DDR technology, including increased bandwidth, lower voltage (1.8V versus the 2.5V of DDR), lower power consumption, and improved packaging. Just as DDR-SDRAM doubled bandwidth over SDR-SDRAM when running at the same clock rate, DDR2-SDRAM doubles bandwidth over DDR-SDRAM by doubling the speed of the electrical interface. DDR2 DIMMs use a new 240-pin connector that is incompatible with the 184-pin DDR-SDRAM and earlier connectors. Table 6-1 lists the important characteristics of DDR2-SDRAM, with PC3200 (DDR400) DDR-SDRAM shown for comparison.

Table 6-1. DDR2 characteristics

Chip	Chip clock	I/O clock	Module name	Module bandwidth
DDR400	200 MHz	400 MHz	PC3200	3,200 MB/s
DDR2-400	100 MHz	200 MHz	PC2 3200	3,200 MB/s
DDR2-533	133 MHz	266 MHz	PC2 4200	4,200 MB/s
DDR2-667	166 MHz	333 MHz	PC2 5300	5,300 MB/s
DDR2-800	200 MHz	400 MHz	PC2 6400	6,400 MB/s
DDR2-1000	250 MHz	500 MHz	PC2 8000	8,000 MB/s

Although Intel has pushed DDR2 hard since its introduction, initial uptake was slow for two reasons. First, DDR2 memory originally sold at a very high premium over DDR memory, sometimes as much as 200% to 300%. By late 2005, that differential had dropped to 15% or 20%, making DDR2 a more reasonable choice. Second, although DDR2 offers much higher bandwidth than DDR, it also suffers from much higher *latency*. In effect, that means that although DDR2 can deliver data at higher speed than DDR, it takes longer to start delivering the data. For applications that use primarily sequential memory access, such as video editing, the bandwidth advantage of DDR2 offers noticeably higher memory performance. For applications that access memory randomly, including many personal productivity programs, the latency advantage of DDR gives it the edge. DDR2-SDRAM DIMMs use 240 pins and can be discriminated from 168-pin SDR-SDRAM and 184-pin DDR-SDRAM memory modules by noting the number of pins and the position of the keying notch.

Rambus RDRAM

Rambus RDRAM is a proprietary RAM standard developed jointly by Intel and Rambus. Rambus RDRAM is packaged in modules called *RIMMs*, which is a tradename rather than an acronym.

There are three types of RDRAM memory, called *Base Rambus*, *Concurrent Rambus*, and *Direct Rambus*. The first two are obsolete, and were used only in devices like game consoles. All RDRAM memory used in PCs is Direct Rambus memory. RDRAM has been made in four speeds, designated PC600, PC700, PC800, and PC1066, although only PC800 and PC1066 remain available. As with DDR-SDRAM, RDRAM modules are named according to their bandwidth, but with a difference. RDRAM uses a 16-bit or 18-bit data path (versus 64-bit for SDRAM) to transfer two bytes at a time, versus the 8-byte bandwidth of DDR-SDRAM. Accordingly, PC800 RDRAM has a bandwidth of only 1.6 GB/s and PC1066 2.133 GB/s, much lower than that of DDR-SDRAM, let alone DDR2-SDRAM.

TWO MODULES IN ONE

RDRAM RIMMs were originally supplied as 16-bit or 18-bit parts. In dual-channel RDRAM motherboards, those modules had to be installed in pairs, one per channel. Currently available PC1066 32/36-bit RDRAM RIMMs are in effect two 16- or 18-bit RIMMs combined into a single package, and can be installed singly in dual-channel RDRAM systems.

RDRAM also suffers from severe latency, and that latency increases as the number of RDRAM devices is increased. Although RDRAM offered potentially higher overall performance at the time it was introduced, faster and much less expensive DDR-SDRAM quickly obsoleted RDRAM for use in desktop systems. RDRAM-based systems are upgradable, barely, but weigh carefully the age of the system and the cost of additional RDRAM memory versus the cost of replacing the motherboard and using DDR-SDRAM or DDR2-SDRAM memory.

RAMBUS ISN'T FOR PCS ANYMORE

Rambus introduced a follow-on to RDRAM called *XDR DRAM*, which is competitive in performance (if not in price) with DDR-SDRAM. XDR DRAM is used in the Sony PlayStation 3 game console, but no existing PC chipset supports XDR DRAM. All of the PCs that were built with Rambus memory are now near the end of their design service life.

You can judge the type of memory likely to be present in a system by knowing that system's age. Figure 6-3 shows a timeline for the types of memory that have been installed in new systems over the last 10 years.

As of late 2005, the memory landscape for PCs appears to be predictable for the next couple of years. PC3200 DDR-SDRAM memory will continue to be used in low-end systems, and will remain widely available for those who are upgrading older systems. DDR2-SDRAM finally gained a foothold in 2005 for Intel-based systems, and as AMD introduces DDR2-compatible processors throughout 2006, DDR2 will become the mainstream memory technology, gradually replacing DDR-SDRAM.

Memory Performance

In addition to the bandwidth rating of a memory module, such as PC3200 or PC2-6400, several other numbers are used to quantify memory performance. These values, known as *timing parameters*, quantify the response time and latency of the module. Memory is structured like a spreadsheet, with many columns and many rows, each of which contains one bit of data. Timing parameters specify the time required to perform such functions as changing the row or column and reading data. (It's not important to understand timing parameters except in a general, overall sense.)

For DDR-SDRAM and DDR2-SDRAM, memory vendors specify values, denominated in whole or fractional clock cycles, for the following four timing parameters:

CAS Latency
   CAS Latency (*Column Access Strobe Latency*), or *tCL*, specifies the number of clock cycles between the column strobe signal and when data is available on the output pins. During sequential memory accesses, the row remains activated and only the column changes, which means that the time required to change columns is critical to overall memory performance. CAS Latency, often abbreviated *CL*, is the most commonly quoted timing parameter and the most important memory timing parameter with respect to overall performance.

RAS to CAS Delay
   RAS to CAS Delay (*Row Access Strobe to CAS Delay*), or *tRCD*, specifies the number of clock cycles between the time a row is activated by the row strobe until the column in that row (which defines a memory cell or bit) can be read or written. When memory is accessed sequentially, the row is already active and only the column changes, so tRCD has little impact on performance. But when memory is accessed randomly, the memory controller must deactivate the old row and activate a new

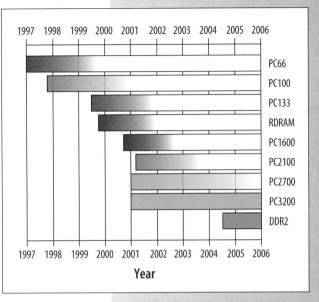

Figure 6-3. Types of memory used in new systems by year

row, which incurs a substantial timing penalty. In that situation, a fast tRCD contributes to faster memory performance.

RAS Precharge Delay

RAS Precharge Delay, or *tRP*, specifies the time required to complete one row access, deactivate that row, reactivate the next row, and begin the next row access. The time required to switch rows and select the next memory cell is therefore the sum of tRP and tRCD. For sequential memory accesses, a slow tRP has little effect; for random memory accesses, a fast tRP contributes significantly to overall memory performance.

Precharge Delay

Precharge Delay, or *tRAS*, specifies the number of clock cycles between the time a row is accessed (activated) and when data can be read from that row. Once the row is activated, data can be read from that row without further overhead until the end of the row is reached, so tRAS ordinarily has little effect on overall memory performance. As with any timing parameter, setting tRAS incorrectly can reduce system stability.

These four memory timing parameters are always listed in the order given, separated by hyphens. For example, a particular PC3200 DDR-SDRAM module may list timings of 2-2-2-5, which means that module is designed to operate with timings of two clock cycles for CAS, tRCD, and tRP, and five clock cycles for tRAS. Similarly, a PC2-3200 DDR2-SDRAM module might list timings of 5-5-5-12, which means that module is designed to operate with timings of 5 clock cycles for CAS, tRCD, and tRP, and 12 clock cycles for tRAS. (Note that DDR and DDR2 timings are not directly comparable, because DDR2 operates on much shorter clock cycles.)

It is important to understand timing parameters only in that the timings you configure your system to use should not be faster than the timings supported by your memory modules. Every modern memory module contains a small chip called the *SPD* (*Serial Presence Detect*) chip, which stores the timing parameters and other characteristics of the module and reports them to the system BIOS. In the ordinary course of things, the module reports its capabilities to the BIOS and the BIOS configures the system to use appropriate settings. However, if a system is producing sporadic memory errors, you can sometimes solve the problem without replacing the memory by using BIOS Setup to specify memory timings that are more relaxed than those nominally supported by the memory modules. This step can allow you to continue using a problem system that requires memory that is unavailable or extremely expensive.

When you are adding or replacing memory in an older system, keep the following memory timing issues in mind:

- Most motherboards can use memory of any CL timing, although some motherboards may not take advantage of the reduced latency. A few motherboards require memory with a specific CL timing. For example, a motherboard that requires CL2.5 DDR memory may not work with CL3 memory, and a motherboard that requires CL3 memory may not work properly with CL2.5 memory. This is a good reason to use the memory configurator utilities provided by Crucial and other memory makers, which take CAS latency issues into account when listing compatible memory modules.

- Some motherboards allow mixing memory with different CL timings, although the faster memory almost always operates at the CAS latency of the slowest module installed. Some motherboards work properly with memory of different CL timings as long as all memory installed has the same CL timing, but misbehave if you install mixed modules of different CL timings. We suspect these problems are caused by minor electrical differences such as capacitance, but have never gotten a good explanation of why this is true. Although problems with mixed CL timings are unusual in our experience, we recommend not mixing CL timings for this reason.

- Most motherboards that support different CL timings automatically configure themselves optimally based on the information reported by the memory module itself, but some require setting memory timings manually in the Chipset Configuration section of BIOS Setup. If you install "fast" modules in a system, it's worth checking BIOS Setup to make sure that the system is configured to use the faster CL timings.

- Using conservative memory timings can increase the stability and reliability of a system at a minimal cost in reduced performance. For example, if a system has DDR CL2.5 memory installed and crashes too frequently, you can increase the stability of that system by configuring CMOS Setup to use CL3 memory timings. CL2.5 memory running as CL3 is more stable than CL2.5 memory running as CL2.5, and probably more stable than CL3 memory running as CL3. The performance hit will be so small that you won't even notice it unless you run a memory benchmark program.

Advice from Ron Morse

Incorrectly set memory timing parameters in BIOS may prevent the machine from operating at all. Some systems with Intel chipsets, when presented with out-of-bounds memory timing parameters during POST, simply lock up. This happens before the video or any other devices are initialized, so the machine appears totally dead. Using the jumper to clear the CMOS to default values is frequently the only remedy.

THE EASY WAY OUT

If all of this discussion of memory minutiae flummoxes you, you can safely ignore it as long as you don't insist on the absolute best memory performance. Simply visit the Crucial (*http://www.crucial.com*) or Kingston (*http://www.kingston.com*) web site and use the memory configurator to specify your motherboard or system model. Choose the least expensive of the modules listed as compatible with your system, install the module, and be done with it.

Other Memory Issues

In addition to memory type, speed, and timings, there are several other issues to consider in choosing proper memory for your system. We'll examine each of those issues in the following sections.

Dual-channel operation

For best performance, modern processors require a great deal of memory bandwidth—more than can be provided by a single memory module. For example, an Intel Pentium 4 processor with an 800 MHz FSB can use memory bandwidth up to 6.4 GB/s, twice that provided by a single PC3200 DIMM. To accommodate this need for greater bandwidth, chipset engineers designed *dual-channel memory controllers* that recognize two physical memory modules as one logical memory module, effectively doubling the data transfer rate between the CPU and memory.

WHEN DUAL-CHANNEL MEMORY MATTERS

Enabling dual-channel memory operation requires that the motherboard have a dual-channel memory controller and that you install memory modules in matched pairs. Ideally, the two memory modules should be identical, but most dual-channel motherboards will accept any pair of DIMMs as long as they are of the same capacity, type, and speed. Most dual-channel memory controllers will operate properly in single-channel mode if you install only one DIMM, but system performance may be significantly degraded.

Dual-channel operation may or may not be important to system performance, depending on the processor you use. For example, the fastest Athlon XP processors use a 400 MHz FSB. Because the Athlon XP uses a 64-bit (8-byte) path between the processor and memory, the maximum memory bandwidth it requires is 3.2 GB/s. That exactly matches the bandwidth of a single PC3200 DIMM, so using dual-channel memory with an Athlon XP system provides little or no performance benefit.

WHEN DUAL-CHANNEL MEMORY DOESN'T MATTER

Despite the lack of any real benefit, many Athlon XP motherboards support dual-channel memory operation, so many people feel obligated to install memory in matched pairs, sometimes discarding the original memory to make room for a new pair of DIMMs. If you are upgrading the memory in a system with an Athlon XP or another processor that does not benefit from dual-channel memory operation, we recommend that you ignore the dual-channel feature and install whatever combination of DIMMs is most cost-effective.

Conversely, if you are upgrading a system that uses a modern processor such as a Pentium 4, Pentium D, or Athlon 64, it's important to make sure that dual-channel memory operation is enabled. Otherwise, you'll cripple system performance, because the processor will waste too much time waiting for memory.

Most dual-channel motherboards provide two or four memory slots. (Some provide only three; populating the third memory slot on such motherboards disables dual-channel memory operation.) Use the following guidelines for upgrading memory in a standard dual-channel motherboard:

- In a motherboard with two or four memory slots, only one of which is populated, install a new memory module that is identical or closely similar to the installed module if doubling the installed memory is sufficient. If you need more memory, remove the original module and install two identical new modules.

- In a motherboard with four memory slots, only two of which are populated, install two or four new matched memory modules, depending on the amount of memory currently installed and the total amount you need after the upgrade.

  - If you are adding two modules, check the motherboard manual to determine whether you can simply install the new modules in the available slots or if you must swap the positions of the old and new modules. Sometimes the higher capacity modules must be installed in channel A and the lower capacity modules in channel B, or vice versa.

  - If you are installing four identical new modules, slot position doesn't matter. If you are installing two pairs of different capacities, check the motherboard manual to see if it matters which you install in channel A and which in channel B.

  - If you are upgrading a system from a relatively small amount of memory to a large amount, check module prices. It's sometimes less expensive to buy four new mid-capacity modules than only two new high-capacity modules.

- In a motherboard with four memory slots, all four of which are populated, install two or four new matched memory modules, depending on the capacity of the currently installed modules and and the total amount of memory you need after the upgrade.

When you are installing fewer modules than the number of memory slots available, it's important to decide which module goes where. Most dual-channel motherboards label the memory slots as follows:

Channel A – DIMM 0 (or 1)
Channel A – DIMM 1 (or 2)
Channel B – DIMM 0 (or 1)
Channel B – DIMM 1 (or 2)

Gold Versus Tin Contacts

Memory modules are available with gold or tin contacts. The type of memory slots in your motherboard determines which you should use. If your motherboard memory slots have tin contacts, use memory modules with tin contacts; if the memory slots use gold contacts, use memory modules that also have gold contacts.

The concern is that placing unlike metals in close contact can cause corrosion, which in turn may cause problems from intermittent memory errors to complete memory failure. Avoid mixing contact metals, particularly if your system operates in a humid environment. Check the motherboard documents to determine which type of memory modules it requires, and buy only compatible modules. (Nearly all recent systems use gold contacts, so if you are in doubt, gold modules are the best choice.)

Unfortunately, it's not always obvious which slot is which. Channel A slots may be grouped together, with channel B slots separated slightly, or DIMM 0 slots for both channels may be together, with DIMM 1 slots separated slightly from them. Many motherboards color-code the DIMM slots, but that coding is not always intuitive. For example, Figure 6-4 shows the four memory slots in an Intel D945PVS motherboard. Two of the slots are blue and two black, but what do the colors indicate? Are both blue slots DIMM 0 (or DIMM 1), or are both blue slots Channel A (or Channel B)?

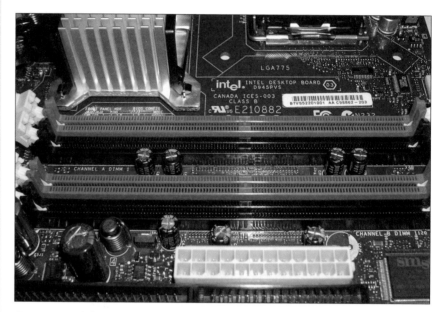

Figure 6-4. Dual-channel DIMM slots, indicated by color

Intel's practice is to color-code DIMM 0 and place Channel A nearer the processor socket, so from top to bottom the slots in this motherboard are Channel A/DIMM 0, A/1, B/0, and B/1. Other motherboard manufacturers use different methods. If you were installing two memory modules in this motherboard, you'd install them in the blue slots, which would put one DIMM on Channel A and the other on Channel B. If instead you installed the two modules in the top two slots, you'd have the same amount of system memory available, but the motherboard would be forced to operate in single-channel memory mode, greatly slowing performance.

Non-parity versus ECC modules

Standard memory, also called *non-parity memory*, uses 8 bits to store an 8-bit byte. *ECC memory* (*Error Correcting Code memory*), sometimes called *parity memory*, uses 9 bits to store an 8-bit byte. The extra bit provided by ECC memory is used to store error detection and correction information.

A non-parity memory module can neither detect nor correct errors. An ECC memory module can detect all multi-bit errors, correct all single-bit errors, and correct some multi-bit errors. Memory errors are so rare that most desktop systems use non-parity memory, which is less expensive and faster than ECC memory. In fact, most desktop chipsets do not support ECC memory. If you install ECC memory in such a system, it may not recognize the memory at all, but more likely it will simply treat the ECC memory as non-parity memory, ignoring the extra bit.

ECC memory is occasionally used in desktop systems, but is much more common in servers and other large, critical systems. Because ECC modules contain additional memory chips, in the ratio of 9:8, they typically cost 10% to 15% more than similar non-parity modules. Also, because the circuitry on ECC modules that calculates and stores ECC values imposes some overhead, ECC modules are marginally slower than similar non-parity modules.

COUNTING CHIPS

You can identify an ECC module visually by counting the number of memory chips on it. If that number is evenly divisible by three or five, it's an ECC module. If not, it's a non-parity module. You can also often identify an ECC module by its part number. ECC modules are 72 bits wide—versus 64 bits for a non-parity module—and usually include that in the model number. For example, the part number of one Crucial 512 MB non-parity module is CT6464Z40B. The part number of the similar ECC module is CT6472Z40B. If the number "72" appears anywhere in a module number, chances are very high that it is an ECC module.

We recommend using ECC memory modules only in the following situations:

- If the currently installed memory modules are ECC, install identical or closely similar modules.

- If you are installing a large amount of memory (2 GB or more), use ECC modules.

Otherwise, save your money and install non-parity modules.

Unbuffered versus registered modules

Unbuffered memory modules allow the memory controller to interact directly with the memory chips on the module. *Registered memory* (also called *buffered memory*) modules place an additional layer of circuitry between the memory controller and the memory chips.

Registered memory is necessary in some environments, because all memory controllers have limitations on how many devices (individual memory chips) they can control, which in turn limits the maximum capacity of the memory modules they can use. When a memory controller interacts with an unbuffered memory module, it controls every memory chip directly. When a memory controller interacts with a registered memory module, it works only with the buffer circuitry; the actual memory chips are invisible to it.

The sole advantage of registered memory is that it permits a system to use higher-capacity memory modules. (The highest capacity modules at any given time are often available only in registered form.) The disadvantages of registered memory are that it is considerably more expensive than unbuffered memory and noticeably slower because of the additional overhead incurred from using a buffer.

Most desktop systems support only unbuffered memory modules. A few can use either registered or unbuffered memory modules. A very few desktop systems—notably, Socket 940 AMD models—require registered memory. If you are upgrading the memory in your system, we recommend that you use registered memory modules only in the following situations:

- The system accepts only registered memory modules.

- The system accepts unbuffered or registered memory modules, but registered modules are already installed.

- The amount of memory you want to install requires using modules that are available only in registered form.

EITHER/OR

Most systems that support unbuffered and registered modules can use only one or the other at a time.

When Fast Isn't Good

Using too much fast memory can cause subtle memory problems. Motherboard and memory manufacturers do not publicize this problem. As a rule of thumb when installing fast memory, use fewer high-capacity modules in preference to more lower-capacity modules. This problem is particularly likely to arise when you "push the envelope"; for example, by installing the fastest memory supported, overclocking your system, or running dual processors.

Motherboard compatibility issues

Motherboards differ in the specific memory configurations they support. It seems reasonable to assume that if a motherboard has unused memory slots, you should be able to upgrade the memory simply by installing any supported memory modules in those empty slots. Unfortunately, that's not always true. Several factors come into play, including the speed, capacity, density, and organization of the memory modules:

Memory speed
    Installing fast memory may reduce the number of DIMMs you can install. For example, a motherboard may have three DIMM slots, all of which can be populated with PC2700 DIMMs. But that motherboard may support at most two PC3200 DIMMs, forcing you to leave the third DIMM slot empty if you install PC3200 memory.

Module capacity
    Not all motherboards support all DIMM capacities. For example, some motherboards may support 256 MB DIMMs, but not 512 MB DIMMs. The allowable mix may also differ. For example, one motherboard may

support 512 MB DIMMs in all four of its memory slots. Another may support 512 MB DIMMs in only two of its four slots, and require that you leave the other two slots vacant or install 256 MB or smaller DIMMs in those slots. Still another may support a maximum of 1 GB of RAM using 512 MB DIMMs, requiring you to leave two of its four memory slots vacant if you install 512 MB DIMMs in the first two slots.

Row limits

Many motherboards limit the number of rows of memory that can be installed to some number smaller than the possible number of rows if all memory slots are populated. Single-sided DIMMs count as one row, and double-sided DIMMs as two rows. If a motherboard has four memory slots and limits installed memory to five rows, for example, that means you could install single-sided DIMMs in all four memory slots (for a total of four rows). Installing two double-sided DIMMs occupies four rows, leaving only one row available. You could install at most one more single-sided DIMM in that system, for a total of five rows.

Memory density and organization

The memory chips used to build memory modules are made in different densities. Current modules use 256 megabit (Mb), 512 Mb, or 1 Gb chips. Older modules use 64 Mb or 128 Mb chips. Non-parity modules use 4, 8, or 16 chips, and ECC modules 5, 9, 10, or 18 chips. For example, a 512 MB non-parity memory module (8 bits per byte) could be made using four 1 Gb chips, eight 512 Mb chips, or sixteen 256 Mb chips. Similarly, a 512 MB ECC memory module (9 bits per byte) could be made using four 1 Gb chips and one 512 Mb chip, nine 512 Mb chips, eight 512 Mb chips and two 256 Mb chips, or eighteen 256 Mb chips.

The chipset memory controller used by an older motherboard may not recognize higher chip densities. For example, the memory controller in a particular motherboard may recognize chip densities of 64, 128, 256, and 512 Mb, but not 1 Gb. If you want to install a 512 MB memory module in that motherboard, you could use a module with eight 512 Mb chips (512X8) or sixteen 256 Mb chips (256X16), but not a module with four 1 Gb chips (1024X4).

Similarly, the memory controller used by a newer motherboard may not recognize low chip densities, which means that older, smaller capacity DIMMs may not work in it. For example, a recent motherboard may recognize only 256 Mb, 512 Mb, and 1 Gb memory chips. If you install an old 128 MB DIMM that uses eight 128 Mb chips in that motherboard, it will not be recognized.

Memory controllers also differ in the types of organization they support. Some controllers support X4, X8, and X16 modules, but many support only one or two of those organizations. For example, the Intel 945P chipset supports only X8 organization. If you install a 512X8

Half What You Paid For

The usual symptom of a chip density problem is that the system recognizes a memory module at some fraction of its nominal size, typically a quarter or a half. For example, if you install a 1 GB DIMM and the system reports it as 512 MB or 256 MB, the problem is almost certainly that the memory controller doesn't support the higher density of the chips on the new memory module. You may be able to get around the problem by substituting a module of the same capacity but a different organization; for example, by substituting a 512X16 module for the 1024X8 module.

512 MB module (eight 512 Mb chips), the motherboard recognizes and uses the full 512 MB capacity. Other 512 MB organizations (1024X4 and 256X8) are not supported. The results of installing a module that uses an unsupported organization are unpredictable. The motherboard may recognize the module at some fraction of its nominal capacity, or it may simply not recognize the module.

GET IT RIGHT THE FIRST TIME

The easiest ways to avoid motherboard compatibility issues are to verify the compatibility of specific memory modules by brand and model on the motherboard web site or to use the memory configurators provided by Crucial (*http://www.crucial.com*) or Kingston (*http://www.kingston.com*). We use the latter method, because the web pages for older motherboards are often not updated to reflect the discontinuation of older memory modules and the introduction of newer memory modules.

Choosing Memory

When you buy memory to upgrade a system, consider the following issues:

Brand matters.

Brand name is important for memory. In our 20+ years of working on PCs, we recall only one high-quality name-brand module that failed other than from lightning damage or other abuse. Conversely, generic memory fails quite frequently. We recall one batch of 20 cheap DIMMs ordered by a client in which fully half of them were dead on arrival and the others failed within a few months. For general-purpose memory, we exclusively use and recommend memory modules from Crucial Technology (*http://www.crucial.com*) and Kingston Technologies (*http://www.kingston.com*).

CHEAP AT HALF THE PRICE

Some companies—including Corsair, KingMax, Mushkin, OCZ, Patriot, and Viking —sell high-performance memory for gamers, overclockers, and other enthusiasts. Crucial also competes in the high-performance segment with its Ballistix modules and Kingston with its HyperX modules. Unless you are trying to eke out the last percent or two of potential system performance, it's seldom worth paying the higher price for these premium modules.

Consider cost per megabyte.

It's generally less expensive to buy mid-capacity modules rather than the equivalent amount of memory in large- or small-capacity modules. For example, if you need 1 GB, two 512 MB DIMMs will probably cost less than four 256 MB DIMMs. Conversely, one 1 GB DIMM may cost

50% more than two 512 MB DIMMs, and a 2 GB DIMM may cost twice as much as four 512 MB DIMMs.

Old memory is a sunk cost.

It's tempting to leave the old memory installed when you are upgrading a system, but it's often a mistake. For example, if you have purchased two 256 MB PC3200 DIMMs for a system that currently has two 64 MB PC1600 SDRAM DIMMs installed, you may be tempted to leave the old DIMMs in place, for a total of 640 MB rather than only 512 MB. After all, you paid good money for those 64 MB DIMMs. The problem is, leaving the old DIMMs installed will cause your new PC3200 DIMMs to run as PC1600 memory, crippling system performance. In general, the best course is to remove old memory rather than retain it.

Decide based on total costs.

Older types of memory may be very expensive per megabyte. For the same cost as adding more old-style memory, you may be able to purchase a new motherboard, processor, and the same amount of newer-style memory. In that case, opt for the wholesale upgrade, which effectively gives you an entirely new system.

Installing Memory

Installing memory modules is straightforward. Most recent motherboards automatically detect installed memory modules regardless of the slot they occupy, but it is good practice to install modules in the lowest numbered slots first. For example, if a single-channel memory motherboard has four memory slots, they will be numbered 0 to 3 (or 1 to 4). Fill slot 0 (or 1) first, then the other slots sequentially as you add modules. If you are installing memory in a dual-channel memory motherboard, install memory modules in pairs, filling the lowest numbered slots first. For example, if the motherboard has two slots each for channel A and channel B, numbered 0 and 1, fill the slots for channel A slot 0 and channel B slot 0 first.

Some motherboards require higher-capacity modules to be installed in lower-numbered slots. For example, if you are installing two 256 MB DIMMs in a dual-channel motherboard that has four DIMM sockets, with 128 MB DIMMs already installed in the 0 slots for channel A and channel B, you may have to move those 128 MB DIMMs to the 1 slots for channel A and channel B and install the new 256 MB DIMMs in the 0 slots for both channels.

That rule is not invariable, though. A few motherboards require smaller modules to be installed in the lower banks. Some motherboards don't care which module you install in which bank. Best practice is to check the manual before installing memory. If no documentation is available, experiment by moving modules around. If some or all of the memory is not recognized during the boot-time memory check or in CMOS Setup, power down the system, rearrange the modules, and restart the system. If all memory is recognized, you can safely assume that you have the modules installed correctly.

Installing and removing a DIMM

To install a DIMM, locate a free memory slot and pivot the ejector arms on each side of the socket as far as possible toward the horizontal. The contact edge of the DIMM module is keyed with notches that correspond to protuberances in the DIMM socket. Align the notches and slide the DIMM straight down into the socket. Position your thumbs on top of the DIMM at each end and press down firmly, as shown in Figure 6-5.

Figure 6-5. Align the memory module and press straight down until it seats

---

DON'T CRACK UP

Some motherboards—particularly cheap ones—are thin and very flexible. The pressure required to seat a DIMM may flex the motherboard enough to crack it. When you install a DIMM in a motherboard that's already in the case, pay close attention to how much pressure you're applying. If the motherboard appears to be flexing too much, remove the motherboard from the case before installing the DIMM. Yes, that takes a lot more time, but it's better than destroying the motherboard.

The DIMM slides (sometimes snaps) into the socket, which automatically pivots the ejector arms toward the vertical. If the ejector arms are not fully vertical, press them toward the DIMM until they lock into the vertical position, as shown in Figure 6-6. Note that some DIMM sockets have minor physical variations. If the DIMM does not fit easily into the socket, do not force it. Contact the vendor who supplied the DIMM for a replacement.

Figure 6-6. When the memory module is fully seated, the ejector arms pivot back to the vertical

To remove a DIMM, pivot both ejector arms simultaneously toward the horizontal position. The DIMM simply pops out.

DON'T FORGET THE CRIMM

If you are installing Rambus RIMMs, also install a Continuity RIMM (CRIMM) in each unused memory slot. Rambus systems malfunction unless all memory slots are occupied, either by a RIMM or a CRIMM. Most Rambus motherboards have enough CRIMMs bundled with the motherboard to populate all but one memory slot. If you run short of CRIMMs, you can buy them online.

Testing and configuring newly installed memory

After you install the new memory modules and verify that all is as it should be, apply power to the system. The memory self-test should increment up to the newly installed amount of memory. (If your system displays a logo splash screen rather than the BIOS boot screen, turn off the splash screen in BIOS Setup so that you can see the BIOS boot screen.) If it instead shows only the original amount of memory, the cause is almost always that you have not seated the new memory module completely. Power down, reseat the module, and try again.

If the memory check shows an amount of memory larger than the original amount but smaller than the expected new amount, the problem is almost always that the BIOS and/or chipset do not support memory modules of the size you've installed. If that occurs, you may need to do one or more of the following things to resolve the problem:

- Check the Chipset Setup portion of CMOS Setup to determine how memory is configured for the newly installed bank(s). Most recent chipsets and BIOSs automatically determine the correct size and configuration parameters for installed modules. But some chipsets, BIOSs, and memory modules do not implement SPD correctly. If this occurs, you may have to set the correct size manually, if indeed the module size you have installed is an available option.

- A limitation on maximum module size may be enforced by the chipset, the BIOS, or both. Before deciding you cannot use the larger module, check the motherboard manufacturer's web site for a BIOS update. If the restriction on module size is enforced by the BIOS but not by the chipset, you may find that a later BIOS revision adds support for the larger module.

- If all else fails, the only alternative may be to return the memory module (you did make sure you had the right to return an incompatible module, didn't you?) and obtain a compatible module.

When Bad Memory Turns Good

As odd as it sounds, faulty memory is seldom the cause of memory problems. When you experience memory errors, the most likely cause is a marginal, failing, or overloaded power supply. The next most likely cause is system overheating. In particular, if the system works normally when first turned on but develops problems after it's been running for a while, power supply or heat problems are the most likely cause. Only after you have eliminated these possibilities should you consider the possibility that the memory itself is defective.

Troubleshooting Memory Installation and Operation

As electronic devices with no moving parts, memory modules seldom malfunction—if they are installed properly. When problems do occur, they may be as obvious as a failed RAM check at boot or as subtle as a few corrupted bits in a datafile. The usual symptom of memory problems is that Windows displays the Blue Screen of Death. Sadly, there are so many other possible causes of a BSOD that it's of little use as a diagnostic aid.

As a first step in diagnosing memory problems, run Memtest86 (*http://www.memtest86.com*). Memtest86 is available as executables for DOS, Windows, and Linux, but the most useful form is the bootable ISO image, which can load even on a system with memory problems so severe that Windows or Linux cannot load and run. If you have a Knoppix disk handy, insert that, power up the system, type `memtest` at the boot prompt, and press Enter. However you get it running, configure Memtest86 to do deep testing and multiple loops. Let it run overnight, and log the results to disk.

When you examine the log, note the addresses where errors occurred. If errors occur reproducibly at the same address or nearby addresses, it's likely that the memory module is defective. If the errors occur at seemingly random addresses, it's more likely that the problem is the power supply or a system temperature that's too high. One possibility, of course, is that the system temperature spikes only when you're gaming or doing graphics work (running the CPU and video card flat out). This effect can make temperature-related component problems difficult to isolate.

If the errors are random, take steps to eliminate the power or heat problem. If the errors occur at reproducible addresses, it's time to start pulling DIMMs. When troubleshooting memory problems, always:

- Use standard antistatic precautions. Ground yourself by touching the case frame or power supply before you touch a memory module.

- Remove and reinstall all memory modules to ensure they are seated properly. While you're doing that, it's a good idea to clean the contacts on the memory module. Some people gently rub the contacts with a pencil eraser. We've done that ourselves, but memory manufacturers recommend against it because of possible damage to the contacts. Also, there is always the risk of a fragment from the eraser finding its way into the memory slot, where it can block one or more contacts. Better practice is to use a fresh dollar bill, which has just the right amount of abrasiveness to clean the contacts without damaging them, as shown in Figure 6-7.

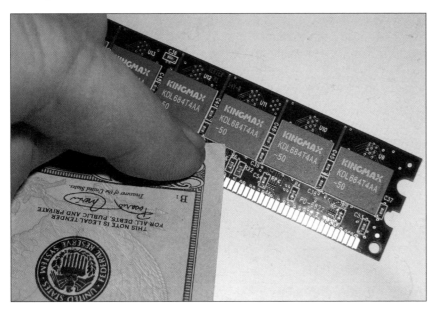

Figure 6-7. Use a new dollar bill to polish the DIMM contacts

The next steps you should take depend on whether you have made any changes to memory recently.

When you have not added memory

If you suspect memory problems but have not added or reconfigured memory (or been inside the case), it's unlikely that the memory itself is causing the problem. Memory does simply die sometimes, and may be killed by electrical surges, but this is uncommon, because the PC power supply itself does a good job of isolating memory and other system components from electrical damage. The most likely problem is a failing power supply. Try one or both of the following:

- If you have another system, install the suspect memory in it. If it runs there, the problem is almost certainly not the memory, but either an inadequate power supply or high temperatures inside the case.

- If you have other memory, install it in the problem system. If it works, you can safely assume that the original memory is defective. More likely is that it will also fail, which strongly indicates power supply or heat problems.

If you have neither another system nor additional memory, and if your system has more than one memory module installed, use binary elimination to determine which module is bad. For example, if you have two modules installed, simply remove one module to see if that cures the problem. If you have four identical modules installed, designate them A, B, C, and D. Install only A and B, restart the system, and run the memory tests again. If no problems occur, A and B are known good and the problem must lie with C and/or D. Remove B and substitute C. If no problems occur, you know that D is bad. If the system fails with A and C, you know that C is bad, but you don't know whether D is bad. Substitute D for C and restart the system to determine if D is good.

WINDOWS XP IS UNFORGIVING

Windows 95, 98, 98SE, and ME do not stress memory. If you upgrade to Windows XP or Linux, memory errors may appear on a PC that seemed stable. People often assume that they did something while installing the new OS to cause the errors, but that is seldom true. Such errors almost always indicate a real problem—a marginal power supply, overheating, or defective memory. The problem was there all along, but Windows 9X simply ignored it.

When adding memory

If you experience problems when adding memory, note the following:

- If a DIMM appears not to fit, there's good reason. DIMMs are available in many different and mutually incompatible types. Every DIMM has one or more keying notches whose placement corresponds to protrusions in the memory slot. If the keying notches in the DIMM match the slot protrusions, the DIMM is compatible with that slot and can be seated. If the DIMM keying notches don't match the socket protrusions, the DIMM is the wrong type and is prevented physically from seating in that slot.

- Make sure that the DIMM seats fully in the memory slot and that the retaining arms snap into place to secure the DIMM. A partially seated DIMM may appear to be fully seated, and may even appear to work. Sooner or later (probably sooner), problems will develop with that module.

- Verify that the modules are installed in the proper slots to match one of the supported memory configurations listed in your motherboard manual.

- If the system displays a memory mismatch error the first time you restart, that usually indicates no real problem. Follow the prompts to enter Setup, select Save and Exit, and restart the system. The system should then recognize the new memory. Some systems require these extra steps to update CMOS.

- If the system recognizes a newly installed module as half actual size and that module has chips on both sides, the system may recognize only single-banked or single-sided modules. Some systems limit the total number of "sides" that are recognized, so if you have some existing smaller modules installed, try removing them. The system may then recognize the double-side modules. If not, return those modules and replace them with single-side modules.

Hard Disk Drives

7

Replacing the original hard disk or adding a hard disk is one of the most common upgrades. It's easy to do and a very cost-effective way to extend the life of a PC. This chapter explains what you need to know to choose, install, and configure hard disks and interfaces.

Hard Disk Drive Interfaces

The hard disk interface defines the physical and logical means by which the hard disk connects to the PC. A modern PC uses one or both of the following hard disk interfaces:

AT Attachment (ATA)

> *AT Attachment (ATA)*, pronounced as individual letters, was by far the most common hard disk interface used in PCs from the early 1990s through 2003. ATA is sometimes called *Parallel ATA* or *PATA*, to differentiate it from the newer *Serial ATA (SATA)* interface. ATA is still used in new systems, although it is being superseded by SATA. ATA is also often called *IDE (Integrated Drive Electronics)*. Figure 7-1 shows two standard ATA interfaces, located at their usual position on the front edge of a motherboard. Note that each interface connector is keyed with a missing pin in the top row and a notch in the connector shroud at the bottom.

Figure 7-1. Standard ATA interfaces

Small Computer System Interface (SCSI)

The *Small Computer System Interface* (*SCSI*) is usually pronounced *scuzzy*, but sometimes *sexy*. SCSI is used in servers and high-end workstations, where it provides two advantages: improved performance relative to ATA and SATA in multitasking, multiuser environments, and the ability to daisy-chain many drives on one interface. Although we formerly recommended SCSI for high-performance desktop systems, the very high cost of SCSI drives and host controllers and the narrowing performance gap between SCSI and SATA has led us to withdraw that recommendation.

ATA VERSUS ATAPI

Technically, only hard drives are ATA devices. Optical drives, tape drives, and similar devices that connect to ATA interfaces use a modified version of the ATA protocols called *ATAPI* (*ATA Packet Interface*). In practical terms, it makes little difference, as you can connect either an ATA hard drive, an ATAPI device, or both at the same time to any ATA interface.

Serial ATA (SATA)

Serial ATA (*SATA*) is a newer technology that is replacing ATA. SATA has several advantages over ATA, including smaller cables and connectors, higher bandwidth, and greater reliability. Although SATA and ATA are incompatible at the physical and electrical levels, adapters are readily available that allow SATA drives to be connected to ATA interfaces and vice versa. SATA is generally compatible with ATA at the software level, which means that the operating system ATA drivers work with either SATA or ATA interfaces and hard drives. Figure 7-2 shows two SATA interfaces, above and below the 32.768 kHz clock crystal at center. Note that each interface connector is keyed with an L-shaped body, which prevents the SATA cable from being connected backward.

Figure 7-2. SATA interfaces

ATA

Before SATA interfaces and drives became common, ATA was used almost universally to connect hard drives. Even today, hundreds of millions of PCs have ATA hard drives. That number will inevitably decline as older systems are upgraded and replaced, but ATA will remain with us for years.

The original ATA specification defined a single interface that supported one or two ATA hard drives. By the early 1990s, nearly all systems had dual ATA interfaces, each of which supported up to two ATA hard drives or ATAPI devices. Ironically, we've come full circle. Many current motherboards provide several SATA interfaces, but only one ATA interface.

If a system has two ATA interfaces, one is defined as the *primary ATA interface* and the other as the *secondary ATA interface.* These two interfaces are identical functionally, but the system assigns a higher priority to the primary interface. Accordingly, the hard drive (a high-priority peripheral) is usually connected to the primary interface, with the secondary interface being used for optical drives and other lower-priority devices.

Assigning masters and slaves

Each ATA interface (often loosely called an *ATA channel*) can have zero, one, or two ATA and/or ATAPI devices connected to it. Every ATA and ATAPI device has an embedded controller, but ATA permits (and requires) only one active controller per interface. Therefore, if only one device is attached to an interface, that device must have its embedded controller enabled. If two devices are attached to an ATA interface, one device must have its controller enabled and the other must have its controller disabled.

In ATA terminology, a device whose controller is enabled is called a *master*; one whose controller is disabled is called a *slave* (ATA predates Political Correctness). In a PC with two ATA interfaces, a device may therefore be configured in any one of four ways: *primary master, primary slave, secondary master,* or *secondary slave.* ATA/ATAPI devices are assigned as master or slave by setting jumpers on the device, as shown in Figure 7-3.

Figure 7-3. Setting the master/slave jumper on an ATA drive

PIO Mode Versus DMA Mode

ATA defines two classes of transfer mode, called *PIO Mode (Programmed I/O Mode)* and *DMA Mode (Direct Memory Access Mode).* PIO mode transfers are much slower and require the processor to arbitrate transfers between the device and memory. DMA mode transfers are much faster and occur without processor intervention. If either device on an ATA channel uses a PIO mode, both devices must do so. That cripples throughput and puts a heavy load on the processor, bogging down the system whenever the drive is accessed.

All modern ATA and ATAPI devices support DMA mode, but for backward compatibility, most can be set to use PIO mode. Using PIO mode is a mistake. When you upgrade a system, if you find any drives that support only PIO mode, replace them. Only very old hard drives and optical drives are limited to PIO mode anyway, so replacing them is a no-brainer.

ATA devices have some or all of the following jumper selections:

Master

Connecting a jumper in the master position enables the on-board controller. All ATA and ATAPI devices have this option. Select this jumper position if this is the only device connected to the interface, or if it is the first of two devices connected to the interface.

Slave

Connecting a jumper in the slave position disables the on-board controller. (One of our technical reviewers notes that he has taken advantage of this to retrieve data from a hard drive whose controller had failed, a very useful thing to keep in mind.) All ATA and ATAPI devices can be set as slave. Select this jumper position if this is the second device connected to an interface that already has a master device connected.

MASTERS ARE MASTERS, AND SLAVES ARE SLAVES

When you jumper a device master or slave, the device assumes that role regardless of which position it connects to on the ATA cable. For example, if you jumper a device as master, it functions as master regardless of whether it is attached to the drive connector at the end of the ATA cable or the drive connector in the middle of the ATA cable.

Cable Select

Most ATA/ATAPI devices have a third jumper position labeled *Cable Select*, *CS*, or *CSEL*. Connecting a jumper in the CSEL position instructs the device to configure itself as master or slave based on its position on the ATA cable. If the CSEL jumper is connected, no other jumpers may be connected. For more information about CSEL, see the following section.

Sole/Only

When functioning as master, a few older ATA/ATAPI devices need to know whether they are the only device on the channel, or if a slave device is also connected. Such devices may have an additional jumper position labeled *Sole* or *Only*. For such a device, jumper it as master if it is the master device on the interface, slave if it is the slave device on the interface, and sole/only if it is the only device connected to the interface.

Slave Present

A few older drives have a jumper designated *Slave Present*, or *SP*. This jumper performs the inverse function of the sole/only jumper, by notifying a device jumpered as master that there is also a slave device on the channel. For such a device, jumper it as master if it is the only device on the interface, or slave if it is the second of two devices on the interface.

If it is the master on a channel that also has a slave installed, connect both the master and slave present jumpers.

Using Cable Select

Most ATA/ATAPI drives provide a Cable Select (CS or CSEL) jumper in addition to the standard master/slave jumpers. If you jumper a drive as master (or slave), that drive functions as master (or slave) regardless of which connector it is attached to on the ATA cable. If you jumper a drive as CSEL, the position of the drive on the cable determines whether the drive functions as a master or a slave.

CSEL was introduced as a means to simplify ATA configuration. The goal was that drives could simply be installed and removed without changing jumpers, with no possibility of conflict due to improper jumper settings. Although CSEL has been around for many years, only in the last few years has it become popular with system makers.

Using CSEL requires the following:

- If one drive is installed on the interface, that drive must support and be configured to use CSEL. If two drives are installed, both must support and be configured to use CSEL

- The ATA interface must support CSEL. Very old ATA interfaces do not support CSEL, and treat any drive configured as CSEL as a slave.

- The ATA cable must be a special CSEL cable. Unfortunately, there are three types of CSEL cable:

  - A 40-wire CSEL cable differs from a standard 40-wire ATA cable in that pin 28 is connected only between the ATA interface and the first drive position on the cable (the middle connector). Pin 28 is not connected between the interface and the second drive position (the end connector on the cable). With such a cable, the drive attached to the middle connector (with pin 28 connected) is master; the drive attached to the connector furthest from the interface (with pin 28 not connected) is slave.

  - All 80-wire (Ultra DMA) ATA cables support CSEL, but with exactly the opposite orientation of the 40-wire standard CSEL cable just described. With such a cable, the drive attached to the middle connector (with pin 28 not connected) is slave; the drive attached to the connector furthest from the interface (with pin 28 connected) is master. This is actually a better arrangement, if a bit non-intuitive—how can a wire be connected to the end connector but not to the one in the middle?—because the standard 40-wire CSEL cable puts the master drive on the middle connector. If only one drive is installed on that cable, that leaves a long "stub" of cable hanging free with nothing connected to it. Electrically, that's a very poor idea, because an unterminated cable allows standing waves to form, increasing noise on the line and impairing data integrity.

- A 40-wire CSEL Y-cable puts the interface connector in the middle with a drive connector on each end, one labeled master and one slave. Although this is a good idea in theory, in practice it seldom works. The problem is that ATA cable length limits still apply, which means that the drive connectors don't have enough cable to get to the drives in all but the smallest cases. If you have a tower, you can forget it.

40-wire CSEL cables are supposed to be clearly labeled, but we have found that this is often not the case. It is not possible to identify such cables visually, although you can verify the type using a digital voltmeter or continuity tester between the two end connectors on pin 28. If there is continuity, you have a standard ATA cable. If not, you have a CSEL cable.

A SHEEP IN WOLF'S CLOTHING

Keep unlabeled 40-wire CSEL cables segregated from standard cables. If you substitute a CSEL cable for a standard cable, drives that are jumpered as master or slave function properly. If you substitute a standard cable for a CSEL cable and connect one drive jumpered as CSEL to that cable, it will function properly as master. But if you connect two CSEL drives to a standard cable, both function as master, which may result in anything from subtle problems to (more likely) the system being unable to access either drive. The best rule is simply never to use a 40-wire cable to connect a hard drive.

Master/slave guidelines

When deciding how to allocate devices between two interfaces and choose master or slave status for each, use the following guidelines:

- Always assign the main hard drive as primary master. Do not connect another device to the primary ATA interface unless both positions on the secondary interface are occupied.

- ATA forbids simultaneous I/O on an interface, which means that only one device can be active at a time. If one device is reading or writing, the other device cannot read or write until the active device yields the channel. The implication of this rule is that if you have two devices that need to perform simultaneous I/O—for example, a DVD writer that you use to duplicate DVDs from a DVD-ROM drive—you should place those two devices on separate interfaces.

- If you are connecting an ATA device (a hard drive) and an ATAPI device (for example, an optical drive) to the same interface, set the hard drive as master and the ATAPI device as slave.

- If you are connecting two similar devices (ATA or ATAPI) to an interface, it generally doesn't matter which device is master and which slave. There are exceptions to this guideline, however, particularly with ATAPI devices, some of which really want to be master (or slave) depending on which other ATAPI device is connected to the channel.

- If you are connecting an older device and a newer device to the same ATA interface, it's generally better to configure the newer device as master, because it is likely to have a more capable controller than the older device.

- Avoid sharing one interface between a DMA-capable device and a PIO-only device. If both devices on an interface are DMA-capable, both use DMA. If only one device is DMA-capable, both devices are forced to use PIO, which reduces performance and increases CPU utilization dramatically. Similarly, if both devices are DMA-capable, but at different levels, the more capable device is forced to use the slower DMA mode. Replace any PIO-only devices if possible.

ATA cables

All desktop ATA cables have three 40-pin connectors: one that connects to the ATA interface and two that connect to ATA/ATAPI drives. ATA cables come in three varieties:

Standard

A standard ATA cable uses a 40-wire ribbon cable and 40-pin connectors in all three positions. All 40 conductors connect to all three connectors. The only real variation, other than cable quality, is the positioning of the three connectors. The two device connectors on a standard ATA cable are located nearer one end of the cable. Either drive may be connected to either drive connector. A standard ATA cable may be used with any ATA/ATAPI device through UltraATA-33 (UDMA Mode 2). If a standard ATA cable is used to connect an UltraATA-66 (UDMA Mode 4) or faster device, that device functions properly, but falls back to operating in UDMA Mode 2 (33 MB/s). A standard ATA cable requires setting master/slave jumpers for connected devices.

Standard/CSEL

A standard/CSEL ATA cable is identical to a standard ATA cable except that pin 28 is not connected between the middle drive connector and the end drive connector. A standard/CSEL ATA cable supports either master/slave jumpering or CSEL jumpering for connected devices. Connector position is significant on a standard/CSEL cable. The interface connector on a CSEL cable is either labeled or is a different color than the drive connectors. The center connector is for the master device, and the end connector opposite the interface connector is for the slave device.

UltraDMA (80-wire)

An *UltraDMA (UDMA)* cable uses an 80-wire ribbon cable and 40-pin connectors in all three positions. The additional 40 wires are dedicated ground wires, each assigned to one of the standard 40 ATA pins. A UDMA cable may be used with any ATA/ATAPI device—and should be for more reliable functioning—but is required for best performance with UltraATA-66, -100, and -133 devices (UDMA Modes 4, 5, and 6, respectively). All UDMA cables are CSEL cables, and may be used in either cable select mode or master/slave mode. Color-coded connectors were not specified for earlier ATA cables. The Ultra DMA cable specification requires the following connector colors:

Blue

One end connector is blue, which indicates that it attaches to the motherboard ATA interface.

Black

The opposite end connector is black, and is used to attach the master drive (Device 0), or a single drive if only one is attached to the cable. If CSEL is used, the black connector configures the drive as master. If standard master/slave jumpering is used, the master drive must still be attached to the black connector, because ATA-66, ATA-100, and ATA-133 do not allow a single drive to be connected to the middle connector, which results in standing waves that interfere with data communication.

Gray

The middle connector is gray, and is used to attach the slave drive (Device 1), if present.

ALL CSEL CABLES ARE NOT THE SAME

Note the difference between using a 40-wire CSEL cable and an 80-wire cable for CSEL operation. Although all Ultra DMA cables support drives jumpered as either master/slave or CSEL, that does not mean you can freely substitute an 80-wire cable for a 40-wire cable. If the drives are jumpered as master/slave, substituting an 80-wire cable works fine. However, if the drives are jumpered as CSEL, replacing a 40-wire CSEL cable with an 80-wire cable causes the drives to exchange settings. That is, the drive that was master on the 40-wire cable becomes slave on the 80-wire cable, and vice versa.

Because an UltraDMA cable is required for UltraATA-66 or faster operation, the system must have a way to detect if such a cable is installed. This is done by grounding pin 34 in the blue connector, which attaches to the interface. Because 40-wire ATA cables do not ground pin 34, the system can detect at boot whether a 40-wire or 80-wire cable is installed. Figure 7-4 shows an 80-wire UltraDMA cable (top) and a 40-wire standard ATA cable for comparison.

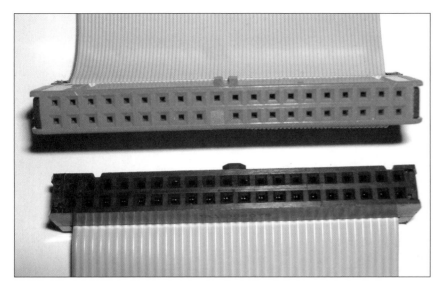

Figure 7-4. UltraDMA 80-wire ATA cable (top) and standard 40-wire ATA cable

Serial ATA

Serial ATA (also known as *SATA* or *S-ATA*) is the successor to the older ATA/ATAPI standards. SATA is intended primarily as a hard drive interface, but may also be used for optical drives, tape drives, and similar devices.

SATA drives and interfaces were originally expected to ship in volume in late 2001, but various issues delayed deployment for more than a year. By late 2002, SATA motherboards and drives were in limited distribution, but it was not until mid-2003 that SATA drives and motherboards with native SATA support became widely available. Despite the slow start, SATA has taken off like gangbusters. Faster, second-generation SATA drives and interfaces began shipping in early 2005.

There are two versions of SATA currently available:

SATA/150

SATA/150 (also called *SATA150*) defines the first generation of SATA interfaces and devices. SATA/150 operates at a raw data rate of 1.5 GB/s, but overhead reduces the effective data rate to 1.2 GB/s, or 150 MB/s. Although this data rate is only slightly higher than the 133 MB/s rate of UltraATA/133, the full SATA bandwidth is available to each connected device rather than being shared between two devices, as is true of PATA.

SATA/300

SATA/300 or *SATA300* (often mistakenly called *SATA II*) defines second-generation SATA interfaces and devices. SATA/300 operates at a raw data rate of 3.0 GB/s, but overhead reduces the effective data rate to 2.4 GB/s, or 300 MB/s. Motherboards based on the NVIDIA

Compatibility Between Old and New IDE Devices

With minor exceptions, there are no outright compatibility conflicts between new ATA devices and old ATA interfaces or vice versa. Newer drives cannot yield their highest performance when connected to an old ATA interface, just as a new interface can't improve the performance of an older drive. But you can connect any ATA or ATAPI drive to any ATA interface with assurance that it will function, albeit perhaps not optimally.

That said, you should not use elderly PIO devices on the same interface as a DMA device. Both devices will function, but the throughput of the DMA device will be crippled. If you're upgrading a system that has a PIO mode device installed, if possible reconfigure it for DMA. Otherwise, replace it with a DMA-capable device.

Also note that an interface supports only one DMA or UltraDMA (UDMA) mode at a time. For example, if you connect a UDMA Mode 4 (66.6 MB/s) Plextor PX-716A DVD writer and a UDMA Mode 6 (133 MB/s) Maxtor hard drive to the same ATA interface, the hard drive operates in UDMA Mode 4 at 66 MB/s, which may hamper hard drive throughput. Similarly, if you install a Plextor PX-740A DVD writer, which supports UDMA Mode 2 (33 MB/s) as its fastest mode, hard drive throughput is crippled at only 33 MB/s.

The 128/137 GB Limit

Older ATA interfaces use 28-bit *Logical Block Addressing* (*LBA*), which limits those interfaces to addressing 2^{28} or 268,435,456 sectors on a hard drive. Because hard drives use 512-byte sectors, that translates to a maximum supported drive size of 137,438,953,472 bytes, or 128 GB. (Drive makers use decimal GB rather than binary GB, and so refer to this limit as 137 GB rather than the 128 GB reported by the BIOS and operating system.) This is a hardware limit, imposed by the interface itself. Current ATA interfaces use 48-bit LBA, which expands the maximum supported drive size by a factor of more than one million, to 128 PB (*petabytes*, where a petabyte is 1,024 terabytes).

If you install a hard drive larger than 128 GB on an older ATA interface, it works properly, but disk space beyond 128 GB is inaccessible. If you really need to support larger drives on what is, after all, an elderly system, one alternative is to install an expansion card that provides one or more 48-bit LBA interfaces for P-ATA hard drives. Better yet, install an SATA adapter card and use SATA hard drives. (All SATA interfaces support 48-bit LBA.) In either case, disable the primary motherboard ATA interface to conserve resources, and run your optical drive and any other ATAPI devices on the secondary motherboard interface.

nForce4 chipset began shipping in early 2005, and were the first SATA/300-compliant devices available. SATA/300 hard drives began shipping in mid-2005. SATA/300 interfaces and drives use the same physical connectors as SATA/150 components, and are backward-compatible with SATA/150 interfaces and drives (although at the lower SATA/150 data rate).

Serial ATA features

SATA has the following important features:

Reduced voltage
> PATA uses a relatively high signaling voltage, which in conjunction with high pin densities make 133 MB/s the highest realistically achievable data rate for PATA. SATA uses a much lower signaling voltage, which reduces interference and crosstalk between conductors.

Simplified cabling and connectors
> SATA replaces the 40-pin/80-wire PATA ribbon cable with a 7-wire cable. In addition to reducing costs and increasing reliability, the smaller SATA cable eases cable routing and improves air flow and cooling. An SATA cable may be as long as 1 meter (39+ inches), versus the 0.45 meter (18") limitation of PATA. This increased length contributes to improved ease of use and flexibility when installing drives, particularly in tower systems.

Differential signaling
> In addition to three ground wires, the 7-wire SATA cable uses a differential transmit pair (TX+ and TX–) and a differential receive pair (RX+ and RX–). Differential signaling, long used for SCSI-based server storage, increases signal integrity, supports faster data rates, and allows the use of longer cables.

Improved data robustness
> In addition to using differential signaling, SATA incorporates superior error detection and correction, which ensures the end-to-end integrity of command and data transfers at speeds greatly exceeding those possible with PATA.

Operating system compatibility
> SATA appears identical to PATA from the viewpoint of the operating system. Thus current operating systems can recognize and use SATA interfaces and devices using existing drivers. (However, if your system uses a chipset or BIOS that does not have native SATA support, or if you are using an operating system distribution disc that predates SATA, you may have to insert a floppy disk with SATA drivers during installation for SATA drives to be recognized.)

External SATA

External SATA (*eSATA*) is intended to replace USB 2.0 and FireWire (IEEE-1394) for connecting external hard drives. eSATA uses a modified SATA connector that is much more robust than the relatively fragile standard SATA connector and is rated for thousands of insertions and removals. eSATA extends the allowable cable length from 1 meter to 2 meters, allowing external hard drives and arrays to be placed conveniently. eSATA is available in 150 MB/s and 300 MB/s variants, both of which support *hot-plugging* (connecting or disconnecting the drive while the system is running).

eSATA provides much higher throughput than USB 2.0 or FireWire, because eSATA lacks the protocol overhead that slows USB 2.0 and FireWire to a fraction of their rated throughput. Performance of an external eSATA hard drive is identical to that of a similar SATA hard drive running internally.

Most current motherboards lack embedded eSATA interfaces, although some motherboards introduced after mid-2005 include such interfaces. If your system lacks an eSATA interface, it's easy enough to add one. eSATA host bus adapters for desktop systems are readily available to fit PCI or PCI Express expansion slots. You can add eSATA support to a notebook system by installing a Cardbus or ExpressCard eSATA card.

Note that some transitional external drive housings and host bus adapters have been sold that allow standard SATA drives to be connected externally using SATA protocols. These devices are not eSATA-compliant. Most use standard SATA connectors, although some substitute USB 2.0 or FireWire connectors and cables (even though the interface is actually SATA). Most do not support hot-plugging.

Francisco García Maceda notes, "I would also mention the cable/bracket combo that some companies (HighPoint and others) are selling so you can make one of your internal SATA ports into an external one. It is a simple cable with a regular SATA connector on one end and an eSATA connector on the other end attached to a regular case bracket; no electronics of any kind. Also, there are external drive enclosures available that allow you to install PATA drives in external eSATA cases; for example, the HighPoint RocketMate 1100. It can be used with the simple cable/bracket combo or with any eSATA card or motherboard."

Point-to-point topology

Unlike PATA, which permits connecting two devices to one interface, SATA dedicates an interface to each device. This helps performance in three ways:

- Each SATA device has a full 150 MB/s or 300 MB/s of bandwidth available to it. Although current PATA drives are not bandwidth-constrained when operating one per channel, installing two fast PATA drives on one channel throttles the throughput of both.

- PATA allows only one device to use the channel at a time, which means that a device may have to wait its turn before writing or reading data on a PATA channel. SATA devices can write or read at any time, without consideration for other devices.

- If two devices are installed on a PATA channel, that channel always operates at the speed of the slower device. For example, installing a UDMA-6 hard drive and a UDMA-2 optical drive on the same

Advice from Francisco García Maceda

I would also mention that most PATA drives have a jumper to limit capacity for the earlier 32 GB BIOS limit. This can save your bacon, because it is becoming increasingly difficult to get disks under 40 GB and if you have to rescue/clone an older drive this might be your only choice.

channel means the hard drive must operate at UDMA-2. SATA devices always communicate at the highest data rate supported by the device and interface.

Support for Native Command Queuing

PATA drives respond to read and write requests in the order they are received, regardless of the location of the data on the drive. This is analogous to an elevator that goes to each floor in the order in which the call buttons were pressed, ignoring people waiting on intermediate floors. Most (but not all) SATA drives support *Native Command Queuing* (*NCQ*), which allows the drive to accumulate read and write requests, sort them into the most efficient order, and then process those requests without consideration for the order in which they were received. This process, also called *elevator seeking*, allows the drive to service read and write requests while minimizing head movements, which results in better performance. NCQ is most important in environments, such as servers, where drives are constantly being accessed, but provides some performance benefits even in desktop systems.

Serial ATA connectors and cables

Relative to PATA, SATA uses thinner cables and smaller, unambiguously keyed connectors. The 7-pin *SATA Signal Connector* is used on both ends of an SATA data cable. Either connector can mate interchangeably with the data connector on the drive or the SATA interface on the motherboard. The 15-pin *SATA Power Connector* uses a similar physical connector, also with unambiguous keying. Figure 7-5 shows an SATA data cable on the left and, for comparison, a UDMA ATA cable on the right. Even allowing for the fact that an ATA cable supports two devices, it's clear that using SATA conserves motherboard real estate and greatly reduces cable clutter inside the case.

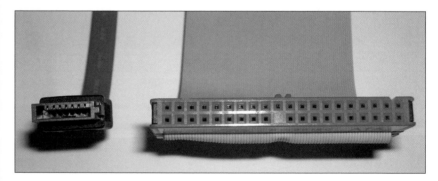

Figure 7-5. SATA data cable (left) and UltraDMA data cable

The SATA specification defines the allowable length of an SATA signal cable as up to 1 meter—more than twice as long as the longest allowable PATA cable. In addition to superior electrical characteristics and greater allowable length, one major advantage of SATA cabling is its smaller physical size, which contributes to neater cable runs and much improved air flow and cooling.

Configuring an SATA hard drive

There's not much to say about configuring an SATA hard drive. Unlike PATA, you needn't set jumpers for master or slave (although SATA does support master/slave emulation). Each SATA drive connects to a dedicated signal connector, and the signal and power cables are completely standard. Nor do you have to worry about configuring DMA, deciding which devices should share a channel, and so on. There are no concerns about capacity limits, because all SATA hard drives and interfaces support 48-bit LBA. The chipset, BIOS, operating system, and drivers on current systems all recognize an SATA hard drive as just another ATA drive, so there's no configuration needed. You simply connect the data cable to the drive and interface, connect the power cable to the drive, and start using the drive. (On older systems, you may have to install drivers manually, and SATA drives may be recognized as SCSI devices rather than ATA devices; this is normal behavior.)

ATA RAID

RAID (*Redundant Array of Inexpensive Disks/Drives*) is a means by which data is distributed over two or more physical hard drives to improve performance and increase data safety. A RAID can survive the loss of any one drive without losing data, because the redundancy of the array allows that data to be recovered or reconstructed from the remaining drives.

RAID was formerly very expensive to implement and therefore used only on servers and professional workstations. That's no longer true. Many recent systems and motherboards have RAID-capable ATA and/or SATA interfaces. The low price of ATA and SATA drives and the built-in RAID support mean that it's now practical to use RAID on ordinary PCs.

There are five defined levels of RAID, numbered RAID 1 through RAID 5, although only two of those levels are commonly used in PC environments. Some or all of the following RAID levels and other multiple-drive configurations are supported by many current motherboards:

JBOD

JBOD (*Just a Bunch Of Drives*), also called *Span mode* or *Spanning mode*, is a non-RAID operating mode that most RAID adapters support. With JBOD, two or more physical drives can be logically melded to appear to the operating system as one larger drive. Data is written to the first drive until it is full, then to the second drive until it is full, and so on. In the past, when drive capacities were smaller, JBOD arrays were used to create single volumes large enough to store huge databases. With 300 GB and larger drives now readily available, there is seldom a good reason to use JBOD. The downside of JBOD is that failure of any drive renders the entire array inaccessible. Because the likelihood of a drive failure is proportionate to the number of drives in the array, a JBOD is less reliable than one large drive. The performance of a JBOD is the same as that of the drives that make up the array.

RAID 0

RAID 0, also called *disk striping*, is not really RAID at all, because it provides no redundancy. With RAID 0, data is written interleaved to two or more physical drives. Because writes and reads are split across two or more drives, RAID 0 provides the fastest reads and writes of any RAID level, with both write and read performance noticeably faster than that provided by a single drive. The downside of RAID 0 is that the failure of any drive in the array causes the loss of all data stored on all drives in the array. That means data stored on a RAID 0 array is actually more at risk than data stored on a single drive. Although some dedicated gamers use RAID 0 in a search for the highest possible performance, we do not recommend using RAID 0 on a typical desktop system.

RAID 0 IS SENSELESS FOR DESKTOP SYSTEMS

RAID 0 actually provides very little performance benefit for a typical desktop PC. RAID 0 comes into its own when the disk subsystem is very heavily used, as with a server that supports many users. Few single-user systems access the disks heavily enough to benefit from RAID 0.

RAID 1

RAID 1, also called *disk mirroring*, duplicates all writes to two or more physical disk drives. Accordingly, RAID 1 offers the highest level of data redundancy at the expense of halving the amount of disk space visible to the operating system. The overhead required to write the same data to two drives means RAID 1 writes are typically a bit slower than writes to a single drive. Conversely, because the same data can be read from either drive, an intelligent RAID 1 adapter may improve read performance slightly relative to a single drive by queuing read requests for each drive separately, allowing it to read the data from whichever drive happens to have its heads nearest to the requested data. It is also possible for a RAID 1 array to use two physical host adapters to eliminate the disk adapter as a single point of failure. In such an arrangement, called *disk duplexing*, the array can continue operating after the failure of one drive, one host adapter, or both (if they are on the same channel).

RAID 5

RAID 5, also called *disk striping with parity*, requires at least three physical disk drives. Data is written block-wise to alternating drives, with parity blocks interleaved. For example, in a RAID 5 array that comprises three physical drives, the first 64 KB data block may be written to the first drive, the second data block to the second drive, and a parity block to the third drive. Subsequent data blocks and parity blocks are written to the three drives in such a way that data blocks and parity blocks are distributed equally across all three drives. Parity blocks are calculated such that if either of their two data blocks is lost, it may be reconstructed using the parity block and the remaining data block. A failure of any one drive in the RAID 5 array causes no data loss, because the lost data blocks can be reconstructed from the data and parity blocks on the remaining two drives. A RAID 5 provides somewhat better read performance than a single drive. RAID 5 write performance is typically a bit slower than that of a single drive, because of the overhead involved in segmenting the data and calculating parity blocks. Because most PCs and small servers do more reads than writes, RAID 5 is often the best compromise between performance and data redundancy.

A RAID 5 can comprise any arbitrary number of drives, but in practice it is best to limit the RAID 5 to three or four physical drives, because the performance of a degraded RAID 5 (one in which a drive has failed) varies inversely with the number of drives in the array. A three-drive RAID 5 with a failed drive, for example, is very slow but is probably usable until the array can be rebuilt. A degraded RAID 5 with six or eight drives is usually too slow to be usable at all.

RAID DOES NOT SUBSTITUTE FOR BACKUPS

Using RAID 1 or RAID 5 is an inexpensive way to protect yourself against data loss from a hard drive failure, but RAID is no substitute for backing up. RAID protects *only* against drive failure. To protect against accidental corruption or deletion of files or loss due to fire, flood, or theft, you still must back up your data.

If your motherboard doesn't have RAID support or if you need a RAID level not provided by the motherboard, you can install a third-party RAID adapter, such as those made by 3Ware (*http://www.3ware.com*), Adaptec (*http://www.adaptec.com*), Highpoint Technologies (*http://www.highpoint-tech.com*), Promise Technology (*http://www.promise.com*), and others. Verify operating system support before you purchase such a card, particularly if you are running Linux or an older version of Windows.

Choosing a Hard Disk Drive

The good news about choosing a hard disk is that it's easy to get a good one. The brand we generally use and recommend, Seagate Technology (*http://www.seagate.com*), is widely available at online and big-box stores, and is competitively priced. Based on our own experience, reports from our readers, and discussions with data recovery firms, we believe that Seagate drives are more reliable than other brands. Seagate drives are quiet, cool-running, and have longer warranties than most competing models. Their speed, if not always best in category, is typically midrange or better.

All of that said, the differences between brands are not huge, whether in reliability, speed, noise level, or some other aspect of hard drive performance. Hitachi (*http://www.hitachigst.com*), Maxtor (*http://www.maxtor.com*), Samsung (*http://www.samsung.com*), and Western Digital (*http://www.wdc.com*) all make good hard drives for desktop systems. You might, for example, choose a Western Digital Raptor drive if speed is the top priority and you are willing to pay more for a drive with lower capacity, higher noise and heat, and lower reliability. Conversely, if price and noise level are top priorities, you might choose a Samsung SpinPoint model.

Manufacturers often offer two or more lines of drives that vary in several respects, all of which affect performance and price. Within a given grade of drive, however, drives from different manufacturers are usually closely comparable in features, performance, and price, if not necessarily in reliability or noise level. Neither is compatibility an issue, as it occasionally was in the early days of ATA. Any recent PATA or SATA hard disk coexists peacefully with any other recent ATA/ATAPI device, regardless of manufacturer.

Use the following guidelines when you choose a hard disk:

Choose the correct interface.

Choose a PATA drive if you are repairing or upgrading an older system that lacks SATA interfaces. Choose an SATA drive if you are repairing or upgrading a system that has SATA interfaces. Many hard drives are available in your choice of PATA or SATA interface, often with nearly identical model numbers. The drives may differ in appearance, but often the only obvious differences may be the data and power connectors, shown in Figure 7-6. More significant differences between models may exist. For example, the SATA model may have a faster seek time, a larger buffer, and support for SATA-only features such as NCQ.

Buy the right capacity drive.

It's tempting to buy the largest capacity drive available, but that's not always the best decision. Very

Figure 7-6. Two Seagate hard drives, with PATA (top) and SATA interfaces

large drives often cost more per gigabyte than midsize drives, and the largest drives may have slower mechanisms than midsize drives. In general, decide what performance level you need and are willing to pay for, and then buy a drive that meets those performance requirements, choosing the model based on its cost per gigabyte. Conversely, if you need a massive amount of disk storage or are implementing RAID, it may make sense to buy the largest drives available despite their high cost per gigabyte and slower performance, simply to conserve drive bays and interface connections.

Get a model with large cache if it doesn't cost much more.

Disk drives use cache (or buffer) memory to increase performance. All other things being equal, the larger the cache, the faster the performance. Inexpensive drives typically have a 2 MB cache, mainstream models an 8 MB cache, and high-performance models a 16 MB cache. Some manufacturers sell the same model drive with differing amounts of cache, often indicated by a different letter on the end of the model number. In our experience, larger caches have a relatively small impact on overall drive performance, and are not worth paying much for. For example, given otherwise identical drives, one with 2 MB cache and the other with 8 MB or one with 8 MB cache and the other with 16 MB, we might pay $5 or $10 more for the model with the larger cache.

Pay attention to power consumption and noise level.

Similar drives can differ significantly in power consumption and noise level. A drive that consumes more power also produces more heat, which contributes indirectly to overall system noise level because the system exhaust fans must work harder. For quiet system operation, it's important to use quiet, low-power hard drives. The power consumption and noise level of a drive are listed in the technical specification sheets available on its web site.

Here are some things that you can safely ignore when shopping for a drive:

Length of warranty

In late 2002, every major drive maker except Samsung reduced their standard warranties from three or five years to one year. All of the mainstream drive makers have returned to offering three-year warranties on their desktop drives, and Seagate offers five-year warranties. In practical terms, the difference is nil. A drive that is four or five years old is due for replacement anyway.

MTBF

Mean Time Between Failures (MTBF) is a technical measure of the expected reliability of a device. All modern drives have extremely large MTBF ratings, often 50 years or more. That doesn't mean that the drive you buy will last 50 years. It does mean that any drive you buy will probably run for years (although some drives fail the day they are installed). The truth is that most hard drives nowadays are replaced not because they fail, but because they are no longer large enough. Ignore MTBF when you're shopping for a drive.

MTTR

Mean Time To Repair (MTTR) is another measure that has little application in the real world. MTTR specifies the average time required to repair a drive. Since nobody except companies that salvage data from dead drives actually repairs drives nowadays, you can ignore MTTR.

Shock rating

Drives are rated in gravities (G) for the level of shock they can withstand in both operating and non-operating modes. For drives used in desktop systems, at least, you can ignore shock rating. All modern drives are remarkably resistant to damage if dropped, but all of them break if you drop them hard enough.

Installing a Hard Disk Drive

The general procedures for installing any hard drive are similar, but the exact steps and the sequence of steps vary depending on the type of drive you are installing—PATA or SATA—and the particulars of your case. The basic steps required to install a hard drive are:

1. Configure the drive as a master or slave device (PATA only).

2. Mount the drive in the chassis.

3. Connect the data cable to the drive and to the PATA or SATA interface.

4. Connect a power cable to the drive.

Before you remove the case panels to install the hard drive:

5. Restart the system and run BIOS Setup. Note the current configuration—which ATA and SATA ports are in use and the descriptions of the devices that are connected to them. Alternatively, use a diagnostic program such as Everest Home Edition to determine the current configuration of your drives and interfaces.

6. If you are also installing a PATA or SATA interface card or RAID adapter, configure that card per the maker's instructions and attach the cables to it. If that card will replace some or all of the embedded PATA or SATA interfaces, use CMOS Setup to disable those interfaces.

Some cases use fixed *drive bays*, which are a fixed part of the chassis structure. A hard drive is installed in a fixed drive bay either by sliding the drive into the bay and securing it by inserting screws through the chassis and into the drive or by attaching drive rails to the drive and sliding the drive and rail assembly into channels in the chassis. Depending on the mounting arrangements, you may or may not need to attach rails to the hard drive before installing it.

Mounting Arrangements

Whatever provisions your case makes for installing hard drives, once you've removed the cover it will almost certainly be obvious how the hard drive mounts within the case. If not, refer to the hardware documentation.

Other cases use removable *drive cage* or *drive tray* assemblies, in which you first secure the drive to the removable assembly and then insert the assembly into the chassis. If your case uses removable drive trays, securing the drive to the tray is one of the first installation steps. Figure 7-7 shows a typical drive tray being removed from the chassis, in preparation for installing the drive in the tray.

Figure 7-7. Removing an internal drive tray

The exact method used to secure the drive in the removable drive tray varies. Many drive trays use four screws that are inserted through the base of the drive tray and into the drive, as shown in Figure 7-8. Other drive trays use screws inserted through the side of the tray. A few use spring-steel clips with projections that seat in the screw holes of the drive, clamps that hold the drive securely with friction, or sliding locking tab arrangements. If your case uses removable drive trays of any sort, make sure to insert the drive oriented so that the data and power connectors are accessible when the tray is reinstalled in the chassis.

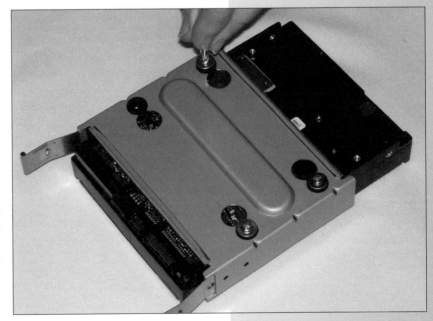

Figure 7-8. Securing a hard drive in a drive tray

Once you remove the cover and decide where and how you will physically install the drive, take the following steps:

1. If you are also adding a PATA or SATA interface card or RAID adapter, install the card in an available slot and route the data cable(s) to the hard drive bay area.

2. (PATA only) If BIOS Setup did not report the details of installed drives, visually examine them to determine how they are configured and to which ATA interface they connect. Depending on the existing configuration, you may be able to add the new drive to a free channel, or you may need to reconfigure existing drives and/or move them to another interface. Follow the recommendations in the earlier section "Assigning masters and slaves" to configure the drive or drives.

3. Decide what to do with the existing hard drive:

   - If you are replacing a failed hard drive, disconnect the data and power cables from the existing drive, and remove the drive from the chassis.

   - If you are replacing a drive that still functions but you need to copy data from it to the new hard drive, leave the old drive in place for the time being. If the old drive occupies the drive bay you need for the new drive, remove the old drive and set it on top of the chassis or elsewhere within reach of the data and power cables. Make sure the drive is oriented normally—horizontal or vertical—rather than at an angle or upside down. If necessary, use a sheet of paper or cardboard underneath the drive to prevent electrical shorts. Connect the data and power cables so that you can use the drive temporarily to copy data from it to the new drive.

   - If you are adding a drive and will continue using the old drive, decide where to install the new drive and whether to make it the primary drive or secondary drive. For example, if you are adding a large drive to store your audio and video collection, you may decide to install the new drive on the secondary channel, leaving the configuration of the old drive unchanged. Conversely, if you plan to use the new drive as the boot drive and for primary storage and the old drive for secondary storage, you may decide to install the new drive on the primary channel and move the old drive to the secondary channel.

4. After you have configured the new drive (and reconfigured the old one, if necessary), mount and secure the new drive and connect the data cable to the drive, as shown in Figure 7-9. If the drive mounts directly to the chassis, it is often easier to connect the data cable to the drive before you mount the drive. If the drive mounts to a removable drive tray, it may be easier to connect the data cable to the drive after you

mount the drive tray in the chassis. If the drive is a PATA model, make sure that the stripe on the data cable is aligned with pin 1 on the drive data connector.

Figure 7-9. Connect the data cable to the hard drive

5. If it is not already connected, connect the other end of the data cable to the motherboard, as shown in Figure 7-10. Connect an SATA drive that is primary to the lowest numbered SATA interface (usually 0, but sometimes 1). Connect an SATA drive that is secondary to the lowest available SATA interface. (On a system with a primary PATA drive and secondary SATA drive, use SATA interface 0 or higher.) Any PATA hard drive should be configured as a master device if at all possible. Connect a PATA drive that is primary as primary master, and a PATA drive that is secondary as secondary master.

Figure 7-10. Connect the data cable to the motherboard interface

Where's the Power Cable?

Many older power supplies do not provide SATA power connectors. The solution is to use an SATA power adapter, one of which may be bundled with the SATA drive. If the drive did not come with an SATA power adapter, you can buy one at any well-stocked computer store or online vendor. Buy two. They're cheap, and you'll probably need the other one eventually.

6. Connect a power cable to the drive, as shown in Figure 7-11. Although it is not a major issue, we prefer to use a dedicated power cable for a hard drive whenever possible, rather than sharing a power cable among two or more drives.

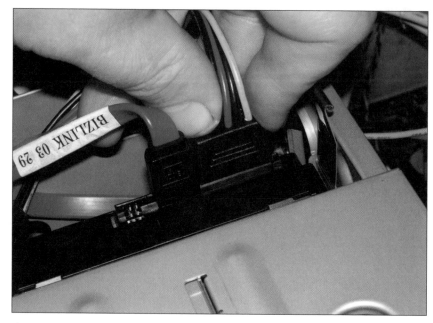

Figure 7-11. Connect the power cable to the drive

7. Leave the cover off for now, and give the system a quick visual check to make sure that everything is connected properly. Connect the keyboard, mouse, and monitor if you'd previously disconnected them, then turn on the power to start the smoke test. You should hear the new drive spin up. If it's difficult to tell (which it often is with newer drives), you can put your fingertip against the drive and feel it spinning up.

8. The new drive should appear on the BIOS boot screen as the system boots. If that screen flashes past too quickly or your system doesn't display configuration details on the boot screen, run CMOS Setup and use it to verify that the new drive is detected correctly. If the new drive is not detected, take the following steps until the problem is resolved:

    a) Restart the system, run BIOS Setup, and look for an option named Auto Detect or something similar. Choose that option to force drive detection.

    b) Power down the system. Verify that the data cable is connected to the drive and interface, that the power cable is connected, and that both cables are seated firmly. If the drive is a PATA model, verify that you are using an 80-wire UltraATA cable and that the colored stripe on the cable corresponds to pin 1 on the drive and interface.

c) Restart the system, run BIOS Setup, and verify that the interface to which you connected the drive is enabled.

d) Power down the system and substitute another data cable.

e) Power down the system and connect the data cable to a different interface.

f) If the drive is a PATA model and shares the cable with another device, power down the system and disconnect the other device temporarily. If the second device is another hard drive that is configured as master, temporarily reconfigure the new drive as master for testing.

g) If the drive is an SATA model and the motherboard uses a chipset that predates SATA, you will need to install SATA drivers from a floppy. Note that even some very recent motherboards use older chipsets that are not SATA-aware, so the age of the system is no indication as to whether it supports SATA natively. These older motherboard designs add SATA support by using a stand-alone SATA controller chip that is not integrated with the main chipset. SATA drives connected to such a motherboard require drivers to be installed manually before the system can access the SATA drive.

9. Once the system recognizes the new drive, use Windows or a third-party utility to partition and format the new drive. We generally use the disk preparation software that is bundled with the hard drive, such as the Maxtor MaxBLAST utility shown in Figure 7-12.

Disk Preparation Software

Disk preparation software is generally manufacturer-specific. For example, Seagate disk preparation software won't run unless there is at least one Seagate hard drive installed. Similarly, Maxtor disk preparation software won't run unless at least one Maxtor drive is present. But, for example, if you are installing a new Seagate hard drive in a system that already has a Maxtor drive installed, you can generally use either manufacturer's disk preparation utility. Look at both, and choose the one you prefer.

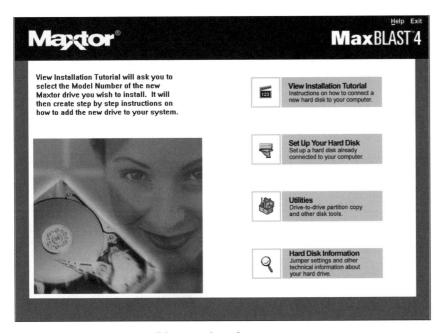

Figure 7-12. Maxtor MaxBLAST disk preparation software

Using SATA with Older Motherboards

Motherboards made before Spring 2003 lack native (chipset-level) SATA support. Transition motherboards produced in late 2002 through mid-2003 use an embedded third-party controller chip such as the Sil 3112A to provide SATA support. Some systems add SATA support with a PCI SATA host adapter. Accessing the SATA drive on such systems may require a driver.

If you are installing Windows XP to boot from the SATA drive, insert the driver diskette when the setup program prompts you to install third-party storage drivers. If the SATA drive is a secondary drive on an existing system, use the OS driver update feature to load the SATA driver after the system boots to the original primary hard drive. If the SATA drive and interface don't appear on the list of IDE/ATA devices, examine the list of SCSI devices.

Some motherboards with embedded SATA interfaces offer SATA configuration options in BIOS Setup, and others do not. If you are adding an SATA drive to an existing system as a secondary drive, you should not have to alter BIOS settings. If you replace the boot drive, you may need to change boot order in BIOS Setup to allow the system to boot from the SATA drive. Depending on the BIOS, the boot order screen may list the SATA boot setting as SATA, the drive model number, or SCSI.

If the motherboard has embedded SATA interfaces, you are normally prompted to install any necessary drivers when you first start the system. If you didn't install these drivers during motherboard installation, you should be prompted for them during Plug and Play enumeration. Before you install an SATA motherboard, it is a good idea to visit the SATA controller manufacturer's web site to download the latest SATA drivers for that controller.

If a properly installed SATA drive is not recognized by the operating system, verify that BIOS Setup is configured properly and that you have loaded and enabled the latest driver for the SATA controller you are using.

Enabling DMA Mode Transfers (PATA Only)

Depending on what level of DMA your hard disk and interface support, enabling DMA transfers may or may not increase disk performance noticeably, but enabling DMA is always worthwhile, because it greatly reduces the burden that PIO transfers place on the processor. If a computer has 75% CPU utilization using PIO transfers, that same computer using DMA transfers may provide the same or better disk performance at perhaps 1.5% CPU utilization. With multitasking operating systems, those extra free CPU ticks translate into faster system response.

To use DMA transfers, the hard drive, BIOS, and chipset must explicitly support DMA, and the operating system must have DMA drivers installed, loaded, and enabled. All recent versions of Windows support DMA transfers, but DMA is not always enabled by default, as follows:

- A fresh Windows install automatically installs DMA-capable drivers and tests the BIOS, interface, and hard drive for DMA compatibility. If any of these tests fail, DMA is disabled. If all three succeed, DMA is enabled automatically at the fastest DMA mode common to the drive and interface.

- Upgrading an existing system to Windows XP automatically enables DMA only if DMA was previously enabled. If DMA was previously disabled, you'll have to enable it manually.

When you install a second hard drive and restart the system, immediately check the current DMA status of that drive and enable DMA if it is not currently enabled. To do so, take the following steps:

1. Right-click My Computer and choose Properties to display the System Properties dialog.

2. Click the Hardware tab and then Device Manager button to display the Device Manager.

3. Locate and expand the IDE ATA/ATAPI controllers item. On a standard system with both ATA controllers enabled, there are three items listed. The first describes the ATA controller itself and may be ignored. The other two items are the *Primary IDE Channel* and *Secondary IDE Channel*.

4. Right-click the channel to which the device for which you want to enable DMA is connected, choose Properties, and then click the Advanced Settings tab to display the dialog shown in Figure 7-13.

5. This dialog displays the Device Type and Current Transfer Mode for Device 0 (master) and Device 1 (slave) on the selected ATA channel. The Current Transfer Mode field shows the transfer mode currently in use, and may be changed as follows:

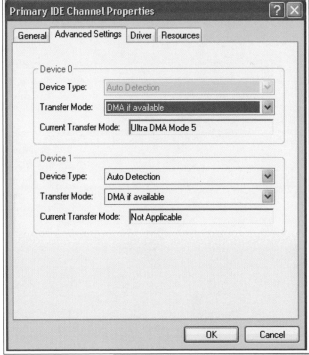

Figure 7-13. Windows XP shows this hard drive is using the UDMA-5 (UltraATA-100) transfer mode

DMA Mode x or Ultra DMA Mode x

Windows is using the indicated MDA or UDMA mode, which is the fastest mode supported by the interface, cable, and device. For example, if the hard drive supports UltraATA-100 and the embedded motherboard interface supports UltraATA-66, but you use a standard 40-wire ATA cable, Windows configures the interface to use UltraATA-33. If you replace that cable with an 80-wire

UltraDMA cable and restart the system, Windows reconfigures the interface to use UltraATA-66. You cannot explicitly choose the UDMA mode to be used.

PIO Mode or PIO Mode x

Windows is using the fastest PIO mode supported by the interface and device, typically PIO-4 (16.7 MB/s). If Transfer Mode is currently set to PIO Only, you may be able to enable DMA by setting Transfer Mode to "DMA if available" and restarting the system. If the Current Transfer Mode for the device still shows PIO Mode after the system is restarted, that device cannot be used in DMA mode. Replace the device with one that supports DMA.

Not Applicable

No device is installed.

All recent versions of Windows automatically disable DMA transfers at boot and revert to PIO transfers if they detect an obvious DMA problem. A DMA checkbox that won't stay checked when you restart the system is a good indication that your computer does not support DMA properly. Unfortunately, this method of determining support is not foolproof. DMA may appear to install successfully, but may have intermittent problems anyway. Any of the following symptoms may (or may not) indicate a DMA problem:

- You cannot access the hard disk at all, or you notice corrupt or missing files.

- The drive sometimes hangs briefly or seems to speed up and slow down during file access.

- The keyboard or the foreground application sometimes stops responding for short periods, or the mouse becomes jerky or nonresponsive.

- Windows locks up during the Plug and Play detection phase of Setup.

- Windows will start only in Safe Mode.

- Windows shutdown takes a lot longer than before you enabled DMA.

If any of these problems occur, it does not necessarily mean that you cannot use DMA with your computer. The following are likely causes of the problems:

Cable

According to the ATA standard, cables can be no longer than 18"(0.45 m), but we often see PATA cables of 24" and even 36". These long cables may not work reliably, if at all, with high-speed DMA modes. Cables also vary greatly in quality. The ones you see for $1.99 in bins at the computer store are less likely to work reliably at high speeds than those that are supplied with a new hard drive. When you're installing a hard drive, always replace the old ATA cable with the cable that comes with the drive. If no cable came with the drive, buy a good-quality DMA cable separately. If you have problems with DMA, replacing the cable with a better cable may solve them.

Drive

All current drives support DMA properly, but some early UltraATA-33 drives did not implement DMA modes correctly. If you reconfigure an older drive to use DMA, first check the manufacturer's web site for details on that model. Software patches for some models are available.

BIOS

Some early BIOS implementations that nominally provide DMA support do not do so correctly. If a more recent BIOS revision is available for your computer, downloading it and installing it may resolve intermittent DMA problems. If your current BIOS does not support DMA, you may find that a revised version is available to add that capability.

SATA MAKES THINGS EASY

Unlike PATA drives and interfaces, which may use various PIO and DMA modes, SATA drives and interfaces use only DMA mode. You don't need to configure settings manually. If the SATA drive is running at all, you can be sure that it's using optimum settings.

Troubleshooting Hard Drive Problems

Problems that occur when you have just installed a hard drive are almost always a simple matter of a bad or incorrectly connected cable, incorrect jumper settings, or some similar trivial problem. If a newly installed drive isn't recognized by the system, turn off the system. Check the cables—make sure that they're aligned properly and seated completely—and replace them if necessary. Make sure that the drive has power, and restart the system.

Once a hard drive is configured properly and recognized by the system, it generally continues working properly until it fails. If you're fortunate, you may get some warning of impending drive failure, such as odd noises coming from the drive, dialogs warning of read or write failures, or a SMART drive failure warning when you start the system. Unfortunately, hard drives often fail like light bulbs—perfect one moment and dead the next.

Isolating the problem

When a functioning drive fails or begins returning read or write errors, there are many possible causes. Take the following steps to isolate the cause of the problem:

1. Before proceeding, note that a failing drive can become a failed drive at any moment. Insofar as is possible, while the drive is still functioning,

Any News Is Bad News

If a hard drive shows even the slightest sign that it has problems, immediately copy the data from that drive to another hard drive or optical disc and replace that drive. Drive makers and third-party utility vendors offer software that claims to repair hard drive problems. Don't believe it. Once a drive has shown signs of impending failure, it will inevitably fail completely, and probably sooner than later. When a hard drive exhibits problems, your only goal should be to rescue your data from that drive. Don't even think about continuing to use a hard drive that has had problems, even if repair utilities swear that the drive is now in perfect condition. It isn't.

copy the important files to another hard drive or an optical disc. If you succeed in copying all of the files you need, copy them again. A particular file may be corrupted on one copy but readable from another. If you get a read failure error while copying a file, choose the Retry option several times until you are sure it won't succeed. At that point, choose the Ignore option to continue copying other files. Sometimes, a file that refuses to copy despite repeated retries on one pass will copy successfully on a subsequent pass, so don't give up too early.

WHERE THERE'S LIFE THERE'S HOPE

Never turn off the system until you have taken every possible step to recover data from a failing drive. A drive that kind of works may stop working entirely and forever if you restart the system.

2. If read/write errors occur only after the system has been running for a while—particularly during warm weather or if you have recently added a fast video card or other heat-producing component—it's possible that the drive is overheating. Remove the case access panel and use your finger as a temperature probe. The hard drive should feel warm (perhaps quite warm) to the touch, but not so hot that it's uncomfortable to press your finger against it for several seconds. If the drive is very hot, leave the side panel off and point a standard house fan directly into the case to cool the drive. If the read/write errors disappear, it's very likely that overheating is causing the problem. Install a hard drive cooler (available from any online or brick-and-mortar computer store) and/or add supplemental cooling fans to the case.

3. One of the most common but little-known causes of hard drive read/write errors is a marginal power supply. Power supplies may begin failing spontaneously and non-obviously, so this problem is always possible. But it's even more likely if you've recently added components to your system; particularly a hot new video adapter or some other component that draws a lot of power. You can eliminate the power supply as the cause of the problem by temporarily (or permanently) replacing it with a high-quality, high-capacity unit. Although it doesn't completely eliminate the power supply as the cause—a power supply can be failing rather than simply being marginal for the load—you can try reducing the load on the current power supply by removing components temporarily; for example, by temporarily reverting from that hot new video adapter to the embedded video or an older, slower video adapter.

4. If the hard drive temperature seems reasonable and the power supply is not the problem, you may have a cable problem. Power down the system and replace the data cable with a new or known-good cable. Also, remove the current power cable and use a different one. (Power cables seldom fail, but we have seen it happen.)

5. Connect the drive to a different interface. Although it's uncommon for a motherboard interface to fail spontaneously, it does happen rarely. If the drive is the PATA primary master, leave it configured as master, disable the primary ATA interface in BIOS Setup, and connect the drive to the secondary interface. For an SATA drive, disable the current SATA interface in BIOS Setup, and connect the drive to another SATA interface. (Don't forget to change the boot device priority.)

6. The drive circuit board may have failed, partially or completely.

   • For a PATA drive configured as master, the circuit board serves two independent functions: acting as the disk controller for all devices connected to that interface, and communicating data between that specific drive and the motherboard. The disk controller function may fail, but the data communication function continue to work. To test for this possibility, reconfigure the drive from master to slave, and connect the drive to an interface that already has a master device present, on the same or another computer. If only the disk controller function of the circuit board has failed, you will be able to access the drive as a slave device and copy the data from it to another drive or optical disc. If the problem drive still cannot be accessed, it's possible that its circuitry has failed completely or that the head-disk assembly (HDA) is physically damaged.

   • For an SATA drive, any circuit board failure makes it difficult to access the drive, because every SATA drive acts as its own disk controller. Even if the data communication function of the controller is working, the drive cannot be accessed if the disk controller function has failed.

7. If you have not already done so, remove the problem drive from the current system and install it in another system. It is possible, although unlikely, that all of the motherboard interfaces have failed in the original system. If so, the drive is not the problem, and it should function normally in the second system.

If none of these nondestructive testing steps allows you to access the drive, it's likely that the drive is physically damaged, which does not bode well for data recovery.

Recovering data from a failed or failing drive

A hard drive failure is annoying, but hard drives are inexpensive and easy to replace. What matters are the files on the drive. The first rule of data recovery is that a microgram of prevention is worth a megaton of cure. The best way to secure your files against loss is to back them up regularly. If you find yourself trying to recover files from a failing or failed hard drive, someone has screwed up.

Cheesy Power Supplies

In particular, the mass-market computers you find at big-box stores and from online vendors such as Dell are often equipped with power supplies that are barely adequate to start with. Something as simple as adding more memory may be the straw that breaks the camel's back. Replacing the cheap, inadequate power supply should be the first upgrade you do on such systems. Power PC and Cooling (*http://www.pcpowercooling.com*) and other vendors offer power supplies designed specifically to replace proprietary units that are incompatible with the standard power supplies available from big-box stores and other local sources.

Still, even if you implement an airtight backup scheme and follow it religiously, excrement happens. Those backup discs you so carefully wrote and verified may turn out to be unreadable, or you may have added or changed critical files since your last backup.

When a drive fails with files on it that haven't been backed up, decide how important those files are and how much you're willing to pay to recover them. If the answer is, "not very and not much," you can take steps to recover the files yourself. But if the files are critical and you are willing to pay someone to recover them for you, the rule is "don't just do something; stand there." Any steps you take yourself to recover the files—such as installing a data recovery program—may make it more difficult or impossible for a professional data recovery firm to retrieve your files.

DON'T GIVE UP TOO SOON

Although we have no direct experience with data recovery firms, our readers have recommended CBL Data Recovery (*http://www.cbltech.com*) and Ontrack (*http://www.ontrack.com*). Check prices and terms carefully before you decide to send your failed drive to a data recovery firm. Policies vary. Some data recovery firms charge a testing fee even if recovery is impossible. Others charge only if data can be recovered. A successful data recovery may cost hundreds or even thousands of dollars, depending on the amount of data and the difficulty involved.

If you decide to attempt to retrieve the data yourself, the steps to take depend on whether the drive is failing or failed:

- If the drive still functions, but returns read errors, attempt to copy the data from the drive before proceeding, as described at the beginning of this section. After you have done as much as possible to copy files from the failing drive, install SpinRite (*http://www.grc.com*) and let it run. It may take a day or more to do a deep analysis and recovery on the drive, but doing so may recover files that are completely unreadable using the standard copy utilities. Copy any files that SpinRite recovers to another hard drive or an optical disc.

- If you determine that the problem is a failed circuit board, and you have or are willing to buy an identical drive, you can replace the failed circuit board with the circuit board from the new drive. Obviously, if you are using a circuit board from an existing drive, be sure to back up the contents of that drive before you proceed.

- If the drive is not accessible and the steps described earlier do not make it so, disconnect the drive from your system and place it in the freezer for at least an hour. (Take steps to avoid condensation; we wrap the drive in plastic with all of the air exhausted and only the data and power connectors exposed, and connect them quickly when we remove the drive from the freezer.) Once the drive is thoroughly chilled, reconnect it to the system immediately and try to read the data from it while it is still cold. The drive warms quickly as it runs, so if this method succeeds you may need to do multiple freezer sessions to recover all of your data.

- Finally, as a last resort—although this sounds bizarre—give the drive a good hard knock against a padded hard surface or strike it with a rubber mallet just as the drive begins to spin up. Hard drives occasionally fail due to *stiction*, which means that the drive motor is no longer capable of starting the drive spinning. Sometimes a hard knock will free things up enough to allow the drive motor to spin the platters. This procedure, of course, risks doing severe damage to the drive, and should be employed only if all other measures fail.

Destroying Data

If you are replacing a failing hard drive or simply discarding a drive that is no longer large enough, you may worry about someone recovering your data from it. If the drive is functional, the best solution is to use a drive wiping utility before you discard the drive. Our favorite wiping utility is the free Darik's Boot and Nuke (DBAN), which you can download from *http://dban.sourceforge.net*. DBAN offers various wiping methods, the strongest of which meet Department of Defense standards and may require a full day to run. (A basic wipe takes only a few minutes, and is good enough for anyone but the truly paranoid.)

If the drive is not functional or if you want one more layer of security after running DBAN, disassemble the drive to expose the platters. Use a screwdriver or a similar tool to make deep scratches in the platters, and then use a hammer to wreak further destruction on the platters. (We know one person who uses a vise to crunch old drives down to twisted hulks and then uses an oxyacetylene torch to melt them into piles of smoking rubble.)

Optical Drives 8

Replacing your optical drive is a fast, easy, inexpensive way to upgrade the capabilities of an older system. And many recent systems include optical drives with limited capabilities, because the manufacturer wanted to save a few dollars. Even if your optical drive is only a year or two old and was a high-end model when new, it may make sense to replace it to gain the additional features and speed of a current model.

Upgrading your optical drive can add many useful features, including the ability to:

- Watch DVD-Video movies on your PC

- Make copies of your audio CDs for your car, or simply to keep the originals in safe storage

- Create custom audio CDs, with a mix of tracks you choose from various sources

- Back up your email, documents, images, and other data to inexpensive optical disks

- Make backup copies of your DVD-Video discs

- Create DVD-Video or Video CD discs from video files you find on the Internet

- Create custom video CDs or DVDs from home video footage

This chapter details what you need to know to choose the best optical drive for your needs, how to install and configure it, and how to troubleshoot it if problems occur.

Optical Drive Types

There are several types of optical drives available. Some can use only CDs, which typically store about 700 MB of data. Other optical drives can use DVDs, which typically store 4,700 MB to 8,500 MB of data. *CD-ROM drives* and *DVD-ROM drives* are read-only (the "ROM" part of the name).

CD writers and *DVD writers* (also called *burners* or *recorders*) can write optical discs as well as read them. DVD is backward-compatible with CD, which means that a DVD drive can also read CD discs, and nearly all DVD writers can also write CD discs.

Roughly in order of increasing price and usefulness, the choices are:

CD-ROM drive

When price is the absolute priority, installing a CD-ROM drive provides basic functionality at minimum cost. CD-ROM drives read only *CD-DA* (audio) discs, *CD-ROM* (data) discs, and (usually) *CD-R/CD-RW* writable discs. CD-ROM drives are commodity items that sell for $15. In fact, manufacturers make so little profit from CD-ROM drives that they have all but disappeared from retail channels. The sole advantage of a CD-ROM drive is its low price. The drawbacks of a CD-ROM drive are that it cannot read *DVD-Video*, *DVD-Audio*, or *DVD-ROM* discs and that it cannot write discs. Choose a CD-ROM drive only as an inexpensive replacement for a failed optical drive on an older system that does not require DVD support or recording features. CD-ROM drive choices are limited and likely to become more so as these drives disappear from the market. We consider any current ATAPI model made by Lite-On, Mitsumi, NEC, Samsung, or Sony acceptable. All are reliable, so buy on price. Unless the small extra cost is a deal-breaker, we strongly suggest installing a more capable optical drive.

DVD-ROM drive

DVD-ROM drives are also commodities, but cost a bit more than CD-ROM drives: $20 or so. Like CD-ROM drives, DVD-ROM drives read CD-DA, CD-ROM, and CD-R/RW discs, but they also read DVD-Video, DVD-ROM, and (sometimes) DVD-Audio discs. Even if you're repairing or upgrading on a tight budget, it usually makes sense to spend an extra $5 to get a DVD-ROM drive rather than a CD-ROM drive so the PC can read DVD-Video and DVD-ROM discs. Like CD-ROM drives, DVD-ROM drives are read-only devices, and cannot write discs. Nearly all current DVD-ROM drives read CDs at 40X or 48X and DVDs at 16X with similar access times and otherwise similar specifications, so there is little reason to choose a brand other than by price and manufacturer reputation. We consider any current ATAPI model made by Lite-On, Mitsumi, NEC, Samsung, Sony, or Toshiba acceptable.

CD-RW drive

CD-RW drives, also called CD writers, CD burners, or CD recorders, sell for $25 or so. CD writers read the same formats as CD-ROM drives—CD-DA, CD-ROM, and CD-R/RW discs—but can also write data to inexpensive CD-R (write-once) and CD-RW (rewritable) discs. Although CD-RW drives do not read DVD discs, they have the advantage of being able to write discs. In addition to being useful for duping

Verify Format Support

If you need a DVD-ROM drive that reads DVD+R/RW and/or DVD-R/RW discs, verify that the model you choose explicitly lists support for the writable DVD formats you need to read. Most current DVD-ROM drives read both "R" (write-once) and "RW" (rewritable) discs in both the "plus" and "minus" formats. Some DVD-ROM drives read "plus" but not "minus" discs, or vice versa. A few drives, mostly older models, read "R" discs, but not "RW" discs. Some models read burned 4.7 GB DVD discs, but not burned dual-layer (8.5 GB) discs. A few drives—notably many Toshiba models—can also read the moribund DVD-RAM format.

audio and data CDs, CD writers also provide an inexpensive backup solution, albeit limited to about 700 MB per disc. Nearly all current CD-RW drives write CDs at 48X, 52X, or 54X and have similar read speeds, access times, and other specifications, so there is little reason to choose a brand other than by price and manufacturer reputation. We consider any current ATAPI model made by Lite-On, Mitsumi, Samsung, or Sony acceptable.

RIPPING MUSIC

If you want the best CD-RW drive available, and are willing to pay the price, choose a Plextor model. Plextor drives are more reliable than any other optical drive we have used, and have the best *digital audio extraction* (*DAE*) for "ripping" audio CD tracks to your hard drive. Unfortunately, they're priced accordingly. A Plextor CD writer sells for more than some DVD writers made by other companies.

DVD-ROM/CD-RW drive

> *Combo drives* combine the functionality of a DVD-ROM drive and a CD-RW drive, and typically sell for $30 to $35. Because they can read nearly any optical disc and write CDs, combo drives were quite popular until the price of DVD writers dropped. At current prices, we'd consider using a combo drive to replace a failed optical drive on an elderly system or in situations where the additional $5 to $40 cost of a DVD writer can't be justified. We consider any current ATAPI model made by Lite-On, Samsung, Teac, or Toshiba acceptable. If you need to read burned DVDs, make sure that the model you choose explicitly lists compatibility with the formats you use. If you need to read DVD-RAM discs, buy a Toshiba model. Otherwise, all are reliable and priced similarly, so buy whatever happens to be the least expensive.

DVD writer

> DVD writers do it all—they both read and write both CDs and DVDs. That flexibility used to come at a high price, but current DVD writers are available for as little as $40 and even the best internal models sell for $100 or less. Here are the issues to consider in choosing a DVD writer:

> *DVD writable formats supported*

>> All current DVD writers can write DVD+R, DVD+RW, DVD-R, and DVD-RW discs interchangeably. Most models can also write dual-layer DVD+R DL and/or DVD-R DL discs—which store about 8.5 GB rather than the 4.7 GB capacity of standard single-layer discs—although the least-expensive models may not support writing DL discs at full speed. A few drives remain available that support the moribund DVD-RAM standard.

Don't Pitch That Old CD-ROM Drive

Although all DVD-ROM drives and DVD writers read CD discs, even premium DVD drives may fail to read scratched or damaged CD discs that an old CD-ROM drive or CD writer may read perfectly. For that reason, we always keep one or two old CD-ROM drives and CD writers installed in older systems, even when we upgrade those systems with a new DVD writer.

If you encounter a CD that your newer optical drives refuse to read or copy, try the disc in an older drive. You may find it reads perfectly in the older drive, and you can make a backup copy to use in your newer drives. In particular, if you are ripping a copy-protected CD, you may find that a newer drive won't touch it, while an older drive copies it perfectly.

WORSE CAN BE BETTER

Although DVD+R and DVD+RW (the *plus formats*) are technically superior to DVD-R and DVD-RW (the *minus formats*), the DVD-R/RW features of a drive may still be important. Although we would never use DVD-R/RW discs for backups or other applications where robust error detection and correction is important, DVD+R/RW discs are incompatible with some older DVD players. If you plan to use your DVD writer to make DVD video discs, check your player's compatibility with the various writable DVD formats. Many older players, and even some newer ones, refuse to read DVD+R discs, so you may have no choice but to write videos to DVD-R discs. Either that, or buy a player that supports the plus formats.

CD writing capabilities

Many people use DVD writers primarily for writing DVDs, and seldom or never write CDs. However, the CD-writing features and performance of a drive are important if you frequently use CD-R or CD-RW discs, perhaps to duplicate your audio CDs or for daily backups. If CD writing is important to you, make sure the drive you buy supports at least 40X CD-R writes and, if you use CD-RW, 24X CD-RW rewrites. Also make sure the drive supports BURN-Proof or a similar anti-coaster technology.

Write speed

Early DVD writers recorded discs at only 1X. As was true of CD writers before them, rapid product development soon boosted the speed of even low-end DVD writers to the maximum practical write speeds for the various formats. In the case of writable DVD, that's 16X for single-layer ±R discs, 8X for DVD+RW and DVD+R DL, and 4X for DVD-RW and DVD-R DL.

If you have an older DVD writer and you write many DVDs, upgrading to a faster current model is probably worth the small cost. Using a 4X DVD writer requires patience; it takes 15 minutes to write a full disc. An 8X writer cuts that to 8 minutes or so, and a 16X writer to about 4.5 minutes. (In each case, the writing speed actually doubles, but writing the table of contents and closing the disc requires a minute or so regardless of writer speed.) Note, however, that for various reasons you may not always write discs at the maximum rated speed of the drive. For example, we often use 8X discs in our 16X writers, because the 8X discs are both less expensive and more reliable. Similarly, when we record video to 8X DVD+R discs, we write them at only 2X or 4X, because discs written at 8X, 12X, or 16X are often rejected by our DVD player or exhibit video and audio artifacts.

Interface

Nearly all internal DVD burners use the standard ATA/ATAPI interface. A few models—notably some Plextor drives—are available in Serial ATA. We suggest you avoid SATA models. The drives themselves are fine, and there's nothing wrong with the SATA interface, but using an SATA optical drive introduces numerous compatibility issues. Very few motherboards, even newer models with full SATA support, work properly with SATA optical drives. Even if the motherboard supports the drive properly, you may find that your operating system and applications don't recognize an SATA optical drive.

Internal versus external

For most systems, an internal ATA/ATAPI DVD burner is the best and most economical choice. However, DVD burners are also available in external variants that connect to a PC using the USB 2.0 and/or FireWire interfaces. Although external drives are more expensive than internal models, they do have a couple of advantages. First, you can share an external drive among several systems, for example for doing periodic backups. Second, an external drive can be used with a notebook computer or other system that doesn't permit installing an internal drive. If an external drive is right for your needs, choosing a model that provides both USB 2.0 and FireWire interfaces offers the most flexibility.

Plextor makes the best DVD writers available. They sell at a premium, but we consider their small additional cost worth paying for their superior reliability and the high quality of the discs they write. The Plextor PX-716A, their flagship model, is superb. It has every imaginable feature, top-notch performance, and is built like a tank. The Plextor PX-740A, their economy model, has a smaller buffer and fewer features, but is built to Plextor's usual high standards. For an external DVD writer, we recommend the Plextor PX-716UF, which provides both USB 2.0 and FireWire interfaces.

DRIVES THAT DON'T DIE

In the decade or more that we've been using (and abusing) Plextor drives, we've had only one Plextor die on us. And that one didn't die of natural causes; it was murdered. (Robert rammed his knee into the drive tray while it was extended, ripping it out of the drive.) During one extended testing session, we used a Plextor PX-716A drive to burn an entire spindle of 50 DVD+R discs one after the other, inserting a new disc as soon as the preceding one ejected. Every disc from first to last was perfect. The drive wasn't even breathing hard.

If you're on a tight budget, a Plextor model may be out of your price range. In that case, we recommend the NEC ND-3550A or the BenQ DW1640.

Unless you're counting pennies, we strongly recommend choosing a DVD writer rather than a less capable optical drive. Other than the SATA issue, you needn't worry about compatibility. Modern DVD writers function properly even in older systems.

Optical Drive Performance

Optical drive speeds are specified using an "X-factor." The earliest CD-ROM drives transferred data at a constant 150 KB/s, the same rate used by audio CDs, which is referred to as 1X. Later CD drives used variable speeds, changing the speed according to where the head was positioned on the CD. It's impossible to assign a single speed rating to such a drive, so manufacturers began specifying the maximum speed those drives used. For example, a CD-ROM drive that transfers data at a maximum rate 52 times the 150 KB/s audio CD rate, or 7,800 KB/s, is called a 52X Max drive.

DVD drives use the same kind of speed rating scheme, but the DVD "X-factor" is different. The 1X DVD rate is 1.321 MB/s, which is the data rate required to store 60 minutes of video on a 4.7 GB DVD disc, or about nine times faster than a 1X CD-ROM drive. For example, a 16X Max DVD drive transfers data as fast as about 21 MB/s, nearly three times the rate of a 52X CD drive.

To complicate matters further, optical drives do different tasks at different rates. For example, a typical early CD writer could write CD-R (write-once) discs at 4X, or 600 KB/s, but read discs at 24X, or 3,600 KB/s. When CD-RW (rewritable) discs were introduced, yet a third number was needed, because most CD writers wrote CD-R discs and CD-RW discs at different speeds. A typical modern CD writer might read CD discs at 52X, write CD-R discs at 52X, and rewrite CD-RW discs at 32X. Such a drive is referred to as a 52-52-32 drive.

SPEED LIMITS

Read speeds may also differ according to the type of disc being read. For example, a particular drive may read data CDs at 52X Max but audio CDs at only 24X, pressed data DVDs at 16X Max, but DVD-Video discs at only 8X, and DVD+R discs at 16X, but DVD+RW discs at only 8X. Similarly, a particular drive may write data CDs at 52X Max, but audio CDs at only 24X.

What About Blu-Ray and HD-DVD?

The next generation of DVD drives and discs will store much more data on a standard-size disc than do current DVD formats, by using a 405 nm blue laser rather than the 650 nm red laser used by current DVD drives and players. The shorter wavelength of the blue laser allows closer track spacing and higher data density within the track.

There is currently a format war going on between two proposed high-capacity DVD standards, which are mutually incompatible. Only one of these standards can prevail, and there are billions of dollars in license fees at stake. The Blu-Ray standard, promoted by the *Blu-Ray Disc Association* (*http://www.bluraydisc.com*), is backed by a group of technology manufacturers and movie studios, led by Philips and Sony. The HD-DVD standard is promoted by the DVD Forum (*http://www.dvdforum.org*)—which owns the patents and trademarks for the original DVD standards—and is backed by another group of technology manufacturers and movie studios, led by NEC and Toshiba. Although Microsoft has not committed exclusively to either standard, it has shown preference for HD-DVD, both by promising HD-DVD support in future versions of Windows and by announcing that future versions of its Xbox console will use HD-DVD.

The major advantage of Blu-Ray is its greater capacity. *BD-ROM* stores 23.3, 25, or 27 GB on a single-layer disc (as compared to 4.7 GB on a single-layer DVD-ROM), and 46.6, 50, or 54 GB on a dual-layer disc (as compared to 9.4 GB on a dual-layer DVD-ROM). *HD DVD-ROM* stores only 15 GB on a single-layer disc and 30 GB on a dual-layer disc. BD-ROM discs that use three or more layers are currently in development, and will expand storage capacity to 100 to 200 GB. Similarly, Toshiba has a three-layer HD DVD-ROM disc in development that will store 45 GB.

Both standards make provision for writable discs. *BD-RE* is the rewritable version of BD-ROM, analogous to DVD+RW. BD-RE recorders will initially ship in single-layer (25 GB) models, with dual-layer 50 GB models to follow. The HD-DVD equivalent is called *HD DVD-Rewritable*. Oddly, these discs store 20 GB per side rather than the 15 GB of the read-only version. *BD-R* is the write-once version of

BD-ROM, analogous to DVD+R. BD-R recorders and drives will be available in 25 GB single-layer models initially with 50 GB dual-layer models to follow. The HD-DVD write-once standard is called *HD DVD-R*, and stores 15 GB in a single layer.

Looking at these specifications, you might wonder how HD-DVD has any chance at all against Blu-Ray. Fortunately for its supporters, HD-DVD has two things going for it. First, HD-DVD discs can be pressed on the existing equipment used to produce DVD-ROM discs, while Blu-Ray requires all new equipment. More important, HD-DVD gained the early support of several movie studios.

Movie studios want one standard, so they won't have to release their films on two different and incompatible types of discs. DVD rental companies like Blockbuster and Netflix want one standard, so they don't have to stock two different copies of the same title. Consumers want one standard, so they don't have to buy two expensive DVD players, one for each format. In fact, everyone wants one standard, but neither the Blu-Ray Disc Association nor the DVD Forum is willing to budge. There's simply too much money at stake.

From a PC perspective, none of this really matters, at least for now. As with any new technology, the prices will initially be astronomical. We expect the first high-capacity PC DVD burners to sell for $1,000, and the discs for $20 each. Then again, the first CD writer we used cost $20,000 and blank discs sold back then for $50 each. Prices will drop rapidly, although we don't expect high-capacity DVD writers for PCs to become mainstream components until at least 2007. And, we wonder how useful they'll be even then. We're not happy at the prospect of using a high-capacity DVD writer that's laden with DRM and produces serialized discs, but that may be the only alternative.

For now, and for the foreseeable future, we think the best choice is a dual-layer DVD+R/RW drive. Standard DVD+R and DVD+RW discs will remain available for many years, long after the high-capacity DVD format war has been decided.

So matters remained, until the first hybrid (or "combo") CD writer and DVD-ROM drive was introduced. At that point, a fourth number was needed to report the DVD-ROM read speed. A typical combo drive might write CD-R discs at 52X, rewrite CD-RW discs at 24X, read CDs at 40X, and read DVDs at 16X. Such a drive is referred to as a 52-24-40-16 drive.

Along came DVD writers, most of which read and write DVD-R, DVD-RW, DVD+R, and DVD+RW, often at different speeds. Most recent DVD writers can also write dual-layer DVD+R/DL and DVD-R/DL discs, also at different speeds. So, the apparently simple question, "Which drive is faster?" often has no simple answer.

Actual read and write speeds also vary from drive to drive, even if the drives have identical speed ratings. In addition to native differences between drives, performance depends on the brand of discs, the firmware version installed, and so on. For example, Drive A, rated to write DVD+R discs at 16X, may write those discs faster than Drive B, which is also rated for 16X DVD+R writes. Conversely, although both drives may be rated for 8X DVD+RW writes, Drive B may write DVD+RW discs faster than Drive A. But if you use a different brand of media or update the firmware in one or both of the drives, the positions may be reversed.

Finally, random access time may matter to you. In general, optical writers have more complex and heavier heads than read-only optical drives. Consequently, optical writers have noticeably slower access times than most read-only drives. For example, the random access time of a fast DVD-ROM drive might be 85 milliseconds, while that of a DVD writer might be twice that. Fast access times don't matter for sequential operations such as burning a disc or watching a DVD video. They do matter when you randomly access data from an optical disc, such as occurs when you play a DVD-based game. That's why serious gamers usually have two optical drives in their gaming systems—an optical writer for general use and a fast DVD-ROM drive for loading games.

Disk or Disc?

With Seagate as the sole exception, hard drive makers refer to their products as "disk" drives. The "disc" spelling is used universally to refer to optical discs.

Optical Disc Types

All mainstream optical discs, from the oldest CDs to the most recent high-capacity DVDs, are based on the original CD specification. The dimensions of a standard CD or DVD are 120 mm in diameter (60 mm radius) by 1.2 mm thick, with a 15 mm diameter central hole that accommodates the rotating center spindle of the drive.

Commercial CDs and DVDs are produced by a physical stamping process, and are referred to as *pressed discs* or *stamped discs*. Commercial discs may be one-sided or two-sided, and the data side or sides are nearly always a reflective silver color. Writable discs are produced by the operation of a relatively high power laser on a layer of dye or another substance that can be altered by light, and are always one-sided. The data side of a writable disc may be nearly any color, from a metallic silver or gold to yellow-green to a dark blue. It is not possible to identify the type or quality of a writable disc by visually examining its data side.

Despite their similarity in appearance, there are many differences between discs. Discs vary in the writable standard they support, the dyes and other materials they use, compatibility with different models of writers and players, archival stability, and overall quality.

Writable CD discs

Although CD writers are obsolescent, writable CD discs continue to sell by the billions. Writable CDs are cheap—even premium brands can be bought in bulk for as little as $0.10 each when they're on sale—and are ideal for duplicating audio CDs, making quick backups of your working data, and other tasks for which their capacity is sufficient. Writable CDs can be written to by CD writers (of course), and by most DVD writers. There are two types of writable CDs:

CD-R discs

CD-R (*CD-Recordable*) discs can, with minor exceptions, be written to only once. Data, once recorded, cannot be overwritten or deleted. Although CD-R discs formerly differed in the maximum write speeds they supported, nearly all CD-R discs currently sold are rated for 48X to 52X writes, and so can be used in nearly any optical writer. CD-R discs can be written by all CD writers and by nearly all DVD writers. CD-R discs can be read by any modern optical drive or player, although some elderly home audio and automobile CD players reject them.

CD-R discs differ primarily in capacity and quality. A standards-compliant CD-R disc stores 74 minutes of audio or about 650 MB of data. Although they are nonstandard, most CD-Rs now sold have a capacity of about 80 minutes of audio or 700 MB of data. In fact, for the same reason 74-minute discs drove 63-minute discs out of the market, it's almost impossible nowadays to find 74-minute discs.

WHEN MORE IS TOO MUCH

Before writable DVDs became affordable, some CD-R drive and disc manufacturers attempted to "push the envelope" on capacity by introducing drives and discs that stored 90 minutes of audio (790 MB of data), or even 99 minutes of audio (870 MB of data). Although some of the drives were excellent and are still usable today, the "extended capacity" discs were unreliable at best, generating frequent read errors even on the drive that wrote them, and often refusing even to load in many drives. Fortunately, extended-capacity CD-R discs died a well-deserved death, and are almost impossible to find today. If you do happen to have any 90- or 99-minute CD-Rs on your shelf, do yourself a favor and pitch them.

Quality differences are harder to pin down, but they are very real nonetheless. Discs differ in the quality of the materials used to make them and the attention paid to quality issues during manufacturing. Even something as trivial as the type of material used to overcoat the reflective layer can have a significant effect on the archival stability of a disc. We recommend CD-R discs made by Taiyo-Yuden. If TY discs are unavailable, CD-R discs made by Maxell, TDK, or Verbatim are also excellent. Note that some manufacturers have an "economy" line and a "premium" line of discs. Don't even consider buying economy discs. It's simply not worth the risk to save pennies per disc.

CD-RW discs

CD-RW (*CD-Rewritable*) discs can be written to repeatedly, by deleting or overwriting old data to make room for new data. CD-RW discs can be rewritten up to 1,000 times.

Rated disc speed is more important for CD-RW than for CD-R. While most writers happily burn (or attempt to burn) any CD-R disc at the highest CD-R speed the drive supports, many writers refuse to burn CD-RW discs at anything faster than the disc's rated speed. There are four types of CD-RW media currently available:

- *Standard Speed CD-RW discs* are rated for 1X to 4X burning, and are usable only in elderly CD-RW writers.

- *High Speed CD-RW discs* are rated for 4X to 12X burning, and are usable in CD-RW writers with the *High Speed CD-RW* logo or *Ultra Speed CD-RW* logo.

- *Ultra Speed CD-RW discs* are rated for 12X, 16X, and 24X burning, and are usable in CD-RW writers with the *High Speed CD-RW* logo or *Ultra Speed CD-RW* logo.

- *Ultra Speed+ CD-RW discs* are rated for 32X burning, and are usable in CD-RW writers with the *High Speed CD-RW* logo or *Ultra Speed CD-RW* logo.

CD-RW discs were always the poor stepchild, and are now much less widely available than CD-R discs, which remain commonplace. Although nearly any recent optical drive and most recent CD and DVD players can read CD-RW discs, there were many early compatibility problems that caused many people to write off CD-RW as a viable technology. At the time CD-RW began to achieve critical mass, many CD-ROM and DVD-ROM drives and most home audio and automobile CD players of the time refused to read CD-RW discs.

As is true of CD-R discs, there are significant quality variations between brands of CD-RW discs. Standard Speed and Ultra Speed+ discs are now difficult to find, and we have no brand recommendations for them. For High Speed CD-RW discs (usually labeled 12X) and Ultra Speed CD-RW discs (usually labeled 24X), we recommend Verbatim.

Binary versus decimal

Manufacturers quote disc capacity in decimal notation. For example, a writable DVD said to have a capacity of 4.7 GB actually stores 4,700,000,000 bytes (give or take a few). Using traditional binary notation, that disc has a capacity of 4,700,000,000 bytes ÷ 1024 = 4,589,843.75 KB ÷ 1024 = 4,482.269+ MB ÷ 1024 = 4.377+ GB, which is often rounded to 4.4 GB.

Writable DVD discs

Unlike writable CDs, for which only the CD-R and CD-RW standards exist, there are numerous standards for writable DVD. This proliferation of writable DVD formats had its origin in the "format wars" that began in the late 1990s and continue even today. As a result, there are three mainstream standards for rewritable DVD discs, and four standards for write-once DVD discs. Interestingly, rewritable standards generally precede the corresponding write-once standards. Here are the primary rewritable standards:

DVD-RAM

> *DVD-RAM* drives first shipped in 1998, beating all other writable DVD standards to market. The *DVD Forum* (*http://www.dvdforum. org*) promoted DVD-RAM, initially for use primarily on PCs, although DVD-RAM later achieved some popularity for recording home video. Although it was first to market, DVD-RAM never really caught on. A combination of high drive prices, expensive media, and slow performance pretty much doomed DVD-RAM right out of the starting gate. It didn't help that the original DVD-RAM specification required discs to be enclosed in cartridges, which kept the price of DVD-RAM discs high and prevented DVD-RAM drives from being used in notebook computers. The one saving grace of DVD-RAM is that it incorporates much more robust error detection and correction than do other writable DVD formats, making DVD-RAM particularly appropriate for backups and similar data-related tasks.

> DVD-RAM drives are still made, and continue to sell in small numbers. DVD-RAM drives write at 5X, slower than other rewritable discs. DVD-RAM discs store 4.7 GB per side—about half the capacity of dual-layer DVD±R DL discs—and are available in single-sided 4.7 GB versions and double-sided 9.4 GB versions. 4.7 GB discs are available bare or in a cartridge. 9.4 GB discs are available only in cartridges. DVD-RAM discs sell for 3 to 10 times the price of DVD+RW or DVD-RW discs, depending on their capacity and whether they are bare or contained in a cartridge. DVD-RAM discs, particularly cartridge-based discs, are compatible only with DVD-RAM drives, some camcorders and personal video recorders, a few DVD-ROM drives (primarily Toshiba models), and a very few DVD players. DVD-RAM discs can be rewritten up to 100,000 times.

> DVD-RAM discs are much harder to find than DVD±R/RW discs. You may find a limited selection at your local big-box store, although they're often not stocked, and even many online vendors do not carry DVD-RAM media. We prefer to use DVD-RAM discs made by Verbatim, Maxell, or TDK.

DVD-RW

> *DVD-RW* is another rewritable standard promoted by the DVD Forum. DVD-RW drives appeared on the market shortly after DVD-RAM drives, and quickly achieved moderate success. Apple adopted and promoted DVD-RW heavily, using drives built by Pioneer. Early 1X drives and discs were soon followed by 2X and then 4X models. Current DVD-RW discs are certified for 4X or (rarely) 6X writes, are rated for up to 1,000 rewrites, and store about 4.7 GB.

A FEW BYTES HERE AND THERE

DVD+RW and DVD+R discs store exactly 2,295,104 2048-byte sectors, or 4,700,372,992 bytes. DVD-RW and DVD-R discs typically store the same amount as DVD+R/RW discs, although the "minus" specifications require only that they store at least 4.7 billion bytes. DVD-RAM discs store 2,295,072 2048-byte sectors, or 4,700,307,456 bytes, ever so slightly less than standard DVD±R/RW discs.

Advice from Jim Cooley

Many DVD-ROM drives and some DVD players can be updated with newer firmware to add read support for formats that were unsupported by the original firmware. You update the firmware for most DVD-ROM drives by running a Windows- or DOS-based installer utility. DVD players are usually updated by burning the new firmware to a disc and loading that disc into the player. See the product manual or manufacturer's web site for detailed instructions.

> DVD-RW has relatively poor error detection and correction, and so is poorly suited for recording data. For a time, DVD-RW discs were considerably less expensive than comparable DVD+RW discs, and so were a reasonable choice for recording television programs, movies, and other noncritical uses. Nowadays, DVD-RW discs sell for the same price as DVD+RW discs, so there is no reason to use them at all unless you have an elderly drive that does not write DVD+RW discs. In that case, we recommend using Verbatim discs.

> DVD-RW discs can be read by any DVD writer other than some elderly DVD+R/RW-only models, and by nearly all recent DVD-ROM drives. Estimates vary for DVD players, but probably 65% to 70% of all installed DVD players play DVD-RW discs correctly. Some DVD players, particularly older models, confuse DVD-RW discs—which have lower contrast and reflectivity than standard discs—for pressed dual-layer discs, and so cannot play them.

DVD+RW

> After several false starts, *DVD+RW* made it to market some months after DVD-RW. DVD+RW originated with a group of companies, led by Sony and Hewlett-Packard, who were dissatisfied with the DVD-RW standard. The DVD Forum was actively hostile to DVD+RW, so the consortium of DVD+RW sponsors created the competing *DVD+RW Alliance* (*http://www.dvdrw.com*) to define the "plus" standards and promote their use.

> Like DVD-RW discs, DVD+RW discs store about 4.7 GB and are rated for 1,000 rewrites. DVD+RW has significant advantages over DVD-RW in performance and reliability. When DVD-RW was limited to 1X writes, DVD+RW already supported 2.4X writes. When DVD-RW reached 2X, DVD+RW leapfrogged to 4X. Soon after DVD-RW

reached 4X, 8X DVD+RW drives and discs began shipping. In addition to being faster, DVD+RW has much more robust error detection and correction. We use and recommend Verbatim DVD+RW discs, although Mitsubishi Chemical Company (MCC) and Ricoh also produce excellent DVD+RW discs.

DVD+RW discs can be read by any DVD writer other than some elderly DVD-R/RW-only models, and by nearly all recent DVD-ROM drives. Again, estimates vary for DVD players, but probably 70% to 80% of all installed DVD players play DVD+RW discs correctly. Some DVD players, particularly older models, confuse DVD+RW discs—which have lower contrast and reflectivity than standard discs—for pressed dual-layer discs, and so cannot play them. Some DVD players, particularly models built by Panasonic, Toshiba, and Hitachi, simply refuse to load DVD+RW (or DVD+R) discs, which is by design.

WHEN PLUS IS BETTER THAN MINUS

We trust DVD+RW sufficiently that we routinely use DVD+RW discs for backing up our data. We wouldn't use DVD-RW for backups on a bet.

As useful as rewritable DVD formats are, there is an even larger demand for write-once formats, which offer higher write speeds, arguably greater archival stability, and lower media costs. There are four mainstream write-once DVD formats:

DVD-R

> *DVD-R* was the first write-once DVD format introduced. DVD-R discs store about 4.7 GB, and are available in versions certified for up to 16X writes. As is true of DVD-RW discs, DVD-R discs have error detection and correction inferior to that of DVD+R/RW discs, so we avoid using DVD-R discs whenever possible, particularly for storing data (as opposed to video). If you own a minus-only recorder, have a DVD player that does not read plus formats, or for some other reason you must use DVD-R discs, we recommend those made by Maxell, TDK, or Verbatim.

> DVD-R discs can be read by any DVD writer other than some elderly DVD+R/RW-only models, and by nearly all recent DVD-ROM drives. More than 90% of all installed DVD players play DVD-R discs correctly, and that percentage will increase as older players are replaced by new units. Some old DVD players are unable to deal with the lower contrast and reflectivity of DVD-R discs relative to pressed discs, but most of those players have long since been replaced.

DVD+R

> After some false starts, *DVD+R* quickly established itself as a superior alternative to DVD-R. DVD+R discs, which store about 4.7 GB, are

available in versions certified for up to 16X writes. DVD+R discs have better error detection and correction than DVD-R discs, and are therefore a better choice for recording data. We use and recommend DVD+R discs made by Maxell or Verbatim, both of which are excellent and well distributed. Ricoh, Taiyo-Yuden and Mitsubishi Chemical Company (MCC, the parent of Verbatim), also produce excellent DVD+R discs, although none of those brands is widely distributed in the U.S.

DVD+R discs can be read by any DVD writer other than some elderly DVD-R/RW-only models, and by nearly all recent DVD-ROM drives. A somewhat lower percentage of DVD players are compatible with DVD+R than DVD-R (perhaps 85%), because even some current DVD players are intentionally made incompatible with DVD+R/RW.

DVD+R DL

The most recent enhancement to the DVD+R standard is *DVD+R DL* (also called *DVD+R9* or *dual-layer DVD+R*), which boosts storage capacity from 4.7 GB to 8.5 GB by adding a second recording layer. Although DVD+R DL compatible drives have been shipping since Summer 2004, initial acceptance of the format was limited because of the very high cost of DL discs. A full year after the introduction of DL drives and discs, name-brand DVD+R discs were readily available for $0.50 each or less, while DL discs sold for 6 to 10 times that price.

Nonetheless, DVD+R DL discs have their place. For backing up data, their higher price may be a small issue when their additional capacity is taken into account. Also, for those who back up their commercial DVD-Video discs, the higher capacity of DVD+R DL allows that video to be duplicated without the compression required to fit it onto 4.7 GB single-layer discs. Our experience with DVD+R DL discs is very limited, but of those we have used we have found Verbatim and TDK discs to be the most reliable.

DVD+R DL compatibility with drives and players other than DVD+R DL writers is problematic. Many recent DVD-ROM drives and DVD players can read DVD+R DL discs, but even some current models cannot. If you plan to use DVD+R DL, we recommend that you first verify compatibility with your other DVD drives and players.

DVD-R DL

DVD-R DL (also called *DVD-R9* or *dual-layer DVD-R*) arrived on the scene some months after DVD+R DL. DVD-R DL has the same issues as DVD+R DL—high disc cost and limited compatibility with older devices. DVD-R DL, like standard DVD-R, has error detection and correction that's inferior to the plus-format versions, so we regard DVD-R DL as unsuitable for recording data. Although DVD-R DL is acceptable for recording video, the superior reliability and features of DVD+R DL make it a better choice. We cannot recommend specific brands of DVD-R DL discs, because we have almost no hands-on experience with that format.

Installing and Configuring an Optical Drive

External optical drives are "installed" simply by connecting them to a USB or FireWire port, as appropriate, and connecting power. Internal optical drives are 5.25" half-height devices, and require the same physical installation steps as any other 5.25" externally accessible drive. The following sections describe the steps required to install and configure an ATAPI (IDE) optical drive.

SATA VERSUS PATA

Serial ATA (SATA) optical drives require the same basic installation steps as standard ATA/ATAPI optical drives, except that SATA drives do not require setting a Master/Slave jumper. We do not recommend using SATA optical drives, because they are plagued with compatibility problems. If you decide to use an SATA optical drive, make absolutely certain that the drive is certified compatible with your motherboard and that you have drivers compatible with your operating system, especially if you will use the drive as a boot device.

Choosing an interface configuration

The first installation decisions are whether to install the drive on the Primary or Secondary ATA interface and whether to configure the drive as the master or slave device. If you are upgrading an existing drive or replacing a failed drive, it might seem reasonable to configure the new drive the same way the old drive was configured. That's not always true. Many systems have non-optimal interface configurations.

The issue is that although PATA interfaces allow two devices to be connected, only one can be active at a time. So, for example, when a hard drive connected to the primary ATA channel is reading or writing data, an optical drive connected to the same channel must wait until the hard drive finishes using the channel before it can read or write data. Each device must take its turn, which slows performance of both devices when they are in use simultaneously.

Use the following guidelines to configure your drives properly:

- If the system uses an SATA hard drive or drives and no ATAPI devices other than the optical drive you are installing, configure the optical drive as the master device on the secondary ATA channel, leaving the primary ATA channel unused. (Windows can become confused if the primary master device is an optical drive rather than a hard drive.)

When There's Only One PATA Channel

If there is only one PATA channel, as is common on recent SATA motherboards, configure the optical drive as the master device on the primary ATA channel.

- If the system has one PATA hard drive—which will always be the primary master—and no ATAPI devices other than the optical drive you are installing, configure the optical drive as the secondary master.

- If the system has two PATA hard drives, they should be configured as primary master and secondary master. Configure the optical drive as the secondary slave.

- If the system has one PATA hard drive, configured as the primary master, and two ATAPI optical drives, for example, a DVD-ROM drive and a DVD writer, use the following guidelines:

  - If you frequently use both optical drives simultaneously—for example, to copy discs from the DVD-ROM drive to the DVD writer—configure the read-only optical drive as the primary slave and the optical writer as the secondary master.

  - If the two optical drives are not used simultaneously—for example, if you use the DVD writer for backups and the DVD-ROM drive for gaming—install the DVD writer as the secondary master and the DVD-ROM drive as the secondary slave.

- If the system has two PATA hard drives, configured as primary and secondary masters, and two ATAPI optical drives, configure the read-only drive as primary slave and the optical writer as the secondary slave.

- If the system has one or two PATA hard drives, an ATAPI optical drive, and another ATAPI device such as a tape drive, use the following guidelines:

  - If possible, install the ATAPI devices on separate channels.

  - If the system has two PATA hard drives, configure both ATAPI drives as slave devices.

  - If you must install one of the ATAPI drives as the secondary master, choose the more recent ATAPI drive for that channel.

  - If you must install two ATAPI drives on the secondary channel, make the newer device the master and the older device the slave.

Installing the optical drive

Installing an optical drive is generally straightforward. If you've ever worked inside a PC before, it should take you 10 minutes or less to install an optical drive. If you've never worked inside a PC, it might take five minutes more. To install an optical drive, proceed as follows:

1. Disconnect all the external cables from the PC and move it to a well-lit work area.

Advice from Brian Bilbrey

Alternatively, put the writer on the channel that does *not* have the drive you back up most: if the system/program drive is primary master and the data drive is secondary master, I'd want to back up from secondary master to primary slave, so I'd configure the writer as primary slave and the read-only drive as secondary slave.

2. Remove the top and/or side panel(s), depending on the design of your case. With some cases, you may also have to remove the front bezel to gain access to the drive bays. Refer to the system or case documentation for details.

3. If you are replacing an existing optical drive, disconnect the data cable and power cable from it and remove the drive from the bay. Depending on case design, the drive may be secured with screws through the drive bay and into the drive, or with rails that secure to the drive with screws and fit channels in the chassis.

4. If you are installing a second optical drive without removing the existing optical drive, remove the drive bay bezel from the position where you intend to install the new drive. You may also have to remove a metal RF shield from behind the bezel. Some cases use snap-in RF shields, as shown in Figure 8-1, which can be removed using your fingers. Other cases secure the RF shields with screws or use twist-off RF shields that are stamped into the chassis when it is made. If your case uses stamped shields, use pliers to grasp the shield and twist it back and forth until it breaks free. Use a file to grind down any sharp burrs that remain, ensuring that no filings remain inside the case on the motherboard where they can cause havoc.

Figure 8-1. Removing an RF shield before installing the drive

5. Remove the new drive from its packaging. If your case uses rails to mount optical drives, install the rails. Rails vary by type of case. Most secure with two screws, as shown in Figure 8-2, but some use a spring

Basic Versus Enhanced Operation

ATAPI optical drives require no special configuration steps to function at a basic level. All modern operating systems, including Windows 2000, Windows XP, and Linux, load ATAPI drivers and recognize ATAPI drives automatically. By default, though, an ATAPI optical drive functions as a simple read-only device. To enable additional features, such as the ability to play DVD movies or burn discs, you'll probably need to install some additional software. Even if the operating system provides some extended function support, such as the CD burning applet included with Windows XP, you'll probably want to install more capable software to take full advantage of the drive's capabilities. Most retail-boxed optical writers include such software, although it may be limited in functionality compared to the full version, or limited to running on the brand of drive with which it is bundled.

steel mechanism that snaps into the screw holes on the drive, and so can be secured without tools. Before you actually connect the rails, eyeball the location of the rail slots in the chassis relative to the various screw holes on the drive. Drives have two sets of rail holes. One places the rails at about the middle of the drive vertically, and the other places the rails at the bottom of the drive. Which set provides proper vertical alignment for the drive depends on the position of the rail slots in the chassis. Rails may also be adjustable for seating depth, so check that positioning to make sure that the drive will seat flush with the front bezel when the drive is installed. Once you think the rails are mounted correctly, test the drive for proper vertical positioning and seating depth by temporarily sliding it into the bay.

Figure 8-2. Mounting a rail on an optical drive

Figure 8-3. The rear panel of a DVD drive, showing the configuration jumper

6. Verify that the drive is configured as Master, Slave, or Cable Select, as appropriate. The configuration jumper is located on the rear panel of the drive, as shown in Figure 8-3. Most drives are configured by default as Master devices. Change the jumper position if necessary to configure the drive to Slave or Cable Select.

7. It's usually easier to connect the ATA cable to the drive before you install the drive in the case. If you are using a new cable, which you should do if the existing cable shows any signs of wear or twisting, connect the new cable before you slide the drive into

the bay. Verify that the pin 1 side of the cable, usually indicated with a red or other colored stripe, corresponds to pin 1 on the drive connector. Then press the cable connector down into the drive connector until it fully seats, as shown in Figure 8-4.

Figure 8-4. Connecting an ATA data cable to an optical drive

When Slow Is Fast Enough

Because optical drives have relatively slow data transfer rates, they can use the standard 40-wire ATA cable shown in Figure 8-4 rather than the 80-wire Ultra-ATA cable used for ATA hard drives. (An 80-wire cable works fine if that's all you have, but it's not necessary.)

FIRST THINGS FIRST

If you have removed an existing optical drive and are using the existing data cable, feed the drive end of the cable out through the drive bay and connect it to the drive before sliding the drive into the bay. If the cable isn't long enough to give you some working slack with the drive outside the case, detach the cable from the motherboard and connect it just as you would a new cable.

---

8. Feed the loose end of the ATA cable through the drive bay from the front. Working from the rear of the drive, feed the cable down into the case, placing the free end near the motherboard ATA connectors.

9. Align the drive rails with the corresponding slots in the case, and press the drive firmly into place until the drive rails seat. If you are using rails that secure with screws, install the screws to lock the drive into place. If you mounted the drive rails correctly, the drive should seat flush with the bezels that cover the vacant drive bays.

10. The ATA interfaces are located near the right front edge of most motherboards. Locate the motherboard ATA interface connector you plan to use (usually the Secondary ATA interface). Locate pin 1 on the

interface, align the ATA cable with its red stripe toward pin 1 on the interface, and press the connector into place, as shown in Figure 8-5.

Figure 8-5. Connecting the optical drive data cable to the motherboard

Advice from Brian Bilbrey

Optical drives installed with spring-lock rails should be braced from the front while applying enough pressure to properly seat the power connector. This prevents the drive from shooting out of the front of the computer when the spring-retention force is overcome, thus propelling the new drive across the room. If your goal is shock-testing equipment, you may omit such bracing.

11. The final step in installing an optical drive—one we forget more often than we should—is to connect power to the drive. Choose one of the power cables coming from the power supply and press the Molex connector onto the drive power connector, as shown in Figure 8-6. It may require significant pressure to get the power connector to seat, so use care to avoid hurting your fingers if the connector seats suddenly. The Molex power connector is keyed, so verify that it is oriented properly before you apply pressure to seat the power cable.

DON'T FORGET THE AUDIO CABLE

Some older systems have an audio cable that links the optical drive to the sound card or motherboard audio connector. This cable was required because older optical drives used a direct connection between the drive and the audio adapter to communicate analog audio to the system. Newer optical drives support digital audio, which is communicated directly over the ATA connection to the bus.

If you install a new optical drive in such an older system, connect the existing audio cable from the new drive to the audio adapter, but also enable digital audio. To do so, open Device Manager, display the Property sheet for the drive, and mark the "Enable digital audio" checkbox.

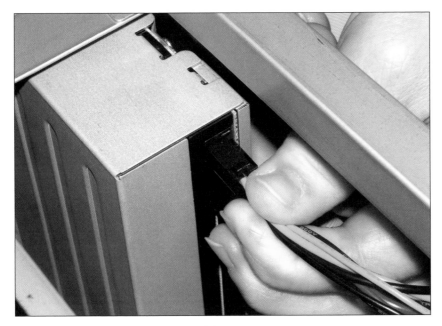

Figure 8-6. Connecting power to the optical drive

That's all there is to installing an optical drive. After you replace the side and/or top panels and the drive bezel, the system is ready to go. Move it back to its original location, reconnect all the external cables, and power it up.

Enabling Bus Mastering (DMA) support

Some older ATAPI optical drives operate in *Programmed I/O (PIO)* mode rather than *Direct Memory Access (DMA)* mode, which is also called Bus Mastering mode. The fastest PIO mode has a maximum data rate slower than that of most DVD drives, so operating in PIO mode reduces drive performance and may result in jerky video display and similar symptoms. More important, PIO mode puts a heavy burden on the CPU. A typical ATAPI optical drive operating in PIO mode may reach 50% to 80% CPU utilization when the drive is being accessed heavily, yet the same drive operating under the same conditions in DMA or Ultra DMA mode may occupy only 1% to 5% of CPU time.

PIO VERSUS DMA

Some optical drives support PIO and DMA modes, but are configured by default for PIO mode. Such drives have a PIO/DMA jumper on the rear panel, near the interface and power connectors. Jumper positions are usually labeled on the top or bottom of the drive. To reconfigure the drive, simply move the jumper from the PIO position to the DMA position.

All modern motherboards, optical drives, and operating systems support DMA modes, but DMA is not always enabled automatically. Windows XP generally manages DMA properly and automatically. During a fresh install, Windows XP tests the ATA interfaces and the connected devices to determine DMA compatibility. If the interface and all connected devices are DMA-compatible, Windows XP enables DMA for that interface. So far, so good.

But a problem may arise if you have upgraded Windows or replaced an older optical drive with a newer model. If the original operating system or optical drive was not configured to use DMA, Windows XP may not enable DMA even though the interface and devices support it. To check DMA status on a Windows XP system, and to enable DMA if necessary, take the following steps:

1. Right-click the My Computer icon and choose Properties to display the System Properties dialog.

2. Click the Hardware tab and then the Device Manager button to display Device Manager.

3. Locate the IDE ATA/ATAPI Controllers entry and click the + icon to expand the listing. There should be three lines visible, assuming that two ATA channels are installed and enabled. The first line describes the ATA controller itself. The two remaining lines are for the Primary IDE Channel and the Secondary IDE Channel. (If you have only one IDE channel line, your motherboard may be a recent model that provides only one PATA interface.)

4. Double-click the channel to which your optical drive is connected—usually the Secondary IDE Channel—to display the Properties dialog for that channel. Click the Advanced Settings tab to display the dialog. This dialog has two sections, one for Device 0 (Master) and another for Device 1 (Slave). The listing for your optical drive should display the Current Transfer Mode as DMA or Ultra DMA. If it does, your drive is operating at peak efficiency, and you can exit the dialog. For example, Figure 8-7 shows that the DVD-ROM drive installed as the master device on the secondary ATA channel is using Ultra DMA Mode 2, which is the fastest DMA mode it supports.

5. If the Current Transfer Mode box for the CD-ROM drive lists PIO Mode, check the setting for that device in the Transfer Mode box.

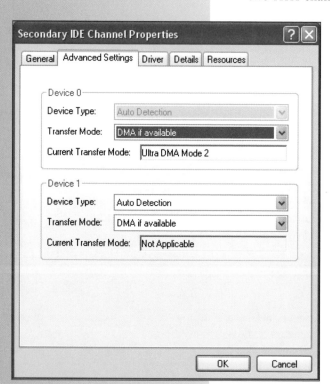

Figure 8-7. The Secondary IDE Channel Properties dialog shows that this drive is operating in Ultra DMA Mode 2

- If the Transfer Mode box is set to "DMA if available," that means that Windows has decided that the interface, the drive, or both do not support DMA. Replace the drive with a newer model that does support DMA. If you are certain that the current drive is DMA-capable, try using another cable or connecting the drive to the other ATA interface.

- If the Transfer Mode box is set to PIO Only, use the drop-down list to change that setting to "DMA if available," save your changes, restart the system, and redisplay that dialog. If the Current Transfer Mode box for the drive now displays DMA mode, the drive is now using DMA. If the box still displays PIO mode, Windows has determined that it is unsafe to use DMA mode. Replace the drive or cable as described in the preceding item.

Advice from Jim Cooley

Reinstalling or updating the chipset drivers may also enable (or re-enable) DMA support for the optical drive under Windows 2000 or XP. Check with your motherboard manufacturer for updated drivers.

DON'T MIX AND MATCH

Regardless of operating system, it's a bad idea to use a PIO-mode device on the same channel as a DMA-capable device. That's because ATA doesn't allow mixing DMA mode and PIO mode on one channel. If one device runs PIO mode, both must do so, which cripples the DMA-capable device. In particular, it's a horrible idea to use a PIO-only optical drive on the same channel as an Ultra DMA hard drive, because that means the hard drive will run in PIO mode. That cuts throughput by 50% to 90% and dramatically increases CPU utilization.

Actually, it's a bad idea to use PIO-mode drives, period. Optical drives are inexpensive. If you have a PIO-only optical drive, the best course is to replace it as soon as possible.

Changing optical drive letter assignments

By default, all versions of Windows assign an optical drive the next available drive letter following those for any local volumes. If you subsequently install an additional hard disk or repartition your drive to create additional volumes, the letter assigned to the optical drive may change, which may confuse installed software that attempts to access the optical drive as the old letter.

You can avoid this "musical chairs" reassignment of optical drive letters by manually assigning the optical drive a drive letter that is higher than the drive letter for any existing local or network volume. Assigning the highest available drive letter, Z, to the optical drive prevents Windows from ever altering that drive letter. If you have two optical drives, assign them Z: and Y:. To assign a different drive letter to the optical drive in Windows XP, proceed as follows:

1. From Control Panel, choose Administrative Tools → Computer Management.

2. Expand the tree if necessary to show items in the Storage branch.

3. Click Disk Management, and locate your optical drive in the lower-right pane, as shown in Figure 8-8.

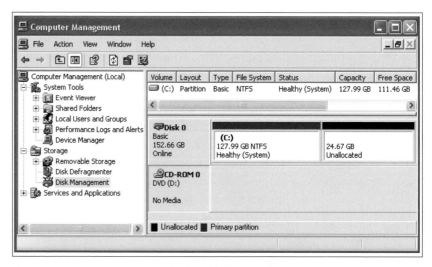

Figure 8-8. Computer Management displays drive letter assignments

4. Right-click the optical drive icon to display the context-sensitive menu, and choose the Change Drive Letter and Paths... menu item to display the Change Drive Letter and Paths dialog.

5. Click the Change button and use the drop-down list to assign an available drive letter to the optical drive.

6. Save your changes and exit. Once you accept the changes, the new drive letter takes effect immediately.

MUSICAL DRIVE LETTERS

If you change the drive letter assignment for an optical drive, do so immediately after installing the drive or the operating system. If you use that drive under its original letter to install software, that software will later attempt to access the drive using the old drive letter.

Troubleshooting Optical Drives

Optical drives generally work or they don't. Assuming the drive is installed and configured properly initially, it should be problem-free throughout its service life.

Use the following guidelines to troubleshoot optical drive problems:

- When an optical drive behaves strangely, the first step is to reboot the system.

- Gross failures, such as the computer BIOS not detecting a drive that formerly worked normally, are usually caused by an outright failure of the drive itself. If you've recently worked inside the system, the most likely cause of a complete drive failure is that you left the power or data cable disconnected or that you damaged the data cable.

HOSTAGE DISCS

Optical drives sometimes refuse to eject a disc, using either software eject or the eject button on the drive itself. If that happens, power down the system completely, allow it to remain off for a minute or so, and then power it back up. If that doesn't solve the problem, the drive itself is probably defective. If the disc being held hostage is valuable, look for a small emergency eject hole in the front panel of the drive. Insert a paper clip into the hole and press firmly to release the drive tray. If the drive has no emergency eject hole, the best option is to disassemble the drive carefully to retrieve the disc.

- If you install an SATA hard drive in a system that was previously all PATA and the optical drive "disappears," make sure that the operating system is fully updated. Older ATA drivers sometimes become confused if SATA and PATA devices are used together. Windows 2000 and Linux distributions that use a kernel earlier than 2.6.11 are particularly subject to this problem.

- If you experience read errors, try a different disc, or clean the current disc. If read errors occur with different discs, use a cleaning disc to clean the drive.

- If a DVD drive refuses to read CDs but will read DVDs, or vice versa, the mostly likely cause is that one of the two read lasers has failed. Replace the drive.

- If an optical writer fails while burning the first disc of a new type of disc or a new batch of your usual type of disc, update the drive firmware. Check the manufacturer's support site to see whether a firmware update is available for download. If not, call their tech support number and ask.

- If the firmware update doesn't solve the problem, try a different brand of disc, preferably one that is recommended by the maker of your optical burner.

A Disc by Any Other Name

There is little relationship between the brand name of a disc and the company that made it. Some companies manufacture discs that are rebranded by several other companies, and may or may not also be sold under the manufacturer's brand name. Some companies put their own brands on discs from different manufacturers. Some companies do both.

It's quite possible to buy two apparently identical spindles of discs, sometimes with the same SKU, and find that one was made in Japan and the other in Taiwan, by different companies. It's also common for spindles of different capacity—25, 50, or 100—all with the same brand name, to contain discs made by different companies. In general, the best discs are made in Japan or Singapore and the worst in Taiwan and Hong Kong.

The best way to determine disc types is to use DVD Identifier (*http://dvd. identifier.cdfreaks.com*) or CD-R Identifier (no web site; search Google). Even these utilities aren't foolproof, because some high-quality disc manufacturers have sold master stamping dies to other companies, whose discs are identified as coming from the company that produced the stamping die rather than the company that actually produced the discs.

Cleaning an optical drive

The first symptom of a dirty optical drive is that you get read errors on a data CD or DVD or degraded sound or video from an audio CD or DVD-Video disc. If this happens, it is often because the disc itself is dirty or scratched, so clean the disc or try a different disc before assuming the drive is at fault.

CLEANING DISCS

We usually clean discs by spraying them lightly with window cleaning solution and gently drying them with a soft cloth. (Wipe straight across the disc rather than in circles.) That method is frowned upon by some, but we've never damaged a disc by cleaning it that way. If you want to use an approved method, buy one of the commercial CD or DVD disc cleaners, which are readily available from big-box stores and other retailers.

Tray-loading optical drives require little cleaning. They are well sealed against dust, and all recent drives incorporate a self-cleaning lens mechanism. For routine cleaning, wipe the external parts of the drive occasionally with a damp cloth. Some drive makers recommend using a drive cleaning kit every month or two, although we usually do so only when we begin getting read errors. To use these kits, which are available in wet and dry forms, insert the cleaning disc and access the drive to spin the cleaning disc for a few seconds. For a particularly dirty drive, you may need to repeat the cleaning process several times. Slot-loading optical drives can be cleaned more thoroughly by vacuuming the interior gently, using a pencil or similar object to hold the slot open, or by using compressed air to blow out the dust and then drenching the interior of the drive with zero-residue cleaner. Most optical drive manufacturers discourage taking more extreme measures, so if you go beyond these routine cleaning steps, you are on your own and may void your warranty.

Updating drive firmware

For any optical drive, but particularly for optical writers, it's important to keep the firmware updated. Firmware updates fix bugs, add features, and add support for new brands and types of optical discs. We generally update the firmware in our optical drives every time we buy a new spindle of discs.

If you're running Windows, visit the manufacturer's web site periodically, and download the latest firmware version for your drive. Most optical drive makers supply firmware updates as executables that can be run directly from Windows or from a command prompt. Verify that there is no disc in the drive, and then just run the executable to update your drive firmware.

Figure 8-9 shows a typical firmware update utility, in this case one for the Plextor PX-716A DVD writer.

If you are running Linux, updating your drive firmware may be problematic. All drive makers supply firmware updaters for Windows. Many also supply OS X updaters. None we know of provides updaters for Linux. If you're dual-booting Linux and Windows, there's no problem. Simply boot Windows and install the Windows version of the firmware update.

But if you're running only Linux, you'll have to jump through a few hoops to get your drive updated. We run Linux on all of our production systems, so we encounter this problem frequently. The best solution is usually just to bite the bullet, pull the optical drive from the Linux box temporarily, connect it to a Windows box, and do the update from there.

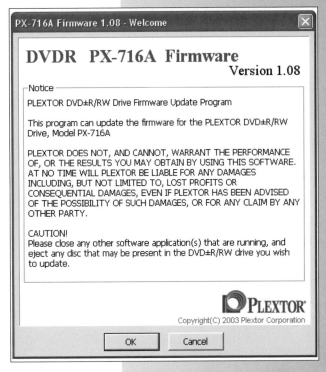

Figure 8-9. A firmware update utility for the Plextor PX-716A DVD writer

---

OLDIES CAN BE GOODIES

When you download the latest firmware update for your drive, also download your current firmware version, just in case. Firmware updates usually fix problems, but they've been known to cause problems of their own. For example, we once updated the firmware in a CD burner, only to find that it would no longer burn a brand of disc that we had been using successfully before the firmware update. We had a nearly full spindle of 100 discs that were now useless. Fortunately, the solution was easy. We simply reinstalled the old version of the firmware, and everything returned to normal.

Determining drive capabilities

Sometimes, an apparent error isn't an error at all. For example, if your optical drive refuses to read, write, or even load a particular type of disc, it may be that the drive simply wasn't designed to accept discs in that format. To determine the capabilities of your optical drive, use Nero InfoTool, shown in Figure 8-10. You can download a free copy of Nero InfoTool from *http:// www.nero.com*.

In our case, the DVD-ROM drive in one of our test-bed systems spit out a DVD+R DL disc someone had sent us. We weren't sure if the problem was the drive, the

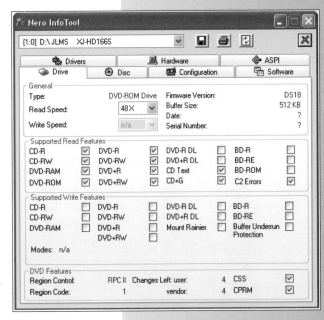

Figure 8-10. Nero InfoTool displays drive capabilities

type of disc, or the individual disc itself. Running Nero InfoTool told us: the drive simply didn't support DL media.

Nero InfoTool also comes in handy when you want to update the firmware in your drive. Some optical drives have no indication of manufacturer or model on the front panel. For example, we decided to upgrade the DVD-ROM firmware to see if the new firmware would add read support for DVD+R DL discs. We thought the unlabeled DVD-ROM drive was a Samsung model. When we ran Nero InfoTool, it listed the drive as an XJ-HD166S, which is a Lite-On model. It's a bad idea to install a firmware update intended for one model of drive to a different model, so ordinarily we'd have had to open the system and remove the drive to verify its model. Instead, we ran Nero InfoTool to find out.

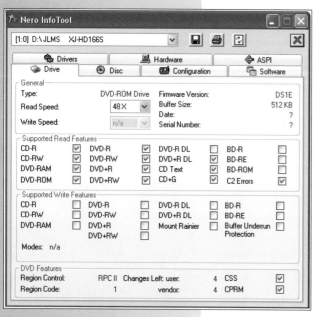

Figure 8-11. Nero InfoTool showing the new firmware's capabilites

We visited the Lite-On site and downloaded the most recent firmware for the drive, which was version DS1E, six versions later than the DS18 firmware currently installed. We ran the firmware update executable and rebooted the system. When we again ran Nero InfoTool, we were pleased to see the change shown in Figure 8-11. Yep, with the firmware update, this drive now reads DVD+R DL discs (although still not DVD-R DL discs).

Verifying quality of burned discs

If you have problems reading a burned disc, the first step is to determine whether the problem is caused by the disc or by the DVD drive or player. Most disc burning applications have a verify feature, but a disc can verify successfully in the drive that burned it and still produce read errors in DVD-ROM drives and players.

If you use high-quality writable discs in a good burner, the disc will seldom be the problem. Still, it's easy enough to check disc quality by doing a surface scan of the burned disc. If you use a Plextor burner, you'll have PlexTools, which can provide more information about disc quality than you ever wanted to know. If you use another brand of burner, download the free Nero CD-DVD Speed utility (*http://www.cdspeed2000.com*).

It's important to use a high-quality DVD-ROM drive to do the scanning, such as one made by Lite-On, Pioneer, NEC, Plextor, or Samsung. To scan a questionable disc, insert it in the DVD drive, start Nero CD-DVD Speed, click the ScanDisc tab, and then click the Start button. Figure 8-12 shows the results from scanning a "perfect" DVD. If there are damaged but readable areas on the disc, they'll be flagged in yellow. Unreadable areas are flagged in red.

We put "perfect" in quotes because few burned optical discs are truly perfect. Running utilities such as PlexTools or Kprobe on nearly any burned disc will find C1/C2 errors (CD) or PI/PO errors (DVD). If the disc has passed a standard surface scan, those errors are generally insignificant. For example, Figure 8-13 shows the result of scanning the same disc shown in the preceding graphic, but with the C1/C2 – PI/PO scan option. Despite the errors shown, this disc is perfectly usable for all practical purposes. We suggest you restrict yourself to standard scans, and leave the highly technical detailed scans to the engineers.

Dealing with Book Type issues

It's not uncommon for burned DVDs that read perfectly in one drive or player to be unreadable in another drive or player, often an older model. Sometimes, the problem is simply a matter of the age of the drive or player. Older read heads may not deal well with some types of discs that were introduced after the player was built, because the newer discs have lower reflectivity and contrast than the pressed DVDs for which the drive or player was designed. For example, most DVD drives and players made before mid-2004 cannot read DVD+R DL discs, although this problem can sometimes be fixed by installing a firmware update. Similarly, many DVD players made before about 2002 will load DVD-R or DVD+R discs, but the playback is jerky and filled with video and audio artifacts.

A complete failure to read is often caused by the *Book Type field*. This field is a half-byte (4-bit) string at the beginning of the physical format information section of the control data block that exists on every DVD, pressed or burned. The purpose of the Book Type field is to identify the type of disc unambiguously so that the the drive or player will know how best to play it. Table 8-1 lists the possible values for the Book Type field.

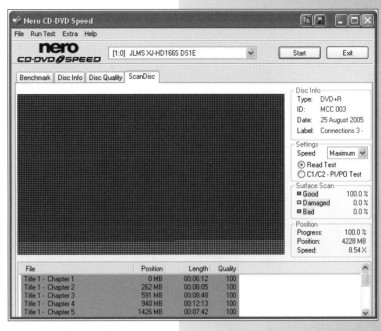

Figure 8-12. Nero CD-DVD Speed displays a perfect disc scan

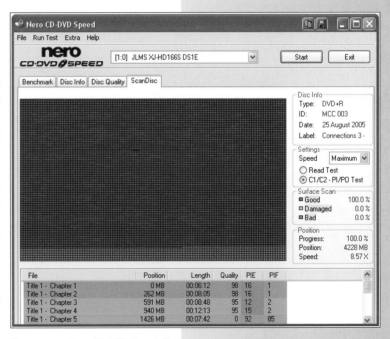

Figure 8-13. Nero CD-DVD Speed displays errors on a PI/PO scan

Table 8-1. Book Type field values

Value	Type	Value	Type	Value	Type	Value	Type
0000	DVD-ROM (SL/DL)	0100	Undefined	1000	Undefined	1100	
0001	DVD-RAM	0101	Undefined	1001	DVD+RW	1101	DVD+RW/DL
0010	DVD-R, DVR-R/DL	0110	Undefined	1010	DVD+R	1110	DVD+R/DL
0011	DVD-RW	0111	Undefined	1011	Undefined	1111	Undefined

If the playback device does not recognize the Book Type field value—either because the drive or player predates a new type of media or because the manufacturer intentionally failed to provide support for particular media types—one of two things happens:

- The playback device makes a best-effort attempt to play the disc. This attempt is usually at least partially successful, and this is the default method used by most current and many older DVD drives and players. Older players and drives may produce read errors and other glitches when attempting to read newer types of discs, but at least they make the attempt.

- The playback device refuses to attempt to read the disc, even if there is no technical reason for doing so. Some DVD drive and player manufacturers refuse to support formats, such as DVD+R and DVD+RW, that are not officially recognized by the DVD Forum. When a disc of an unsupported type is inserted, these drives and players simply eject it, without attempting to read it.

As a workaround, some DVD writer makers have enabled a feature in their firmware called compatibility bit-setting. A drive that supports this feature can record DVD+R, DVD+RW, and DVD+RW DL discs with the Book Type field set to 0000. In other words, these drives lie to the playback device by causing the discs they write to report themselves as DVD-ROM discs.

Some DVD writers automatically write any "plus format" disc with the Book Type field set to identify the disc as a DVD-ROM. Other DVD writers support *compatibility bit-setting*, but make using it optional (and require that the burning software explicitly support the feature). Still other DVD writers do not support compatibility bit-setting. Plextor, for example, long refused to support this feature (although their PX-740A does support it). If you need compatibility bit-setting, make sure that any drive you install explicitly lists support for that feature, and, if necessary, that your burning software also supports it.

Our opinion is that compatibility bit-setting is pretty much obsolete. In an era of $25 DVD players and $40 DVD writers, it makes more sense just to replace older, incompatible hardware with newer models that eliminate the compatibility issues.

External and Removable Storage Devices

9

Adding an external or removable storage device is an easy, inexpensive way to supplement the storage of your PC. By definition, external storage devices do not require installation, and most do not require even installing a device driver or other software. Even internal removable storage devices—tape drives and removable hard drives—are easy to install, no more difficult than a standard hard drive or optical drive. By using external or removable storage devices, you can expand the storage of your system to whatever capacity you need.

Uses for External and Removable Storage

The potential uses of external and removable storage devices are as many and as varied as the people who use them. Here are just a few:

Expanding storage on notebook systems
> Replacing the hard drive in a desktop system is easy and inexpensive, but options for notebook systems are much more limited. Notebook hard drives are expensive, have relatively small capacities, and are slow. Adding an external hard drive to a notebook system addresses all of these problems. If the notebook has a USB 2.0, FireWire, or External SATA port, you can use one of the many models of external hard drives that support one or more of those interfaces. If your notebook has only slow USB 1.1 ports, you can install a USB 2.0, FireWire, or External SATA PC Card adapter to take advantage of the much higher transfer speeds of those interfaces.

Transporting or shipping large amounts of data
> If you need to transport or ship large amounts of data, an external or removable hard drive is often the best solution. External hard drives are available in very high capacities. A frame/carrier removable hard drive system uses standard hard drives, and so is limited in capacity only by the size of the largest standard hard drives available.

In This Chapter

Uses for External and Removable Storage

External Hard Drives

External Drive Enclosures

Removable Hard Drive Enclosures

USB Flash Memory Drives

Tape Drives

MOVIES ON DISK

For example, one of our readers works for a company that produces digital special effects for movies, always on very short deadlines. That company formerly used expensive, high-capacity tape drives to duplicate their 100 GB to 500 GB video sequences to multiple tapes and shipped the tapes to the movie production company. Nowadays, they just copy a video sequence to one FireWire external hard drive and FedEx the drive to the production company. When the drive arrives, the production company staff plugs it into a PC and copies the data from the external hard drive to a server. The external drives are so inexpensive compared to the value of the data on them that the drives are treated as consumables and are sent in duplicate to make sure that at least one copy arrives on time.

Using one computer for multiple operating systems

Software development and similar work that requires using multiple operating systems always presents a problem. You can configure one PC to multiboot different operating systems, but that is seldom entirely satisfactory. You can install a dedicated computer for each OS, but doing that is expensive, generates a lot of noise and heat, and means you're soon covered up in computers. Using a frame/carrier removable hard drive system solves all the problems. Installing each OS on its own hard drive means that you can simply insert the carrier with the appropriate OS, restart the system, and have the equivalent of a dedicated PC running that OS. We use frame/carrier units on our main test-bed systems for that reason.

Sharing one computer among several people

Using a frame/carrier removable hard drive system allows one computer to be shared among several people. Inserting the drive and restarting the system presents each user with his own desktop environment, programs, and data, with no concerns about conflicts or accidentally damaging someone else's data or configuration.

FAMILY HARMONY

One married couple with three teenagers reports that they used to have five PCs, all of which were getting old. They considered buying or building five new systems, but the configurations they wanted—fast video cards, large flat-panel displays, and so on—would have cost more than they wanted to spend. Instead, they built only three new systems, each configured lavishly, and equipped each new system with a frame/carrier removable hard drive system. As it turned out, the couple ended up sharing one of the systems—he runs Linux and she runs Windows XP—while the three kids share the two other systems. Everyone is happier than they would have been with five inexpensive systems. (They also installed a gaming console, which keeps scheduling conflicts to a minimum.)

Supporting multiple large data sets

Some scientists, market researchers, and others need to manipulate extremely large data sets—sometimes in the 250+ GB range. Although it may be possible to build a PC with sufficient disk space to store all the data sets on internal hard drives, it's usually cheaper and more efficient to swap those data sets in and out as needed. If there are many such data sets, using external or removable hard drives may be the only practical option.

Backing up

Tape drives, optical drives, and other traditional backup solutions are too slow and have too little capacity to be practical for doing complete backups of today's huge hard drives. What's needed is something that's fast, stores a lot of data, and doesn't cost much per byte stored. In other words, a hard drive. In addition to their speed and capacity advantages, removable hard drives have a major advantage if you experience catastrophic system failure, because you can simply connect the backup hard drive and boot it directly, without spending the time needed to rebuild the system, reinstall the operating system and applications, and recover from tape.

Offline data storage

Even the largest hard drive eventually fills up, particularly if you're a pack rat like Robert. External or removable hard drives allow you to store unlimited amounts of data offline. For example, one of our readers ripped his entire DVD movie collection to several external hard drives, and stored the original discs safely. Each external drive stores between 40 and 100 movies, depending on the capacity of the drive, the size of the movies, and the level of compression he used when ripping the movies. He keeps a rotating selection of two or three of these external hard drives plugged into his home-theater PC, and always has a selection of between 100 and 250 movies available for immediate viewing simply by choosing from a directory listing. If a movie he wants to view is on an offline drive, it takes only seconds to plug in that drive and access the movie. Others use external or removable hard drives for storing collections of music, digital images, or home videos. One person we know records an entire season of his favorite television programs, stores them to external hard drives, and watches them in a marathon session after the season has ended.

Sneakernetting data

In olden days, the ubiquitous floppy disk was the medium of choice for sneakernetting data between systems that weren't networked. Nowadays, the 1.44 MB capacity of a standard floppy is ridiculously small, and even a writable CD or DVD disc may have too little capacity.

USB 2.0 flash drives, which are available in capacities as large as 16 GB, and external or removable hard drives are capacious enough and fast enough to make it practical to transfer amounts of data that are impractical to transfer via optical disc.

Securing data

If you work with extremely sensitive data—such as payroll information—using an external or removable hard drive allows you to secure that data by taking it with you or by storing it in a vault.

BEWARE TEMPORARY FILES

If you use an external or removable hard drive to store sensitive data, that drive must be bootable and should be the only hard drive in the system. If the external or removable hard drive is a secondary drive, the internal hard drive may retain temporary files, backup data files, OS swap files, and similar files that could compromise the security of your data. For absolute data security, configure the system without a permanent hard drive and always power down the system when you disconnect the external or removable hard drive. Also consider using good encryption (think AES) at the filesystem level for securing the data on a drive that may be vulnerable to theft or loss.

Advice from Jim Cooley

Portability is a key advantage of external and removable storage devices, but portability also means that these devices are easily misplaced or stolen. Always take steps to ensure that such devices are properly secured when unattended, and that the data on them is encrypted or otherwise protected against being accessed by unauthorized people.

Advice from Brian Jepson

You may want to look into TrueCrypt, an open source tool for creating encrypted images that can be mounted as drives. I use it on a laptop that came with XP Home, because encrypted NTFS files are supported only on Pro. I've grown extremely fond of it: *http://www.truecrypt.org*.

It's also survived numerous XP crashes (that weren't caused by TrueCrypt as best as I can tell) that happened while the virtual drive was mounted. In theory, I should dismount my TrueCrypt drive before launching a buggy game like Temple of Elemental Evil, but I forget sometimes.

External Hard Drives

External hard drives are external peripherals that comprise a standard desktop or notebook hard drive contained within a portable enclosure that provides one or more types of interface connector to link the external hard drive to a desktop or notebook computer. Many external hard drives include backup software that features a "one-button" means of backing up data from your internal hard drive.

External hard drives may use any of three interfaces:

USB 2.0

USB 2.0 is by far the most common interface supported by external hard drives. USB 2.0 nominally provides 60 MB/s bandwidth, but overhead typically reduces this to an effective 25 MB/s to 30 MB/s. Because standard hard drives can use 50 MB/s or more bandwidth, the USB 2.0 interface throttles throughput noticeably for the fastest external hard drives, making them "feel" somewhat slower than an internal drive. The advantage of USB 2.0 is that it is ubiquitous, so a USB 2.0 external hard drive can be connected to nearly any notebook or desktop system.

ALWAYS FLUSH

Although data corruption is possible with any external hard drive, it is particularly likely to occur with USB 2.0 external hard drives. Data corruption occurs if the drive is turned off or disconnected before buffered data is written to it. To avoid data corruption, always flush the buffer before you turn off or disconnect the drive. To do so, use the Windows Safely Remove Hardware Wizard, which notifies you when it is safe to remove the drive.

FireWire

> FireWire (*IEEE-1394a* or *IEEE-1394b*) is similar functionally to USB 2.0, but faster in real terms. Most FireWire external hard drives use IEEE-1394a S400, which provides nominal bandwidth of about 400 Mb/s, or 50 MB/s. True throughput is somewhat smaller, but sufficient to make throttling relatively minor. Most IEEE-1394b external hard drives support the S800 data rate, which eliminates throttling completely. The disadvantage of FireWire is that relatively few systems, notebook or desktop, provide an S400 FireWire interface port, and almost none provide an S800 port. Few FireWire-only external hard drives are available. Most drives that support FireWire also include a USB 2.0 interface. If you plan to use a small FireWire drive with your notebook computer, you'll probably want bus power. Not all FireWire ports deliver bus power.

External SATA

> External SATA (*eSATA*) is the least common interface supported by external hard drives, but is fast gaining popularity. eSATA provides 150 MB/s or 300 MB/s bandwidth, and the high efficiency of the eSATA protocol means that nearly all of that bandwidth is actually available to the drive. An eSATA external hard drive has the same performance as the same drive used internally. The disadvantage of eSATA is that only a tiny percentage of systems have eSATA ports.

eSATA AFTER THE FACT

You can add eSATA support to an existing system by installing an eSATA host bus adapter in a desktop system or by using a Cardbus or ExpressCard eSATA card in a notebook. For desktop systems, you can instead use an inexpensive adapter that connects to an internal standard SATA port and provides an eSATA port on an expansion card bracket.

Advice from Ron Morse

If you use a USB 2.0 High Speed device, make sure not only that your system BIOS supports USB 2.0 High Speed transfers but also that High Speed support is enabled in BIOS Setup. The default BIOS setting on some ASUS motherboards, for example, is for "Full Speed" USB transfers. High Speed capability must be enabled manually via the BIOS Setup routine. The motherboard manual indicates the default setting and how to change it if necessary.

Advice from Brian Jepson

You can also go into Device Manager, open up Properties for the drive, choose Policies, and select Optimize for Quick Removal. It claims you can yank the drive out without dismounting, but, well . . . it's Windows.

Advice from Brian Jepson

Drawing power from the interface doesn't always work with USB 2.0, since it delivers less power than FireWire. I tested this with four different 2.5" drives, and looked into the power consumption issue. In theory, there is enough juice coming via USB 2.0 to run the drive, but not enough for the spinup.

There are two kludges that enclosure makers push, and both of them stink. The first is the USB Y adapter: you plug one end into your drive, and the other two ends into two separate USB ports. It rarely works, as it's not unusual to find that both USB ports are on a single USB root hub, and are sharing the voltage.

The other kludge is to include a small rechargeable battery in the enclosure. Surprisingly, this works pretty well, because the drive really only needs the extra power in short bursts. But it still freaks me out; the consequences of the battery draining in the field are unacceptable.

The only reliable solution for USB bus power I've found is 1.8" drives. Even Seagate claims that only one line of their 2.5" drives will run via USB power, and that's "in the majority of systems": *http://www.seagate.com/docs/pdf/whitepaper/TP-535.pdf*.

Broadly speaking, there are three categories of external hard drive:

Full-size external hard drives

> *Full-size external hard drives* are about the size of a thick hardback book (or a Mac Mini). Because they use standard 7200 RPM 3.5" desktop ATA or SATA drives, these drives have high capacities—from 120 GB to 500 GB or more—and very high disk performance. They are readily available in USB and/or USB/FireWire interfaces, and by mid-2006 will be available in eSATA models. Because full-size external hard drives use standard 3.5" desktop hard drives, they require more power than can be provided by the interface cable. Accordingly, full-size external drives always use a power brick. Figure 9-1 shows a 500 GB Seagate external hard drive, a typical full-size model.

Figure 9-1. Seagate 500 GB full-size external hard drive (image courtesy of Seagate Technology LLC)

Portable external hard drives

> *Portable external hard drives* are smaller than a paperback book, and about an inch thick. Because they use 4200 RPM 2.5" notebook hard drives, these drives have smaller capacities—typically 40 GB to 120 GB—and lower disk performance than full-size models. Their low power consumption means they can be powered directly by the interface and so require no power brick. Most portable models are USB-only. Figure 9-2 shows a 120 GB Seagate portable external hard drive, a typical model.

Figure 9-2. Seagate 120 GB portable external hard drive (image courtesy of Seagate Technology LLC)

Pocket external hard drives

Pocket external hard drives are a solution in search of a problem. Because they use 3600 RPM 1" hard drives, these models have tiny capacities—typically 5 GB or less—and much lower disk performance than even portable models. We see no point to buying one of these drives. USB flash drives, described later in this chapter, are smaller, faster, cheaper, and hold more data. Figure 9-3 shows a 5 GB Seagate pocket external hard drive, a typical model. (Note that models based on 1.8" hard drives have substantially higher capacities, are much less expensive per gigabyte than USB flash drives, and are often small enough to qualify as "pocket" drives.)

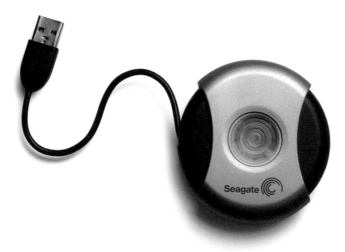

Figure 9-3. Seagate 5 GB pocket external hard drive (image courtesy of Seagate Technology LLC)

External hard drives of various types are made by Iomega, Maxtor, Seagate, Western Digital, and other companies. We prefer the Seagate models.

(REALLY) EXTERNAL HARD DRIVES

Don't overlook the advantages of a *Network Attached Storage* (*NAS*) device, also called a *Network Hard Drive*. These devices resemble standard external hard drives, but instead of connecting to a PC via USB or FireWire to provide local storage on that PC, they connect directly to your network with an Ethernet cable, providing storage that is accessible to any PC on the network. NAS devices are made by Maxtor, Western Digital, D-Link, NETGEAR, Buffalo, and many other manufacturers.

External Drive Enclosures

You don't have to buy an external hard drive; you can roll your own. External drive enclosures are an economical alternative to commercial external hard drives, which sometimes sell at a high premium over the cost of a bare hard drive. These enclosures, most of which cost $20 to $40, accept standard ATA or SATA drives and provide internal power and data connectors for the drive. They also include ATA-to-USB and/or ATA-to-FireWire interface circuitry and an external jack or cable by which the enclosure can be connected to a PC. Models that accept 2.5" notebook hard drives are powered by the USB cable (usually a USB Y-cable, which draws power from two USB ports) or a 6-wire FireWire cable. Models that accept 3.5" hard drives use a separate power brick to supply the higher current needed by standard ATA/SATA hard drives.

Installing a hard drive in one of these enclosures is easy: you simply open the enclosure, secure the hard drive with the supplied mounting screws, connect the internal power and data cables to the drive, and put the cover back on the enclosure. Most enclosures use rubber shock mounting and other means to protect the drive if the enclosure is dropped.

WARRANTY ADVANTAGES

One advantage to rolling your own is that commercial external drives usually have only a one-year warranty. If you build your own external drive with an enclosure and a standard hard drive, the drive has its standard warranty, which may be as long as five years.

External drive enclosures are made by Belkin, IOGEAR, Kingwin, ThermalTake, Vantec, and others, and are widely available online and at big-box retailers. Price is a good indicator of quality. The $20 units we've seen appear fragile and shoddily made. The $30 and $40 products use more metal and less plastic, and appear to be considerably more reliable. The better units sometimes include a cooling fan, which may improve the reliability and service life of the drive.

MORE POWER

Some external enclosures can also accept a DVD writer or other drive that uses removable media. If you mount a DVD writer in such an enclosure, make sure the power brick is rated to supply the peak amperage required by the drive, which may be considerably higher than the draw of a hard drive.

Removable Hard Drive Enclosures

Frame/carrier removable hard drive enclosures are actually just modified drive bays that allow a standard hard drive mounted in a carrier assembly to be inserted and removed easily. In effect, you use a frame/carrier system to convert an internal hard drive into a removable hard drive.

The frame resides permanently in an externally accessible drive bay, and is connected permanently to power and to the ATA or SATA interface. The carrier assembly contains power and data cables, which remain permanently attached to the hard drive. The rear of the carrier assembly contains a custom connector that routes power and data signals from the PC through the frame and carrier to the hard drive. The connector that mates the carrier to the frame is designed for durability, and is typically rated for thousands of insertions and removals.

These devices are simply physical modifications that allow internal hard drives to be inserted and removed easily. The computer sees the drive as just another hard drive because it *is* just another hard drive. Frame/carrier assemblies are available for any hard disk interface, including PATA and SATA. More sophisticated units support such functions as hot-swapping, sparing, and RAID, if your host adapter, drivers, and operating system also support those functions.

Figure 9-4 shows three components of the StorCase (*http://www.storcase.com*) DE-100 frame/carrier system. The assembly at the top is a frame with an empty carrier partially inserted. (In actual use, the frame would be secured within a 5.25" externally accessible drive bay and the carrier would contain a hard drive.) The carrier provides standard power and data cables, which connect to the hard drive contained in the carrier. Below is the rear side of a second carrier, showing the proprietary connector that joins the carrier to the frame when the carrier is fully inserted. The rear of the frame provides standard connectors for power and data cables.

Figure 9-4. StorCase Data Express DE-100 frame with two carriers

Similar frame/carrier systems are available from other manufacturers, including Kingwin, Lian Li, Vantec, Vision, and others. (A frame from one manufacturer is almost certainly incompatible with a carrier from another manufacturer, even if the carrier appears to fit the frame.) Some carriers include one or two front-mounted cooling fans, which are often rather ineffective and sometimes quite loud. Fortunately, it's usually easy to disable these fans by unplugging their power connectors. Other models use a rear-mounted fan, which is usually reasonably quiet and effective.

USB Flash Memory Drives

USB flash memory drives are known by many names, both generic and trademarked. These devices are sometimes called *keychain drives*, *watch-fob drives*, *key drives*, *pen drives*, *pocket drives*, *USB sticks*, *memory sticks*, *flash drives*, *USB mass storage drives*, and so on. To the displeasure of the manufacturers, trade names for these devices are often used generically, including *ThumbDrive* (Tech 2000), *JumpDrive* (Lexar), and *Gizmo!* (Crucial Technology). Whatever you call them, they've become ubiquitous.

Figure 9-5 shows a collection of typical USB flash drives, with a Swiss Army Knife (not one of the models with a flash memory drive incorporated) shown for scale. The flash drives on the left are inexpensive and reliable Crucial Gizmo! units. Those on the right are a Kingston DataTraveller II (top) and the premium DataTraveller Elite.

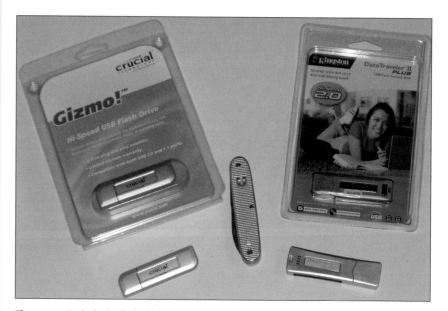

Figure 9-5. Typical USB flash drives

USB flash drives are conceptually simple. They comprise a physical housing that contains a USB interface connector, some flash memory, and the circuitry needed to interface the memory to the USB connector. Some drives include additional circuitry, such as support for hardware-based encryption or an LCD display. The drive plugs into and is powered by a USB port, and the flash memory is nonvolatile. Data written to the USB flash drive is retained permanently until it is manually deleted or overwritten. USB flash drives are most commonly used for backup and to "sneakernet" data between unconnected machines.

A SHEEP IN WOLF'S CLOTHING

You may already own a USB flash drive without being aware of it. Most digital cameras, digital voice recorders, and MP3 players can also be used as USB flash drives. Just plug them into a USB port on your computer, open them in Explorer as removable drives, and copy your files back and forth.

Here are the important characteristics of USB flash drives:

Price

Current-generation USB 2.0 flash drives are available at prices ranging from $10 or so for low-capacity no-name units to $300 or more for the largest capacity name-brand drives. In general, within a particular manufacturer's line, price is closely related to capacity and speed, but there are very wide variations between manufacturers. A fast, name-brand 256 MB model, for example, may sell for about the same price as a slower, no-name 512 MB model.

Interface

First-generation USB flash drives used the USB 1.1 interface, which limited the effective data transfer rate to about 1 MB/s, too slow to be useful for transferring large amounts of data. Most current USB flash drives use the Hi-Speed USB 2.0 interface, which offers a theoretical data transfer rate of 60 MB/s, and real-world data transfer rates that may approach 25 MB/s under ideal conditions.

WHEN HIGH SPEED IS LOW SPEED

Not all USB 2.0 flash drives support Hi-Speed operation. Some inexpensive models support only Full Speed operation, which limits data transfer rates to 1 MB/s or thereabouts. Although these drives are technically USB 2.0 devices, the Full Speed limitation means that for all practical purposes, they can be considered USB 1.1 devices.

Capacity

Current USB 2.0 flash drives are available with capacities ranging from 128 MB to 16 GB. First-generation USB 1.1 drives, some of which are still available at fire sale prices, typically have capacities from 16 MB to 128 MB.

A Flash Drive with Infinite Capacity

Most flash drives are of fixed capacity, but there is at least one exception. Bonzai USB 2.0 Upgradeable Flash Drives (*http://www.simpletech.com*) provide unlimited expandability by the simple expedient of accepting standard Secure Digital (SD) or MultiMediaCard (MMC) flash memory cards. If your digital camera uses either of these two types of flash memory, you can make your collection of memory cards serve two purposes.

Read and write performance

The read and write speeds of USB flash drives are quantified using the CD-ROM X-factor, where 150 KB/s (153,600 bytes/s) is defined as 1X. As is common practice for hard drives, USB flash drives define a kilobyte as 1,000 bytes and a megabyte as 1,000,000 bytes, and consider 1X speed to be 150,000 bytes/s rather than 153,600. For example, a USB flash drive that reads at 15,000,000 bytes/s is described as having 100X read speed.

Read performance—transferring data from the drive to the host—is affected by many factors, including the speed of the flash memory and interface circuitry used by the drive, the number and size of files being read, and the operating system being used. Every USB flash drive we tested reads a few large files faster than it reads many smaller files that total the same number of bytes, sometimes much faster. Absolute read performance differs dramatically from model to model, with less-expensive models typically offering half or less the speed of premium models.

Write performance—transferring data from the host to the drive—is generally lower than read performance. On slower drives, write speed may be 90% of read speed, while on fast drives, write speed is often not much more than 50% of read speed. (Of course, read speed on fast drives may be three or four times faster than on slower drives.)

Encryption and password protection

A basic flash drive allows data to be written and read, but provides no other functions. More expensive models may include built-in encryption and/or password or biometric protection, provided by a dedicated chip on the drive and accessed by a driver that must be installed on any PC that is to read or write data on that drive. Frankly, we don't trust the encryption functions of such drives. We worry that our data will somehow become locked up and inaccessible. Fortunately, such drives function as standard USB flash drives if you simply don't install the encryption drivers. If we're concerned about the security of data that we've stored on a USB flash drive, we use standard encryption utilities to protect it. We recommend that you do the same.

U3 Smart USB Drives

U3 Smart USB Drives began shipping in October 2005. Although U3 drives provide standard USB flash drive storage functions, they are more than just storage devices. They allow you to carry your complete working environment with you, including data, programs, and personal preference settings. When you boot a system with a U3 Smart USB Drive installed, that system loads the data, programs, and settings stored on the drive. When you shut down the system, the system automatically synchronizes changes to the flash drive. The major limitation of U3 flash drives is their limited software support. They can be used only with Windows 2000 or Windows XP and, for example, support Outlook but not other popular email clients such as Thunderbird. For more information, see *http://www.u3.com*.

A THREAT TO NATIONAL SECURITY?

Users love USB flash drives, but computer security people hate them. One of our sources tells us that the NSA (National Security Agency) uses epoxy cement to plug the USB ports in their desktop systems to prevent their data from being carried away in these tiny, easily concealable devices.

Tape Drives

Although corporate data centers still use tape drives for backing up, tape drives are no longer a mainstream technology for home and small business PCs, if indeed they ever were. For corporations, the advantages of high-end tape drives—extreme reliability, robust error detection and correction, high capacity, and speed—outweigh the disadvantages. For homes and small businesses, the disadvantages of consumer-grade tape drives—low capacity and speed, high cost, and the physical fragility of the tapes—outweigh the advantages.

Figure 9-6. Certance Travan 40 internal tape drive (image courtesy of Certance LLC)

Consumer-grade tape drives have always lagged behind hard drives in capacity, and that gap remains today. The highest-capacity consumer-grade tape drives, Travan 40 models, store only 20 GB natively, although they are advertised as storing 40 GB with compression. (Realistically, you can expect to store about 30 GB on a "40 GB" tape, less for incompressible data, such as image files.) Consumer-grade tape drives use the ATA or USB 2.0 interface—so even the internal models are as easy to install as an optical drive—but they require many hours to write and verify a tape. Also, tapes are quite expensive, at $30 to $40 each, which translates to a media cost of $1/GB or more. Figures 9-6 and 9-7 show Certance Travan 40 tape drives, internal and external models, respectively.

If you are considering buying a tape drive—or if you currently use one for backup—consider the following:

Figure 9-7. Certance Travan 40 external tape drive (image courtesy of Certance LLC)

- If your working data set—with or without compression—fits on one DVD, we recommend using a DVD writer with DVD+R or DVD+RW discs. (That's what we use for our own backups, after years of using tape drives.) DVD writers are much faster than tape. Backing up and verifying 4,400 MB to a DVD+R disc takes only a few minutes, versus an hour or more to back up and verify the same amount of data to a consumer-grade tape drive. If 4,400 MB isn't quite enough, you can use DVD+R/DL dual-layer discs, which store up to 8,500 MB. Although optical discs have less robust error detection and correction than tape

Proprietary Removable Storage Systems

Over the years, many companies have tried and failed miserably to develop a market for proprietary external or removable storage systems. The most successful of the bunch—the Iomega ZIP and Jaz drives—were never more than niche products, and are now merely footnotes in computer history. Other products, such as the LS-120 high-capacity floppy drive and cartridge-based storage systems from SyQuest, Castlewood, and others, sold in small numbers and are long obsolete.

The problem with most of these products was that their makers attempted to use the King Gillette scheme of giving away the razor and selling the blades. Accordingly, these companies sold their drives at a low price—often below their cost—expecting to recoup their investment by selling lots of high-profit disk cartridges. Alas, users never bought as many disk cartridges as the manufacturers thought they would, so, with the exception of Iomega, most of these companies have disappeared.

If you are still using one of these obsolete drives, do yourself a favor. Get your data off the proprietary disk cartridges while you still can and write it to your hard drive or optical discs. Then, do a favor for a stranger. Sell the drive on eBay so that someone else who has a nonfunctioning drive and a bunch of disks can salvage his data.

drives, that problem is easily solved by making more frequent backups and keeping older backup discs for redundancy. Media costs range from $0.05/GB to $0.50/GB, depending on the media you use.

ONE CENT PER GIGABYTE?

The cost/capacity equation will change as high-capacity Blu-Ray and HD-DVD writers become mainstream products, which we don't expect to occur until at least mid-2007. Although Blu-Ray and HD-DVD drives and discs will be very expensive initially, we expect eventually to see 50 GB writable optical discs selling for $0.50 apiece. Of course, by that time we'll probably all have a terabyte or more of hard disk storage in our systems.

- If your working data set is too large for one DVD, we recommend using full-size external hard drives or a frame/carrier removable hard drive system for backup. Depending on the number and type of files to be backed up, real-world throughput may be 30 GB/hour or more, which makes it practical to back up and verify large data sets even if your backup window is short. Hard drives have less robust error detection and correction than tape drives, but again that problem is easily solved by using redundancy. Media costs are roughly $1/GB, depending on the size and type of external or removable hard drive you choose.

FUNNY-LOOKING TAPES

For the same cost as a consumer-grade tape drive and enough tapes to implement a reasonable rotation, you can buy three or four external hard drives that are specifically designed for backing up. These drives—sold by Seagate, Maxtor, Western Digital, Fantom, and others—include backup software such as Dantz Retrospect, which allows you to back up your system by pressing one button. The size of your backup set is limited only by the total capacity of the external hard drive, and multiple backup sets can be written to the drive until its capacity is reached.

Whatever you do, don't buy just one external hard drive for backup. If you have only one backup drive, Murphy's Law predicts that when your internal hard drive fails, you'll somehow break the external hard drive as well. Use at least two external hard drives for backup, and alternate backups between them.

Video Adapters

10

A *video adapter*, also called a *graphics adapter*, renders video data provided by the processor into a form that the monitor can display. Many motherboards provide an integrated video adapter. Most also provide a special video expansion slot that accepts a standalone video adapter card. A standalone video adapter is called a *video card* or *graphics card*. Upgrading video is fast, easy, and generally inexpensive. There are several good reasons to do so, including:

- Your current video card or integrated video has failed.

- You've installed a larger display and require higher-resolution video than the old adapter provides.

- You need a digital video (DVI) connector to drive a flat-panel LCD display.

- You want to record television programs or other video sources to your hard drive.

- You want to watch DVD-Video discs or other fast-motion video sources without jerkiness.

- Your current video adapter is too slow for or incompatible with the games you want to play.

DIRECTX COMPATIBILITY

DirectX (DX) is a Microsoft graphics standard that's particularly important to gamers. The oldest video cards still being produced support DX7. Entry-level video adapters usually support DX8. Current midrange and high-end video adapters support DX9.0a, DX9.0b, DX9.0c, or DX9.0L. DX10, originally called *Windows Graphics Foundation*, and DX11 will be released with Windows Vista.

In this chapter, we tell you what you need to know to choose and install a video adapter, and to troubleshoot video adapter problems.

Video Adapter Interfaces

Every video adapter, integrated or standalone, has at least two interfaces:

- One interface between the PC and the video adapter
- At least one interface between the video adapter and the display(s).

Some video adapters provide some combination of interfaces for two or more computer displays (analog and/or digital), TV-Video RF In, TV-Video RF Out, S-Video (Y/C) In, S-Video (Y/C) Out, or others.

Small but Good

Nearly all PCIe video cards fit only the standard full-length PCIe x16 slot shown in Figure 10-1. One oddball video adapter, the Matrox Millennium G550 PCIe (*http://www.matrox.com*), fits any PCIe slot—including x1, x4, x8, and x16—and its low profile means that it will fit in any SFF system. This card supports dual high-resolution analog or digital displays, and is narrowly targeted at people who don't care about 3D graphics performance or DX level, but want the best 2D text quality available.

PC adapter interfaces

The first consideration in upgrading video is the type of PC-to-video adapter interface provided by your motherboard. Depending on the age and type of motherboard, it will provide one or more of the following interfaces, which are listed in decreasing order of desirability:

PCI Express
   PCI Express (*PCIe*) is the current video interface standard. Video card manufacturers devote most of their resources to developing new, faster PCIe adapters. PCIe video cards run the gamut from sub-$50 entry-level cards to fire-breathing $500+ cards designed for playing 3D graphics-intensive games such as Doom 3, Half-Life 2, and others. If your motherboard has a PCIe slot, you have literally hundreds of models to choose among. The PCIe standard is rigidly defined, so there's little doubt that any PCIe video adapter you buy will be physically and electrically compatible with the PCIe slot on your motherboard. Most PCIe video cards support DX9 or higher. Figure 10-1 shows a standard black PCI Express x16 video expansion slot, located between the two white PCI slots and the chipset heatsink at the top of the image.

Figure 10-1. A PCIe x16 video expansion slot

PCIe RETENTION MECHANISMS

Note the retention mechanism on the right end of the slot. When you install a PCIe video adapter, the retention mechanism snaps into place, mating to a slot in the video adapter and securing it in the slot. When you remove a PCIe video adapter, make sure to release the retention mechanism before you attempt to pull the card from the slot. Otherwise, you may damage the card and/or the motherboard.

AGP 3.0 (8X/4X)

    AGP 3.0 (*Accelerated Graphics Port* or *Advanced Graphics Port*), also called *AGP 8X/4X*, immediately preceded the PCIe standard, and AGP 3.0 motherboards and video cards will remain available for some time to come. Although PCIe is the future, video card makers can't afford to ignore the huge installed base of AGP 3.0 systems. Available AGP 3.0 video cards span the range from $20 entry-level cards to high-end 3D gaming cards. Most current AGP 3.0 video adapters support DX9, but older models may support only DX8 or DX7. Figure 10-2 shows a standard brown AGP 3.0 video expansion slot, located between the white PCI slot and the chipset heatsink at the top of the image. Note the keying tab in the body of the slot, located to the right of center, toward the front of the system.

AGP RETENTION MECHANISMS

Note the retention mechanism on the right end of the slot, which is similar to the PCIe retention mechanism. When you install an AGP adapter, make sure the retention mechanism locks to secure the adapter in the slot; when you remove an AGP adapter, release the mechanism before you pull the card.

Figure 10-2. An AGP 3.0 video expansion slot

AGP 2.0 (4X/2X)

    AGP 2.0, also called *AGP 4X/2X* or *AGP 1.5V*, is functionally obsolete, although millions of AGP 2.0 motherboards are in use and a few AGP 2.0 video cards remain on the market. AGP 2.0 video adapters support

DX8 or DX7, and use very old chipsets that no longer provide competitive 3D graphics performance. AGP 2.0 motherboards use the same slot as AGP 3.0 motherboards, including the same keying, so it's impossible to differentiate the two visually. That matters little, however, because many current AGP video cards can be used in AGP 2.0 motherboards.

AGP 1.0 (1X)

AGP 1.0, also called AGP 3.3V, is \long obsolete, and most motherboards that used it have been retired from service. If you have an AGP 1.0 motherboard that you want to continue using, though, don't despair. Many current AGP video cards can be used in AGP 1.0 motherboards. Figure 10-3 shows a standard light-brown AGP 1.0 video expansion slot. You can differentiate an AGP 1.0 slot visually by noting that the keying tab in the slot body is offset to the left (toward the rear of the system), and that there is no retention mechanism.

Figure 10-3. An AGP 1.0 expansion slot

PCI

Last (and least) is the PCI interface. Unlike cards built to later video standards, PCI video cards are not matched to a dedicated video slot. Instead, they can be installed in any available standard PCI slot. Although a few PCI video cards remain on the market, a system whose motherboard has only PCI slots is probably too old to be economically upgraded.

PCI-X VERSUS PCIe

PCI-X (not to be confused with PCI Express or PCIe) is an enhanced version of PCI that is used primarily on servers and workstations. Although a (very) few PCI-X video adapters are available, these are not mainstream devices and should never be installed, even on a desktop system that happens to have a PCI-X slot.

AGP compatibility considerations

AGP cards and slots may run at 8X, 4X, 2X, or 1X speed, with 1X defined as 266 MB/s. All AGP cards and slots are backward-compatible in terms of speed. For example, an 8X AGP card can also run at 4X, 2X, and 1X. AGP cards and slots can operate at 3.3V, 1.5V, or 0.8V. (Older components use the higher voltages.) AGP cards and slots may be designed to be compatible with one, two, or all three of these voltages. Speeds and voltages are related as follows:

- An AGP 8X device must use 0.8V.

- An AGP 4X device may use 1.5V or 0.8V.

- An AGP 2X or 1X device may use 3.3V or 1.5V.

AGP cards and slots are keyed to prevent installing a card in an incompatible slot, which could damage the card, the motherboard, or both. Figure 10-2 shows the 1.5V keying tab that is used in AGP 2.0 and AGP 3.0 slots. This keying divides the AGP slot contacts into groups of 21 and 41 pins, with the smaller group toward the rear of the system. Figure 10-3 shows the 3.3V keying tab that is used in AGP 1.0 slots. This keying also divides the AGP slot into groups of 21 and 41 pins, but with the smaller group toward the front of the system.

There are six types of AGP motherboards and six types of AGP video cards. Table 10-1 lists the speeds, keying, and voltages by AGP motherboard type, and Table 10-2 by video adapter type.

Table 10-1. Motherboard AGP compatibility

Motherboard type	Speeds	Key tab	Voltage(s)
AGP 3.3V (AGP 1.0)	2X, 1X	3.3V	3.3V
AGP 1.5V (AGP 2.0)	4X, 2X, 1X	1.5V	1.5V
Universal AGP	4X, 2X, 1X	none	3.3V, 1.5V
AGP 3.0	8X, 4X	1.5V	0.8V
Universal 1.5V AGP 3.0	8X, 4X, 2X, 1X	1.5V	1.5V, 0.8V
Universal AGP 3.0	8X, 4X, 2X, 1X	none	3.3V, 1.5V, 0.8V

Table 10-2. Video adapter AGP compatibility

Video adapter type	Speeds	Key slot(s)	Voltage(s)
AGP 3.3V (AGP 1.0)	2X, 1X	3.3V	3.3V
AGP 1.5V (AGP 2.0)	4X, 2X, 1X	1.5V	1.5V
Universal AGP	4X, 2X, 1X	3.3V, 1.5V	3.3V, 1.5V
AGP 3.0	8X, 4X	1.5V	0.8V
Universal 1.5V AGP 3.0	8X, 4X, 2X, 1X	1.5V	1.5V, 0.8V
Universal AGP 3.0	8X, 4X, 2X, 1X	3.3V, 1.5V	3.3V, 1.5V, 0.8V

BE WARY OF VERY OLD AGP CARDS AND MOTHERBOARDS

Some early AGP 1.0 and 2.0 cards and slots were keyed incorrectly. Before you install a new AGP card in a very old motherboard, or vice versa, check the card and motherboard documentation to verify that the card is in fact compatible with the slot.

If you're paying careful attention, you may have noted one ambiguity in Tables 10-1 and 10-2. It's physically possible to install a 0.8V AGP 3.0 video card in an AGP 1.5V motherboard that does not support 0.8V cards. If you do that, the video card won't be damaged, but it may not function properly (or at all).

UNIVERSAL AGP

Some AGP slots and cards support only one standard—AGP 1.0, AGP 2.0, or AGP 3.0—but most recent cards and slots you're likely to encounter are universal. To summarize:

- *Universal 1.5V AGP 3.0 (U1.5VAGP3.0)* slots and cards support 1X, 2X, 4X, or 8X operation at 1.5V or 0.8V, using a universal connector. A U1.5VAGP3.0 card can be installed in any AGP slot except a 3.3V AGP 1.0 slot. A U1.5VAGP3.0 slot accepts any AGP card except a 3.3V AGP 1.0 card.

- *Universal AGP 3.0 (UAGP3.0)* slots and cards support 1X, 2X, 4X, or 8X operation at 3.3V, 1.5V, or 0.8V, using a universal connector. A UAGP3.0 card can be used in any AGP slot. A UAGP3.0 slot supports any AGP card.

You can verify the type of AGP slot and card by checking the documentation provided with the component or available on the manufacturer's web site.

Figure 10-4 shows the AGP connector portion of an ATI All-In-Wonder 9800 Pro AGP graphics card. The presence of both keying slots on the contact edge establishes that this is either a Universal AGP card or a Universal AGP 3.0 card. That means this card can be installed in any AGP slot without fear of damage. (A Universal AGP 3.0 card will operate properly in any AGP slot; a Universal AGP card may not operate properly in a 0.8V-only AGP 3.0 slot, but nothing will be damaged.) Note also the hook-shaped portion at the far right of the contact edge. This part of the connector locks into the AGP retention mechanism on the motherboard to secure the card in the slot.

Figure 10-4. A Universal AGP card, showing the two keying slots on the AGP connector

Adapter/display interfaces

A video adapter is useless without some means of connecting it to the display or displays. Accordingly, every video adapter includes at least a primary video output, and some contain a secondary video output as well. These outputs are one or both of the following types:

DB-15 Analog
   Older video adapters and some current models provide the familiar *DB-15 analog video connector*, usually called a *VGA connector*. Nearly all CRT monitors and many digital flat-panel displays can be connected to a VGA connector. (Inexpensive flat-panel displays may have *only* an analog video connector.)

DVI Digital
   Many recent video adapters provide a *DVI* (*Digital Visual Interface*) connector. DVI defines three types of connectors. These connectors are keyed to prevent an analog display from being connected to a digital-only interface or vice versa, which could destroy the display, the interface, or both.

   DVI-Analog
      The *DVI-Analog* (*DVI-A*) connector, shown in Figure 10-5, supports only analog displays and is keyed to prevent a digital (DVI-D) display cable from being connected.

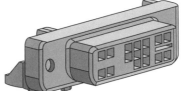

Figure 10-5. DVI-A analog-only connector

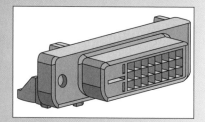

Figure 10-6. DVI-D digital-only connector

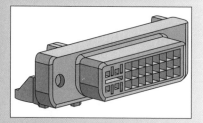

Figure 10-7. DVI-I hybrid analog/digital connector

DVI-Digital

The *DVI-Digital* (*DVI-D*) connector, shown in Figure 10-6, supports only digital displays and is keyed to prevent an analog (DVI-A) display cable from being connected.

DVI-Integrated

The *DVI-Integrated* (*DVI-I*) connector, shown in Figure 10-7, supports analog and digital displays, and accepts either a DVI-A or a DVI-D cable.

Connecting a DB-15 analog display to a DVI-A or DVI-I interface requires an adapter like the one shown in Figure 10-8. Nearly all standalone video adapters that provide a DVI interface use the DVI-I variant, and include such an adapter. If your adapter doesn't include one, you can buy an DVI-VGA adapter from most online computer component vendors.

Figure 10-8. A DB-15 to DVI-A/I adapter

Choosing a Video Adapter

Years ago, Proctor & Gamble, RJ Reynolds, and other consumer products giants discovered that the best way to increase their sales was to go into competition with themselves. Instead of making only one or two brands of laundry detergent or breakfast cereal or floor wax or cigarette, they started making dozens of brands, all similar, but each appealing to a different type of buyer. Just as important, the flood of brands meant the giants could stifle competitors by monopolizing scarce retail shelf space.

The two major video card makers, ATI and NVIDIA, have taken this scheme to ridiculous extremes. Each produces two dozen or more video chipsets, from old, slow models that are used in $20 video cards to models that are used in $700 gaming cards. Any particular chipset may be available in variants that run at different clock speeds, and any of these may be used to build video adapters with different amounts, types, and speeds of memory, and so on. Many different companies use ATI and/or NVIDIA video chipsets to build their own branded video cards, further increasing the number of choices and the level of confusion. (When we checked NewEgg.com while writing this paragraph, we found an incredible 569 different video cards for sale—238 PCIe, 283 AGP, and even 48 PCI models.)

INTEL VIDEO

By unit volume, Intel is by far the largest maker of video adapters, but all of their adapters are integrated into system chipsets. Intel video adapters provide excellent 2D display quality, but only pedestrian 3D graphics performance. In late 2005, Intel announced that it would no longer produce low-end chipsets with integrated graphics, leaving that segment of the market to other chipset makers such as ATI and SiS. We believe that Intel made this decision because they understood that their current integrated graphics products were inadequate to support the advanced video requirements of Windows Vista, and we expect Intel to remedy that problem in 2006 and 2007 with new series of chipsets that include integrated graphics sufficient for Vista.

We were about to say that even we can't keep everything straight, but in fact it's worse than that. Based on conversations with some of our contacts at ATI and NVIDIA, we don't think *they* can keep everything straight. So which video card should you buy? Here are some guidelines:

Decide how much to spend.

If you don't play 3D games, 3D graphics performance doesn't matter, unless you plan to upgrade to Windows Vista. Any current video card, even a $35 model, is fast enough to run productivity software and similar 2D applications under Windows XP or Linux.

If you're a casual gamer, spending $75 to $100 buys you much faster 3D graphics performance. If you're a serious gamer, plan to spend at least $150 to $250 to be able to play recent games at reasonable frame rates. If you're a rabid gamer, well, the sky's the limit.

If you are upgrading a system to be compatible with Windows Vista, choose a card with at least midrange 3D graphics performance, something like an NVIDIA 6800GT or better with at least 128 MB of video memory.

Consider a motherboard replacement.

Rather than replace a failed video card or integrated video, consider spending a bit more to replace the motherboard instead. The integrated video on current motherboards is more than sufficient for anything other than gaming (or Vista), and by replacing the motherboard you also get a newer chipset, a new BIOS, new features such as SATA, and a new motherboard that has a warranty and will probably last for years.

DON'T BUY A VIDEO-SLOTLESS MOTHERBOARD

Make sure that any motherboard you buy allows embedded video to be disabled and provides an AGP or PCIe slot. That way, you can upgrade the video later if you need to.

Don't overbuy.

If you buy a standalone video adapter, remember that video is just one part of your system. It makes no sense to buy a fast gaming video card for an older system. You'll see some video performance benefit, certainly, but the card can't reach anything near its real potential when hampered by the relatively slow processor, memory, and other components in the older system. Other than for gaming or to add extra features, such as TV capture, we recommend spending no more than $50 on a video adapter to upgrade an older system.

INEXPENSIVE DOESN'T NECESSARILY MEAN SLOW

If you need better 3D graphics performance than embedded video provides but you don't want to spend much, look at "obsolescent" 3D video adapters—those a couple generations out of date. For example, in late 2005 ATI RADEON 9250-series adapters were available for $30 or so. The RADEON 9250 or a similar obsolescent NVIDIA adapter can't compare in graphics performance to a current $400 gaming card—or even to a $100 midrange adapter—but for many people, it's just the right compromise between cost and performance.

If you buy an older adapter, make sure to verify the level of DirectX it supports. The RADEON 9250, for example, supports DX8. If you plan to play a game that requires DX9, the older adapter will be of little benefit. This problem is self-limiting, though. You are unlikely to want to run 3D applications that require the most recent version of DirectX on an older card. Such applications require more graphics power than older cards can provide.

Buy only a Universal AGP 3.0 or PCI Express x16 video adapter.

If you decide to install a standalone video adapter, buy only a Universal AGP 3.0 or an x16 PCIe adapter. Check the motherboard manual to verify which type or types of adapter it supports, and then buy accordingly. Most recent AGP motherboards use either 0.8V AGP 3.0 cards only or 1.5V AGP 2.0 and 0.8V AGP 3.0 cards interchangeably. Fortunately, the PCI Express standard has not yet fragmented, so any PCIe adapter works with any PCIe motherboard.

Unless you are a gamer, give more weight to 2D display quality than to 3D performance.

Display quality is subjective and very difficult to quantify, but a real issue nonetheless. Matrox video adapters have always been the standard by which we judge 2D display quality, but Matrox adapters are no longer competitive in terms of 3D performance. The three major video chipset companies are ATI and NVIDIA, both of which provide chipsets that are used both for standalone AGP adapters and for embedded video, and Intel, whose video adapters are available only in integrated form. ATI and Intel video adapters have always provided excellent 2D display quality—just a half-step behind Matrox—so we don't hesitate to recommend either of those brands to anyone who is concerned about

2D quality. Older NVIDIA adapters, especially high-performance models, often favored 3D performance at the expense of 2D image quality. NVIDIA 6000-series and later video adapters have excellent 2D display quality.

If you buy a high-performance video card, make sure it has a good warranty.
Video cards used to be among the most reliable components of a PC. This is changing, not because manufacturers are cutting corners, but because new high-performance video cards are pushing hardware technology to the limit. Having a video card die after only six months or a year is now relatively common, particularly for those who push the card past its limit by overclocking it in pursuit of the highest possible performance. We've seen video cards with 90-day warranties, which is completely unacceptable. Regard one year as an absolute minimum, and longer is better.

Make sure that the video adapter supports the display settings you need.
Video adapters differ in the resolutions and refresh rates they support. It's important to make sure that the video adapter you buy supports resolutions and refresh rates appropriate for your display.

Resolution

Resolution describes the maximum number of pixels the adapter can display, horizontally and vertically. For example, an inexpensive display adapter may support resolutions of 640×480 (640 pixels horizontally by 480 pixels vertically), 800×600, 1024×768, 1280×1024, and 1600×1200. If you have a large CRT monitor that supports 1920×1440 resolution (and you use that resolution), the maximum resolution of this video card is too low to be optimum for your monitor. Not all video adapters support all intermediate resolutions. For example, although the adapter we're discussing supports 1024×768 and 1280×1024, it may not support the intermediate 1152×864 resolution. If you have a display that is optimized for that resolution, you may want to look for a different video adapter that also supports 1152×864.

Refresh rate

Refresh rate is the number of times the image is renewed per second. If the refresh rate is too low, the image on a CRT monitor flickers. (Flat-panel LCD displays operate at low refresh rates without flickering.) The minimum refresh rate necessary to avoid flicker depends on many factors, including the phosphors used in the monitor, the size and resolution of the monitor, ambient lighting conditions, and your own vision. Most people consider 72 Hz the minimum acceptable refresh rate on small to midsize CRT monitors, and 85 Hz is better. On large CRT monitors, a 100 Hz or higher refresh rate may be necessary to avoid flicker. The maximum refresh rate supported by a video adapter is related to the resolution you use. For example, a particular video adapter may support a 120 Hz refresh rate at 1024×768, but only 85 Hz at 1280×1024 and 60 Hz at 1600×1200. Despite the fact that the adapter technically supports 1600×1200, most people will find the 60 Hz refresh rate unacceptable, so in practical terms that adapter is limited to 1280×1024.

Make sure the video adapter provides the interface(s) you need.

Most analog CRT monitors use the familiar high-density DB15 VGA connector, although a few high-end models also support RGB component video. Flat-panel displays (FPDs) use a variety of connectors, including the analog VGA connector (typically used by low-end FPDs), or one of three different types of DVI connectors described earlier in this chapter. Midrange and higher FPDs normally provide a DVI-D or DVI-I digital connector, and may also provide a DB-15 analog connector. If you plan to run dual displays, make sure the video adapter you choose has dual connectors of the type(s) needed by your displays, and that those connectors can be used simultaneously.

Advice from Jim Cooley

Before you buy a dual-DVI video adapter, verify the type of cables it uses. Some video adapters that support dual-DVI displays don't use two ordinary DVI cables. Instead, they require a special dual-DVI cable with a custom connector on the video adapter end. A dual-DVI cable for my Matrox video adapter set me back $100.

USE A DIGITAL VIDEO CARD WITH A DIGITAL DISPLAY

If you plan to use an FPD, whenever possible choose an FPD and a video adapter that both support digital (DVI-I or DVI-D) connectors. FPD image quality is hit-or-miss if you use an analog connection, because video data originates in digital form, is converted to analog by the video adapter, and is then converted back to digital by the FPD. These multiple AD/DA conversions can introduce various artifacts, none of which is pleasing. The inferiority of an analog video connection is particularly noticeable with 19" and larger flat-panel displays.

Also, some analog video adapters simply don't "play nice" with some FPDs, and there's enough variation from one sample to another that about the only way to know for sure is to try it. This problem seems to be worse with DB-15 analog connections than with DVI-A connections, but the only sure way to avoid it is to use a digital path end-to-end.

TV Tuner/Capture Cards

At first glance, it seems reasonable that a computer video adapter should also be compatible with television video, but in fact computer video standards are so different from television video standards that few PC video adapters handle TV-video. There are exceptions, though, and they fall into two categories:

Dedicated TV tuner/capture cards

These cards tune a television signal and capture it for recording to disk, but do not provide standard video adapter functions. Installing one of these cards with appropriate software allows your PC to function like TiVo or another *PVR/DVR* (*personal video recorder/digital video recorder*). Hauppauge (*http://www.hauppauge.com*) is the best-known vendor of such cards, with their various WinTV-PVR models.

Video adapters with integrated TV tuning/capture functions

These cards combine TV tuner/capture functions with standard PC video adapter functions. ATI dominates this market segment with its RADEON All-In-Wonder (AIW) series cards. These cards are optimized for use with ATI's MultiMedia Center software, which provides PVR/DVR functions as well as other multimedia features.

The plethora of functions supported by these cards means that card bracket real estate is at a premium, as shown in Figure 10-9. This model, an ATI AIW 9800 Pro AGP card provides, from left to right, a purple Video-In connector, a standard RF-In F-connector, a black Video-Out connector, and a standard DVI-I computer video connector. Some models don't even attempt to fit all the necessary connectors on the card bracket. Instead, they provide a proprietary connector that links to an external break-out box, usually called an *octopus connector*.

Figure 10-9. The I/O ports of an ATI RADEON All-In-Wonder 9800 Pro AGP video card

Which, if any, of these cards makes sense for you depends on your priorities and habits. If you primarily time-shift TV programs, a $99 DVD recorder is probably a better choice than a TV tuner/capture card. These devices are essentially VCR replacements that record directly to writable DVD discs rather than VHS tapes. More expensive models include a hard drive that can store many hours of programming.

If you want more than a simple VCR replacement and you dislike, as we do, TiVo policies and practices (not to mention their high fees), installing a TV tuner/capture card in your primary PC or a secondary PC is a good alternative. If you prefer to use Windows, we recommend an ATI AIW card used with their bundled MultiMedia Center software. If you want more flexibility and are willing to learn a bit about Linux, we recommend a Hauppauge PVR-250 or PVR-350 card—or cards; you can install multiple tuner cards if you want to record multiple programs simultaneously—on a Linux box running MythTV (*http://www.mythtv.org*).

Installing a Video Card

Installing a video card is generally straightforward, but there are a couple gotchas to watch out for:

- If you are installing an AGP card on a motherboard with a non-Intel chipset, you may need to install a GART driver before you physically install the video card or its drivers. Skipping this step can cause Windows to black-screen at boot. Follow the instructions supplied with the new video card to install the GART driver.

- The presence of old video drivers may cause problems with the installation of the new card. You may need to use Safe Mode (press F8 while the system boots and choose Safe Mode from the menu) to uninstall the old video drivers before installing the new video card or, if the current video adapter is dead, as the first step after installing the new video card.

SAFE MODE VERSUS VGA MODE

Pressing F8 during boot displays the Windows Advanced Options Menu, which offers several choices. The first option, Safe Mode, starts the system with everything disabled except the essentials—no networking or sound, only a vanilla 640×480 VGA video driver, and so on. We use Safe Mode during troubleshooting to minimize the number of variables that may be causing the problem. If for some reason you prefer to start the system in what we call Safe Video Mode—with all drivers loading normally except that the vanilla 640×480 video driver is used—choose Enable VGA Mode instead of Safe Mode.

If you buy a retail-boxed video card, it will include a comprehensive manual. If you buy an OEM video card that arrives without a manual, your first step should be to download the PDF manual from the maker's web site. (You may also need to download drivers if no driver disc is provided.) The exact sequence of installation steps, including loading drivers, varies from card to card, so follow the instructions provided in the manual.

Here are the top mistakes to avoid when installing a new video card:

Failing to read the manual
    Most people don't bother to *Read the Fine Manual* (RTFM), which is a mistake. If you don't read the manual, you're likely to do something

wrong; most commonly, people install drivers too early, too late, or the wrong way. That's best case. Worst case, you may destroy your expensive new video card instantly when you turn on the power. So, RTFM.

Failing to seat the video card

Video cards, both AGP and PCIe, may require significant pressure to seat fully. You may think the card is seated. You may even have heard it snap into place. That doesn't mean it's fully seated. Always verify visually that the card is seated fully in the connector and that the retention mechanism has latched the card in place. A partially seated video card may not work at all. Worse still, it may kinda, sorta work, leaving you with a difficult troubleshooting problem.

Failing to connect supplemental power

Many recent video cards, particularly high-performance models, require more power than the video slot can provide. These cards have a supplemental power connector designed to accept either a special PCIe power connector or a standard Molex hard drive power connector. Failing to connect supplemental power can have several results, none of them good. At best, the video card simply won't work, but nothing will be damaged. At worst, the card may attempt to draw too much power from the video connector, damaging the card and/or the motherboard. (If your card requires a PCIe power connector and your power supply doesn't provide one, there are adapter cables available with standard Molex hard drive power connectors on one end and PCIe power connectors on the other.)

Failing to connect power to the fan

Fast video cards generate a lot of heat. Instead of depending on a passive heatsink for cooling, many recent video cards use a small fan to cool the video processor. Failing to connect power to this fan will cause the video processor to overheat, perhaps catastrophically. Running a fast video adapter without its fan for even a few seconds can literally burn the video processor to a crisp. (We try to avoid using such cards, because fans fail unpredictably, and a failed fan can have the same result. If you do purchase such a card, be sure to clean it regularly. Not only does the fan motor have to work harder to spin dusty blades, but its cooling capacity is greatly diminished.)

To physically install a video card, proceed as follows (deferring to conflicting instructions in the manual):

1. Disconnect the display and other external cables and move the system to a well-lit work area. Remove the case access panel(s) to gain access to the case interior. Now, as always when you have the case open, is a good time to clean the system.

2. If you are replacing an existing video card, remove the screw that secures the video card to the chassis, release the retention mechanism,

if any, and pull the video card. If you are upgrading integrated video, align the video card with the motherboard video slot to determine which slot cover you need to remove (it's not always obvious.)

3. Remove the correct slot cover. You may also need to loosen the screw for the adjacent slot cover temporarily in order to free the slot cover you want to remove. Carefully slide the rear bracket of the video card into place, making sure that the external connectors on the bracket clear the edges of the slot. Carefully align the connector on the video card with the AGP or PCIe slot and use both thumbs to press the video card down until it snaps into the slot, as shown in Figure 10-10.

Figure 10-10. Insert the video card and press down firmly to seat it

4. Verify visually that the card contacts have fully penetrated the video slot, and that the base of the video card is parallel to the slot and in full contact with it. Verify that the retention mechanism, visible here as two brown tabs to the lower right of the heatsink, mates to the corresponding notch on the video card, snapping into place as the card is seated. If you need to remove the adapter later, remember to press those tabs to unlock the retaining bracket before you attempt to pull the card.

5. After you are certain that the video adapter is fully seated, secure it by inserting a screw through the bracket into the chassis, as shown in Figure 10-11.

Figure 10-11. Secure the video card with a screw

DANGER, WILL ROBINSON!

If the video card has a supplemental power connector and/or a fan power connector, make certain to connect power to them before proceeding. It's always embarrassing to burn a new video card to a crisp, and it isn't covered by warranty.

6. Replace the access panel(s), move the system back to its original location, reconnect all the external cables, and turn on the power. Follow the instructions that came with the video card to install and configure the video drivers and any other software supplied with the adapter, such as a DVD-Video player or TV capture program. If you intend to view DVDs on your PC, the DVD-Video player is essential, because Windows cannot play DVDs without it (and in fact, the player software includes a decoder that even Windows Media Player relies on to play DVDs). You should be sure to visit the decoder software vendor's web site for updates, as they may not be automatically provided through Windows update or the video card manufacturer's periodic driver updates.

Configuring Windows Video

The first step in configuring video is to install the video drivers. The exact procedure required to install video drivers varies from card to card, but is described in the manual that accompanies the card or can be downloaded from the manufacturer's web site. Follow those instructions exactly, especially with regard to the sequence required for removing the old video drivers. Although most video cards come with a driver disc, we recommend installing the updated drivers available on the manufacturer's web site. Note, however, that you may have to install the drivers from disc before you can install updated drivers. Also, the driver disc may include a DVD player and other utilities that are not available for download.

Windows video is configured from the Settings page of the Display Properties dialog, shown in Figure 10-12, and the Advanced Settings dialog, one page of which is shown in Figure 10-13 (the exact pages in this dialog vary according to the video adapter and driver installed). To view Display Properties, run the Display applet from Control Panel or right-click on a vacant area of the desktop and choose Properties. To view the Advanced Settings dialog, click the Advanced button in the Settings page of Display Properties.

Figure 10-12. Use the Display Properties Settings page to configure hardware settings for your video adapter and monitor

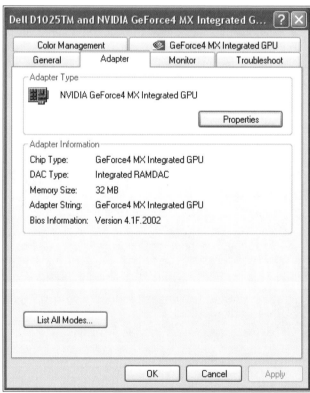

Figure 10-13. Use the Advanced Settings dialog to configure specific settings for the adapter and monitor, enable or disable video acceleration settings, and choose Color Management options

Troubleshooting Video Adapter Problems

If you experience video problems, first check the obvious things—that the display has power and is connected properly to the adapter, that no one has changed settings for the adapter or display, and so on. Boot the system in Safe Mode (press F8 during boot to display the Windows boot menu) to load the vanilla Windows display drivers and verify that the adapter and display are functioning properly. If you have another display handy, try connecting it to the problem system to eliminate the display as a possible cause.

Once you eliminate those possible causes, the next consideration is whether you've made any recent changes to your video hardware, software, or configuration. If so, that is a likely cause. Sometimes, problems caused by such a change don't manifest immediately. We have, for example, seen an updated Windows video driver function perfectly until one particular program was loaded or another piece of hardware was installed, which caused the system to crash and burn horribly.

That means the next step is to change video drivers. If a later driver is available, download and install it. If no later driver is available, try reinstalling the current driver. If problems manifest soon after installing an updated driver, try reinstalling the older driver.

Once they are installed and running properly, video adapters seldom fail, short of something like a lightning strike or abusing the adapter by overclocking it. Over 20 years' experience with hundreds of systems, we remember only a few instances when a functioning video adapter just died. Hardware failures are more likely today, not because newer video adapters are inferior to older models, but because they're now pushed harder. High-end video adapters nowadays come with at least a heatsink for the graphics processor, and it's not unusual to see a video adapter on a gamer's system with a fan or even a Peltier cooler installed. If you install a high-performance adapter, make absolutely certain that the fan, if any, has power, and that there is free air flow to the heatsink. Many video problems on systems so equipped are due to simple overheating.

Here are some specific problems you may encounter and how to remedy them:

No video or severe video problems occur with a newly installed card.

The usual cause is that the video card isn't seated properly. Verify that the video card is fully seated and latched. Make sure the display has power and the video cable is connected. Some systems with integrated video automatically disable the integrated video if a standalone video card is detected, but others require you to disable integrated video manually and enable the AGP or PCIe video card in BIOS Setup. Nearly all video adapters that have analog and digital outputs automatically detect the type of connected display and configure themselves properly, but a few require changing a switch or jumper to select the active output

Advice from Brian Jepson

You may also want to try the most recent WHQL (Windows Hardware Quality Labs) driver–this may be older than the most current driver. Sometimes, the latest driver posted on the vendor's web site still has some bugs that need to be ironed out while they are working on certification from Microsoft. I think WHQL certification is far from a guarantee of trouble-free operation, though, but it's worth a try if you think you have a buggy driver.

port. Similarly, if the video adapter supports dual displays or if you have two video adapters installed, you may have to specify whether your display is connected to the primary or secondary port.

"Out of scan range" or similar message is displayed.

The display isn't connected to the video adapter or the video adapter is providing a signal at a resolution and/or refresh rate that is not supported by the display. Verify that the display is connected. Restart the system in Safe Mode and select a supported resolution and refresh rate.

Text is too large or too small.

The video adapter is set for too high or too low a resolution for the monitor size, or Windows is configured to use nonstandard (Large or Very Large) fonts. Right-click on an unused area of the desktop, choose Properties, and modify the settings in the Display Properties dialog and subdialogs to correct the problem. Depending on your preferences and your visual acuity, we recommend running a 17" CRT monitor at 800×600 or 1024×768; a 19" monitor at 1280×1024 or 1600×1200; and a larger monitor at 1600×1200 or higher.

FLAT-PANEL DISPLAYS AND TEXT SIZE

CRT monitors can use any of a range of resolutions while maintaining high video quality. Flat-panel LCD displays are designed to operate at one specific resolution (the *native resolution*), and provide poor image quality at anything other than native resolution. Rather than change resolution with an FPD, change the font-size options in Windows and/or your applications to display text at optimum size.

Text is scrambled or appears distorted or in an odd font.

The probable cause is incorrect video drivers. Download and install the most recent stable drivers for your adapter. If it occurs on a system that had been working correctly, there are several possible causes. If text entered in an application appears in a strange font, but menus and other system fonts are correct, use preferences or options within the application to choose another font. If menus are scrambled only within one application, uninstall and then reinstall that application. If the problem occurs in multiple applications and system applets, system font files may have been corrupted or replaced with older, incompatible versions. The surest cure is to reinstall Windows.

Video problems occur in hot weather or after the system has been running for a while.

The video card is overheating, for which there are numerous possible causes. If the video card has a fan, make sure that it has power and is spinning freely. If the video card uses a passive heatsink, make sure that the heatsink is not blocked with dust. Verify that the case air vents are not blocked by dust and that the supplemental case fans, if any, are operating properly.

The display shows random black, white, or partial/colored blocks.

These screen artifacts may appear only when using certain combinations of resolution and color depth, and are not affected by mouse movement or by running a different application. They may be persistent or may appear and disappear seemingly at random. This problem is a result of malfunctioning video memory. Possible causes include an improperly seated video card, overheating, and defective memory on the card. Remove the video card, clean the contacts by polishing them with a new dollar bill, and reinsert the video card. Verify that the heatsink or fan on the card is operating properly and that the interior case temperature is not too high. If none of these actions solve the problem, the video card needs to be replaced.

Video is usually fine but becomes jerky during DVD-Video playback.

This may result from a slow processor or video adapter, inadequate memory, or by having too many other programs running, but if it occurs on a relatively recent system there are a couple of hardware configuration issues that are more likely causes. First, verify that the DVD drive is operating in DMA mode rather than PIO mode. Second, if you are using a flat-panel display with a digital connector, this problem may be caused by a conflict with USB devices (yes, we know that sounds odd). Disconnect all USB devices, including the keyboard and mouse if you have PS/2 substitutes. Restart the system and check DVD-Video playback. If the problem disappears, try plugging USB devices in separately until you discover which USB device or port is causing the problem.

Displays

11

For most people, a display is something that came with the last computer they bought—or the one before that. Few people ever think about upgrading their displays, and that's unfortunate. Even the newest, fastest system is hampered by an old, small, dim, fuzzy display. Fortunately, upgrading your display is easy—usually it's a simple matter of buying it and plugging it in—and nowadays it's cheaper than ever. Unless your current display is top-notch, consider upgrading it. Your eyes will thank you.

Two display technologies compete for consumers' dollars. A *CRT display* (*Cathode Ray Tube*) uses the older technology, but CRTs have significant price and other advantages and so retain significant market share. An *LCD display* (*Liquid Crystal Diode*) uses the newer technology and has advantages all its own. After you read this chapter, you'll know which of these two technologies is the right choice for you.

In This Chapter

CRT Displays

LCD Displays

Troubleshooting Display Problems

MONITOR OR DISPLAY?

For some reason, most people refer to a CRT display as a monitor and an LCD monitor as a display, although in fact the terms are interchangeable.

Figure 11-1. Samsung 997DF 19" CRT display (image courtesy of Samsung)

CRT Displays

CRT displays use the same picture tube technology—with many enhancements—as the first color televisions did more than half a century ago. But old doesn't necessarily mean obsolete. A good CRT display, such as the Samsung 997DF 19" model shown in Figure 11-1, provides excellent image quality at a reasonable price. CRT displays are an excellent choice for many people, and will remain so for years.

OLD FRIENDS AND NEW ONES

In autumn 2005, Robert finally replaced his beloved Hitachi SuperScan Elite 751 19" CRT display—which he had been using as his primary display for six years—with a 19" Samsung 930BF LCD display. The Hitachi is a top-notch display, and Robert would have sworn that its image quality was as good then as the day it was first installed. Until, that is, he connected the Samsung 930BF. The difference was startling. The Samsung provided much better brightness, contrast, and color saturation.

Does that mean that a good LCD display always beats a good CRT display, or that current display technology is worlds better than that of six years ago? Nope. It just means that every CRT display—even the best models—decreases in brightness, contrast, and saturation as it ages. From day to day, the difference is imperceptible, but as the months and years pass the accumulated difference becomes large.

There is a happy ending to this story, though. Robert had been running the Hitachi CRT at 50% brightness and 85% contrast for years. Boosting brightness to 75% and contrast to 100% greatly improved the display quality, so there's life in it yet. Barbara promptly grabbed the Hitachi for her own office, where it will probably live for another few years.

CRT monitors use the following major components:

CRT

The CRT is essentially a large glass bottle, flat or nearly so on one end (the screen), tapering to a thin neck at the back, and with nearly all air exhausted. The inside of the screen end is covered with a matrix of millions of tiny *phosphor* dots (or stripes). A phosphor is a chemical compound that, when struck by electrons, emits visible light of a particular color. Phosphors are organized by groups of three, collectively called a *pixel*. Each pixel contains one phosphor dot that emits each of the additive primary colors, red, green, and blue. By choosing which dots to illuminate and how brightly to illuminate each, any pixel can be made to emit any one of thousands or millions of discrete colors. The distance between nearest neighbors of the same phosphor color on adjacent rows is called the *dot pitch* or *stripe pitch*. A smaller pitch results in a sharper image and the ability to resolve finer detail.

Electron guns

The phosphor dots are excited by one or more electron emitters, called *electron guns*, located in the neck at the back of the monitor. A gun comprises a heated cathode, which emits electrons, and circuitry that focuses the free electrons into a thin beam.

Deflection yoke

The *deflection yoke* is located around the tapered portion of the CRT, between the guns and the screen. This yoke is actually a large electromagnet, which, under the control of the monitor circuitry, is used to steer the electron beam(s) to impinge on the correct phosphor dot at the correct time and with the correct intensity.

Mask

The *mask* sits between the electron guns and the phosphor layer, very close to the latter. This mask may be a sheet of metal with a matrix of fine perforations that correspond to the phosphor dot triads on the screen, called a *shadow mask*, or a series of fine vertical wires that correspond to phosphors laid down in uninterrupted vertical stripes, called an *aperture grill*. In practice, and despite the marketing efforts of manufacturers to convince us otherwise, we find that the mask type makes little real difference. Good (read: more expensive) monitors produce good images, regardless of their mask type. Inexpensive monitors produce inferior images, regardless of their mask type.

CRT Characteristics

Here are the important characteristics of CRT monitors:

Screen size

Screen size is specified in two ways. The nominal size—the size by which monitors are advertised and referred to—is the diagonal measurement of the tube itself. However, the front bezel of the monitor conceals part of the tube, making the usable size of the monitor less than stated. Various consumer lawsuits have resulted in monitor manufacturers also specifying the *Viewable Image Size* (*VIS*), which is the portion of the tube that is actually visible. Typically, VIS is an inch or so less than nominal. For example, a nominal 17" monitor may have a 15.8" VIS. Small differences in VIS—for example, 15.8" versus 16"—make little practical difference. The smallest monitors still available are 15". While 17" remains the most popular size, 19" models are now so inexpensive that they have nearly overtaken 17" models in unit sales. Monitors 21" and larger are still relatively expensive, and are used primarily by graphics artists and others who require huge displays.

Dot/stripe pitch

Dot pitch or *stripe pitch* is measured in millimeters, and specifies the center-to-center distance between the nearest neighboring phosphor dots or stripes of the same color. Smaller pitch means a sharper image that resolves finer detail. Unfortunately, dot pitch, which is used to describe shadow mask monitors, cannot be compared directly to stripe pitch, which is used to describe aperture grill monitors. For equivalent resolution, stripe pitch must be about 90% of dot pitch. That is, a 0.28 mm dot pitch monitor has resolution similar to a 0.25 mm stripe pitch monitor.

Maximum resolution

Maximum resolution specifies the maximum number of pixels that the monitor can display, which is determined by the physical number of pixels present on the face of the tube. The maximum resolution of many low-end monitors is identical to the optimum resolution for that monitor size. For example, 1024×768 is optimum for 17" monitors, so many low-end 17" monitors provide 1024×768 maximum resolution. Conversely, midrange and high-end monitors may have maximum resolutions higher than practically usable. For example, a high-end 17" monitor may support up to 1600×1200. There is no real benefit to such extreme resolutions, although it can be useful to have one step higher than optimum (e.g., 1280×1024 on a 17" monitor or 1600×1200 on a 19" monitor) available for occasional use for special purposes.

Synchronization range

The *synchronization range* specifies the bandwidth of the monitor, which determines which combinations of resolution, refresh rate, and color depth can be displayed. Synchronization range is specified as two values:

Vertical Scanning Frequency

Vertical Scanning Frequency (VSF) is the inverse of the time the monitor requires to display one full screen. VSF (also called *refresh rate*) is measured in hertz (Hz) and specifies the number of times per second the screen can be redrawn. To avoid screen flicker, the monitor should support at least 70 Hz refresh at the selected resolution. Within reason, higher refresh rates provide a more stable image, but rates beyond 85 or 90 Hz are necessary only for specialized applications such as medical imaging. Most monitors support a wide range of refresh rates, from very low (e.g., 50 Hz) to very high (e.g., 120 to 160 Hz).

Horizontal Scanning Frequency

Horizontal Scanning Frequency (HSF) is the inverse of the time the monitor requires to display one full scan line. HSF is measured in kilohertz (KHz), and specifies the overall range of bandwidths supported by the monitor. For example, a monitor running 1280×1024 at 85 Hz must display 1024 lines 85 times per second, or 87,040 scan lines per second, or about 87 KHz. In fact, some overhead is involved, so the actual HSF for such a monitor might be 93.5 KHz.

Resolution and refresh rate are interrelated parts of synchronization range of an analog monitor. For a given resolution, increasing the refresh rate increases the number of screens (and accordingly the amount of data) that must be transferred each second. Similarly, for a given refresh rate, increasing the resolution increases the amount of data that must be transferred for each screen. If you increase resolution or refresh rate, you may have to decrease the other to stay within the HSF limit on total bandwidth.

Note that manufacturers often specify maximum resolution and maximum refresh rate independently, without consideration for their interrelatedness. For example, specifications for a 19" monitor may promise 1600×1200 resolution and 160 Hz refresh. Don't assume that means you can run 1600×1200 at 160 Hz. 160 Hz refresh may be supported only at 640×480 resolution; at 1600×1200, the monitor may support only 70 Hz refresh.

COLOR DEPTH AND BANDWIDTH

Resolution and refresh rate alone determine the required bandwidth for an analog monitor. Color depth is immaterial, because the color displayed for a given pixel is determined by the analog voltages present on the red, green, and blue lines at the time that pixel is processed. Therefore, at a given resolution and refresh rate, an analog monitor uses exactly the same bandwidth whether the color depth is set to 4, 8, 16, 24, or 32 bits, because the video card converts the digital color data to analog signals before sending it to the monitor. For purely digital monitors, such as LCD displays, greater color depth requires greater bandwidth, because color information is conveyed to a digital monitor as a digital signal.

Tube geometry

Monitors use one of three geometries for the front viewing surface. Older monitors used spherical tubes or cylindrical tubes, both of which have noticeably curved surfaces. *Flat square tubes* (*FST*) are nearly flat. Other than some "value" models, all current monitors use an FST. Don't consider buying a monitor that is not FST.

CRT advantages

CRT displays have many advantages relative to LCD displays.

Price

CRTs cost less than LCDs. For the same price as an entry-level 17" LCD, you can buy a midrange 19" CRT or two good 17" CRTs. The pricing differential has somewhat narrowed recently, but LCDs are likely for the foreseeable future to cost more than CRTs with similar size, features, and quality.

Variable resolution

LCDs are designed to operate at one resolution, typically 1024×768 for 15" models and 1280×1024 for 17", 18", and 19" models. Although you can run an LCD at lower resolution than it was designed to use, you don't want to. At nonnative resolution, you must choose between having a sharp image that occupies only a portion of the screen or using pixel extrapolation, which results in a full-screen image with significantly degraded image quality. CRTs, conversely, can operate at various resolutions, which means that you can choose the resolution that suits your own preferences and vision.

Service life

A high-quality CRT normally lasts for many years. It's common for a CRT to remain in use for five years or more, and even ten years is not unheard of. LCDs use an array of *cold cathode ray tubes* (*CCRTs*), which are similar to fluorescent tubes, to provide the backlight required to view the image. A failed CCRT is not economically repairable. When a CCRT burns out, the LCD display must be replaced.

ONLY THE BAD DIE YOUNG

Not all CRTs have a long service life. High-quality models typically live a long time; cheap models often die after only a year or two of use.

Superior display of fast-motion video

CRTs use phosphor pixels, which can be turned on or off almost instantly. LCDs use transistorized pixels that respond more slowly. This slower response may be visible as a smearing or ghosting effect when an LCD displays fast-motion video, such as DVD video or graphics-intensive games. Although better LCDs don't exhibit this problem, at least not as severely as cheaper models, it is common and intrusive with entry-level LCDs.

Larger viewing angle

CRTs present essentially the same image quality regardless of viewing angle. Conversely, LCDs present their best image quality only within a relatively small viewing angle, although midrange and better LCD models typically have larger viewing angles than entry-level models.

Accurate color reproduction

Many graphic artists refuse to use LCDs because the appearance of colors and the relationship between them changes with viewing angle. This problem is particularly acute with inexpensive LCDs, although even premium units exhibit it at least to some extent. The best LCD models are good enough in this respect for routine use, but most who insist on accurate color reproduction still prefer high-quality CRT monitors.

No pixel defects

A CRT never has defective pixels. An LCD panel is manufactured as a monolithic item that contains more than a million pixels, and on some LCD panels one or a few of those pixels are defective. Defective pixels may be always-on (white), always-off (black), or some color. People vary in their reaction to defective pixels. Many don't even notice a defective pixel or two, while others, once they notice a defective pixel, seem to be drawn to that pixel to the exclusion of all else. Most manufacturer warranties specifically exclude some number of defective pixels, typically between five and ten, although the number may vary with display size and, sometimes, with the location of the defective pixels and how closely they are clustered. As long as the display meets those requirements, the manufacturer considers the display to be acceptable. You may or may not find it acceptable.

Vibrant color rendering

Although the contrast and brightness of recent high-end LCDs are excellent, most LCDs provide subjectively less vibrant color than a good CRT. This is particularly evident in the darkest and lightest areas, where tones seem to be compressed, which limits subtle gradations between light tones or dark tones that are readily evident on a good CRT. Also, some LCDs add a color cast to what should be neutral light or dark tones. For example, dark neutral tones may appear shifted toward the blue (cooler) or red (warmer) ranges. This problem is less prevalent in high-quality LCDs than in entry-level units, and is also more likely to occur if you are using an analog interface rather than a digital interface.

If your budget is limited, a CRT offers far more bang for the buck than an LCD and, particularly for entry-level models, overall display quality will also be higher.

Choosing a CRT display

Use the following guidelines when choosing a CRT display:

- Remember that a CRT display is a long-term purchase. Even with heavy use, a high-quality CRT can be expected to last five years or more, so buy quality and choose a model that's likely to keep you happy not just for your current system, but for one or even two systems after that.

- Make sure the CRT is big enough, but not too big. We consider 17" models suitable only for casual use or those on the tightest of budgets. For not much more, you can buy a 19" model that you'll be much happier with. Conversely, make sure your desk or workstation furniture can accommodate the new CRT. Many people have excitedly carried home a new 21" CRT only to find that it literally won't fit where it needs to. Check physical dimensions and weight carefully before you buy. Large CRTs commonly weigh 50 lbs. or more, and some exceed 100 lbs. That said, if you find yourself debating 17" versus 19" or 19" versus 21", go with the larger model. But note that if your decision is between a cheap larger CRT and a high-quality smaller one for about the same price, you may well be happier with the smaller CRT. A $130 17" CRT beats a $130 19" CRT every time.

- Stick with good name brands and buy a midrange or higher model from within that name brand. That doesn't guarantee that you'll get a good CRT, but it does greatly increase your chances. The CRT market is extremely competitive. If two similar models differ greatly in price, the cheaper one likely has significantly worse specs. If the specs appear similar, the maker of the cheaper model has cut corners somewhere, whether in component quality, construction quality, or warranty policies.

RECOMMENDED BRANDS

Our opinion, which is shared by many, is that NEC-Mitsubishi, Samsung, and ViewSonic make the best CRTs available. Their CRTs, particularly midrange and better models, provide excellent image quality and are quite reliable. You're likely to be happy with a CRT from any of these manufacturers.

- If possible, test the exact CRT you plan to buy (not a floor sample) before you buy it. Ask the local store to endorse the manufacturer's warranty—that is, to agree that if the CRT fails you can bring it back to the store for a replacement rather than dealing with the hassles of returning it to the manufacturer. Mass merchandisers like Best Buy usually won't do this—they try to sell you a service contract instead, which you shouldn't buy—but small local computer stores may agree to endorse the manufacturer's warranty. If the CRT has hidden damage from rough handling during shipping, that damage will ordinarily be apparent within a month or two of use, if not immediately.

BUY CRTS LOCALLY

After shipping costs, it may actually cost less to buy locally, but that is not the main reason for doing so. Buying locally gives you the opportunity to examine the exact CRT you are buying. CRTs vary more between samples than other computer components. Also, CRTs are sometimes damaged in shipping, often without any external evidence on the CRT itself or even the box. Damaged CRTs may arrive DOA, but more often they have been jolted severely enough to cause display problems and perhaps reduced service life, but not complete failure. Buying locally allows you to eliminate a "dud" before you buy it, rather than having to deal with shipping it back to the vendor or manufacturer.

- Most mainstream CRT manufacturers produce three—Good, Better, and Best—models in 17", 19", and 21". In general, the Good model from a first-tier maker corresponds roughly in features, specifications, and price to the Better or Best models from lower-tier makers. For casual use, choose a Good model from a first-tier maker, most of which are very good indeed. If you make heavier demands on your CRT—such as sitting in front of it eight hours a day—you may find that the Better model from a first-tier maker is the best choice. The Best models from first-tier makers are usually overkill, although they may be necessary if you use the CRT for CAD/CAM or other demanding tasks. Best models often have generally useless features like extremely high resolutions and unnecessarily high refresh rates at moderate resolutions. It's nice that a Best 17" model can display 1600×1200 resolution, for example, but unless you can float on thermals and dive on rabbits from a mile in the air, that resolution is likely to be unusable. Similarly, a 17" CRT that supports 115 MHz refresh rates at 1024×768 is nice, but in practical terms offers no real advantage over one that supports an 85 or 90 MHz refresh.

- Choose the specific CRT you buy based on how it looks to you. Comparing specifications helps narrow the list of candidates, but nothing substitutes for actually looking at the image displayed by the CRT. For example, CRTs with Sony Trinitron tubes have one or two fine horizontal internal wires whose shadows appear on screen. Most people don't even notice the shadow, but some find it intolerable.

- Make sure the CRT has sufficient reserve brightness. CRTs dim as they age, and one of the most common flaws in new CRTs, particularly those from second- and third-tier manufacturers, is inadequate brightness. A CRT that is barely bright enough when new may dim enough to become unusable after a year or two. A new CRT should provide a good image with the brightness set no higher than 50%.

Like all other component manufacturers, CRT makers have come under increasing margin pressures. A few years ago, we felt safe in recommending any CRT from a first-tier maker, because those companies refused to put their names on anything but top-notch products. Alas, first-tier makers have been forced to make manufacturing cost reductions and other compromises to compete with cheap Pacific Rim CRTs.

Accordingly, low-end models from first-tier makers may be of lower quality than they were in the past. The presence of a first-tier maker's name plate still means that CRT is likely to be of higher quality than a similar no-name CRT, but is no longer a guarantee of top quality. Many first-tier CRTs are actually made in the same Pacific Rim plants that also produce no-name junk, but don't read too much into that. First-tier CRTs are still differentiated by component quality and the level of quality control they undergo. There is no question in our minds that the first-tier CRTs are easily worth the 10% to 20% price premium they command relative to lesser brands. In fact, we think it is worth the extra cost to buy not just a first-tier CRT, but a midrange first-tier CRT.

LCD Displays

LCD displays use a relatively new technology, but all of the early teething problems have long been worked out and the prices of LCD displays have fallen to the point that they are now mainstream products. A good LCD display, such as the ViewSonic VP191 19" model shown in Figure 11-2, provides top-notch image quality in a compact package. Although traditional CRTs have advantages of their own, most people who experience the bright, contrasty image of a good LCD display will never return to using a CRT monitor.

Figure 11-2. ViewSonic VP191 19" LCD display (image reprinted with permission from ViewSonic Corporation)

WHY ARE THOSE STRAIGHT LINES CURVED?

If you convert from a standard CRT display to a flat-screen CRT display or (particularly) an LCD display, you may notice an odd effect. Your eye and brain become used to seeing the curved surface of the old display as flat. The new display, which truly is flat, looks concave! Straight lines appear to bow inward, particularly if you work close to the display. The effect is so convincing that Robert actually held a straight-edge up to his new LCD display. Sure enough, the "bent" lines were straight. Don't worry, though. The optical illusion disappears after only a couple hours' use.

CRT monitors were the dominant PC display technology until recently, but that has changed. For displays bundled with new PCs, LCDs exceeded CRTs in popularity by late 2002. By 2005, LCDs had also begun to outsell CRTs in retail channels. Lower cost and other advantages of CRTs ensure that they'll remain available for years to come, but the emphasis has definitely shifted to LCDs.

LCD display characteristics

Here are the important characteristics of LCDs:

Resolution

Unlike CRT monitors, which have a maximum resolution but can easily be run at lower resolutions, LCDs are designed to operate at one resolution, called the *native resolution*. You can run an LCD at lower than native resolution, but that results in either the image occupying only part of the screen at full image quality or, via pixel extrapolation, the image occupying the full screen area but with greatly reduced image quality.

Interface

LCDs are available in analog-only, digital/analog hybrid, and digital-only interfaces. Using an analog interface requires converting the video signal from digital to analog inside the PC and then from analog to digital inside the monitor, which reduces image quality, particularly at higher resolutions. Synchronization problems occur frequently with analog interfaces, and can cause various undesirable display problems. Finally, analog interfaces are inherently noisier than digital interfaces, which causes subtle variations in display quality that can be quite disconcerting.

Refresh rate

Whereas CRT monitors require high vertical refresh rates to ensure stable images, LCDs, because of their differing display technology, can use much lower refresh rates. For example, at 1280×1024 resolution on a CRT monitor, you'll probably want to use an 85 Hz or higher refresh rate for good image quality. At the same resolution on an LCD, 60 Hz is a perfectly adequate refresh rate. In fact, on LCDs, a lower refresh rate often provides a better image than a higher refresh rate.

Response time

Unlike CRT monitors, whose phosphor-based pixels respond essentially instantaneously to the electron beam, LCD panels use transistors, which require time to turn on or turn off. That means there is a measurable lag between when a transistor is switched on or off and when the associated pixel changes to the proper state. That lag, called *rise time* for when the transistor is switched on and *fall time* for when it is switched off, results in a corresponding lag in image display.

Everything You Always Wanted to Know About LCD Response Time

Fast LCD response time is a Good Thing. Fast response means smoother scrolling and no ghosting or smearing, even when you view fast-motion video. Unfortunately, there's no standard way to measure or specify response time, so different LCD makers use different methods. That means you can't necessarily compare the response time specified by one LCD maker directly with that specified by another. (Actually, it's worse than that; you can't necessarily compare response times for two different models made by the same company.)

When LCDs first appeared, most makers specified *rise-and-fall* response in milliseconds (ms), the time required for a pixel to change from black to white (*rise time*) and then from white to black (*fall time*), also called the *black-white-black* (*bwb*) response. Nowadays, in addition to or instead of bwb, many LCD makers specify *white-black-white* (*wbw*) response and/or *gray-to-gray* (*gtg*) response, the time required to go from one level of gray to another.

And gtg times are not necessarily comparable between different brands, or even between different models from the same company, because gtg time depends on which particular levels of gray are tested. Do we specify gtg response for going from an almost-black gray to an almost-white gray, or for going from one almost-middle gray to another almost-middle gray? It makes a difference.

Some makers also specify the rise time separately. For example, we found one display that was advertised as having a 4 ms response time, but the product data sheet on the

maker's web site listed that display as having an 8 ms response time. Both numbers were accurate, as far as they went. The 4 ms time quoted in the ad referred to rise time (black to white). The 8 ms time quoted in the technical documents referred to bwb response.

It is not safe to make assumptions about one type of response time based on another type. For example, one LCD may have response times of 20 ms bwb and 8 ms gtg, while another model from the same manufacturer may have response times of 16 ms bwb and 12 ms gtg. So, is the second LCD slower or faster than the first? It depends on which numbers you decide to use. Advertisers use the fastest numbers available. Count on it.

All of these response-time numbers can be different, and there's no direct relationship among them. If you look only at ads (as opposed to technical documentation), it's often not clear what type of response time is being specified. If a response time is quoted without qualification, such as "16 ms," that ordinarily (but not always) refers to bwb response.

A fast bwb (or wbw) response time is more important for general use, while a fast gtg response time is more important for gamers and graphic artists. For general use, bwb response of 25 ms to 30 ms is acceptable to most people, and 16 ms to 20 ms preferable. For gaming and other demanding applications, bwb response of 12 ms is generally acceptable and 8 ms preferable, with gtg response no slower than 8 ms and 4 ms or less desirable.

LCD advantages

Relative to CRT displays, LCD displays have the following advantages:

Brightness

> LCDs are brighter than CRTs. A typical CRT has brightness of about 100 candelas/square meter, a unit of measurement called a *nit*. (Some displays are rated in *foot Lamberts* (*fL*); one fL equals about 3.43 nits). A typical LCD is rated at 250 to 350 nits, roughly three times as bright as a typical CRT. CRTs dim as they age, although a brightness control with enough range at the upper end can often be used to set an old CRT

to near original brightness. The CCRTs used to backlight LCDs also dim as they age, but generally fail completely before reduced brightness becomes a major issue.

Contrast

Contrast measures the difference in luminance between the brightest and dimmest portions of an image, and is expressed as a ratio. The ability to display a high-contrast image is an important aspect of image quality, particularly for text. An average CRT may have a contrast ratio of 200:1, and a superb CRT 250:1. An inexpensive LCD may have a contrast ratio of 400:1, and a superb LCD 1,000:1. In other words, even an inexpensive LCD may have higher contrast than an excellent CRT.

Usability in bright environments

Even good flat-screen CRTs are subject to objectionable reflections when used in bright environments, such as having the screen facing a window. Good LCDs are much superior in this respect. Short of direct sunlight impinging on the screen, a good LCD provides excellent images under any lighting conditions.

Size and weight

A typical CRT is about as deep as its nominal screen size. For example, a 19" CRT may be 19" from front to back. Large CRTs may be difficult to fit physically in the available space. Conversely, LCDs are quite shallow. The panel itself typically ranges from 1.5" to 3" deep, and even with the base most LCDs are no more than 7" to 8" deep. Also, where a large CRT may weigh 50 to 100 pounds or more, even large LCDs are quite light. A typical 17" LCD might weigh 10 pounds, and even a 23" unit may weigh less than 20 pounds. That small size and weight means that it's possible to desk- or wall-mount an LCD with relatively inexpensive mounting hardware, compared to the large, heavy, expensive mounting hardware needed for CRTs.

NOMINAL VERSUS ACTUAL SIZE

Stated LCD display sizes are accurate. For example, a 19" LCD has a display area that actually measures 19" diagonally. CRT sizes, on the other hand, are nominal because they specify the diagonal measurement of the entire CRT, part of which is covered by the bezel. For example, a nominal 19" CRT might have a display area that actually measures 18.1" diagonally. A couple of lawsuits several years ago convinced CRT makers to begin stating the usable size of their CRTs. This is stated as *VIS* (*viewable image size or visible image size*), and is invariably an inch or so smaller than the nominal size.

This VIS issue has given rise to the belief that a 15" LCD is equivalent to a 17" CRT, a 17" LCD to a 19" CRT, and so on. In fact, that's not true. The image size of a typical 17" CRT is an inch or so larger than that of a 15" LCD, as is the image size of a 19" CRT relative to a 17" LCD.

Power consumption

Depending on size and other factors, a typical CRT consumes 100 to 160 watts while operating, while an LCD consumes only a quarter to a half as much power. Using an LCD reduces your electricity bill directly by consuming less power and indirectly by reducing the heating load on your air conditioning during hot weather.

Choosing an LCD display

If you've decided that an LCD is right for you, use the following guidelines to choose one:

- Current LCDs are available in analog-only, digital-only, and models with both analog and digital inputs. Analog input is acceptable for 15" (1024×768) models, but for 17" (1280×1024) models analog video noise becomes an issue. At that screen size and resolution, analog noise isn't immediately obvious to most people, but if you use the display for long periods the difference between using a display with a clean digital signal and one with a noisy analog signal will affect you on almost a subconscious level. For a 19" (1280×1024) LCD, we regard a digital signal as extremely desirable but not absolutely essential. For a larger display or above 1280×1024, we wouldn't consider using analog signaling.

- Insist on true *24-bit color support*, which may be described as support for *16.7 million colors*. Most current LCDs support 24-bit color, allocating one full byte to each of the three primary colors, which allows 256 shades of each color and a total of 16.7 million colors to be displayed. Many early LCDs and some inexpensive current models support only six bits per color, for a total of 18-bit color. These models use extrapolation to simulate full 24-bit color support, which results in poor color quality. If an LCD is advertised as "24-bit compatible," that's good reason to look elsewhere. Oddly, many LCDs that do support true 24-bit color don't bother to mention it in their spec sheets, while many that support only 18-bit color trumpet the fact that they are "24-bit compatible."

- Most LCD makers produce three or more series of LCDs. Entry-level models are often analog-only, even in 19" and 21" sizes, and have slow response times. Midrange models usually accept analog or digital inputs, and generally have response times fast enough for anything except 3D gaming and similarly demanding uses. The best models may be analog/digital hybrids or digital-only, and have very fast response times. Choose an entry-level model only if you are certain that you will never use the display for anything more than word processing, web browsing, and similarly undemanding tasks. If you need a true CRT-replacement display, choose a midrange or higher model with a digital interface and the fastest response time you are willing to pay for.

- Decide what panel size and resolution is right for you. Keep in mind that when you choose a specific LCD model, you are also effectively choosing the resolution that you will always use on that display.

- Buy the LCD locally if possible. Whether or not you buy locally, insist on a no-questions-asked return policy. LCDs are more variable than CRT monitors, both in terms of unit-to-unit variation and in terms of usability with a particular graphics adapter. This is particularly important if you are using an analog interface. Some analog LCDs simply don't play nice with some analog graphics adapters. Also, LCDs vary from unit to unit in how many defective pixels they have and where those are located. You might prefer a unit with five defective pixels near the edges and corners rather than a unit with only one or two defective pixels located near the center of the screen.

- If you buy locally, ask the store to endorse the manufacturer's warranty —that is, to agree that if the LCD fails you can bring it back to the store for a replacement rather than dealing with the hassles of returning the LCD to the maker.

- If possible, test the exact LCD you plan to buy (not a floor sample) before you buy it. Ideally, and particularly if you will use the analog interface, you should test the LCD with your own system, or at least with a system that has a graphics adapter identical to the one you plan to use. We'd go to some extremes to do this, including carrying our desktop system down to the local store. But if that isn't possible for some reason, still insist on seeing the actual LCD you plan to buy running. That way, you can at least determine if there are defective pixels in locations that bother you. Also, use a neutral gray screen with no image to verify that the backlight evenly illuminates the entire screen. Some variation is unavoidable, but one or more corners should not be especially darker than the rest of the display, nor should there be any obvious "hot" spots.

- Stick with good name brands and buy a midrange or higher model from within that name brand. That doesn't guarantee that you'll get a good LCD, but it does greatly increase your chances. The LCD market is extremely competitive. If two similar models differ greatly in price, the cheaper one likely has significantly worse specs. If the specs appear similar, the maker of the cheaper model has cut corners somewhere, whether in component quality, construction quality, or warranty policies.

Recommended Brands

Our opinion, confirmed by our readers and colleagues, is that NEC-Mitsubishi, Samsung, Sony, and ViewSonic make the best LCDs available. Their LCDs—particularly their midrange and better models —provide excellent image quality and are quite reliable. You're likely to be happy with an LCD from any of these manufacturers.

Troubleshooting Display Problems

Troubleshooting CRTs versus LCDs begins with similar steps, but diverges due to the differing natures of the two display types. The first trouble-shooting steps are similar for either display type: power down the system and display and then power them back up; make sure the power cable is connected and that the outlet has power; verify that the signal cable is connected firmly to both video adapter and display and that there are no bent pins; verify that the video adapter is configured properly for the display; try the problem display on a known-good system, or try a known-good display on the problem system; and so on. Once you've tried the "obvious" trouble-shooting steps, if the problem persists, the next step you take depends on the type of display. The following sections cover basic troubleshooting for CRTs and LCDs.

Troubleshooting CRTs

CRTs seldom fail outright without obvious signs, such as a loud snap or a strong odor of burning electrical components. Most CRT problems are really problems with the power, video adapter, cable, or hardware/software settings. To eliminate the CRT as a possible cause, connect the suspect CRT to a known-good system, or connect a known-good display to the suspect system.

If the CRT is the problem, it is often not worth repairing. If the CRT is out of warranty, parts and labor may cost more than buying a new CRT, which also gives you better specs and a warranty. About the only CRTs we'd even consider repairing out-of-warranty are high-end 21" or larger models, and even there the economics are dubious.

Even if the CRT is in warranty, the shipping costs may exceed the value of the CRT. For example, shipping a CRT both ways can easily cost $75 or more. If that CRT is a year-old 17" model, you're probably better off spending $100 to $200 for a new 17" or 19" CRT than paying $75 in shipping to have the old one repaired. CRTs have many components, all of which age together. Fixing one is no guarantee that another won't fail shortly. In fact, that happens more often than not in our experience.

DON'T FSCK WITH CRTs

Never disassemble a CRT. At best, you may destroy the CRT. At worst, it may destroy you. Like televisions, CRTs use extremely high voltages internally, and have large capacitors that store that energy for days or even weeks after the CRT is unplugged. Robert once literally burned a screwdriver in half when working inside a color television that had been unplugged for several days. Also, the large, fragile tube may implode, scattering glass fragments like a hand grenade. People who repair CRTs and televisions for a living treat them with great respect, and so should you. If you must repair a CRT, take it to someone who knows what she is doing. You have been warned.

Here are some common CRT problems:

CRT displays no image

Check the obvious things first. Verify that the CRT is plugged in (and that the receptacle has power), the video cable is connected to the video card, the computer and CRT are turned on, and the brightness and contrast settings are set to the middle of their range. If none of these steps solves the problem, your CRT, video card, or video cable may be bad. Check the suspect CRT on a known-good system or a known-good CRT on the problem system.

POWER MISMANAGEMENT

If you have ACPI or APM power management enabled, it may be causing the problem. Some systems simply refuse to wake up once power management puts them to sleep. We have seen such systems survive a hardware reset without restoring power to the CRT. To verify this problem, turn off power to the system and CRT and then turn them back on. If the CRT then displays an image, check the power management settings in your BIOS and operating system and disable them if necessary.

CRT displays only a thin horizontal line or a pinpoint at the center

This is a hardware problem. The flyback transformer or high-voltage circuitry is failing or has failed. Replace the CRT.

CRT flashes one color intermittently, even when the screen is blanked

This is a hardware problem with one of the electron guns. Replace the CRT. This problem may also manifest as a strong color cast during normal operation that is not correctable using the normal color balance controls.

CRT snaps, crackles, or pops when powered up, or emits a strong electrical odor

Catastrophic CRT failure is imminent. The noises are caused by high-voltage arcing, and the smell is caused by burning insulation. Unplug the CRT from the wall before it catches fire, literally.

CRT emits a very high-pitched squeal

There are two likely causes. First, you may be driving the CRT beyond its design limits. Some CRTs display a usable image at resolutions and/or refresh rates higher than they are designed to use, but under such abuse the expected life of the CRT is shortened dramatically, perhaps to minutes. To correct this problem, change video settings to values that are within the CRT's design specifications. Second, the power receptacle may be supplying voltage lower than the CRT requires. To correct this problem, connect the CRT to a different circuit or to a UPS or power conditioner that supplies standard voltage regardless of input voltage.

CRT displays some colors incorrectly or not at all

This is usually a minor hardware problem. The most likely cause is that the signal cable is not connected tightly to the CRT and/or video card, causing some pins to make contact intermittently or not at all. Verify that no pins are loose, bent, or missing on the cable or the connectors on the CRT and video card, and then tighten the cable at both ends, If that doesn't fix the problem, open the computer, remove the video card, and reseat it fully.

In elderly systems, another possible cause is that some hardware DVD decoder cards "steal" one color (usually magenta) and use it to map the DVD video signal onto the standard video signal. Remove the DVD decoder card. If your video adapter includes hardware DVD support, or if you are upgrading to such an adapter, you don't need a DVD decoder card.

Image rolls or a horizontal line scrolls constantly down the screen

The most likely cause is that the CRT is receiving inadequate power. Connect it to a different circuit or to a backup power supply that provides correct voltage regardless of fluctuations in mains voltage.

Image flickers

The most likely cause is that the refresh rate is set too low. Change the refresh rate to at least 75 Hz. Flicker also results from interaction with fluorescent lights, which operate on 60 Hz AC and can heterodyne visually with the CRT. This can occur at 60 Hz (which is far too low a refresh rate anyway), but can also occur at 120 Hz. If you're running at 120 Hz refresh and experience flicker, either use incandescent lighting or reset the refresh rate to something other than 120 Hz.

Image is scrambled

The video card settings are likely outside the range supported by the CRT, particularly if you have just installed the CRT or have just changed video settings. To verify this, restart the system in Safe Mode (press F8 during boot to display the Windows boot menu and choose Safe Mode). If the system displays a VGA image properly, change your display settings to something supported by the CRT.

Image displays rectilinearly, but is incorrectly sized or aligned on screen

Most modern CRTs can display signals at many different scan frequencies, but this doesn't mean that the CRT will necessarily automatically display different signals full-screen and properly aligned. Use the CRT controls to adjust the size and alignment of the image.

Image displays other than rectilinearly (trapezoid, parallelogram, barrel, or pincushion)

Depending on the CRT, video card, and video settings, this may be normal behavior, adjustable using the CRT controls. If the distortion is beyond the ability of the controls to correct, the problem may be with the video card, the CRT, or the driver. First try changing video settings. If the problem persists at several settings, move that CRT to a different system (or use a different video card) to determine whether the problem is caused by the CRT or video card. Repair or replace the faulty component.

Image wavers or shimmers periodically or constantly

This is usually caused by RF interference from another electrical or electronic device, particularly one that contains a motor. Make sure such devices are at least three feet from the CRT. Note that such interference can sometimes penetrate typical residential and office walls, so if the CRT is close to a wall, check the other side. Such image problems can also be caused by interference carried by the power line or by voltage variations in the AC power supply. To eliminate interference, plug the CRT into a surge protector. Better still, plug it into a UPS or power conditioner that supplies clean power at a constant voltage.

This problem may also be caused by using a video cable that is too long or of poor quality or by using a poor-quality *KVM switch (keyboard/video/mouse switch)*. Manual KVM switches are particularly problematic.

Colors are "off" or smearing appears in some areas

The CRT may need to be degaussed. A CRT that sits in one position for months or years can be affected even by the earth's very weak magnetic field, causing distortion and other display problems. Exposing a CRT to a strong magnetic field, such as unshielded speakers, can cause more extreme image problems. Many modern CRTs degauss themselves automatically each time you cycle the power, but some have a manual degauss button that you must remember to use. If your CRT has a manual degauss button, use it every month or two. The degaussing circuitry in some CRTs has limited power. We have seen CRTs that were accidentally exposed to strong magnetic fields, resulting in a badly distorted image. Built-in degaussing did little or nothing. In that case, you can sometimes fix the problem by using a separate degaussing coil, available at RadioShack and similar stores for a few dollars. We have, however, seen CRTs that were so badly "magnet burned" that even a standalone degaussing coil could not completely eliminate the problem. The moral is to keep magnets away from your CRT, including those in speakers that are not video-shielded.

Troubleshooting LCD displays

If you've tried the basic troubleshooting steps and your LCD still doesn't work properly, you may have one or more of the following problems:

No image

   If your LCD displays no image at all and you are certain that it is receiving power and video signal, first adjust the brightness and contrast settings to higher values. If that doesn't work, turn off the system and LCD, disconnect the LCD signal cable from the computer, and turn on the LCD by itself. It should display some sort of initialization screen, if only perhaps a "No video signal" message. If nothing lights up and no message is displayed, contact technical support for your LCD manufacturer. If your LCD supports multiple inputs, you may need to press a button to cycle through the inputs and set it to the correct one.

Screen flickers

   Unlike CRTs, where increasing the refresh rate always reduces flicker, LCDs have an optimal refresh rate that may be lower than the highest refresh rate supported. For example, a 17" LCD operating in analog mode may support 60 Hz and 75 Hz refresh. Although it sounds counterintuitive to anyone whose experience has been with CRTs, reducing the refresh rate from 75 Hz to 60 Hz may improve image stability. Check the manual to determine the optimum refresh rate for your LCD, and set your video adapter to use that rate.

The screen is very unstable

   First, try setting the optimal refresh rate as described above. If that doesn't solve the problem and you are using an analog interface, there are several possible causes, most of which are due to poor synchronization between the video adapter clock and the display clock, or to phase problems. If your LCD has an auto-adjust, auto-setup, or auto-synchronize option, try using that first. If not, try adjusting the phase and/or clock settings manually until you have a usable image. If you are using an extension or longer than standard video cable, try connecting the standard video cable that was supplied with the display. Long analog video cables exacerbate sync problems. Also, if you are using a KVM switch, particularly a manual model, try instead connecting the LCD directly to the video adapter. Many LCDs are difficult or impossible to synchronize if you use a KVM switch. If you are unable to achieve proper synchronization, try connecting the LCD to a different computer. If you are unable to achieve synchronization on the second computer, the LCD may be defective. Finally, note that some models of video adapter simply don't function well with some models of LCD.

Poor image

   If the screen is displaying a full, stable image, but that image is of poor quality, first verify that the display is not connected through a KVM switch or using an extension cable. If so, connect the display directly to the video adapter using the standard cable. If that is already the case, adjust the brightness, contrast, and focus controls. If you are unable to get a proper image using these controls, the problem is most likely a clock or phase mismatch, which you can cure by taking the steps described in the preceding item.

ADJUSTING CLOCK AND PHASE

The best way to adjust clock and phase is to use auto-adjust first. Check the utility and driver CD that came with the monitor. It may have a wizard or at least the appropriate background screens to use while adjusting phase and clock settings. If not, go to the Windows Start menu and select Shutdown. When the screen goes gray and the Windows Shutdown dialog appears, leave that dialog onscreen, but ignore it. Use the gray screen to adjust clock and phase manually. Any problems with clock and phase and any changes you make to the clock and phase settings are clearly evident on the gray screen.

Always adjust clock first. Clock is usually not a problem if you have used the auto-adjust feature of your monitor, but if you do have clock problems they will be evident as large vertical bars on your screen. Tweak the clock setting until those bars disappear. Then adjust phase. Phase problems are evident as thin black lines running horizontally across the screen. Adjust phase until the lines disappear or are minimized.

Not all analog video cards synchronize perfectly with flat panels. The gray Shutdown screen exaggerates the problem, so don't worry if very tiny movements are visible after you've adjusted clock and phase as well as possible. After you've set the clock and phase controls for the best image possible on the gray screen, cancel Shutdown and the image should be optimized.

"Signal out of range" message

Your video card is supplying a video signal at a bandwidth that is above or below the ability of your LCD to display. Reset your video parameters to be within the range supported by the LCD. If necessary, temporarily connect a different display or start Windows in Safe Mode and choose standard VGA in order to change video settings.

Text or lines are shadowed, jaggy, or blocky

This occurs when you run an LCD at other than its native resolution. For example, if you have a 19" LCD with native 1280×1024 resolution but have your display adapter set to 1024×768, your LCD attempts to display those 1024×768 pixels at full screen size, which physically corresponds to 1280×1024 pixels. The pixel extrapolation needed to fill the screen with the smaller image results in artifacts such as blocky or poorly rendered text, jaggy lines, and so on. Either set your video adapter to display the native resolution of the LCD, or set your LCD to display the lower-resolution image without stretching the display (a feature sometimes referred to as display expansion), so that pixels are displayed 1:1, which results in the lower resolution using less than the entire screen.

Some pixels are always on or always off

This is a characteristic of LCDs, particularly older and inexpensive models, caused by defective pixels. Manufacturers set a threshold number below which they consider a display acceptable. That number varies with the manufacturer, the model, and the size of the display, but is typically in the range of 5 to 10 pixels. (Better LCDs nowadays usually have zero dead pixels.) Nothing can be done to fix defective pixels. Manufacturers will not replace LCDs under warranty unless the number of defective pixels exceeds the threshold number.

A persistent after-image exists

Again, this is a characteristic of LCDs, particularly older and inexpensive models. The after-image occurs when the display has had the same image in one place for a long time. The after-image may persist even after you turn the display off.

Moving images blur, smear, or ghost

Transistor-based pixels in an LCD respond more slowly than the phosphors in a CRT. The least-expensive LCDs exhibit this problem even with slow image movement, as when you drag a window. Better LCDs handle moderately fast image movement without ghosting, but exhibit the problem on fast-motion video. The best LCDs handle even fast-motion video and 3D gaming very well. The only solution to this problem is to upgrade to an LCD with faster response time.

Dim image

Use the brightness control to increase image brightness. If you have set brightness to maximum and the image is still too dim, contact the display manufacturer. The CCRTs used to backlight the screen have a finite lifetime and may begin to dim as they near the end of their life.

Image is only partially backlit

One or more of the CCRTs that provide the backlight have failed. Contact the display manufacturer.

Horizontal or vertical lines appear

If one or more horizontal and/or vertical lines appear on the display, first power-reset the computer and display. If the lines persist, run the auto-setup function of your display. If that does not solve the problem, power the system and display down, remove the video cable, and verify that the video plugs and jacks on both computer and display ends do not have broken or bent pins. Even if all appears correct, try a different video cable. If the problem persists, contact the display manufacturer.

Advice from Ron Morse

Some people claim that leaving the unit powered off for a day or two will "erase" a persistent after-image. Others suggest leaving a neutral gray screen (like the one used for phase adjustment) up on the screen to "equalize" the display. I dunno. FWIW, I've seen this problem on older Samsung panels but never on the Sony or NEC/LaCie panels I use.

Audio 12

When they designed the original PC 25 years ago, IBM didn't foresee audio as a business necessity, so the only provision early PCs made for audio was a $0.29 speaker driven by a square-wave generator to produce beeps, boops, and clicks sufficient for prompts and warnings. Reproducing speech or music was out of the question. Doing that required an add-on sound card, and those were quick to arrive on the market as people began playing games on their PCs. Early sound cards were primitive, expensive, difficult to install and configure, and poorly supported by the OS and applications. By the early 1990s, however, sound cards shipped with most PCs. By 2001 most motherboards included at least basic integrated audio, and by 2003 it was difficult to find a mainstream system or motherboard that did not have excellent integrated audio.

AUDIO/SOUND ADAPTER/CARD

Properly, the term *audio card* or *sound card* refers to an expansion card, while *audio adapter* or *sound adapter* refers to any component used to produce audio, whether an expansion card or a device integrated on the motherboard. Like most people, we use these terms interchangeably.

An audio adapter by itself is useless without some means to hear the sound produced by the adapter. The usual solution is a set of speakers, although many people use headphones instead of or in addition to speakers. You can also use a headset, which is a set of headphones with a microphone added.

There are many good reasons to upgrade your audio adapter or speakers, including:

- Your current audio adapter or speaker set has poor audio quality or has failed.

- Your current audio adapter supports fewer speakers than you would like to use.

- You want to use *VoIP* (*Voice over Internet Protocol*) services such as Skype (*http://www.skype.com*) for free worldwide telephone service, but your current audio adapter doesn't support the required full-duplex operation.

- You need a digital audio-out connector to connect to home audio components and your current audio adapter doesn't provide one.

- You play games that require *hardware audio acceleration* or other features that are not supported by your current audio adapter.

The following sections describe what you need to know to choose, install, configure, troubleshoot, and use an audio adapter and speakers effectively.

Audio Adapters

Standalone sound cards are a dying category, killed by the ubiquity and high quality of integrated audio. Of the many companies that formerly specialized in sound cards, only Creative Labs, M-AUDIO, and Voyetra/Turtle Beach retain a significant retail market presence.

Figure 12-1. M-AUDIO Revolution 5.1 (left) and 7.1 sound cards

Still, there is a place for standalone sound cards. Gamers use them, because they provide features not available with integrated audio, such as hardware acceleration of gaming audio standards like EAX, and because their onboard processors relieve the main system processor of processing audio data streams. Audiophiles use them, because good sound cards provide better audio quality than even the best integrated audio. Upgraders use them, because adding an inexpensive sound card is an easy way to add functions, such as surround sound, that are not provided by the integrated audio in some older motherboards. Figure 12-1 shows a pair of M-AUDIO Revolution sound cards, a popular (and good) choice among both gamers and audiophiles.

CREATIVE LABS VERSUS M-AUDIO

The general consensus, with which we agree, is that Creative Labs sound cards are excellent for gaming, but don't have the best sound quality. Conversely, M-AUDIO sound cards have superb sound quality, but have slightly inferior gaming support. Accordingly, if you're a dedicated gamer, we recommend using a Creative Labs model. If you're an audiophile, go with an M-AUDIO model. If you're a gamer and an audiophile, pick one. You won't be disappointed in either.

Audio adapter components

The key function of an audio adapter is playback—accepting a digital data stream from the PC and converting it to an analog audio signal that can be reproduced on speakers or headphones. Most audio adapters can also do the converse—accept an analog audio signal and convert it to a digital data stream that can be stored on a PC. Audio adapters use the following components to provide these functions:

Converters

Audio adapters contain at least one *Digital-to-Analog Converter* (DAC) and one *Analog-to-Digital Converter* (ADC) for each of the two stereo channels, and at least one DAC for each additional audio channel. (Many audio adapters can output 5, 6, 7, or 8 channels, but few can record more than two-channel stereo sound.) A DAC converts a digital audio stream into the analog audio delivered to the Line-out port. An ADC digitizes analog sound received from the Line-in or Microphone port. CD-Audio sound, generally the highest quality supported by audio adapters, requires 16-bit resolution. The converters used in better-quality audio adapters usually support higher resolution, typically 18- or 20-bit. Some expensive cards use 24-bit or higher resolution for both recording and playback. Resolution sometimes differs between the DAC and ADC. For example, a card might use an 18-bit DAC and a 20-bit ADC. Internal resolution is often higher than that supported by the DAC/ADC, typically 24- or 32-bit.

Sample rate generator

The *sample rate generator* provides the clock for the converters under the control of the PC. While nothing prevents using arbitrary or continuously variable sample rates, most sample rate generators instead support discrete sample rates, which are usually even fractions of 44,100 Hz and 48,000 Hz. A sample rate generator might support sample rates of 48,000, 44,100, 32,000, 24,000, 22,050, 12,000, 11,025, and 8,000 Hz. Many audio adapters support differing rates for recording versus playback. For example, a card may support playback rates of 48,000,

44,100, 22,050, 11,025, and 8,000 Hz, but record only at 44,100 Hz. High-end cards may support sampling rates as high as 96 KHz in Dolby Digital 5.1 mode and 192 KHz in stereo mode.

SAMPLING RATE AND RESOLUTION

Sampling is the process by which a continuously varying analog source, such as an audio stream, is converted to discrete digital data. Sampling takes "snapshots" of the analog source stream and digitizes them to represent the whole. *Resolution* specifies the amount of data captured in each snapshot, specified in bits, which may also be referred to as *sample size.* A larger sample size captures more data about the audio stream, and results in higher fidelity. *Sampling rate* specifies how often samples are captured, and is specified in hertz (Hz) or kilohertz (KHz). A faster sampling rate captures more data and also results in higher fidelity. CD-DA audio is sampled in stereo with 16-bit resolution at 44,100 Hz. Voice-only sampling is often done at much lower resolution and sampling rates; for example, a mono 8-bit 8,000 Hz sample, results in much smaller digital file sizes.

Processor

The *processor* (also called the *sound generator* or *synthesis engine*) performs general audio processing tasks and creates analog output from MIDI input by reading, interpolating, and combining wavetable samples into the composite audio waveform represented by the MIDI instructions. Most audio adapters use a custom *digital signal processor* (*DSP*) like the E-mu Systems EMU10K1 or EMU10K2, or the Crystal/Cirrus Logic CS4630 or CS8420. The processor used directly or indirectly determines several key capabilities of the audio adapter, including how many MIDI channels, voices, hardware-accelerated sound streams, and so on it supports. DSPs provide useful supplementary capabilities in hardware, such as reverb and chorus effects, text-to-speech processing, and compression. Because a DSP is programmable, some DSP-based audio adapters support related functions, such as fax-modem or telephone answering machine functions.

WHAT'S MIDI?

There are two types of sound files. *Waveform audio files*, also called simply *sound files*, store actual binary audio data that can be played back directly. Common waveform audio file formats include .wav, .mp3, and .ogg. *MIDI (Musical Instrument Digital Interface) files* store instructions that audio adapters use to create synthesized audio on the fly, using wavetable samples and other methods to produce music that sounds more or less natural. MIDI synthesis is commonly used to produce music, sound effects, and other audio for games and other applications.

Connectors

Audio adapters typically provide the following connectors:

Line-out

> *Line-out* is a line-level (unamplified) stereo output intended to be connected to line-in on amplified speakers, headphones, home audio equipment, or a recorder. Most audio adapters provide one stereo Line-out port, but some provide two mono Line-out ports, designated left and right. Audio adapters that support four speakers usually have two stereo Line-out ports, one each for front and rear speakers. Audio adapters that support surround sound may provide three or four Line-out connectors to support six or eight speakers. The standard color code for Line-out is lime, although for this and other color codes makers often pay scant attention to the exact hue. The standard icon usually stamped into the card bracket is three concentric circle segments (to represent audio vibrations) with an outward-pointing arrow anchored in the center.

Line-in

> *Line-in* is a line-level stereo input intended to be connected to Line-out of external analog audio sources such as a CD player or VCR. Some microphones can also be connected to Line-in. The standard color is light blue. The standard icon is the same as for Line-out, but with the arrow head pointing to the center.

Microphone-in

> *Microphone-in*, sometimes labeled *Mic*, is a monaural input that supports inexpensive microphones for recording voice. The standard color is pink, although red is commonly used, and the standard icon resembles a microphone.

Subwoofer

> *Subwoofer* is a line-level monaural output intended to be connected to a powered subwoofer, which may also be called an *LFE* (*Low-Frequency Emitter*). Standard color is orange.

S/PDIF

> *Sony-Philips Digital InterFace* (*S/PDIF*) is an RCA coax jack or optical jack that provides a direct digital connection between the audio adapter and an external device with an S/PDIF jack. S/PDIF is a standard feature on most high-end audio adapters, and may be an option on midrange audio adapters. Some audio adapters have both S/PDIF input and output ports, but others have only an S/PDIF output. Because of limited room on the expansion bracket of the audio adapter, S/PDIF ports are often present as a header connector on the audio adapter, which uses an extender cable to a cliffhanger bracket where the S/PDIF connectors reside. Some audio adapters use a proprietary connector that joins the audio adapter to a

Advice from Ron Morse

The only microphones that should be attached directly to a Line-in connector are the ones with integral pre-amplifiers. Generally, if your microphone needs a battery, it connects to Line-in; otherwise it goes to "mic."

remote head, which often contains S/PDIF connector(s), Line-in connector(s), and MIDI connector(s).

Figure 12-2 shows the audio connectors on an M-AUDIO Revolution 7.1, which are typical for a premium sound card. From left to right are a coax S/PDIF jack, Microphone-in, and Line-in, followed by four Line-out jacks to connect the eight speakers supported by this card.

Figure 12-2. M-AUDIO Revolution 7.1 audio connectors

Audio Adapter Characteristics

Here are the important characteristics of audio adapters:

Audio channels
>   It's important that the audio adapter support your speaker configuration. Audio adapters may support any combination of the following configurations:
>
>   2.0 – front left and right satellites
>
>   2.1 – 2.0 with a subwoofer
>
>   4.1 – 2.1 with a rear left/right satellite pair added
>
>   5.1 – 4.1 with a front center-channel speaker added
>
>   6.1 – 5.1 with a rear center-channel speaker added
>
>   7.1 – 5.1 with a side left/right satellite pair added
>
>   8.1 – 7.1 with a rear center-channel speaker added

Frequency response

The range of human hearing is usually stated as 20 Hz to 20 kHz. All current audio adapters nominally support this range or close to it. However, few cards state ±dB for that range, which specifies how flat the frequency response curve is. A good card may have frequency response of 20 Hz to 20 kHz at ±3 dB. A professional-level card may have frequency response of 20 Hz to 20 kHz at 1 dB down. Inexpensive cards may claim frequency response of 20 Hz to 20 kHz, but that range may turn out to be stated at 10 dB down or some similarly absurd number, which in effect means that actual usable frequency response may be something like 100 Hz to 10 kHz.

Signal-to-noise ratio

Signal-to-noise ratio (*S/N ratio*), stated in dB, specifies the amount of signal (data) relative to noise, with higher numbers indicating better performance. A low S/N ratio translates to audible hiss. The best audio adapters have 95 dB or greater S/N for analog audio; midrange adapters about 90 dB; and inexpensive adapters may have 85 dB or less. It's not unusual for a card to have somewhat lower S/N ratio for digital recording and digital playback. For example, an excellent consumer-grade audio adapter may specify an S/N ratio of 96 dB FS A-weighted for analog audio, 93 dB FS A-weighted for digital recording, and 90 dB FS A-weighted for digital playback. In a typical PC environment, noise level (both ambient external audible noise and the electrically noisy inside of the PC) and the typical use of low-quality speakers or headphones make it unlikely that anyone could differentiate between cards with S/N ratios of 80 dB or higher if that were the only difference. However, cards with higher S/N ratios are generally better shielded and use better components, which translates to better sound and less hiss.

Duplex mode

Half-duplex audio adapters can either play sound or capture sound, but not both at the same time. *Full-duplex* audio adapters do both simultaneously. For simple tasks—listening to CDs or playing games—a half-duplex card is adequate. More advanced audio functions, such as VoIP telephony and voice recognition, require a full-duplex card. Most midrange and all high-end audio adapters support full-duplex.

Standards compatibility

In the distant past, software wrote directly to the audio adapter. That meant that compatibility with proprietary standards—initially AdLib and later Sound Blaster—was important, because if your game or application didn't explicitly support your audio adapter, you simply couldn't use sound with that software. Microsoft took the initiative away from audio adapter manufacturers by incorporating standard sound APIs into Windows. Here are the standards you should be aware of:

Microsoft DirectSound

> Microsoft DirectSound (*DS*) is a component of DirectX. Developers can write to the DS API, rather than to the underlying hardware, with the assurance that their software will function with any DS-compatible audio adapter. DS compatibility is an absolute requirement for any audio adapter.

Microsoft DirectSound3D

> Microsoft DirectSound3D (*DS3D*) is an extension to DS that supports 3D positional audio, which is a technology that manipulates sound information to extend stereo imaging to full surround sound, allowing sounds to appear to come from any position around you. For example, when in an air combat game your missile hits a bandit in front of you, the sound of that explosion comes from the front. But if you didn't notice his wingman on your six, the sound of his missile blowing off your tail comes from behind. The realism of DS3D imaging in any given situation depends on how many speakers you use and the hardware capabilities of the audio adapter. If you intend to use DS3D-enabled software, it's important to have hardware support for DS3D in your audio adapter, because DS3D positional effects that cannot be processed in hardware are processed by the main CPU, which can bog down system performance.

Creative Labs EAX

> Creative Labs *EAX* (*Environmental Audio Extensions*) is a proprietary Creative Labs extension to DS3D. EAX 1.0, used by older Creative Labs sound cards, provides reasonable 3D imaging. EAX 2.0 and EAX Advanced HD Multi-Environment are significant enhancements that provide unmatched positional audio performance. Given the dominance of Creative Labs, the various flavors of EAX are widely supported by game software.

Hardware acceleration

> Midrange and high-end audio adapters have an onboard DSP, which is a general-purpose CPU optimized for processing digital signals, such as audio. In 2D mode, the DSP provides enhanced audio effects like chorus, reverb, and distortion. In 3D mode, it processes 3D-positional audio (e.g., DirectSound3D or EAX) algorithms locally, removing that burden from the main CPU. Inexpensive audio adapters use the host CPU, which reduces performance significantly, particularly during complex operations such as 3D rendering. Any accelerated audio adapter should accelerate 32 or more DS and DS3D sound streams in hardware.

Choosing an Audio Adapter

Use the following guidelines when choosing an audio adapter:

Don't buy too much audio adapter.

When you add or replace an audio adapter, don't pay for features you won't use. Don't buy an expensive audio adapter if you'll use it only for playing CDs, casual gaming, VoIP telephony, and so on. Even $30 sound cards include most of the features that more expensive cards provide, and are more than adequate for most purposes.

Don't buy too little audio adapter.

If you use your sound card for 3D gaming, buy one with hardware acceleration and other features that support what you use the card for. Capable consumer-grade audio adapters like the M-AUDIO Revolution 5.1 and Creative Labs Audigy2 series sound cards sell for under $100, and are suitable for anything short of professional audio production.

Avoid no-name audio adapters.

Stick to name-brand audio adapters. We frequently hear horror stories from readers who have purchased house-brand audio adapters—outdated drivers, missing or inadequate documentation, poor (or no) tech support, shoddy construction, incompatibilities with Windows, and on and on. What's particularly ironic is that you may pay more for a house-brand audio adapter than for a low-end name-brand card. You can buy decent name-brand audio adapters for $30 from reputable companies. Don't buy anything less.

Installing a Sound Card

An audio adapter physically installs just as any other expansion card does. Some audio adapters require many system resources, so keep the following guidelines in mind:

If you are rebuilding your system

Install the audio adapter before you install other components such as network adapters, allowing the audio adapter to make first claim on system resources. Although Windows and recent motherboards usually do a good job of juggling resources, we have experienced resource conflicts when installing an audio adapter in a system that was already heavily loaded with other adapters. If that happens, the best course is to disable all adapters in Device Manager (except essential ones like the video card and disk interfaces), then physically remove those adapters, then install and configure the audio adapter, and finally reinstall the other adapters one by one. If you have problems, try installing the audio adapter in a different PCI slot.

External USB Sound Adapters

Several companies, including Creative Labs, M-Audio, and Turtle Beach, manufacture external audio adapters that connect to a PC via a USB port. The advantage of these devices is easy installation—you just connect the box to a USB port and install the drivers; no need to open the case. The disadvantage is that you have one more box cluttering up your desk.

If you are replacing an existing audio adapter

Before you remove the card, use the Control Panel Add/Remove Programs applet to remove audio drivers and supporting software, delete the audio adapter in Device Manager and delete all remaining drivers from the hard disk. Turn the PC off (even though Windows or the driver's uninstall program may advise you to reboot, don't reboot yet, or Windows will try to reinstall the drivers), take off the cover, physically remove the old audio adapter, and start the PC. Verify that all vestiges of the old audio adapter are gone. If the audio adapter is embedded, run BIOS Setup and disable it. With all that done, turn off the PC again and physically install the new audio adapter. Start the system again and install the drivers for it.

OUT WITH THE OLD

Except for physically removing and replacing the audio adapter, we recommend following the same procedure when updating audio drivers. That is, never upgrade audio drivers. Instead, remove the old ones and install the new ones as a clean install. We have encountered problems more than once when attempting to upgrade existing drivers. A clean install avoids those.

If you are installing an audio adapter in a motherboard that has integrated audio

Before you install an audio adapter in a system with embedded audio, disable the integrated audio adapter either in BIOS Setup or by changing a jumper on the motherboard (or both). Every motherboard we know that includes integrated audio allows you to disable sound in BIOS. Enabling or disabling sound usually has no effect on interrupts, because embedded PCI sound uses one or two shareable PCI interrupts. Older motherboards, however, may have embedded ISA sound adapters, which may use fixed ISA interrupts. Such motherboards may or may not allow sound to be disabled and the interrupt made available for other adapters. If it is possible to disable the interrupt, doing so usually requires removing a physical jumper on the motherboard.

THE CD AUDIO CABLE

All recent optical drives support digital audio, which means that they deliver the digital audio stream directly from a disc to the system via the ATA interface. Old CD-ROM drives did not support digital audio, and required a separate cable from the drive to an audio input on the motherboard or sound card. If you are upgrading a system with such a drive, don't forget to install this CD Audio cable. Better yet, replace the old optical drive with a current model.

Configuring an Audio Adapter Card Under Windows

To configure an audio adapter under Windows, take the following steps:

1. Before you install the new adapter, remove the existing audio adapter and drivers, if any, and verify that all vestiges of the old audio adapter drivers are gone. Install the new sound card and restart the system.

2. Windows should recognize that the new audio adapter is present and display the Add New Hardware Wizard. Although Windows includes drivers for many audio adapters, you are usually better off using the drivers supplied by the audio adapter manufacturer. To do so, mark the Search for... option button and click Next.

WINDOWS AUDIO DRIVERS VERSUS GOOD AUDIO DRIVERS

Windows audio drivers may have limited functionality, such as supporting only stereo sound on an 8-channel sound card or not fully supporting the hardware acceleration features of the adapter. We strongly recommend downloading drivers from the sound card maker rather than using those provided with Windows.

---

3. When Windows displays the next dialog, either specify the location of the drivers or tell it which drives to search for them. Click Next to continue.

4. Windows should locate the proper drivers and load them. When the process completes, reboot the system. Most audio adapters include an automated installation procedure for bundled applications, which usually autoruns immediately after the system restarts. Follow the prompts, and provide any necessary information to complete the installation.

5. Right-click My Computer, choose Properties, click the Hardware tab, and then click the Device Manager button. Expand the "Sound, video and game controllers" branch and verify that the sound card is installed properly and that no conflicts exist. Most sound cards have a test utility that you should run to verify that all aspects of the audio hardware and drivers are operating properly.

6. From Control Panel, double-click Multimedia to display the Volume page of the Sounds and Audio Devices Properties dialog, shown in Figure 12-3. Set the Device volume slider to the its highest setting

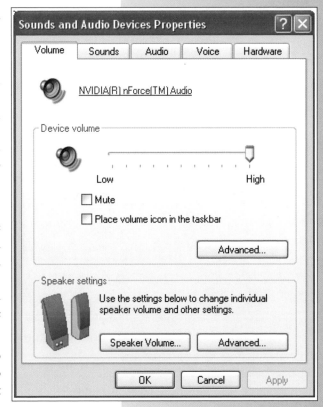

Figure 12-3. Sounds and Audio Devices Properties dialog

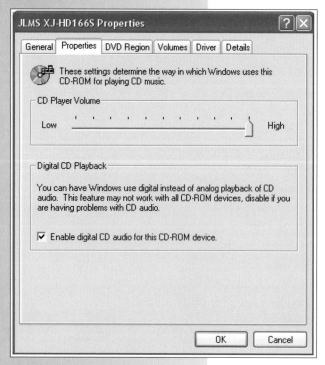

Figure 12-4. Enable digital audio in the optical drive device properties dialog

and use the Speaker settings section to configure your speaker setup and audio playback performance settings.

7. Click the Audio tab to display the Audio page of the Sounds and Audio Devices Properties dialog. If you have more than one audio device in your system, use the Preferred device drop-down lists in the Playback and Recording sections to select one of the installed audio devices as the default for each. Click the Advanced Properties buttons in the Playback and Recording sections to configure driver-specific options.

8. Right-click My Computer and choose Properties to display the System Properties dialog. Click the Hardware tab and then the Device Manager button to display Device Manager. Expand the DVD/CD-ROM drives item and double-click each optical drive entry to display the Properties dialog for that optical drive, as shown in Figure 12-4. On the Properties page, verify that the "Enable digital CD audio for this CD-ROM device" checkbox is marked.

Speakers and Headphones

No matter how good your audio adapter is, it's useless unless you have speakers or headphones to listen to the audio it produces. Computer speakers span the range from $10 pairs of small satellites to $500+ sets of up to nine speakers that are appropriate for a home theater system.

As is true of displays and input devices, personal preference is the most important factor in choosing speakers. Speakers that render a Bach concerto superbly may not be the best choice for playing a first-person shooter game like Unreal Tournament. For that matter, speakers that one person considers perfect for the Bach concerto (or the UT game), another person may consider mediocre. For that reason, we strongly suggest that you listen to speakers before you buy them, particularly if you're buying an expensive set.

Speaker and headphone characteristics

Here are the important characteristics of speakers:

Number
Speaker sets are designated by the total number of satellite speakers, followed by a period and a "1" if the set includes a subwoofer. Choose a

speaker set configuration that your audio adapter supports. For example, there is no point to buying a 7.1 speaker set if your audio adapter supports at most a 5.1 configuration.

The price of a speaker set has little bearing on the number of speakers in the set. For example, there are $75 7.1 speaker sets available, and $500 2.0 sets. We recommend that you decide on the number of speakers according to your budget. If you have $75 to spend, for example, you're much better off buying a decent 2.1 speaker set than a cheesy 7.1 speaker set.

RARE BIRDS

Only 2.0, 2.1, 4.1, 5.1, and 7.1 sets are common; 6.1 and 8.1 speaker sets are rare. If your sound card supports a 6.1 or 8.1 configuration—those with a rear center-channel output—buy a 5.1 or 7.1 speaker set and add an individual center-channel speaker to fill out the configuration.

Frequency response

Frequency response is the range of sound frequencies that the speaker can reproduce. The values provided for most speakers are meaningless, because they do not specify how flat that response is. For example, professional studio-monitor speakers may provide 20 Hz to 20 kHz response at 1 dB. Expensive home audio speakers may provide 20 Hz to 20 kHz response at 3 dB, and 40 Hz to 18 kHz response at 1 dB. Computer speakers may claim 20 Hz to 20 kHz response, but may rate that response at 10 dB or more, which makes the specification meaningless. A reduction of about 3 dB halves volume, which means that sounds below 100 Hz or above 10 kHz are nearly inaudible with many cheap computer speakers. The only sure measure of adequate frequency response is that the speakers sound good to you, particularly for low bass and high treble sounds.

Amplifier power

Manufacturers use two means to specify output power. *Peak power*, which specifies the maximum wattage the amplifier can deliver instantaneously, is deceptive and should be disregarded. *RMS power (Root Mean Square)*, a more accurate measure, specifies the wattage that the amplifier can deliver continuously. Listening to music at normal volume levels requires less than one watt. Home audio systems usually provide 100 watts per channel or more, which allows them to respond instantaneously to transient high amplitude peaks in the music, particularly in bass notes, extending the dynamic range of the sound. The range of computer speakers is hampered by their small amplifiers, but computer speakers also use small drivers that cannot move much air, so their lack of power is not really important. Typical dual-speaker sets provide 4 to 8 watts RMS per channel, which is adequate for normal sound reproduction. Typical subwoofers provide 15 to 40 watts, which, combined with the typical 5" driver, is adequate to provide flat bass response down to 60 Hz or so (although subwoofers often misleadingly claim response to 20 Hz). Headphones are not amplified, but use the line-level output of the audio adapter.

Connectors

Most 2.0 sets place the amplifier in one speaker, which has connections for Line-in (from the audio adapter), Speaker (to the other speaker), and DC Power (to a power brick). Many speakers also provide an output for a subwoofer. Sets that include a subwoofer usually put the amplifier in the subwoofer, which has connections for the other speakers in the set. Some sets also provide a second Line-in jack. This jack is quite useful if you want to connect both your PC and a separate line-level audio source, such as a CD player or another PC, to the amplified speakers, allowing you to listen to either source separately or both together. An increasing number of high-end speakers—particularly six-channel Dolby Digital 5.1 systems—provide direct digital inputs via a Digital DIN connector, an S/PDIF connector, or both.

Choosing Speakers and Headphones

Use the following guidelines when selecting computer speakers or headphones:

Choose speakers appropriate for your listening preferences and audio adapter capabilities.

Picking suitable speakers requires considering what you listen to, how you listen to it, and the features of your audio adapter. For example, if you listen mostly to classical music at low to moderate volume, powerful bass is less important than flat, transparent frequency response in the midrange and highs. A high-quality set of dual speakers with frequency response from 90 to 18,000 Hz and 4 or 5 watts RMS per channel will serve. Conversely, if you listen to rock or heavy metal, or if you play games and want to shake the walls, crystalline highs are less important, but bass is critical. You'll want speakers that include a powerful subwoofer. Similarly, if you have a 3D audio adapter, it makes little sense to couple it to a two-piece or three-piece speaker set. Buy a speaker set with enough speakers to take advantage of the 3D positional audio capabilities of the card.

Avoid cheap speakers.

The very cheapest speakers, those that sell for $5 or $8 or are bundled with inexpensive PCs, have sound quality noticeably inferior to speakers that sell for even a little more. Speakers in the $15 range and above use better (and more powerful) amplifiers, better-quality drivers (typically separate midrange/woofers and tweeters), and provide additional features, such as the ability to connect more than one sound source or a separate subwoofer.

Stick with name brands.

Altec-Lansing, Creative Labs, Labtec, and Logitech are the best-known names in inexpensive computer speakers. Each produces a broad range of speaker models, one of which should be appropriate for almost anyone. Increasingly, well-known names in home audio—such as Bose, JBL, Klipsch, and Polk Audio—are entering the computer speaker market. Ironically, their background in high-quality home audio means that they tend to publish realistic specifications for their computer speakers, which make them look inferior to lesser speakers for which the makers publish inflated specifications.

Make sure to buy speakers with the correct interface.

Most computer speakers use an analog audio interface, which allows them to connect directly to the Line-out jack of your sound adapter. Some computer speakers—particularly high-end four-, five-, and six-speaker sets—instead use a direct digital connection via a Digital DIN connector, an S/PDIF connector, or both. If you are using a traditional sound adapter, make sure that your sound adapter and speakers share a common interface method.

Consider using headphones instead of speakers.

Even inexpensive headphones often provide a better listening experience than good computer speakers, both because the cushions isolate you from ambient noise and because it's easier to render very high fidelity sound with the small speakers and tiny power levels used by headphones. Headphones also allow you to work (or play) without disturbing others. If you're going to buy headphones, consider instead buying a headset, which adds a microphone to support such functions as voice/speech recognition, VoIP telephony, and adding voice annotations to documents. The only drawback to headphones is that most are not well suited for use with 3D audio adapters, although some specialized four-channel headphones are available.

Get a no-questions-asked money-back guarantee.

With speakers more so than any other computer component except perhaps input devices, personal preference must rule. Speakers that sound great to us may sound mediocre to you, and vice versa. The only way to know for sure is to listen to the speakers in your own environment. If they turn out to be unsuitable, you don't want to be stuck with them, so make sure you can return them without a hassle.

Troubleshooting Audio Problems

Most audio problems are a result of improper, defective, or misconnected cables; incorrect drivers; or resource conflicts. Audio problems that occur when you have made no changes to the system are usually caused by cable problems or operator error (such as accidentally turning the volume control down). Audio problems that occur when you install a new audio adapter (or when you add or reconfigure other system components) are usually caused by resource conflicts or driver problems.

To troubleshoot audio problems, always begin with the following steps:

1. Shut down and restart the system. Surprisingly often, this solves the problem.

2. Verify that all cables are connected, that the speakers have power and are switched on, that the volume control is set to an audible level, that you haven't muted audio in Windows, and so on.

3. Determine the scope of the problem. If the problem occurs with only one program, visit the web sites for Microsoft, the software company, and the audio adapter maker to determine if there is a known problem with that program and audio adapter combination. If the problem occurs globally, continue with the following steps.

4. Verify that the audio adapter is selected as the default playback device. If you have more than one audio adapter installed, verify that the default playback device is the audio adapter to which the speakers are connected.

5. If your audio adapter includes a testing utility, run it to verify that all components of the audio adapter are operating properly.

6. If you have another set of speakers and/or a spare audio cable, substitute them temporarily to eliminate the speakers as a possible cause. If you have a set of headphones, connect them directly to Line-out on the audio adapter to isolate the problem to the system itself. Alternatively, connect the questionable speakers to another system with a known-good audio adapter, or even an MP3 player or portable CD player.

If the problem is occurring on a new system, or one in which you have just added or replaced an audio adapter, take the following steps in order:

1. Verify that the speakers are connected to the correct jacks. Connecting speakers to the wrong jacks is one of the most common causes of sound problems. We do it ourselves from time to time.

2. Check the troubleshooting sections of the Microsoft web site and the web sites for your motherboard and audio adapter manufacturer. Some audio adapters, for example, have problems with motherboards with

certain Via chipsets, while other audio adapters have problems when used with certain AGP video cards.

3. Remove the drivers, restart the system, and reinstall the drivers from scratch.

4. Remove the drivers, shut down the system, and relocate the audio adapter to a different PCI slot. When the system restarts, reinstall the drivers from scratch.

5. If none of that works, suspect either a defective audio adapter or a fundamental incompatibility between your audio adapter and the rest of your system. Remove the drivers, shut down the system, remove the audio adapter, install a different audio adapter, and reinstall the drivers for it. If the replacement audio adapter is the same model and exhibits the same symptoms, try installing a different model of audio adapter.

If the problem occurs on a previously working system, take the following steps in order:

1. If you have recently added or changed any hardware, check Device Manager to verify that no resource conflicts exist.

2. If you have recently installed or uninstalled any software, it's possible that Setup installed DLLs that are incompatible with your audio adapter, or removed DLLs that your audio adapter or applications require. Remove the audio adapter drivers and reinstall them from scratch.

3. If the sound still does not function properly, suspect an audio adapter failure.

Here are some specific common sound problems and their solutions:

There's no sound.
> This is probably the most common sound problem, and can have many causes. Following the troubleshooting steps just listed should resolve the problem.

Sound is scratchy or intermittent.
> This problem can also have many causes. Perhaps the most common is the audio adapter itself. Older and inexpensive audio adapters often have poor audio quality. Other common causes include a defective or low-quality audio cable, speakers placed too close to the monitor or other source of electrical noise, and the placement of the audio adapter within the system. If you have a choice, locate an audio adapter as far as possible from other expansion cards. Another possible cause is that some video card drivers are optimized for benchmark tests by having them keep control of the bus. The result can be intermittent dropouts and scratchiness in the sound.

Computer sounds are audible but audio CDs are not.

Computer sound is digital, and is delivered directly to the audio adapter via the bus. Some old CD-ROM drives require a separate internal cable joining the audio-out connector on the back of the CD-ROM drive to the CD-audio connector on the audio adapter. If you do not have the necessary cable, you can temporarily fix the problem by connecting a standard stereo audio cable from the headphone jack on the front of the CD-ROM drive to the Line-in jack on the audio adapter. Note that modern motherboards and optical drives can deliver CD audio as a digital signal directly to the audio adapter, obviating the need for a separate CD audio cable.

A channel or channels are inaudible.

If you have another set of speakers or headphones, connect them directly to the audio adapter Line-out port to isolate the problem to either the audio adapter or the speakers. Roughly in order of decreasing probability, the most likely causes and solutions are:

- The Windows audio balance control is set fully in one direction. Double-click the speaker icon in the System Tray and verify balance settings in the Volume Control dialog (or the replacement applet installed with your audio adapter drivers).

- The balance control on your speakers, if present, may be set fully in one direction. This happens commonly when someone blindly attempts to change volume or tone and turns the wrong knob. Center the speaker balance control.

- The audio cable is defective. Many audio cables, particularly those supplied with inexpensive speakers, are constructed poorly. Replace it with a high-quality, shielded audio cable, available for a few dollars from computer stores, audio specialty stores, and big-box stores.

- The audio cable is not fully seated in either the audio adapter jack or the speaker jack. Verify that the cable is fully seated at both ends.

- You are using a mono rather than stereo audio cable to connect Line-out on the audio adapter to the speakers. Replace the cable.

- The audio adapter driver is not installed, is installed improperly, or is the wrong driver. Some audio adapters may function partially under these conditions, and the most common symptom is single-channel audio. Uninstall any driver currently installed, and then reinstall the proper driver.

- Although it is rare, we once encountered a set of amplified speakers with one channel dead and the other working. Replace the speakers.

After installing an audio adapter, your PC speaker no longer works.

This is by design in some audio adapters. Installing the card and driver intentionally disables the PC speaker and routes sounds that would ordinarily go to the PC speaker to the audio adapter instead.

Windows suddenly loses sound.

On Windows systems with properly configured and functioning audio adapters, sound may disappear entirely for no apparent reason. This has happened to us on many different systems, under different versions of Windows, using different motherboards and audio adapters. The audio adapter still shows as installed, and everything appears perfectly normal, but the system simply stops sending audio to the speakers. This problem may or may not be accompanied by the speaker icon disappearing from the system tray. We have no idea what causes this, and we've never been able to get a satisfactory explanation from Microsoft. Restarting the system normally solves the problem, until next time. On systems where "next time" is all too frequent, we have occasionally had some success by removing and then reinstalling the sound drivers.

The system locks up when you boot or blue-screens immediately after booting.

This problem normally results from a severe resource conflict or an improperly installed card. Verify first that the card is seated fully. If so, boot the system in Safe Mode or using the Last Known Good Configuration. With the system booted, determine which devices and resources are conflicting, resolve the conflicts, and restart the system.

The system makes a ticking sound.

This is usually caused by an interrupt conflict, often with the keyboard. Remove the keyboard in Device Manager, shut down and power off, and restart with just the mouse connected. If that solves the problem, turn off the system, reconnect the keyboard, and restart. If the problem persists, try moving the audio card to a different PCI slot or using a USB keyboard.

Input Devices

13

The ancient Romans had a saying—"de gustibus non est disputandum"—or, loosely translated, "there's no arguing matters of taste." When it comes to input devices—keyboards, mice, trackballs, and game controllers—that's indisputably true. An input device that one person loves another may hate, and vice versa. So, although we won't presume to recommend specific models in this chapter, we will tell you what to look for when you are choosing one for yourself.

Few people ever think about upgrading their input devices. That's unfortunate, because, along with your display, the quality of your input devices have more impact on system usability and comfort than any other component. We have seen people using cheap, sticky keyboards and mice so worn their pointers jump around, apparently unaware that for $25 and 30 seconds' work they could swap those shoddy old parts for a modern keyboard and optical mouse.

Nor is the problem limited to old components. Cheap consumer-grade systems often include keyboards and mice we wouldn't use on a bet. We once unpacked a keyboard that had come with a consumer-grade system and made the mistake of turning it upside down to look for the label. Several of the keys fell off. We don't know how much they pay for these components, but on the cheapest consumer-grade systems we'd be surprised if the keyboard and mouse together cost $5. Replacing the keyboard and mouse on even a new consumer-grade system can be the best $25 upgrade you can make.

Keyboards

Keyboards are available in two distinct styles. A *traditional keyboard* is rectangular and has a constant slope, from highest at the rear to lowest at the front. These keyboards are available in various footprints, including standard (19"×8"); mid-size (18"×7"); and space-saver (17"×6.5" or less).

Size is important to the extent that large keyboards occupy considerable desk space and may not fit some keyboard drawers. Figure 13-1 shows a Microsoft MultiMedia Keyboard, a typical traditional keyboard. This model, like many, has a detachable wrist rest that you can remove if space is limited.

Figure 13-1. Microsoft MultiMedia Keyboard (image courtesy of Microsoft Corporation)

An *ergonomic keyboard* uses a split face and variable slopes, which allow more natural and comfortable hand and wrist positions. Most ergonomic keyboards are as large as or larger than standard traditional keyboards. Some claim that ergonomic keyboards help reduce *Repetitive Stress Injury (RSI)* problems such as *Carpal Tunnel Syndrome (CTS)*, but we have seen no credible evidence to support these claims. The secret to avoiding such problems, regardless of what keyboard style you use, is to take frequent breaks and to avoid using the keyboard continuously for more than an hour or so at a time. Figure 13-2 shows a Microsoft Natural MultiMedia Keyboard, a typical ergonomic keyboard.

YOUR MILEAGE MAY VARY

One of our reviewers notes that the wrist pain resulting from the combination of full-time job and a book deal was certainly eased by making the transition to an ergonomic keyboard. However, we've also heard from people who were experiencing pain with an ergonomic keyboard and found that changing to a standard keyboard relieved the pain. We suspect it's a change, any change, that helps. After all, the "R" in RSI stands for "repetitive."

Figure 13-2. Microsoft Natural MultiMedia Keyboard (image courtesy of Microsoft Corporation)

Advice from Nancy Kotary

It's worth mentioning that some non-traditional or self-taught typists tend to have more trouble with the split keyboards. Although I am a fairly fast typist, I type a few letters in the middle of the keyboard with the "wrong" hand, so the split keyboards don't work for me. As mentioned elsewhere in this book, the best advice is "try before you buy."

Some people strongly prefer one or the other style. Barbara, for example, dislikes ergonomic keyboards, which she refers to as "melted" or "deformed." Robert, on the other hand, doesn't care which style he uses. He uses ergonomic keyboards on several systems and straight keyboards on others. If you've never used an ergonomic keyboard, give one a try before you buy your next keyboard. You may hate it—everyone does at first—but then again after you use it for an hour or so you may decide you love it.

Choosing a keyboard

Keyboards vary in obvious ways—style, size, and form—and in subtle ways like key spacing, angle, dishing, travel, pressure required, and tactile feedback. People's sensitivity to these differences varies. Some are keyboard agnostics who can sit down in front of a new keyboard and, regardless of layout or tactile response, be up to speed in a few minutes. Others have strong preferences about layout and feel. If you've never met a keyboard you didn't like, you can disregard these issues and choose a keyboard based on other factors. If love and hate are words you apply to keyboards, use an identical keyboard for at least an hour before you buy one for yourself.

That said, here are several important characteristics to consider when you choose a keyboard:

Consider layout.

The position of the primary alphanumeric keys is standard on all keyboards other than those that use the oddball Dvorak layout. What varies, sometimes dramatically, is the placement, size, and shape of other keys, such as the shift keys (Shift, Ctrl, and Alt), the function keys (which may be arrayed across the top, down the left side, or both), and the cursor control and numeric keypad keys. If you are used to a particular layout, purchasing a keyboard with a similar layout makes it much easier to adapt to the new keyboard.

Consider weight.

Although it sounds trivial, the weight of a keyboard can be a significant issue for some people. The lightest keyboard we've seen weighed just over a pound, and the heaviest was nearly eight pounds. If your keyboard stays on your desktop, a heavy keyboard is less likely to slide around. Conversely, a very heavy keyboard may be uncomfortable for someone who works with the keyboard in his lap.

Avoid multifunction keyboards.

Keyboards are low-margin products. As a means to differentiate their products and increase margins, some manufacturers produce keyboards with speakers, scanners, and other entirely unrelated functions built in. These functions are often clumsy to use, fragile, and have limited features. If you want speakers or a scanner, buy speakers or a scanner. Don't get a keyboard with them built in.

Consider a wireless keyboard for special purposes.

Various manufacturers make wireless keyboards, which are ideal for home theater setups, presentations, or if you just like working with the keyboard in your lap. Wireless keyboards include a separate receiver module that connects to a USB port or the PS/2 keyboard port on the PC. The keyboard and receiver communicate using either radio frequency (RF) or infrared (IR). IR keyboards require direct line-of-sight between the keyboard and receiver, while RF keyboards do not. Most IR keyboards and many RF keyboards provide very limited range—as little as five feet or so, which limits their utility to working around a desk without cables tangling, although Bluetooth models often offer at least across-the-room ranges. Some RF keyboards and a few IR keyboards use higher power to provide longer range, up to 50 feet or more. These are often quite expensive and provide relatively short battery life. Whichever type of wireless keyboard you get, make sure it uses standard (AA/AAA/9V) alkaline or NiMH batteries rather than a proprietary NiCd battery pack, which is subject to the infamous NiCd memory effect, whereby NiCd batteries soon begin to lose the ability to hold a charge.

NORTHGATE OMNIKEY REDUX

The Northgate OmniKey keyboard, with its function keys down the left and a satisfyingly clacky feel, has attained nearly cult status among some users, although Northgate itself is long gone. The same is true of the ancient mechanical IBM Model M keyboards. (Our copyeditor apparently has her own personal stock of Model Ms, which we suspect she stores in her wine cellar and rotates regularly.)

Original OmniKey and IBM Model M keyboards haven't been produced for years, so remaining working examples are sought after like Old Masters. Fortunately, there's an alternative. Creative Vision Technologies, Inc. (*http://www.cvtinc.com*) makes the Avant Stellar keyboard, which is more or less a clone of the Northgate OmniKey Plus. At $190, it isn't cheap, but it's as close as you'll find to the OmniKey in a current keyboard. If you prefer the IBM Model M, the Avant Prime is a near-copy of it, and costs a bit less than the Stellar.

Which Brand of Keyboard to Buy?

Logitech and Microsoft both produce a wide range of excellent keyboards, one of which is almost certainly right for you. Even their basic models are well built and reliable. The more expensive models add features such as RF or Bluetooth wireless connectivity, programmable function keys, and so on.

We used Microsoft keyboards almost exclusively for many years, and continue to recommend them. However, when we tested Logitech keyboards recently, we found that we actually preferred their features and feel. We currently use Logitech keyboards on many of our primary systems, although we also use various Microsoft keyboards, both older and current models, on several systems.

Avoid inexpensive, no-name keyboards.

Advice from Jim Cooley

If you don't need these special functions, and most don't, consider not installing additional programs beyond the driver. Many leave programs running in the background which can consume valuable CPU resources.

Configuring a keyboard

Windows allows you to customize some aspects of keyboard behavior, such as repeat rate, key mappings, and so on. To configure your keyboard, open Control Panel and double-click the Keyboard applet to display the Keyboard Properties dialog.

Installing a programmable keyboard and driver may install a separate management application, or may simply add pages and options to the standard Keyboard Properties dialog. For example, Figure 13-3 shows the additional page of the extended Keyboard Properties dialog that results from installing the Microsoft IntelliType Pro driver. If you install a programmable keyboard, make sure to locate and explore the options its driver provides. The default driver installation for some programmable keyboards leaves some very useful options disabled or set to less than optimum values.

Figure 13-3. The Windows XP Keyboard Properties dialog as modified by installing the Microsoft IntelliType Pro driver

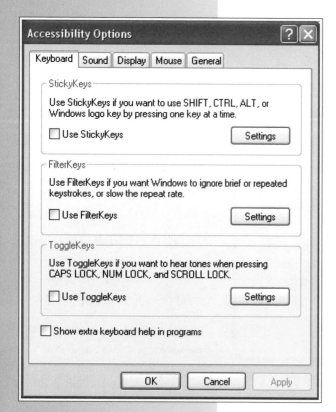

Figure 13-4. The Windows XP Accessibility Options dialog

Choose Accessibility Options from Control Panel to display the Accessibility Options dialog, shown in Figure 13-4. Although intended primarily to aid people with various disabilities, some options available here may be useful to anyone. In particular, anyone who has accidentally toggled Caps Lock on will appreciate the audible warning provided by ToggleKeys.

Cleaning a keyboard

Keyboards collect all manner of dirt, dust, and sticky spills, particularly if you eat, smoke, or drink near them. For routine cleaning, turn the keyboard upside down and shake it vigorously, which causes an incredible amount of stuff to fall out. Monthly, use your vacuum cleaner to do a thorough job. It's a good idea to shut down the system (or at least close all files) before you start vacuuming. Otherwise, the random series of keystrokes that vacuuming generates can have some unexpected results. In one case, we deleted a document. Formula 409 and similar commercial cleaners do a good job of removing grunge, but make sure the system is turned off while you use them, and try to avoid allowing too much to run down inside the keyboard. It's better to spray cleaner on a paper towel and then wipe than to spray the cleaner directly on the keyboard.

All of that presupposes that your keyboard is just normally dirty. For cleaning seriously dirty keyboards (see Figure 13-5), we've been using the dishwasher method for more than 20 years. Most people think we're kidding when we recommend it, but it works for us. We've used it successfully with both mechanical and membrane-based keyboards. Proceed as follows:

1. Disconnect the keyboard from the computer. We probably shouldn't have to mention this step, but we don't want to get hate mail from someone who didn't realize it wasn't a good idea to run his system unit and monitor through the dishwasher.

2. Place the keyboard, keys down, in the top rack of the dishwasher. Secure the keyboard cable with a rubber band or tie wrap to keep it from becoming entangled in the moving parts of the dishwasher.

Set the dishwasher for gentle cycle and coolest water temperature, if those options are available. Make sure to select the option for air dry rather than a heated drying cycle. (We use dishwasher detergent and run the keyboards just as we would a load of dishes, but, if you're more cautious, using just warm water seems to work about as well.)

3. Run the keyboard through an entire wash cycle, using dishwasher detergent. When the cycle finishes, remove the keyboard and douse it with at least a gallon of water, making sure to repeatedly flood the keys themselves. For safety's sake, we always recommend using distilled water, but in fact we always use ordinary tap water and have never had a problem. (If your tap water is particularly hard, it's a good idea to use distilled or de-ionized water instead.) After rinsing, turn the keyboard this way and that and shake it to drain as much water as possible. Use a towel to dry the accessible parts. At this point, your keyboard should look like new (see Figure 13-6).

Figure 13-5. A keyboard after more than a year without cleaning

4. Set your oven to 150 degrees (or its lowest setting). We have no idea what the melting point of the plastic used in keyboards is, but we haven't melted one yet. Bake keyboard until done, usually one to two hours. Let the keyboard cool, remove, and serve.

We generally put the clean keyboard back in our stock of spares, where it may have another month or three to air dry naturally, but we've also reconnected a keyboard immediately after such treatment without any problems. We used to be concerned that puddles might still be lurking inside the keyboard, so we'd disassemble it and dry it thoroughly before reconnecting it. But we've found that a couple hours inside a 150-degree oven does a pretty good job of evaporating any residual water. Your mileage may vary. If you hear a sloshing sound after drying, it's probably a good idea to disassemble the keyboard and check further. The important thing is to make sure the keyboard is completely dry internally before you connect it to the computer.

Figure 13-6. The same keyboard after a trip through the dishwasher

DIFFERENT STROKES

One of our readers notes, "I still like the idea of giving the keyboard a last flush, or rinse, with rubbing alcohol. The alcohol will displace most of the residual water and it will evaporate much faster. After draining out as much of the alcohol as I can, I stick it on top of the hot water heater for the night."

Another says, "I never use powdered dishwasher soap, always gel or liquid. I always run them through a normal (hot water) cycle and have used both heated drying and unheated drying cycles with no obvious difference. I always shake out as much water as I can after removing them form the dishwasher. I've never flushed a washed keyboard with water or alcohol after removing it from the dishwasher. No visible impact. After a couple of unfortunate experiences with mice and keyboards in a 'low' heat oven I no longer oven dry. Oven thermostats can vary quite a bit. I air dry keyboards and mice for at least a couple of days and more typically at least two weeks. No problems observed."

Advice from Ron Morse

It is possible for Windows to find itself in a state where it no longer recognizes the machine's USB ports (usually as the result of a failed install of a new USB device). Recovery from this condition may be difficult if you use a USB keyboard and mouse, short of reinstalling the operating system. While admittedly a rare occurrence, most computer shops sell inexpensive USB to PS/2 connector converters that don't take up too much space in the toolkit. You may not need one very often, but it's invaluable when you need it.

Troubleshooting and repairing keyboards

Decent keyboards are so inexpensive that it's not worth spending much time troubleshooting or repairing them.

If a keyboard stops working or behaves strangely, take the following steps:

1. Reboot the system (this step usually solves the problem).

2. Turn the keyboard upside-down and shake it; a paperclip or other object may have become lodged under a key.

3. Check to make sure the cables are connected properly.

4. If it is a USB keyboard, try plugging it into a different USB port.

5. Try the problem keyboard on another system, or a known-good keyboard on the problem system. If the problem is the keyboard, replace the keyboard.

6. If the problem is the PS/2 keyboard connector on the system, replace the current keyboard with a USB model.

Mice and Trackballs

Mice and trackballs are members of a class generically described as *pointing* devices. All pointing devices have the same purpose—allowing you to move the cursor (or pointer) around the screen and to click to select items or perform other functions. A great variety of fiendishly clever pointing devices are built into notebook computers, but nearly all desktop systems use mice. Those few that don't use a trackball, which is essentially a mouse turned on its back.

All modern mice and trackballs are optical, which provides better precision than earlier mechanical models and eliminates the need for cleaning. Don't even consider buying a mechanical mouse or trackball, no matter how little it costs.

Choosing a mouse or trackball

Use the following guidelines when choosing a mouse or trackball:

Get the right size and shape.

Mice are available in various sizes and shapes, including very small mice intended for children, small mice intended for use with notebooks, the mainstream ergonomic mouse, and some very large mice that have many buttons and extra features. Most people find nearly any mouse comfortable to use for short periods, but if you use a mouse for extended periods small differences in size and shape often make a big difference in comfort. Pay particular attention to mouse shape if you are left-handed. Although makers of asymmetric ergonomic mice may claim that their mice are equally usable by left- and right-handers, many lefties find them uncomfortable and so resort to right-handed mousing. Some manufacturers produce symmetric mice for which chirality is not an issue.

SMALL HANDS, BIG MOUSE?

Don't assume that hand size and mouse size are necessarily related. For example, Barbara, who has small hands, prefers the Microsoft IntelliMouse Explorer, which is an oversized mouse. She found that using a standard or small mouse for long periods caused her hand to hurt. Changing to a large mouse solved the problem.

Get a wheel mouse.

Although some applications do not support the wheel, those that do are the ones most people are likely to use a great deal—Microsoft Office, Internet Explorer, Mozilla, and so on. Using the wheel greatly improves mouse functionality by reducing the amount of mouse movement needed to navigate web pages and documents.

Consider a mouse with extra buttons.

Mice typically have two buttons and a scroll wheel, but some have three or more buttons. Standard two-button mice (three, counting the wheel) are adequate for most purposes. However, five-button mice are ideally suited to some applications, such as games and web browsing. For example, the two extra buttons can be mapped to the Back and Forward browser icons, eliminating a great deal of extraneous mouse movement.

Advice from Nancy Kotary

Don't dismiss trackballs, especially if you have any kind of RSI (repetitive stress injury) or general hand or wrist trouble. Many sufferers have switched over to the trackball, with good results and less pain. Sometimes they had to take test runs with several different models, but it saved them from cortisone shots or surgery. There's a big difference between models from one manufacturer, even; I hate the Logitech Marble Mouse but absolutely cannot work without the Logitech TrackMan Wheel. And others in my office feel just the opposite. Now all we need is for someone to make a Bluetooth trackball to get the last cord off my desk.

Make sure the cord is long enough.

We have seen mice with cords ranging in length from less than 4 feet to about 9 feet. A short mouse cord may be too short to reach the system, particularly if it is on the floor.

Consider a cordless model.

If your desktop is usually cluttered, consider buying a cordless mouse. The absence of a cord can make a surprising difference, more so for the mouse than the keyboard. Cordless mice devour batteries, though, so either buy NiMH batteries and a charger or a cordless mouse that includes a recharging cradle.

Try a trackball.

Trackballs have never really caught on, probably because people who are used to a mouse find trackballs awkward, at least initially. In our experience, about 10% of those who try a trackball become trackball converts. But trackballs sell probably only 0.1% the volume of mice, which means there are a lot of people who don't know what they're missing.

Trackballs are made in two styles. The Microsoft Trackball Explorer, shown in Figure 13-7, represents the first style, in which the index finger operates the trackball and the thumb operates the mouse wheel and buttons. The Microsoft Trackball Optical, shown in Figure 13-8, illustrates the second style of trackball, in which the index finger operates the mouse wheel and buttons and the thumb operates the trackball. Some people adapt quickly to either type of trackball; others find one or the other type intolerable. If you've never used a trackball, try both types if possible before you buy one.

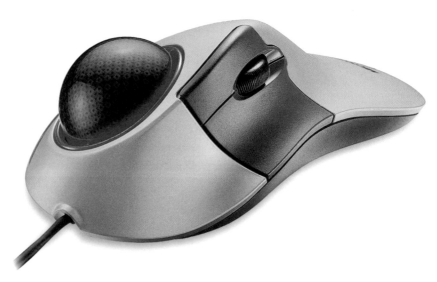

Figure 13-7. Microsoft Trackball Explorer mouse (image courtesy of Microsoft Corporation)

Figure 4-15. Press the new I/O template into place

Figure 13-8. Microsoft Trackball Optical mouse (image courtesy of Microsoft Corporation)

Which Brand of Mouse to Buy?

Logitech and Microsoft both produce a wide range of excellent optical mice, in corded and cordless models. One of them is almost certainly right for you. Even their basic models are well built and reliable. The more expensive models have more features, are more precise, and are probably more durable.

We used Microsoft optical mice almost exclusively for many years, and continue to recommend them. However, when we tested the superb Logitech MX-series optical mice, we found that we preferred their shape and feel. We now use Logitech optical mice on many of our primary systems, although we also use various Microsoft optical mice, both older and current models, on several systems.

Avoid inexpensive, no-name mice. If someone attempts to sell you a mechanical "ball" mouse, run away.

Configuring a mouse or trackball

Windows allows you to customize how your mouse behaves, including scrolling settings, point speed, acceleration, type, button mappings, and so on. To configure your mouse, open Control Panel and double-click the Mouse applet to display the Mouse Properties dialog.

Installing a new mouse or upgrading the driver may install a separate management application, or may simply add pages and options to the standard

Mouse Properties dialog. For example, Figure 13-9 shows the additional button-mapping functions that appeared when we installed the Microsoft IntelliPoint 5.0 driver with our IntelliMouse Explorer. If you install a new mouse driver, locate and explore the options it provides. The default settings for such things as button definitions are probably useful, but one of the alternative options may better suit your work habits.

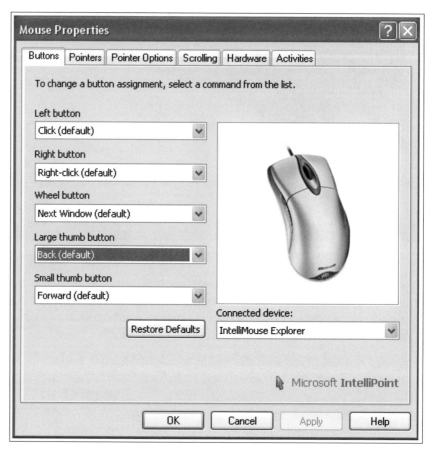

Figure 13-9. The Windows Mouse Properties dialog as modified by installing the Microsoft IntelliPoint mouse driver

Troubleshooting a mouse

If a mouse malfunctions, make sure that the cable is connected properly and clean the mouse. If it still doesn't work, replace it.

Game Controllers

A *game controller* is a specialized input device optimized for use with games. Unlike keyboards, mice, and trackballs, which are relatively standardized in form and function, game controllers run the gamut in shape, size, features, and purpose. Some game controllers sit on the desktop. Others clamp to the desk, and still others are held in both hands and manipulated directly. Game controllers may provide a joystick, a steering wheel, a flight yoke, foot pedals, or may be what we call "grab, twist, and squeeze" controllers.

A particular game controller may be well suited for one game and entirely inappropriate for another. For example, a game controller with a steering wheel may be perfect for an automobile racing game, but unusable for a first-person shooter (FPS) game like Doom 3. Serious gamers who play diverse games often own several game controllers and use the one most appropriate for the game they are playing at the moment.

Older game controllers used analog sensors and the analog "game port" interface, both of which caused no end of problems. Analog controllers drifted and required frequent recalibration. The game port interface—originally designed for analog data acquisition and to support two simple paddles for playing Pong—was never intended to support the numerous sophisticated features of modern game controllers, and did so poorly. Nearly all current models use digital sensors, and all of them use the USB interface. Although conflicts still arise, particularly if you install multiple game controllers on a system, the USB interface has eliminated most of the problems that formerly made configuring game controllers more a black art than a science.

The following sections tell you what you need to know to choose a game controller.

Game controller characteristics

Here are the important characteristics of game controllers:

Type

> The first game controllers were *joystick controllers*, which are still popular and still most appropriate for playing flight simulator and air combat games. Some are marginally usable for some driving, racing, action/adventure, and sports games. *Steering wheel controllers*, many of which include foot pedals, are ideal for driving/racing games and some flight simulators, but ill-suited to other games. *Gamepad controllers* are suitable for action games, including first-person shooters, sports, and most arcade-style games.

Number of axes

> An *axis* is a line drawn through the center of the joystick (or the D-pad on a gamepad) that defines the directions that one can move by manipulating the controls. All controllers have an *x-axis* (side to side movement) and a *y-axis* (front to back). Some controllers add a *z-axis* (up and down) and/or a *throttle axis*. Depending on the controller type, the third and/or fourth axes may also be called a *yoke control* or *rudder control*, for their intended function, or a *twist control*, for the method used to activate the axis.

Throttle

The *throttle* is a variable input, present on most joysticks and some gamepads, and normally assigned to the third or fourth axis on the controller. The throttle is usually used to control vehicle speed, and may be a slider, wheel, pedal, or variable-pull trigger, depending on the controller.

Response type

Motion along an axis can be tracked in two ways. *Proportional response* (common with joysticks) offers finer control, because small stick movements result in small incremental movements onscreen. *Non-proportional response* (common with gamepads) is all-or-nothing—any movement of the control along an axis results in full motion on that axis, offering faster response at the expense of fine control. Some controllers are programmable to allow choosing between proportional and nonproportional modes.

Number of buttons

All controllers have buttons, which are momentary-on switches used to fire weapons and perform similar on/off functions.

Hat switch

A *hat switch*, sometimes called a *POV hat*, a *Point of View hat*, or just a *hat*, is called that because it usually resides on the head of the joystick, where it's easily manipulated by the thumb. The hat switch is a directional rocker switch (usually four-way, but sometimes eight-way) that allows you to rapidly change your point of view to face front, rear, left, or right. Games that do not support POV may use the hat to provide four extra buttons.

Force feedback

Recent high-end game controllers have force-feedback technology, which uses small servo motors built into the game controller itself to provide physical feedback under the control of game software designed to use force feedback. For example, with a force-feedback joystick, as you pull a 7G turn you feel the joystick jerk and jitter as the aircraft control surfaces lose laminar flow, but as you extend to gain airspeed, the controls settle down again. When you come up on the six of a bandit and begin hosing him down with your 30 mm rotary cannon, the joystick stutters as the gun recoils.

Well-implemented force feedback greatly enhances the ambiance of games that support it properly. The only real drawback to force feedback is that it is expensive. A $50 controller without force feedback might cost $100 with it. Interestingly, this same technology (in much enhanced form) is used in current fly-by-wire combat aircraft.

Programmability

All current game controllers include DirectInput drivers or are compatible with standard Windows drivers. A DirectInput-compliant controller can be programmed within any DirectInput-compliant game. However, DirectInput provides only basic functionality, so many controllers come with their own programming software that provides extended functionality, including:

Cross-game commonality

By default, games may use different buttons for similar purposes. For example, one air combat game may use button 1 to fire guns, button 2 to launch a Sidewinder, and button 3 to launch a Sparrow. Another air combat game may offer similar weapons selection, but use different buttons. Programmable game controllers allow you to redefine button functions so that the same button performs similar actions in different games.

Stored profiles

Many modern game controllers are quite flexible and may be used with diverse games. Optimal controller configuration for one game, however, may be less desirable for another. Better game controllers can store multiple groups of configuration settings, called *macros* or *profiles*, that allow you to quickly load whichever settings are most appropriate for the game you're about to play, rather than having to reprogram the controller manually each time. Most such controllers come with predefined settings for various popular games.

Choosing a game controller

More so than for any other input device, the "best" game controller is a matter of personal preference. If it feels right to you, it probably is right. If it feels wrong, it's probably wrong, no matter how much someone else may like it. Use the following guidelines when choosing a game controller:

Get the right type(s).

Make sure the game controller type is appropriate for the games you play most often. If you frequently play two or more games that are ill-suited to using the same controller, buy two or more controllers, and use the type most suited to whatever game you play.

Buy a force-feedback model.

If an appropriate force-feedback model is available and is within your budget, buy it rather than the cheaper model. Many games support force feedback, and that support is of a higher quality with each upgrade of many games.

Solicit advice from friends.

Friends are among the best sources of information about game controllers. You'll get a great deal of feedback from them, much of it conflicting, but valuable nonetheless. Not the least advantage of this method is that they'll probably let you play a few games with their controllers, giving you the opportunity to judge the merits for yourself in a realistic environment.

Installing a game controller

Physically installing a game controller is straightforward: plug it into the USB port. Before you connect the game controller, however, we suggest that you visit Microsoft and update Windows to the latest drivers, particularly DirectX.

Troubleshooting game controllers

It's impossible to provide comprehensive information about troubleshooting game controllers because both the controllers themselves and the problems you may encounter are so diverse. A cheap game controller is probably going to physically break or otherwise fail sooner rather than later. There's not much we can say about that, except to suggest that you buy a better-quality game controller in the first place. If you experience problems with a good game controller, here are some actions to take:

Install the latest release of DirectX.

DirectX is a work in progress. If you have problems with a game controller, particularly a new model or one you have just installed, download and install the latest version of DirectX. Before you install the update, review the DirectX FAQ (*http://go.microsoft.com/ ?linkid=664008&e=9797*) carefully to discover issues pertinent to your own configuration. It's also a good idea to review the FAQs posted by the makers of your video card, sound card, and game controller to discover any potential conflicts or interdependencies such as a need to update drivers for those devices.

Install the latest drivers.

Some game controllers provide basic functionality using the default drivers provided with Windows. If your game controller appears to be only partially functional, you may need to install a driver to support its enhanced functions. Most game controller vendors frequently update drivers to fix bugs, add support for new games, and so on, so it's a good idea to check the vendor support page frequently.

Update your system BIOS.

If you have problems with a game controller connected to an older system, update the system BIOS. For example, on one older system, we installed a joystick that the driver insisted on recognizing as a gamepad.

We tried updating the driver software, DirectX, and so on, all to no avail. Then we noticed after updating the main system BIOS for unrelated reasons that the driver now recognized the joystick as a joystick. We reflashed the BIOS to its original level, and the problem recurred. We re-reflashed the BIOS to the updated level, and the problem went away again.

Make sure the game controller is configured for the game.

If the game controller appears to work properly for one game but not others, make sure that you've used the programmable functions of the game controller to configure it properly to support the other games. Most programmable game controllers include predefined profiles for popular games. If no profile is included for a game you purchase, check the vendor web site to see if an updated profile for that game is available.

Make sure the game is configured for the game controller.

The default configuration settings for some games are inappropriate for some game controllers. For example, although many first-person shooter (FPS) games disable the freelook/mouselook feature by default, some gamepads require it to be enabled for proper functioning. Each time you install a new game, check the game controller manual or web site to see if there are specific instructions to configure the controller optimally for that game.

The following material describes some specific problems you may encounter and some possible solutions. As always, the best way to troubleshoot problems is to swap components. If you have another system and/or another game controller available, try swapping controllers back and forth between the system to determine if the problem is caused by the system or the controller. Most problems occur with older controllers that use the gameport interface. The best solution is often to replace your game controller with a new USB model.

No controller applet appears in Control Panel.

Install the software for your game controller. If you have already done that, install DirectX manually. Although most controller software installs DirectX, some requires you to install it yourself. Installing DirectX adds the Control Panel applet.

Installing a DirectX update causes problems.

Reinstalling the latest version of your controller software after installing the DirectX update almost always fixes the problem. If that doesn't work, visit the controller maker's web site for additional information. If the web site offers no fix and you are using a gameport controller, try uninstalling your sound card drivers completely. Once you've eradicated all traces of the sound card drivers, shut down the system and physically remove the sound card. Then power the system back up (without the sound card) and shut it down again. Reinstall the sound card, restart the system, and reinstall the sound card drivers.

DON'T REVERT DIRECTX

Never try to downgrade DirectX by installing an earlier version over a later version. It just doesn't work, and attempting to do it causes worse problems than the one you're trying to solve. If you absolutely must revert to an earlier DirectX version, the only way we know to do so reliably is to strip the hard drive down to bare metal and reinstall Windows and all applications.

Installing a new sound card or updating sound drivers disables force feedback.

Gameport DirectInput force-feedback controllers use MIDI signals to control feedback. If you didn't completely remove all vestiges of the old sound card drivers, the new card or drivers may not be configured to use MIDI correctly. Uninstall the sound card and drivers (as described earlier) and reinstall them.

Controller doesn't work on gameport switch or with extension cables.

To make it easier to switch among controllers, some people install a gameport switchbox or extension cables. If you are having problems with a controller connected via a switchbox or extension cable, try connecting it directly to the system. Switches work with most analog controllers, but don't work with analog force-feedback controllers or any digital controller. Extension cables also often cause problems. The controller may not function at all, or it may function sporadically. Either dispense with the extension cables, or buy better-quality cables.

Y-cable doesn't work with two controllers.

A Y-cable should allow you to share one gameport between two analog game controllers for head-to-head play. However, the pinouts of Y-cables are nonstandard and a given Y-cable may not work with a particular type of controller. If the controllers are different models, it may be impossible to find a Y-cable that allows you to use both. Even if the Y-cable works properly with the controllers, each controller will be limited to a subset of the functions that it supports when it is the only controller connected. The best solution is to use two identical controllers that have pass-through ports—which allows you to use the full feature set of both controllers—or to use USB controllers.

USB game controller does not work properly.

Problems are infrequent with recent USB ports and USB game controllers, but occur more often with older USB ports and/or game controllers. If your USB controller is functioning improperly or not at all and installing the latest version of DirectX and the controller drivers doesn't solve the problem, there are several possible hardware problems:

Defective USB port

If you're sure software isn't the problem, first try plugging the controller into a different USB port. We've encountered few bad root USB ports on motherboards, but bad ports are not uncommon on inexpensive USB hubs.

Incompatible USB controller, port, or device

Modern USB 2.0 devices are rigidly standardized, but older USB 1.1 devices were plagued by incompatibilities. Early USB motherboards—particularly those based on older VIA chipsets—have USB bugs that frequently cause problems with USB game controllers, even current models. Nor is the fault always with the motherboard. Some early USB game controllers were not fully compliant and may or may not function properly when connected to a particular USB port. If the motherboard is at fault, you can solve the problem by replacing the motherboard or by disabling the motherboard USB ports and adding a PCI expansion card that provides USB 2.0 root ports. If the device itself is the problem, the only solution may be to replace the device.

Inadequate USB power

Some USB game controllers draw more power than an unpowered USB hub or USB keyboard jack can supply. If your game controller doesn't work when connected to an unpowered USB hub, try connecting it to a root hub port on the PC or to a powered USB hub port. Note that not all motherboard USB ports are fully powered, and sometimes two USB ports share power. A good rule of thumb is to try to figure out which USB ports are on separate root hubs when you use USB-powered stuff, and connect power-hungry USB devices to different root hub ports. If your game controller doesn't work when connected to a motherboard USB port but works when connected to a motherboard USB port on another system, using a powered USB hub will likely solve the problem.

Bad USB cable

Surprisingly often, USB cables are defective; particularly those you find for $3 in a bin at the computer store. But we've encountered defective USB cables of all sorts, including those bundled with motherboards and USB devices. We generally keep a couple of spare Belkin USB cables on hand for such eventualities (*http://www.belkin.com*).

Game controller fails to work when daisy-chained.

The way USB is supposed to work and the way USB actually works are two entirely different things. Although you should in theory be able to daisy-chain USB devices freely, in practice it often doesn't work out that way. If your USB game controller doesn't work when daisy-chained, try connecting it to a root hub port or to a powered USB hub.

Force-feedback controller does not center properly.

With the game controller active, open the controller applet in Control Panel. Disconnect the controller, recenter it while disconnected, and then reconnect it. Refresh or update the controller in the applet.

Older gameport controller fails on newer systems.

Older gameport controllers were designed for the gameports on ISA sound adapters, which use 5V logic. Newer PCI adapters typically deliver only 3.3V to the gameport, which may be inadequate to drive the older controller. The only practical fix is to replace the controller.

Wireless Networking

14

When we outlined this chapter, we devoted significant space to standard wired Ethernet networking. After all, we've been running a wired network in our house since about 1985—the days of ARCNet on RG-62 coax cable—and have about a mile (literally) of cable running through our walls, attic, and basement. But then we realized that people nowadays usually don't want to run network cables throughout their homes.

Wireless networking is where the action is. If we had any doubts, a quick trip to Best Buy quashed them. The shelves were full of wireless networking gear. There were few wired networking components in stock, and those were gathering dust. So we decided to refocus this chapter on wireless networking.

Wireless networking has some key advantages relative to wired networking:

Flexibility

> A wireless network is, by definition, flexible. You're not tethered by a cable to the nearest network jack. You can install a new PC in the kids' bedroom without having to drill holes in the walls and run a cable down to your office. You can carry your notebook from your office to the den to the deck, with your network connection active the whole time. You can relocate or add systems without worrying about how to get them connected to the network.

Simplicity

> Wireless networks are very simple to install and maintain. Once your wireless network is set up, all you need do is install a wireless network card and enter your passphrase to put that system on the network.

SAF

> *SAF (Spousal Acceptance Factor)* is higher with wireless networking. With wired networking, you may find yourself explaining to your spouse why you can't put his system exactly where he wants it, or what those ugly wires hanging out of the walls are for. With wireless, you never have to apologize or explain.

In This Chapter

Neighborhood Area Networking (NAN)

If you have a wired network and your cable modem goes down, you're out of luck until the cable company gets around to fixing the problem. With wireless networking, you can set up a *NAN* (*Neighborhood Area Network*). If your cable modem goes down, you just connect to a neighbor's wireless network and share his DSL connection until your cable modem is back up. When his DSL is down, you return the favor. With a NAN, Internet outages are pretty much a thing of the past. (Note that some service providers look askance upon connection sharing, particularly if two or more households share and pay for only one connection.)

Wireless networking also has a couple of disadvantages relative to wired networking:

Throughput

Wired 100BaseT Ethernet has a nominal data rate of 100 megabits/second (Mb/s) and actual throughput of roughly 80 Mb/s, or 10 megabytes/second (MB/s). Gigabit Ethernet (1000BaseT) is theoretically 10 times faster, and is actually 3 to 5 times faster. If you use an Ethernet hub, that bandwidth is shared among all systems connected to the network. If you use a nonblocking Ethernet switch, each system has a dedicated, full-speed communication channel. The wireless networking technologies we describe in this chapter provide either 54 Mb/s or 108 Mb/s nominal bandwidth, with actual throughput of roughly 25 Mb/s or 50 Mb/s respectively, and that bandwidth is always shared among all the systems on the network.

If you are using a network only to share an Internet connection, the lower throughput of wireless is unimportant because even the slowest wireless connection is much faster than most broadband Internet service. However, if you do heavy data transfers across the network, such as backing up files from one PC to another, the lower throughput of wireless may become problematic. Also, because wireless bandwidth is shared among all active wireless clients, doing a heavy data transfer between two clients leaves other clients with very little available bandwidth.

Security

Wired networking is inherently secure, in the sense that outsiders cannot easily gain access to the systems on your network or to internal traffic, assuming, of course, that your Internet connection is properly secured. Wireless networks are by default insecure, because wireless equipment vendors ship their products with security features disabled. Some credible estimates say that nearly 100% of all residential wireless networks run wide open, with no security at all. Fortunately, that's attributable to laziness or ignorance, because modern wireless networking gear can be secured nearly as well as a wired network. But all the security features in the world won't help if you don't use them, so make securing your network a high priority.

WHAT ABOUT COST?

At first glance, wireless networking seems noticeably more expensive than wired networking. After all, most computers already have a free Ethernet port, so all you need to buy is some $10 Ethernet cables and a $30 Ethernet switch. To install wireless networking, you'll probably have to buy a $35 wireless networking adapter for each computer and a $50 wireless access point or wireless router. Wired networking is definitely cheaper, right? Well, maybe.

The putative cost advantage of wired networking assumes that all of your computers and your Internet connection are in one room (or that your spouse doesn't mind Ethernet cables draped over doorways and hanging out of the walls). In a typical household, doing the job right means you're going to need some supplies and equipment. At a minimum, you'll want a spool of Category 6 or better networking cable, modular connectors for both ends of each cable run, modular faceplates to hold the modular connectors, old-work boxes to hold the modular faceplates, drop cables for each end of each cable run, a good wire stripping/crimping tool, a drill and other hand tools, and so on. You may even need a $50 bellhanger bit (a standard 3/8" to 5/8" drill bit on the end of a six-foot flexible rod that you use to drill in inaccessible locations.) By the time you add everything up–even assuming you have or can borrow part of what you need–doing a wired network properly often costs as much or more than using wireless networking instead.

We recommend using wireless networking unless you have a good reason to use wired networking. It makes sense to use wired networking:

- To link systems that transfer large amounts of data, particularly streaming video.

- To connect desktop computers and other devices that are in close proximity to each other and do not require mobility.

- To extend your wireless network to cover areas that are prevented by obstructions or distance from joining your primary wireless network.

- To connect devices, such as network printers or surveillance cameras, that do not support wireless connections (although you can connect such devices to a wireless bridge device that converts them to wireless operation).

Don't overlook alternatives to a permanently installed wired network. For example, if you infrequently need to transfer large files from one system to another, it may be easier to copy those files to a writable DVD or an external USB hard drive and sneakernet them to the other machine.

A temporary wired network can also be useful at times. All recent motherboards include integrated Ethernet, so there's a fallback position when you need wired networking temporarily for a particular task. Keep a long Category 6 *Ethernet cross-over cable* handy for such times. (We have a 100-footer.) With a cross-over cable, you can connect two systems directly to each other, without using a hub or switch. Do the transfer across the cable, and then roll up the cable and put it back in the closet until next time.

WHAT'S A CROSS-OVER CABLE?

There are two types of Ethernet cable. A standard Ethernet cable is used to connect a network adapter to a hub (or switch). Ethernet adapters send on some wires and receive on others. Hub ports reverse the two, so everything works. The adapters send on the wires that the hub receives on, and vice versa. A standard cable can't be used to connect two standard Ethernet adapters directly, because both adapters send on one set of wires and receive on another. Nobody hears anybody. A cross-over cable swaps the send/receive wires at one end, so the two adapters are able to communicate. (Auto-sensing Ethernet adapters automatically detect which pairs to send and receive on, and so can be used with either type of cable; however, a cross-over cable works with any type of Ethernet adapter, auto-sensing or not.)

If you buy a cross-over cable, pay attention to the category rating. A Category 5 or 5e cable is rated for a 100 Mb/s 100BaseT connection. If your systems have Gigabit Ethernet—which you should always choose if you have the option—you'll need a Category 6 or better cable. (Actually, Gigabit Ethernet usually works fine on a 50- or 100-foot Category 5e cable, but better safe than sorry.)

Wireless Networking Standards

Current wireless networking components use one or more of the following standards, which are referred to collectively as standards:

802.11b

> The 802.11b specification was released in mid-1999, and devices based upon it soon flooded the market. 802.11b supports a maximum data rate of 11 Mb/s, comparable to 10BaseT Ethernet, and has typical real-world throughput of about 5 Mb/s. 802.11b uses the unlicensed 2.4 GHz spectrum, which means that it is subject to
> interference from microwave ovens, cordless phones, Bluetooth adapters and gadgets, and other devices that share the 2.4 GHz spectrum. 802.11b is functionally obsolete, because components that use faster standards and have much better security are now available at reasonable cost. Millions of 802.11b adapters remain in use, primarily as embedded or PC Card adapters in notebook computers.

802.11a

> The 802.11a standard was released concurrently with 802.11b, but 802.11a was slower to catch on, because it originally required an FCC license and because 802.11a components were significantly more

expensive than 802.11b components. 802.11a supports a maximum data rate of 54 Mb/s, and has typical real-world throughput of about 25 Mb/s. It uses a portion of the 5 GHz spectrum that was formerly licensed, which limited interference from other devices. Unlike the wild-and-woolly 2.4 GHz spectrum, where anyone at all could play without permission, the 5 GHz spectrum was tightly regulated to avoid interference. Although that portion of the spectrum is now unlicensed, it remains relatively uncluttered. The real downside of 802.11a is that a 5 GHz signal has shorter range and is more easily obstructed than a 2.4 GHz signal. However, 802.11a, which for a time seemed moribund, is seeing a renaissance that is primarily driven by home users who have found that the 5 GHz spectrum used by 802.11a is much more reliable for such tasks as streaming video wirelessly.

802.11g

The most recent wireless standard is 802.11g, which combines the best features of 802.11a and 802.11b. Like 802.11b, 802.11g works in the 2.4 GHz spectrum, which means it has good range but is subject to interference from other 2.4 GHz devices (such as cordless telephones). Because they use the same frequencies, 802.11b components can communicate with 802.11g components, and vice versa. Like 802.11a, 802.11g supports a maximum data rate of 54 Mb/s, and has typical real-world bandwidth of about 25 Mb/s. In the absence of interference, that is sufficient to support real-time streaming video, which 802.11b cannot. 802.11g components are now inexpensive, and have made 802.11b obsolete.

MIXING AND MATCHING WIRELESS COMPONENTS

In theory, 802.11b and 802.11g components are standards-based, so components from different manufacturers should interoperate. In practice, that is largely true, although minor differences in how standards are implemented can cause conflicts. In particular, some high-end 802.11b/802.11g components include proprietary extensions for security, faster performance, and similar purposes. Those components do generally interoperate with components from other vendors, but only on a "least common denominator" basis—that is, using only the standard 802.11 features. The best way to ensure that your wireless network operates with minimal problems is to buy all of your wireless components from the same vendor.

"802.108g"

Several manufacturers, including D-Link and NetGear, produce wireless components that claim to provide 108 Mb/s bandwidth. In fact they do, but only by "cheating" on the 802.11g specification. Such components, colloquially called "802.108g" devices, work as advertised, but using them may cause conflicts with 802.11g-compliant devices operating in the same vicinity.

The problem is this: 802.11g defines 11 channels (13 in Europe), each with 22 MHz of bandwidth. Each 22 MHz channel can support the full 54 Mb/s bandwidth of 802.11g. But these channels overlap, as shown in Figure 14-1. Three of the channels—1, 6, and 11—are completely non-overlapping, which means that three 802.11g-compliant wireless networks in the same vicinity—one assigned to each of the three non-overlapping channels—can share the 2.4 GHz spectrum without conflicts. Alternatively, two 802.11g-compliant networks can be assigned to two channels that do not overlap each other, for example, Channels 2 and 8.

Unfortunately, the design of 802.108g devices is such that they claim not just 2/3 of the available spectrum, but all of it. Rather than use the top 2/3 or the bottom 2/3 of the range, current 802.108g devices use the middle 2/3, leaving only small spectrum segments at either end of the range unused. Because the spectrum segments left unused by 802.108g are not a full channel wide, no other 2.4 GHz 802.11 devices can operate without interference in the vicinity of an 802.108g device that is operating in full-speed 108 Mb/s mode.

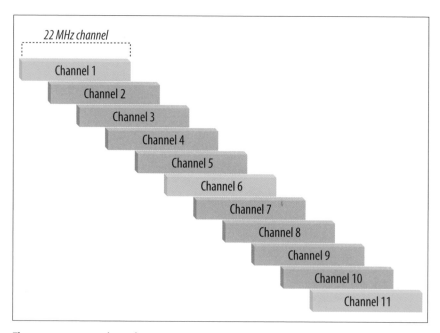

Figure 14-1. 802.11g channels

Wireless Components

Wireless networks use an *access point* (*AP*), also called a *wireless access point* (*WAP*), to provide a gateway to the wired network and a *wireless local area network adapter* (*WLAN adapter* or simply *wireless adapter*) to provide a link between a wireless client PC and the AP.

DO IT ALL WITH ONE BOX

Wireless routers combine an access point with a router, and are a good choice for a home or SOHO (small office/home office) network. Most wireless routers also include several Ethernet hub or switch ports to allow connecting wired Ethernet adapters to the router, providing an all-in-one solution. The router protects your network from intrusions, the wireless AP hosts your wireless clients, and the Ethernet hub or switch ports provide a place to connect your wired PCs. Because wireless routers cost only a few dollars more than single-purpose components, they are extremely popular. We use a D-Link DI-624 wireless router to manage our SOHO network.

Access points

An AP connects to the wired network (or directly to a cable/DSL modem) and can simultaneously provide wireless links to many wireless adapters. A typical AP allows 32 or 64 wireless adapters to be connected simultaneously. All wireless adapters that connect to an AP share the wireless bandwidth provided by that AP. For example, if the AP provides 54 Mb/s of wireless bandwidth, all connected wireless adapters share that 54 Mb/s even though each adapter may have a maximum individual bandwidth of 54 Mb/s or more.

If only one wireless adapter is transferring data at a particular moment, that adapter gets the full available bandwidth. If several adapters are transferring data simultaneously, the available bandwidth is shared among them. Accordingly, the instantaneous bandwidth available to any particular adapter varies dynamically, depending on how many other adapters are also using bandwidth at that moment and how much bandwidth they are using.

IT'S NOT NICE TO SHARE

Bandwidth sharing means that wireless networking may be a poor choice for applications, such as streaming video, that require real-time, high-bandwidth communications. The bandwidth of modern wireless components is barely sufficient to stream DVD-quality video under ideal conditions. If one or more other wireless clients are also using bandwidth, the delivered video will be choppy. For that reason, we always recommend using wired networking for video or, alternatively, a dedicated or 802.11a wireless networking connection.

Advice from Jim Cooley

Many cable/DSL modems now ship with just a USB output jack, which makes it difficult to connect to a WAP/router. You may need to purchase a replacement modem that also provides an Ethernet jack. Alternatively, some cable/DSL providers offer a choice of modems. If your provider offers that choice, ask for a modem that includes an Ethernet jack.

A wireless network may have one or many APs. Although most home or SOHO networks get along fine with one AP, using a second AP provides additional area coverage, allows more wireless adapters to connect to the network simultaneously, and provides additional shared bandwidth. For example, one AP might have insufficient range to cover a large home, particularly one built with stone, steel studs, heavy plaster walls, or other materials that block radio waves. We can't imagine that the limit of 32 or 64 connected wireless adapters would be a problem in any home or SOHO environment, but the limited shared bandwidth might be.

Adding a second AP at some distance from the first AP extends the coverage area and doubles the bandwidth available to be shared among the wireless clients. Depending on their location, some wireless adapters may be within range of both APs, while others will be in range of only one or the other AP. If the wireless network is properly configured, client wireless adapters simply connect transparently to an available AP without user intervention. If the client is mobile—for example, a notebook computer being carried from room to room—the connection automatically hops from one AP to the next as the client moves within the coverage area.

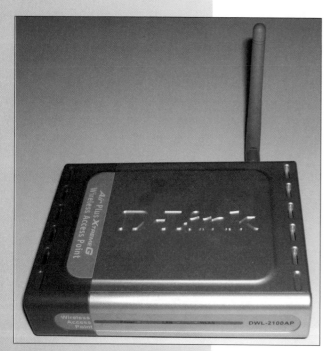

Figure 14-2. The D-Link DWL-2100AP, a typical AP

Figure 14-2 shows a typical AP intended for home or small-business use. This AP, a D-Link DWL-2100AP model, uses the ubiquitous low-gain, omnidirectional "rubber duck" antenna used by most wireless devices. The mounts used for these antennae allow the antennae to be oriented in all three dimensions to maximize signal strength and optimize coverage area. Some APs use permanently affixed antennae. Others, including this model, provide a socket for an external antenna. Various external antennae are available, including models suitable for outdoor mounting, models that provide higher gain than standard rubber duck antennae, and models that are highly directional.

Wireless adapters

Clients connect to the wireless network using wireless adapters, which are functionally analogous to the standard Ethernet adapters used in a wired network. Wireless adapters are available in various interfaces, including PCI (for desktop systems), *CardBus* (for notebooks), *PCMCIA* (*People Can't Memorize Computer Industry Acronyms*) card adapters (for older notebooks and handheld devices), and USB (for any system). Like APs, PCI and USB wireless adapters are normally supplied with a low-gain, omnidirectional rubber-duck antenna that can usually be replaced with an external high-gain or unidirectional antenna. Figure 14-3 shows a D-Link AirPlus ExtremeG DWL-G520, which is a typical PCI wireless adapter. CardBus wireless adapters, like the D-Link DWL-G650 shown in Figure 14-4, have an internal, low-gain, omnidirectional antenna, and make no provision for using an external antenna. However, certain models of CardBus (or PCMCIA) adapters, such as some Proxim Orinoco cards, include an external antenna port.

Figure 14-3. The D-Link DWL-G520, a typical PCI wireless adapter

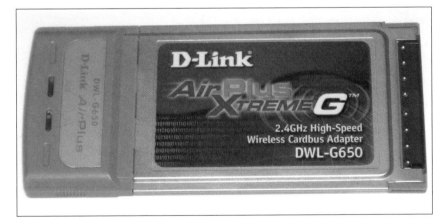

Figure 14-4. The D-Link DWL-G650, a typical CardBus wireless card

Wireless Component Interoperability

APs and wireless adapters support one or more 802.11 standards, and may also support proprietary protocols. Standards-based APs and wireless adapters from different companies generally interoperate well, with minor exceptions. You can, for example, usually connect to a D-Link AP with a NETGEAR or wireless adapter or vice versa, assuming that both products are designed for the same standard or standards. Some APs and wireless adapters are single-standard (i.e., 802.11g or 802.11a), and other APs and wireless clients support multiple standards (e.g., 802.11a/b/g).

Some wireless vendors—particularly those who focus on businesses—anticipate the standards-making process by adding proprietary features that have not yet been ratified as a standard (and may never be ratified). Such enhanced products are attractive to businesses for their added features and are usually able to interoperate with standards-based products, but generally only at a least-common-denominator level. For example, Belkin jumped the gun on the emerging 802.11n standard by introducing so-called "Pre-N" APs and wireless adapters. These Pre-N products—which may or may not end up being compatible with the 802.11n standard when it is finalized—provide higher speed and longer range when they are used together, but when they are used with 802.11g or earlier components, they function as standard components.

In general, we recommend avoiding whenever possible wireless components that depend on proprietary extensions to provide the required level of functionality. Current standards-based wireless components provide adequate security and manageability for any home or small business environment.

Transmitter power, receiver sensitivity, and antenna considerations

The range of a wireless connection depends on many factors, including its speed, amount of interference, obstructions in the signal path, and the types of antennae used. All other things being equal, though, the range of a connection is determined by how powerful the transmitter is and how sensitive the receiver. Different brands and models of wireless components may differ significantly in both respects.

Transmitter power

The transmitter power of wireless networking components is usually stated in *dBm*, and may range from 0 dBm (defined as 1 milliwatt or mW) to 30 dBm (just over 1,000 mW). An increase or decrease of about 3 dBm corresponds to a doubling or halving of transmission power. For example, an output of 3 dBm corresponds to about 2 mW. An increase or decrease of 10 dBm corresponds to increasing or decreasing transmitter power by a factor of 10. For example, an output of 10 dBm is about 10 mW; 20 dBm about 100 mW; and 30 dBm about 1,000 mW. All other things being equal, increasing power output increases range and transmission speed.

Wireless devices may use fixed transmission power, set transmission power dynamically under firmware control, or allow transmission power to be set manually. The amount of transmission power needed varies with the distance between devices, the sensitivity of the receiver, the data rate of the link, the amount of obstruction in the signal path, and other factors. In general, longer distances between devices and higher data rates require more transmission power.

You might think the best idea would be for all devices to use maximum transmission power all the time, but high power is not always desirable. Using more power than needed does not improve the speed or quality of the wireless link; it simply introduces unnecessary RF into the environment, where it may interfere with other wireless devices that would otherwise be able to use the same channel without conflicts.

Accordingly, the firmware of some wireless devices is programmed to negotiate link characteristics with other wireless devices, including transmitter power, to establish an optimum connection at the minimum required power level. This negotiation can be done at very low data rates, so the initial contact between the devices can occur at low power. Each device tells the other about its own capabilities, including the fastest link speed it supports. The devices then increase their transmitter power to the minimum level needed to support the highest common data rate. If the maximum available transmitter power is insufficient to support their highest common data rate, they fall back to a lower data rate, using whatever power level is needed to support that lower data rate.

Other wireless devices allow transmission power to be set manually, usually within a range of a few mW up to perhaps 100 or 200 mW. Often, the output power is not stated numerically, but instead is named (Full, Half, Quarter, Eighth, and so on) or as a maximum output power with options to reduce output by a series of 3 dB steps, each of which halves output power. Still other wireless devices make no provision for adjusting transmission power, instead using a fixed transmission power, usually 30 mW or so.

Receiver sensitivity

The flip side of transmitter power is receiver sensitivity. All other things being equal, a more sensitive receiver can sustain a connection with a weaker signal than a receiver with lower sensitivity. A sensitive receiver is as important as a powerful transmitter, because signal strength drops rapidly with increasing distance from the transmitter and because higher data rates require stronger signals.

If you are building a wireless network for which range is critical, particularly if your signal paths are obstructed, it's worth paying attention to the receiver sensitivity of components you are considering using. For example, the D-Link DWL-2100AP has excellent receiver sensitivity. A cheap, no-name component might have actual receiver sensitivity 10 dBm lower than the D-Link model (the documentation for the cheesy AP probably won't admit that, but we're talking real-world here). That means when the D-Link AP is at its maximum range to sustain a 54 Mb/s link, the cheap AP might sustain only a 24 or 36 Mb/s link. Worse still, if the D-Link AP is at its maximum range to support a 36 Mb/s link, the cheap AP might sustain only a 6 or 9 Mb/s link.

Antenna considerations

Most mainstream wireless components are supplied with a standard "rubber duck" antenna, which is usually described as omnidirectional. That's true in a sense, but the standard antenna radiates omnidirectionally primarily in one plane. For example, with the antenna oriented vertically (at 90°, relative to the horizontal plane), as shown in Figure 14-5, the radiation pattern resembles a doughnut extending horizontally outward in all directions. If this AP were installed on one floor of a home, for example, its coverage area might include all rooms on that same floor, but rooms on floors above and below its location would receive a weak signal.

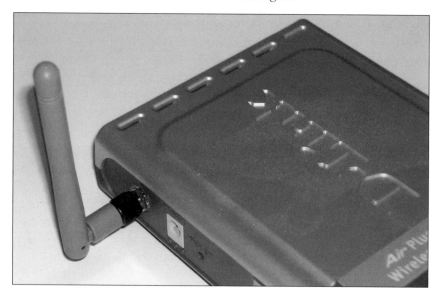

Figure 14-5. Antenna oriented vertically to maximize horizontal coverage

Because antenna orientation has a major effect on coverage area, most antenna mounts permit the antenna to be rotated in all dimensions. For example, Figure 14-6 shows the antenna in the same vertical plane as the preceding image, but oriented at 45°, relative to the horizontal plane. With the antenna oriented this way, the AP provides a smaller coverage area on the floor where it is located, with added coverage on that portion of the floor above located to the right of the AP and added coverage on that portion of the floor below located to the left of the AP.

Figure 14-6. Antenna tilted to provide additional vertical coverage at the expense of horizontal coverage

Similarly, Figure 14-7 shows the antenna tilted at 45° in both the horizontal and vertical planes relative to the first image. With the antenna oriented this way, the AP provides some horizontal coverage on the floor where it is located, with added coverage on that portion of the floor above located to the right front of the AP and added coverage on that portion of the floor below located to the left rear of the AP.

Figure 14-7. Antenna tilted to provide additional front-to-rear vertical coverage at the expense of horizontal and vertical right-to-left coverage

AP antenna orientation has a major impact on coverage area. Changing antenna orientation by even a few degrees can make major differences in signal strength throughout the coverage area, benefiting some areas at the expense of others. Also, obstructions are not necessarily equally obstructive at different antenna orientations. When you install a wireless network, don't simply orient the AP antenna vertically and hope for the best. Spend some time playing around with antenna orientation to see how it affects signal strength throughout your coverage area. Use a notebook with a wireless adapter and run the site-survey software provided with the wireless adapter, or a package such as Network Stumbler (*http://www.stumbler.net*), to optimize the coverage area.

But Wait, There's More!

We ran out of space before we ran out of words. Originally, this chapter was much longer, and included detailed instructions for installing, configuring, and securing a wireless network. Alas, we had to cut that material to fit the available space. But all is not lost.

You can download this additional material in PDF form at *http://www.oreilly.com/catalog/repairpc/*.

THE WILD, WOOLLY 2.4 GHZ BAND

Most forms of wireless use the 2.4 GHz band, which is unlicensed and can be used freely by anyone. Wireless components must share this band with millions of other electronic components—everything from microwave ovens to baby monitors to cordless phones to wireless security systems to garage door openers—which means there's a lot of interference.

This fact was brought home to us, in spades, when Robert happened to be using his notebook computer to shoot some screen captures of a Super G wireless adapter configuration utility. Signal quality and data rate were at their highest, until Barbara turned on the microwave oven. The D-Link wireless adapter and AP held the connection, but the signal quality and data rate plummeted. It was as though someone had turned on a jammer, which of course is exactly what happened.

If you use wireless networking, be prepared to make compromises to deal with spectrum conflicts. You may even need to replace some of your other electronic gear, such as swapping out your 2.4 GHz cordless phones for 900 MHz or 5.8 GHz models.

Cases 15

At first glance, it might seem odd to suggest upgrading a system by replacing the case. When you think about it, though, there are some good reasons to replace your computer case, including:

Noise level

    Older and inexpensive cases were designed with little concern for noise level. Many modern cases are engineered to reduce noise levels, with features such as sound-deadening panels, unobstructed air intake vents, large fan grills, and rubber drive mounting blocks to isolate vibration and noise. By itself, a good case can't make a loud system quiet, but it can help reduce the din. When combined with other "Quiet PC" features such as a quiet power supply, quiet CPU cooler, quiet case fans, and so on, a well-designed case can help you build a nearly silent system.

Cooling efficiency

    Modern processors, video cards, and other components run hot. Older cases, designed in a time of 30W processors and 10W video cards, don't cope well with the heat load produced by modern 130W processors and 100W video cards. Modern cases are engineered with unobstructed air flow, shrouds, and other features designed to maximize cooling efficiency.

Appearance

    Standard computer cases are, not to put too fine a point upon it, ugly. Nowadays, good case companies have engineers to worry about noise levels and cooling efficiency, but they also employ industrial design experts to make sure that their products are also visually attractive. The best modern cases are attractive enough not just to have on display in your office, but in your living room.

And, of course, most new cases come with a new, higher-capacity power supply, which is no bad thing. If you're not prepared to replace your case, though, there are several improvements you can make to your existing case.

In This Chapter

Case Characteristics

Tweaking Your Current Case

Case Characteristics

Here are the important characteristics of cases.

Form factor

Form factor is the most important thing about a case, because it determines which motherboards and power supplies fit that case. Mainstream cases are available in *ATX* and *microATX* and *Extended ATX* form factors. ATX (sometimes called *Full ATX*) cases accept full-size ATX or smaller microATX motherboards and full-size ATX or smaller SFX power supplies. microATX (sometimes called μATX) cases accept only microATX motherboards. Some microATX cases accept either ATX or SFX power supplies; others accept only SFX power supplies. Extended ATX cases accept full ATX and oversize ATX motherboards and ATX power supplies, and are ordinarily used only for workstations and servers.

What the Heck Is BTX?

In mid-2004, Intel began shipping products based on their new *Balanced Technology Extended* (*BTX*) form factor, which will eventually replace ATX and its variants. BTX and its smaller variants, *microBTX* and *picoBTX*, are primarily a response to cooling problems and other inadequacies in the ATX specification that became evident as the power consumption and heat production of modern processors has continued to increase.

Although BTX motherboard sizes differ little from ATX and its variants, BTX specifies many changes in component layout and orientation, cooling, physical mounting, and so on. BTX motherboards and cases are of similar size and appearance to their ATX analogs, but are physically incompatible with ATX components.

In practical terms, the arrival of BTX is likely to have little short-term effect. Migration to BTX will not occur overnight—although Intel would like it to—but will take place gradually. ATX motherboards, cases, power supplies, and other components will remain available for years to come. For now, BTX components are scarce and sell at a premium. As we move into 2007 and 2008, BTX components will become mainstream, with ATX gradually relegated to upgrade-only status.

In short, you needn't be concerned about upgrading or repairing an ATX-based system now, because upgrade components are likely to remain available for the usable life of the system. In fact, we are likely to continue recommending ATX in preference to BTX for new systems into 2007, based on the lower cost and wider component availability of ATX components. For more information about BTX, see the Balanced Technology Extended (BTX) Interface Specification Version 1.0 at *http://www.formfactors.org*.

Style

Cases are available in many styles, including *low-profile desktop*, *standard desktop*, *micro-tower* (for microATX boards), *mini-tower*, *mid-tower*, and *full-tower*. Low-profile cases are popular for mass-market and business-oriented PCs, but we see little purpose for them. They take up more desk space than towers, provide poor expandability, and are difficult to work on. Micro-tower cases take up very little desk space, but otherwise share the drawbacks of low-profile cases. Mini/mid-tower styles—the dividing line between them is nebulous—are the most popular, because they consume little desktop space while providing good expandability. Full-tower cases take up no desk space at all, and are tall enough that optical drives are readily accessible. Their cavernous interiors make it very easy to work inside them, and they often provide better cooling than smaller cases. The drawbacks of full-tower cases are that they are more expensive (and heavier!) than other cases, sometimes significantly so, and that they may require using extension cables for keyboard, video, and/or mouse.

Figure 15-1. Antec Aria SFF case (image courtesy of Antec)

TAC-compliance

TAC (*Thermally-Advantaged Chassis*) cases cope with the high temperatures of modern processors by exhausting CPU heat directly to the exterior rather than inside the case. To accomplish this, TAC cases use a shroud that covers the processor and CPU cooler and a duct that connects the shroud to the side panel of the case. Because the location

Small Form Factor (SFF) Cases

A proprietary case style called *Small Form Factor* (*SFF*) is fast gaining popularity, primarily due to the efforts of Shuttle. Such systems are generally called "cubes," although they're really about the shape and size of a shoebox. SFF systems use standard Pentium 4 or Athlon 64 processors, and are designed to cram the power of a full-size PC into the smallest possible box.

SFF PCs have two important drawbacks. First, the form factor is nonstandard, which means you can use only motherboards that are designed to fit the specific case. Leading motherboard makers do not make SFF motherboards, so you are limited to motherboards from second- and third-tier makers. Second, cooling is critical when a high-performance processor, a fast hard drive, and a power supply of sufficient wattage are crammed into a shoebox-size enclosure. Although we do not have sufficient data to make an absolute prediction, we expect that the higher operating temperature of SFF PCs will lead to increased instability and a shorter life relative to similar components enclosed in a standard case. We recommend avoiding SFF PCs unless system size is your absolute highest priority.

One exception to the proprietary nature of SFF cases is the Antec Aria, shown in Figure 15-1. The Aria is slightly larger than proprietary SFF cases, which allows it to accept standard microATX motherboards.

of the processor is standardized on ATX-family motherboards and the TAC shroud and duct are adjustable, a TAC-compliant case can be used with nearly any motherboard, processor, and CPU cooler. Figure 15-2 shows the TAC-compliant Antec SLK2650BQE case, a popular mini-tower model, with the TAC vent visible on the left-side panel.

Why Antec?

Readers sometimes ask us why we endorse Antec products so strongly. The answer is simple: Antec products are high-quality, rock-solid reliable, competitively priced, and very widely distributed both online and in local stores. Local availability is an important consideration, because it can cost $25 or more to ship a case. Local big-box stores get deliveries in pallet loads, so the shipping cost for an individual case is small. That often means the total cost of a case is less at a local store than from online vendors with nominally lower prices.

Figure 15-2. Antec SLK2650BQE mini-tower case (image courtesy of Antec)

Figure 15-3 shows the TAC shroud and duct arrangement on the side panel of an Antec SLK2650BQE case. Like most TAC cases, this one uses a passive duct arrangement, depending on the CPU cooler fan to move air from the CPU cooler to the case exterior. But Antec makes provisions for mounting an optional supplemental fan between the side panel and duct to move more air.

Figure 15-3. Detail of TAC shroud/duct on an Antec SLK2650BQE case (image courtesy of Antec)

UPGRADING TO TAC

Some case makers, including Antec, offer replacement side panels for some of their older case models. The new side panel includes a TAC duct and shroud. If your case has a replacement side panel available, you can upgrade the case to TAC compliance simply by installing the new side panel. Of course, there aren't any TAC Police breaking down doors to check for TAC compliance, so the real reason for upgrading to TAC is to keep your processor running cooler and more reliably.

Some cases are not technically TAC-compliant but are designed to accomplish the same goal. For example, the Antec Sonata II, shown in Figure 15-4, is not TAC-compliant. Instead, Antec designed this case with a chassis air duct, visible as the dark gray area at the left of the case, that enhances cooling of both the processor and the video card.

Figure 15-4. Interior view of the Antec Sonata II mini-tower case (image courtesy of Antec)

Similarly, the Antec P180, shown in Figure 15-5, is not TAC-compliant, but is engineered to minimize noise and maximize cooling. The P180 reverses the usual arrangement, putting the power supply at the bottom of the case instead of at the top. The power supply is contained within its own air chamber to keep the heat produced by the power supply out of the main area of the case interior, and is cooled by a dedicated 120 mm fan. The motherboard and drive areas are cooled by two standard 120 mm fans (rear and top), with provision for adding a third 120 mm fan at the front and an 80 mm fan for the video card.

Figure 15-5. Interior view of the Antec P180 tower case (image courtesy of Antec)

Drive bay arrangement

The number and arrangement of drive bays may be unimportant if the system is unlikely to be upgraded later. Even the smallest cases provide at least one 3.5" external bay for a floppy drive, one 5.25" external bay for an optical drive, and one 3.5" internal bay for a hard disk. For flexibility, we recommend buying a case that provides at least one 3.5" external bay, two 5.25" external bays, and three or more 3.5" internal bays.

Accessibility

Cases vary widely in how easy they are to work on. Some use thumb screws and pop-off panels that allow complete disassembly in seconds without tools, while disassembling others requires a screwdriver and more work. Similarly, some cases have removable motherboard trays or drive cages that make it easier to install and remove components. The flip side of easy access is that unless they are properly engineered, easy-access cases are often less rigid than traditional cases. Years ago we worked on a system that experienced seemingly random disk errors. We replaced the hard disk, cables, disk controller, power supply, and other components, but errors persisted. As it turned out, the user kept a stack of heavy reference books on top of the case. As she added and removed books, the case was flexing enough to torque the hard disk in its mounting, causing disk errors. Rigid cases prevent such problems. The other aspect of accessibility is sheer size. It's easier to work inside a large case than a smaller case simply because there's more room.

Provisions for supplemental cooling

For basic systems, the power supply fan and CPU cooler fan may suffice. More heavily loaded systems—those with fast processors, multiple hard drives, a hot video card, and so on—require supplemental fans. Some cases have little or no provision for adding fans, while others provide mounting positions for half a dozen or more fans. In addition to the number of fans, the size of fans the case is designed to accept is important. Larger fans move more air while spinning more slowly, which reduces noise level. Look for a case that has mounting positions for at least one 120 mm rear fan and one 120 mm front fan (or already has one or both of those installed). Provisions for additional fans are desirable.

Construction quality

Cases run the gamut in construction quality. Cheap cases have flimsy frames, thin sheet metal, holes that don't line up and razor-sharp burrs and edges that make them dangerous to work on. High-quality cases have rigid frames, heavy sheet metal, properly aligned holes, and all edges rolled or deburred.

Material

PC cases have traditionally been made of thin sheet steel panels, with a rigid steel chassis to prevent flexing. Steel is inexpensive, durable, and strong, but it is also heavy. In the last few years, the popularity of LAN parties has increased, fueling a demand for lighter cases. A steel case light enough to be conveniently portable is insufficiently stiff, which has led case makers to produce aluminum cases for this specialty market. Although aluminum cases are indeed lighter than equivalent steel models, they are also more expensive. Unless saving a few pounds is a high priority, we recommend you avoid aluminum models. If weight is important, choose an aluminum LAN party case, such as the Antec Super LANBOY case, shown in Figure 15-6.

Figure 15-6. Antec Super LANBOY LAN party case (image courtesy of Antec)

Tweaking Your Current Case

If you're not prepared to replace your case, there are other things you can do to improve the cooling efficiency and reduce the noise level.

Improving cooling efficiency

The most important thing you can do to improve cooling efficiency is to keep the case clean, particularly the air intake grills and the fans themselves. Test your system periodically to determine its cooling efficiency. Use an ordinary thermometer to determine ambient room temperature and then measure the temperature of the air being exhausted by the rear case fan (not the power supply fan). If the exhaust air is 5° C (9°F) or more warmer than ambient room temperature, you need more or better fans.

DRESSING CABLES

One quick, easy, cheap thing you can do to improve air flow and cooling is to dress the cables. Before you declare your upgrade or repair complete, tie off all of the internal cables into neat bundles and tuck them out of the way. Use cable-ties or those yellow plastic thingies that come with garbage bags to secure the cables to the case frame or otherwise out of the way. Dressing the cables neatly does more than just improve air flow and cooling. It also prevents loose cables from fouling fans.

But you can't just add fans willy-nilly and expect your case to be cooled optimally. You have to consider the air flow pattern inside the case, and install fans to direct that air flow for optimum cooling. Ideally, you want cool room air to enter through the front of the case, be directed over the drives, expansion cards, memory, processor, and other heat-producing components, and then be exhausted from the rear of the case. The power supply fan provides some general system cooling, but its primary purpose is to cool the power supply itself. For general cooling, you need supplemental case fans, which are readily available from online vendors and local stores.

Your goal should be to use a combination of intake and exhaust fans to provide air movement through the case. If all of your fans blow in (intake), you pressurize the case and limit air flow to whatever can escape through the vents and other gaps in the case. If all of your fans blow out (exhaust), you create a vacuum, and again limit air flow to whatever can enter through the various gaps in the case. An ideal fan pattern puts one or two intake fans at the front of the case, and one or more exhaust fans at the back of the case. (The power supply fan is also usually an exhaust fan.)

I'D LIKE ONE INTAKE FAN AND ONE EXHAUST FAN, PLEASE

You can't buy an intake fan or an exhaust fan. These aren't different types of fans; a fan functions as an intake or exhaust fan depending on which direction you mount it. Look for an arrow or arrows on the body of the fan. If there is only one arrow, it indicates the direction of air flow. Some fans have two arrows, one for air flow direction and one for blade rotation direction. Which is which will be obvious when you look at the fan.

Supplemental case fans have these characteristics:

Size

Supplemental case fans are available in various standard sizes, including 80 mm, 90 mm, 92 mm, and 120 mm. Unless you are willing to do surgery on your case, select the size or sizes of fans that fit your existing mounting positions. If you have a choice of mounting positions that accept different-size fans, always choose the larger size. If they have the same design and rotation speed, a larger fan moves more air than a smaller fan, or, alternatively, moves the same amount of air at a lower rotation speed (and noise level).

Rotation speed

The rotation speed of a fan, specified in revolutions per minute (RPM), is stated for the nominal voltage (usually +12V) that the fan is designed to use and when it is running in free air. All other things being equal, a faster-running fan moves more air and produces more noise.

Some fans have variable speeds, set either via a multiposition switch—usually high, medium, and low—or a knob that sets fan speed over a continuously variable range. Even single-speed fans can be made variable, however, by altering the feed voltage. A fan designed to run on +12V, for example, can be run instead at +7V, which slows its speed significantly. The only limit to voltage adjustments is the required startup voltage, below which the fan may run if started spinning manually, but will not start spinning on its own. For most +12V fans, that limit is +7V.

Voltage can be adjusted in several ways. You can add a fixed resistor pack, available from online sources such as *http://www.endpcnoise.com* and *http://www.frozencpu.com*, that drops the +12V supply voltage to +7V or so. There are also fan-speed control consoles available, which fit an unused external 5.25" drive bay and provide a knob for adjusting fan speeds by increasing or decreasing the voltage. Finally, some power supplies provided dedicated "fan-only" power connectors that vary the voltage to the fan, under the control of the power supply.

Air flow rate

The *air flow rate* of a fan is specified in cubic feet per minute (CFM), and depends on the size, speed, and design of the fan. Variable-speed fans specify a range of flow rates from their minimum speed setting to the maximum, such as 10 CFM to 25 CFM. Nominal flow rates are invariably optimistic, as they assume an unobstructed fan. Actual flow rates are normally about half nominal.

Noise level

Noise level is specified in A-weighted decibels or dB(A), with lower numbers meaning a quieter fan. Once again, the noise level of variable-speed fans is specified as a range from lowest to highest speeds (and air flow rates), such as 20 dB(A) to 28 dB(A). If you are interested in reducing the noise level of your system, look for fans that are rated for 30 dB(A) or less at maximum speed. If your goal is a "silent PC," look for fans rated at 20 dB(A) or less. Nominal noise level ratings are also invariably optimistic, as they assume no contribution from grill noise, which may be substantial.

Power type

Most case fans are designed to be connected to a standard Molex (hard drive) power connector. Some are instead designed to connect to a 3-pin motherboard power header, which has the advantage of putting fan voltage/speed under motherboard controller. Before you buy a fan of the latter type, however, make sure you have an available motherboard power header to provide power to it. Alternatively, you can buy an adapter to convert a 4-pin Molex power cable to a 3-pin fan connector.

Bells and whistles

Some fans are designed to be visually attractive—for example, by using transparent blades and body—or to attract attention with LED illumination, fluorescent dyes, and similar gew-gaws. We have no general objection to these fancy fans, but some transparent fans use brittle plastic, which seems to resonate and increase fan noise. If you choose such a fan, try to get one with flexible blades.

Installing a supplemental case fan isn't difficult. Fans are ordinarily supplied with mounting screws or bolts, rubber isolation pads or a foam sound-deadening surround, and similar accessories. To install the fan, orient it inside the case, with its mounting hole locations aligned with the holes in the case. (Make sure it's oriented to blow in the right direction.)

Some fans secure with screws, which are driven through the mounting holes in the case and into the body of the fan. Others use bolts, which are inserted from outside the case, through holes in the body of the fan, and are secured by nuts on the inner surface of the fan. Neither of these methods isolates the fan from the case, so fan noise and vibration can be transferred to the case. We prefer to use flexible pull-through fan mounting connectors, as shown in Figure 15-7. To use these, pull the flexible connector through the body of the fan and case mounting hole until it snaps into place and then trim off the excess, leaving perhaps a quarter of an inch protruding to retain the fan. Trim them flush only if you want the fan to fall inward onto the motherboard. In conjunction with rubber isolation blocks or a foam surround, these flexible connectors reduce fan noise, sometimes noticeably. You can buy flexible fan mounts from companies that specialize in quiet PC components, such as EndPCNoise.com (*http://www.endpcnoise.com*) or FrozenCPU (*http://www.frozencpu.com*).

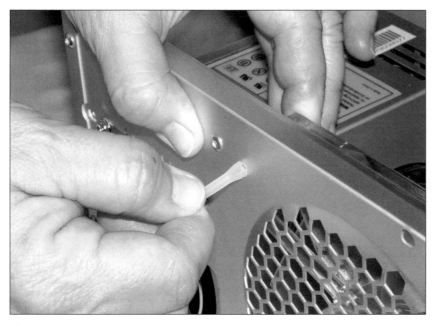

Figure 15-7. Using flexible pull-through fan mounting connectors

RUNNING GRILL-LESS

Fan grills protect fingers from spinning fan blades, but they reduce air flow and increase noise significantly. Depending on the fan and grill, it's not unusual for noise level to be doubled.

You can have safety and efficiency with a little effort. Remove the fan grill—you may have to cut it out—and substitute a 4" to 6" piece of PVC tubing of the appropriate diameter, secured with screws or adhesive. The PVC tubing presents very little resistance to air flow, so the fan can operate at maximum efficiency with minimal noise. (Make sure to increase the clearance between the back of the system and the wall to provide adequate room for the air to be exhausted.)

Although adding supplemental case fans is an easy and inexpensive way to improve cooling, there are other steps you can take:

TAC-in or TAC-out?

TAC systems are ordinarily designed to draw in cool outside air through the TAC duct and direct it onto the top of the CPU cooler. Thinking about that, we wondered why we'd want to exhaust CPU waste heat inside the case. Wouldn't it be better to exhaust the warm air from the CPU cooler directly to the outside of the case? After all, in a properly cooled system, the air temperature inside the case isn't much higher than ambient room temperature.

So we did some testing by reversing the usual direction of the air flow, exhausting hot air through the TAC duct rather than drawing in cool air. For most systems, we found little difference in CPU temperature either way, but for some systems, exhausting the warm air through the TAC duct allowed the CPU to run noticeably cooler. Only in systems with a "hot" video card did running TAC in standard intake mode yield lower CPU temperatures.

If you decide to run your TAC system "backwards," make sure the CPU fan is set to push air into the TAC shroud rather than drawing it in (you can do this simply by reinstalling the CPU cooler fan "upside-down"). Also, if you use a supplemental fan in the TAC housing, make sure that fan is set to exhaust air from the case rather than pushing it into the case. The last thing you want is two fans pushing in opposite directions.

Install a TAC side panel.

If you're upgrading an older system with a hot new processor, check to see whether there's a replacement side panel available for your case that adds a TAC shroud and duct. Removing CPU heat directly can reduce interior case temperatures by several degrees. With that excess heat disposed of by the TAC vent, case fans can run slower and quieter.

Make your own TAC panel.

If your current case is otherwise suitable and there's no replacement TAC side panel available for it, consider making your own. To do so, mark the location of the CPU on the side panel, and use a hole saw to cut a hole of appropriate size in the side panel. Measure the depth from the inside of the side panel to the top of the CPU cooler, and cut a tube of appropriate length from PVC pipe or other material of a diameter large enough to slide down over the top of the CPU cooler, being careful to allow clearance for air to be drawn in around the CPU cooler. (The material you use for the tube is not critical; even a cardboard tube works fine.)

Mount the tube to the side panel using screws or adhesive. If you want a finished appearance, you can buy some grill material at the hardware store. For even better cooling, you can install a case fan of the appropriate size between the side panel and the tube, making sure that this fan works with the CPU cooler fan, not against it.

Build your own chassis air duct.

You can build your own chassis air duct, similar to the duct shown with the Sonata II case, using cardboard, foamboard, or a similar material. Your goal should be a duct that covers the processor and CPU cooler, memory, and video card. Make sure to allow sufficient clearance between the duct and the motherboard for air to be drawn in. Design the duct to route that air over the CPU and other heat-producing components and then to be exhausted by the rear case fan.

Reducing noise level

Although case design has a limited impact on noise level, there are some changes you can make to your current case to reduce noise level:

Use mouse pads to isolate the case.

One of the easiest, cheapest ways to reduce system noise is to isolate the case from the floor or desk surface. Most cases have rubber or plastic feet, but these are often too hard to absorb the noise and vibration that the system transfers to the surface it sits upon. Use mouse pads or similar soft spongy material between the case feet and the floor or desktop to eliminate this source of noise. The improvement is usually minor, but sometimes it is quite noticeable.

Replace the power supply.

The power supply is one of the largest noise sources in most computers (the CPU cooler fan is the other). You can reduce the noise level of most systems significantly by replacing the original power supply with a quiet or silent model. Quiet power supplies—such as various models made by Antec, Nexus, PC Power & Cooling, Seasonic, Zalman, and others—are much quieter than standard power supplies, although they are audible if you are near the system and in a quiet room. Silent power supplies have no fans or other moving parts, and are completely silent.

Replace noisy old case fans.

The stock case fans in most systems were chosen for their low cost rather than for their noise level or cooling efficiency. Replacing the stock fans with better models can reduce noise level, sometimes dramatically.

Open up the air intakes.

Air moving through a grill or holes produces noise. If your case air intakes are small and/or obstructed by grills, that not only harms cooling efficiency by restricting air flow, it also adds to the noise level. By opening up these intakes, you can improve cooling and reduce noise at the same time. (We have on occasion taken a hacksaw to a case that had inadequate air intakes.)

Install sound-deadening material.

Online sources such as *http://endpcnoise.com* sell sound-absorbing insulation that can be applied to case panels and other interior case surfaces. We're of two minds about this stuff. While it's undoubtedly true that adding insulation can reduce noise levels significantly, it's also true that sound-deadening material also functions as thermal insulation, increasing interior case temperatures. If you choose to install sound-deadening material, don't overdo it. Make sure not to block air intakes, and keep a careful eye on system temperature.

Power Supplies and Power Protection

16

It's easy to forget that computers depend on a reliable, steady source of electric power. Power isn't sexy. PC enthusiasts talk for hours about the latest processor or video card, but seldom give a thought to such boring issues as power supplies and power protection. Experts, on the other hand, recognize that reliable power is the foundation of a reliable computer. If you take a peek at experts' computer rooms, you'll find that all of their systems have top-notch, high-capacity power supplies, backed up by industrial-strength power protection. If your computer and data are important to you, you would do well to emulate them.

Power Supplies

Power supplies lack glamour, so nearly everyone takes them for granted. That's a big mistake, because the power supply performs two critical functions: it provides regulated power to every system component, and it cools the computer. Many people who complain that Windows crashes frequently understandably blame Microsoft. But, without apologizing for Microsoft, the truth is that many such crashes are caused by low-quality or overloaded power supplies.

If you want a reliable, crash-proof system, use a high-quality power supply. In fact, we have found that using a high-quality power supply allows even marginal motherboards, processors, and memory to operate with reasonable stability, whereas using a cheap power supply makes even top-notch components unstable.

The sad truth is that it is almost impossible to buy a computer with a top-notch power supply. Computer makers count pennies, literally. Good power supplies don't win marketing brownie points, so few manufacturers are willing to spend $30 to $75 extra for a better power supply. For their premium lines, first-tier manufacturers generally use what we call midrange power supplies. For their mass-market, consumer-grade lines, even name-brand manufacturers may compromise on the power supply to meet a price point, using what we consider marginal power supplies both in terms of output and construction quality.

The following sections detail what you need to understand how to choose a good replacement power supply.

Power supply characteristics

The most important characteristic of a power supply is its *form factor*, which defines its physical dimensions, mounting hole locations, physical connector types and pinouts, and so on. All modern power supply form factors derive from the original *ATX form factor*, published by Intel in 1995.

When you replace a power supply, it's important to use one with the correct form factor, to ensure not only that the power supply physically fits the case, but also that it provides the correct types of power connectors for the motherboard and peripheral devices. Three power supply form factors are commonly used in current and recent systems:

ATX12V

ATX12V power supplies are the largest physically, available in the highest wattage ratings, and by far the most common. Full-size desktop systems use ATX12V power supplies, as do most mini-, mid-, and full-tower systems. Figure 16-1 shows an Antec TruePower 2.0 power supply, which is a typical ATX12V unit.

Figure 16-1. Antec TruePower 2.0 ATX12V power supply (image courtesy of Antec)

SFX12V

SFX12V (s-for-small) power supplies look like shrunken ATX12V power supplies, and are used primarily in small form factor microATX and FlexATX systems. SFX12V power supplies have lower capacities than ATX12V power supplies—typically 130W to 270W for SFX12V versus up to 600W or more for ATX12V—and are generally used in entry-level systems. Systems that were built with SFX12V power supplies can accept an ATX12V replacement if the ATX12V unit physically fits the case.

TFX12V

TFX12V (t-for-thin) power supplies are physically elongated (versus the cubic form of ATX12V and SFX12V units) but have capacities similar to SFX12V units. TFX12V power supplies are used in some small form factor (SFF) systems with total system volumes of 9 to 15 liters. Because of their odd physical shape, you can replace a TFX12V power supply only with another TFX12V unit.

Although it is less likely, you may encounter an *EPS12V* power supply (used almost exclusively in servers), a *CFX12V* power supply (used in microBTX systems), or an *LFX12V* power supply (used in picoBTX systems). Detailed specification documents for all of these form factors can be downloaded from *http://www.formfactors.org*.

THE 12V MODIFIER

In 2000, to accommodate the +12V requirements of their new Pentium 4 processors, Intel added a new +12V power connector to the ATX specification and renamed the specification ATX12V. Since then, each time Intel has updated a power supply specification or created a new one, it required this +12V connector, and used the 12V modifier in the name of the specification. Older systems use non-12V ATX or SFX power supplies. You can replace an ATX power supply with an ATX12V unit, or an SFX power supply with an SFX12V (or possibly an ATX12V) unit.

The changes from older versions of the ATX specification to newer versions and from ATX to smaller variants such as SFX and TFX have been evolutionary, with backward compatibility always kept firmly in mind. All aspects of the various form factors—including physical dimensions, mounting hole locations, and cable connectors—are rigidly standardized, which means you can choose among numerous industry-standard power supplies to repair or upgrade most systems, even older models.

ALL THE JUICE THAT FITS

When you replace your power supply, it's important to get a replacement unit that fits your case. If your old power supply is labeled ATX 1.X or 2.X or ATX12V 1.X or 2.X, you can install any current ATX12V power supply. If it is labeled SFX or SFX12V, you can install any current SFX12V power supply or, if the case has enough clearance, an ATX12V unit. If the old power supply is labeled TFX12V, only another TFX12V unit will fit. If your old power supply is not labeled with specification and version compliance, search the maker's web site for the model number of your current power supply. If all else fails, measure your current power supply and compare its dimensions with those of the units you are considering buying.

Chapter 16: Power Supplies and Power Protection

Here are some other important characteristics of power supplies:

Rated wattage

The nominal wattage that the power supply can deliver. Nominal wattage is a composite figure, determined by multiplying the amperages available at each of the several voltages supplied by a PC power supply. Nominal wattage is mainly useful for general comparison of power supplies. What really matters is the individual amperage available at different voltages, and those vary significantly between nominally similar power supplies.

TEMPERATURE MATTERS

Wattage ratings are meaningless unless they specify the temperature at which the rating was done. As temperature increases, the output capacity of a power supply decreases. For example, PC Power & Cooling rates wattage at 40° C, which is a realistic temperature for an operating power supply. Most power supplies are rated at only 25° C. That difference may seem minor, but a power supply rated at 450W at 25° C may deliver only 300W at 40° C. Voltage regulation may also suffer as temperature increases, which means that a power supply that nominally meets voltage regulation specifications at 25° C may be outside specifications during normal operation at 40° C or thereabouts.

Efficiency

The ratio of output power to input power expressed as a percentage. For example, a power supply that produces 350W output but requires 500W input is 70% efficient. In general, a good power supply is between 70% and 80% efficient, although efficiency depends on how heavily the power supply is loaded. Calculating efficiency is difficult, because PC power supplies are *switching power supplies* rather than *linear power supplies*. The easiest way to think about this is to imagine the switching power supply drawing high current for a fraction of the time it is running and no current the remainder of the time. The percentage of the time it draws current is called the *power factor*, which is typically 70% for a standard PC power supply. In other words, a 350W PC power supply actually requires 500W input 70% of the time and 0W 30% of the time.

Combining power factor with efficiency yields some interesting numbers. The power supply supplies 350W, but the 70% power factor means that it requires 500W 70% of the time. However, the 70% efficiency means that rather than actually drawing 500W, it must draw more, in the ratio 500W/0.7, or about 714W. If you examine the specifications plate for a 350W power supply, you may find that in order to supply 350W nominal, which is 350W/110V or about 3.18 amps, it must actually draw up to 714W/110V or about 6.5 amps. Other factors may increase that actual maximum amperage, so it's common to see 300W or 350W power supplies that actually draw as much as 8 or 10 amps maximum. That variance has planning implications, both for electrical circuits and for UPSs, which must be sized to accommodate the actual amperage draw rather than the rated output wattage.

High efficiency is desirable for two reasons. First, it reduces your electric bill. For example, if your system actually draws 200W, a 67%-efficient power supply consumes 300W (200/0.67) to provide that 200W, wasting 33% of the electricity you're paying for. An 80%-efficient power supply consumes only 250W (200/0.80) to provide that same 200W to your system. Second, wasted power is converted to heat inside your system. With the 67%-efficient power supply, your system must rid itself of 100W of waste heat, versus half that with the 80%-efficient power supply.

Regulation

One of the chief differences between premium power supplies and less expensive models is how well they are regulated. Ideally, a power supply accepts AC power, that is possibly noisy or outside specifications, and turns that AC power into smooth, stable DC power with no artifacts. In fact, no power supply meets the ideal, but good power supplies come much closer than cheap ones. Processors, memory, and other system components are designed to operate with pure, stable DC voltage. Any departure from that may reduce system stability and shorten component life. Here are the key regulation issues:

Ripple

A perfect power supply would accept the AC sine wave input and provide an utterly flat DC output. Real-world power supplies actually provide DC output with a small AC component superimposed upon it. That AC component is called *ripple*, and may be expressed as *peak-to-peak voltage* (p-p) in millivolts (mV) or as a percentage of the nominal output voltage. A high-quality power supply may have 1% ripple, which may be expressed as 1%, or as actual p-p voltage variation for each output voltage. For example, at +12V, a 1% ripple corresponds to +0.12V, usually expressed as 120mV. A midrange power supply may limit ripple to 1% on some output voltages, but soar as high as 2% or 3% on others. Cheap power supplies may have 10% or more ripple, which makes running a PC a crapshoot.

Load regulation

The load on a PC power supply can vary significantly during routine operations; for example, as a DVD burner's laser kicks in or an optical drive spins up and spins down. *Load regulation* expresses the ability of the power supply to supply nominal output power at each voltage as the load varies from maximum to minimum, expressed as the variation in voltage experienced during the load change, either as a percentage or in p-p voltage differences. A power

Power Factor

Power factor is determined by dividing the true power (W) by the apparent power (Volts × Amps, or VA). Standard power supplies have power factors ranging from about 0.70 to 0.80, with the best units approaching 0.99. Some newer power supplies use passive or active *power factor correction* (*PFC*), which can increase the power factor to the 0.95 to 0.99 range, reducing peak current and harmonic current. In contrast to standard power supplies that alternate between drawing high current and no current, PFC power supplies draw moderate current all the time. Because electrical wiring, circuit breakers, transformers, and UPSs must be rated for maximum current draw rather than average current draw, using a PFC power supply reduces the stress on the electrical system to which the PFC power supply connects.

supply with tight load regulation delivers near-nominal voltage on all outputs regardless of load (within its range, of course). A top-notch power supply regulates voltages on the critical *voltage rails*—+3.3V, +5V, and +12V—to within 1%, with 5% regulation on the less critical –5V and –12V rails. An excellent power supply might regulate voltage on all critical rails to within 3%. A midrange power supply might regulate voltage on all critical rails to within 5%. Cheap power supplies may vary by 10% or more on any rail, which is unacceptable.

Line regulation

An ideal power supply would provide nominal output voltages while being fed any input AC voltage within its range. Real-world power supplies allow the DC output voltages to vary slightly as the AC input voltage changes. Just as load regulation describes the effect of internal loading, *line regulation* can be thought of as describing the effects of external loading; for example, a sudden sag in delivered AC line voltage as an elevator motor kicks in. Line regulation is measured by holding all other variables constant and measuring the DC output voltages as the AC input voltage is varied across the input range. A power supply with tight line regulation delivers output voltages within specification as the input varies from maximum to minimum allowable. Line regulation is expressed in the same way as load regulation, and the acceptable percentages are the same.

Noise level

The power supply fan is one of the major noise sources in most PCs. If your goal is to reduce the noise level of your system, it's important to choose an appropriate power supply. *Noise-reduced power supplies*—models such as the Antec TruePower 2.0 and SmartPower 2.0, Enermax NoiseTaker, Nexus NX, PC Power & Cooling Silencer, Seasonic SS, and Zalman ZM—are designed to minimize fan noise, and can be the basis of a system that is nearly inaudible in a quiet room. *Silent power supplies*, such as the Antec Phantom 350 and the Silverstone ST30NF, have no fans at all and are almost totally silent (there may be a minor buzzing from the electrical components). In practical terms, there's seldom much advantage in using a fanless power supply. They are quite expensive relative to noise-reduced power supplies, and the noise-reduced units are sufficiently quiet that whatever noise they make is subsumed by the noise from case fans, the CPU cooler, hard drive rotation noise, and so on.

Power supply connectors

In the last few years, there have been some significant changes in power supplies, all of which have resulted directly or indirectly from the increased

Flying Off the Rails

Load regulation on the +12V rail became much more important when Intel shipped the Pentium 4. In the past, +12V was used primarily to run drive motors. With the Pentium 4, Intel began using 12V VRMs to supply the higher currents that Pentium 4 processors require. Recent AMD processors also use 12V VRMs to supply power to the processor. ATX12V-compliant power supplies are designed with this requirement in mind. Older and/or inexpensive ATX power supplies, although they may be rated for sufficient amperage on the +12V rail to support a modern processor, may not have adequate regulation to do so properly.

power consumption and changes in the voltages used by modern processors and other system components. When you replace a power supply in an older system, it's important to understand the differences between the older power supply and current units, so let's take a brief look at the evolution of ATX-family power supplies through the years.

For 25 years, every PC power supply has provided standard Molex (hard drive) and Berg (floppy drive) power connectors, which are used to power drives and similar peripherals. Where power supplies differ is in the types of connectors they use to provide power to the motherboard itself. The original ATX specification defined the 20-pin *ATX main power connector* shown in Figure 16-2. This connector was used by all ATX power supplies and early ATX12V power supplies.

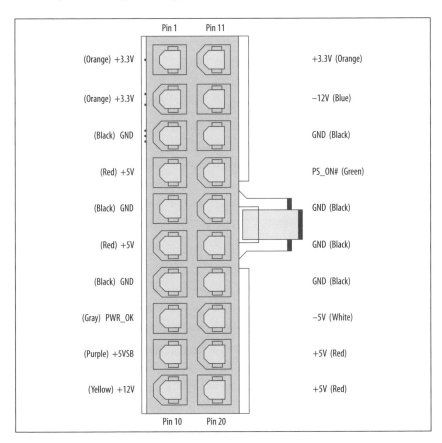

Figure 16-2. The 20-pin ATX/ATX12V main power connector

The 20-pin ATX main power connector was designed at a time when processors and memory used +3.3V and +5V, so there are numerous +3.3V and +5V lines defined for this connector. The contacts within the connector body are rated to carry at most 6 amps. That means the three +3.3V lines can carry 59.4W (3.3V × 6A × 3 lines), the four +5V lines can carry 120W, and the one +12V line can carry 72W, for a total of about 250W.

Chapter 16: Power Supplies and Power Protection

That setup sufficed for early ATX systems, but as processors and memory became more power-hungry, system designers soon realized that the 20-pin connector provided inadequate current for newer systems. Their first modification was to add the *ATX auxiliary power connector*, shown in Figure 16-3. This connector—defined in ATX specifications 2.02 and 2.03 and in ATX12V 1.X, but dropped from later versions of the ATX12V specification—uses contacts rated for 5 amps. Its two +3.3V lines therefore add 33W of +3.3V carrying capacity, and its one +5V line adds 25W of +5V carrying capacity, for a total addition of 58W.

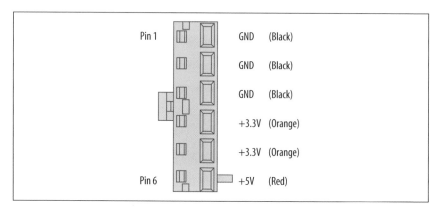

Figure 16-3. The 6-pin ATX/ATX12V auxiliary power connector

Intel dropped the auxiliary power connector from later versions of the ATX12V specification because it was superfluous for Pentium 4 processors. The Pentium 4 used +12V power rather than the +3.3V and +5V used by earlier processors and other components, so there was no longer any need for additional +3.3V and +5V. Most power supply makers stopped providing the auxiliary power connector soon after the Pentium 4 shipped in early 2000. If your motherboard requires the auxiliary power connector, that is sufficient evidence that that system is too old to be economically upgradable.

While the auxiliary power connected provided extra +3.3V and +5V current, it did nothing to increase the amount of +12V current available to the motherboard, and that turned out to be critical. Motherboards use *VRMs* (*voltage regulator modules*) to convert the relatively high voltages supplied by the power supply to the low voltages required by the processor. Earlier motherboards used +3.3V or +5V VRMs, but the increased power consumption of the Pentium 4 made it necessary to change to +12V VRMs. That created a major problem. The 20-pin main power connector could provide at most 72W of +12V power, much less than needed to power a Pentium 4 processor. The auxiliary power connector added no +12V, so yet another supplementary connector was needed.

Intel updated the ATX specification to include a new 4-pin 12V connector, called the *+12V Power Connector* (or, casually, the *P4 connector*, although recent AMD processors also use this connector). At the same time, they renamed the ATX specification to the ATX12V specification to reflect the addition of the +12V connector. The +12V connector, shown in Figure 16-4, has two +12V pins, each rated to carry 8 amps—for a total of 192W of +12V power—and two ground pins. With the 72W of +12V power provided by the 20-pin main power connector, an ATX12V power supply can provide as much as 264W of +12V power, more than sufficient for even the fastest processors.

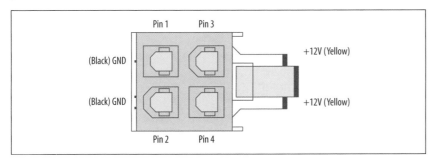

Figure 16-4. The 4-pin +12V power connector

The +12V power connector is dedicated to providing power to the processor, and attaches to a motherboard connector near the processor socket to minimize power losses between the power connector and the processor. Because the processor was now powered by the +12V connector, Intel removed the auxiliary power connector when they released the ATX12V 2.0 specification in 2000. From that time, all new power supplies came with the +12V connector, and a few to this day continue to provide the auxiliary power connector.

These changes over time mean that a power supply in an older system may have one of the following four configurations (from oldest to newest):

- 20-pin main power connector only
- 20-pin main power connector and 6-pin auxiliary power connector
- 20-pin main power connector, 6-pin auxiliary power connector, and 4-pin +12V connector
- 20-pin main power connector and 4-pin +12V connector

Unless the motherboard requires the 6-pin auxiliary connector, you can use any current ATX12V power supply to replace any of these configurations.

That brings us to the present ATX12V 2.X specification, which made more changes to the standard power connectors. The introduction of the PCI Express video standard in 2004 again raised the old issue of the +12V current available on the 20-pin main power connector being limited to 6 amps (or 72W total). The +12V connector can provide plenty of +12V current, but it is dedicated to the processor. A fast PCI Express video card can easily draw more than 72W of +12V current, so something needed to be done.

Intel could have introduced yet another supplementary power connector, but instead it decided this time to bite the bullet and replace the aging 20-pin main power connector with a new main power connector that could supply more +12V current to the motherboard. The new 24-pin *ATX12V 2.0 main power connector*, shown in Figure 16-5, was the result.

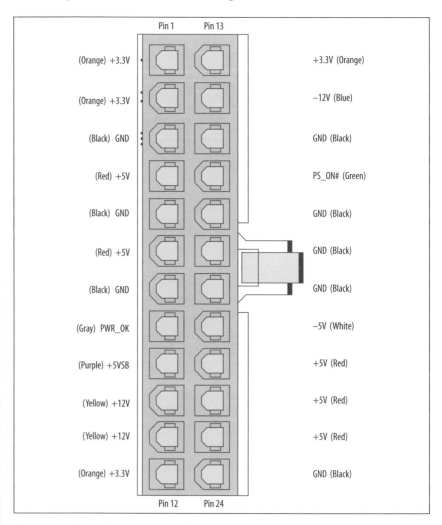

Figure 16-5. The 24-pin ATX12V 2.0 main power connector

The 24-pin main power connector adds four wires to those of the 20-pin main power connector, one ground (COM) wire, and one additional wire each for +3.3V, +5V, and +12V. As is true of the 20-pin connector, the contacts within the body of the 24-pin connector are rated to carry at most 6 amps. That means the four +3.3V lines can carry 79.2W (3.3V × 6A × 4 lines), the five +5V lines can carry 150W, and the two +12V lines can carry 144W, for a total of about 373W. With the 192W of +12V provided by the +12V power connector, a modern ATX12V 2.0 power supply can provide a total of up to about 565W.

One would think 565W would suffice for any system. Not true, alas. The problem, as usual, is a question of which voltages are available where. The 24-pin ATX12V 2.0 main power connector allocates one of its +12V lines to PCI Express video, which at the time the specification was released was thought to be sufficient. But the fastest current PCI Express video cards can consume far more than the 72W that dedicated +12V line can provide. For example, we have an NVIDIA 6800 Ultra video adapter that has a peak +12V draw of 110W.

Obviously, some means of providing supplemental power was necessary. Some high-current AGP video cards addressed this problem by including a Molex hard drive connector, to which you could attach a standard peripheral power cable. PCI Express video cards use a more elegant solution. The 6-pin *PCI Express graphics power connector*, shown in Figure 16-6, was defined by PCISIG (*http://www.pcisig.org*)—the organization responsible for maintaining the PCI Express standard—specifically to provide the additional +12V current needed by fast PC Express video cards. Although it is not yet an official part of the ATX12V specification, this connector is well-standardized and present on most current power supplies. We expect it to be incorporated in the next update of the ATX12V specification.

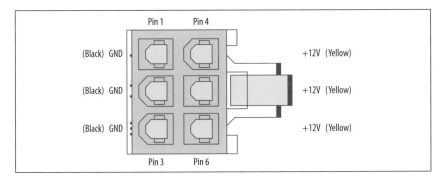

Figure 16-6. The 6-pin PCI Express graphics power connector

The PCI Express graphics power connector uses a plug similar to the +12V power connector, with contacts also rated to carry 8 amps. With three +12V lines at 8 amps each, the PCI Express graphics power connector can provide up to 288W (12 × 8 × 3) of +12V current, which should suffice for even the fastest future graphics cards. Because some PCI Express motherboards can support dual PCI Express video cards, some power supplies now include two PCI Express graphics power connectors, which boosts the total +12V power available to graphics cards to 576W. Added to the 565W available on the 24-pin main power connector and the +12V connector, that means an ATX12V 2.0 power supply could be built with a total capacity of 1,141W. (The largest we know of is a 1,000W unit available from PC Power & Cooling.)

With all of the changes over the years, device power connectors had been neglected. Power supplies made in 2000 included the same Molex (hard drive) and Berg (floppy drive) power connectors as power supplies made in 1981. That changed with the introduction of Serial ATA, which uses a different power connector. The 15-pin *SATA power connector*, shown in Figure 16-7, includes six ground pins, and three pins each for +3.3V, +5V, and +12V. In this case, the high number of voltage-carrying pins is not intended to support higher current—an SATA hard drive draws little current, and each drive has its own power connector—but to support the make-before-break and break-before-make connections needed to allow hot-plugging, or connecting/disconnecting a drive without turning off its power.

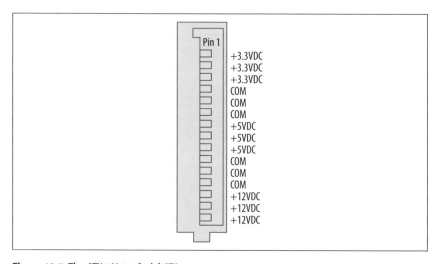

Figure 16-7. The ATX12V 2.0 Serial ATA power connector

Despite all of these changes throughout the years, the ATX specification has gone to great lengths to ensure backward compatibility of new power supplies with old motherboards. That means, with very few exceptions, you can connect a new power supply to an old motherboard, or vice versa.

BEWARE OLDER DELL SYSTEMS

For a few years in the late 1990s, Dell used standard connectors on its motherboards and power supplies, but with nonstandard pin connections. Connecting a standard ATX power supply to one of these nonstandard Dell motherboards (or vice versa) could destroy the motherboard and/or power supply. Fortunately, these systems are now so old that they are no longer economically upgradable. Still, if you find yourself replacing the power supply or motherboard in an older Dell system, be absolutely certain that it is not one of the nonstandard Dell units. To do so, check the model number of the system on the PC Power & Cooling web site (*http://www.pcpowerandcooling.com*). PC Power & Cooling sells replacement power supplies for these nonstandard Dell systems, but given that the youngest such system is now quite old, it's anyone's guess how long PC Power & Cooling will continue to sell these nonstandard power supplies.

Even the change in the main power connector from 20 to 24 pins presents no problem, because the newer connector keeps the same pin connections and keying for pins 1 through 20, and simply adds pins 21 through 24 onto the end of the older 20-pin layout. As Figure 16-8 shows, an old 20-pin main power connector fits the 24-pin main power connector perfectly. In fact, the main power connector socket on all 24-pin motherboards we have seen is designed specifically to accept a 20-pin cable. Note the full-length ledge on the motherboard socket in Figure 16-8, which is designed to allow a 20-pin cable to latch into place.

Figure 16-8. A 20-pin ATX main power connector connected to a 24-pin motherboard

Of course, the 20-pin cable doesn't include the extra +3.3V, +5V, and +12V wires that are present on the 24-pin cable, which raises a potential problem. If the motherboard requires the extra current available on the 24-pin cable to operate, it can't run using on the 20-wire cable. As a workaround, most 24-pin motherboards provide a standard Molex (hard drive) connector socket somewhere on the motherboard. If you use that motherboard with a 20-wire power cable, you must also connect a Molex cable from the power supply to the motherboard. That Molex cable provides the extra +5V and +12V (although not +3.3V) needed by the motherboard to operate. (Most motherboards do not have +3.3V requirements higher than the 20-wire cable can meet; those that do can use a supplemental VRM to convert some of the additional +12V supplied by the Molex connector to +3.3V.)

Because the 24-pin ATX main power connector is a superset of the 20-pin version, it's also possible to use a 24-pin power supply with a 20-pin motherboard. To do so, seat the 24-pin cable in the 20-pin socket, with the

Figure 16-9. A 24-pin ATX main power connector connected to a 20-pin motherboard

four unused pins hanging over the edge. The cable and motherboard socket are keyed to prevent installing the cable improperly. One possible problem is illustrated in Figure 16-9. Some motherboards put capacitors, connectors, or other components so close to the ATX main power connector socket that there's insufficient clearance for the extra four pins of the 24-pin power cable. In Figure 16-9, for example, those extra pins intrude on the secondary ATA socket.

Fortunately, there's an easy workaround for this problem. Various companies produce 24-to-20-pin adapter cables like the one shown in Figure 16-10. The 24-pin cable from the power supply connects to one end of the cable (the left end in this illustration), and the other end is a standard 20-pin connector that plugs directly into the 20-pin socket on the motherboard. Many high-quality power supplies include such an adapter in the box. If yours doesn't and you need an adapter, you can purchase one from most online computer parts vendors or a well-stocked local computer store.

Figure 16-10. An adapter cable to use a 24-pin ATX main power connector with a 20-pin motherboard

Choosing a Power Supply

Use the following guidelines to choose a power supply appropriate for your system:

Choose the correct form factor.

Above all, make sure the power supply you buy fits your case.

Choose a name-brand power supply.

There are literally scores of brands of power supplies available, many of which are made in the same Chinese factories and simply have different labels attached to them. Most of those are of mediocre quality or worse, but some good name-brand power supplies are made in China. For years we have exclusively used and recommended units from two companies, Antec (*http://www.antec.com*) and PC Power & Cooling (*http://www.pcpowerandcooling.com*). Both produce a wide range of models in different capacities. One of them is probably right for your needs.

Choose a power supply with sufficient capacity.

When it comes to power supplies, too much capacity is far better than too little. Using a 450W power supply on a system that draws only 250W does no harm; assuming equal efficiencies, the 450W unit consumes the same amount of power as would a 250W unit. Using a higher-capacity power supply than necessary costs a bit more, but has several advantages. The larger power supply generally runs cooler, because its fans were designed to cool the unit when it runs at full capacity. The larger unit typically provides tighter voltage regulation because it's not being stressed. And when it's time to add a faster processor or video card, the larger power supply has enough excess capacity to handle the additional load.

It's possible to add the maximum current draws for all system components and size the power supply on that basis. The problem with that method is that it can be nearly impossible to determine those draws for all components, especially motherboards and expansion cards. If you want to keep it simple, size your power supply according to the following configurations:

Basic system

For a system with a slow processor, 256 MB to 512 MB of RAM, embedded video, one hard drive, one optical drive, and zero or one expansion card, install a 300W or larger power supply.

Mainstream system

For a system with a midrange processor, 512 MB to 1 GB of RAM, a midrange video adapter, one or two hard drives, one or two optical drives, and one or two expansion cards, install a 400W or larger power supply.

High-performance system

For a system with a fast processor, more than 1 GB of RAM, one or two fast video adapters, two or three hard drives, one or two optical drives, and two or more expansion cards, install a 500W or larger power supply.

Choose a high-efficiency power supply.

Don't buy any power supply, particularly a high-capacity unit, that is rated at less than 70% efficiency at moderate to high loads. (Power supplies are typically less efficient at very light loads.)

Choose a quiet power supply.

Noise-reduced power supplies used to sell at significant premiums over standard power supplies. That's no longer true. Mainstream "quiet" power supplies such as the Antec TruePower 2.0 and PC Power & Cooling Silencer series sell for little or no more than standard power supplies of equal quality that produce considerably more noise. Even if your goal is not to produce a quiet PC, there's little point to choosing a noisy unit when quieter units are so readily available.

Installing a power supply

Before you do anything else, verify that the new power supply is set to the correct input voltage. Some power supplies detect the input voltage and set themselves automatically, but some must be set manually. If your power supply is of the latter type, check the position of the slide switch to make sure it's set for the correct input voltage, as shown in Figure 16-11.

Figure 16-11. Verify that the power supply is set for the proper input voltage

AVOID FIREWORKS

If you connect a power supply set for 230V to a 115V receptacle, no harm is done. The system receives half the voltage it requires, and won't boot. But if you connect a power supply set for 115V to a 230V receptacle, the system receives twice the voltage it's designed to use, and is destroyed instantly in clouds of smoke and showers of sparks.

Standard power supplies are secured with four screws. To remove a power supply, disconnect the AC supply cord, the motherboard power cable(s), and all device power cables. Use one hand to hold the power supply in place while removing the four screws that secure it, and then lift it straight out. Some power supplies use a locking tab and slot arrangement, so you may have to slide the power supply a short distance to clear the tab before lifting it out. To install a power supply, reverse that process. Slide the power supply into place, as shown in Figure 16-12, making sure that the locking tab, if present, mates with the slot.

Figure 16-12. Slide the power supply into place

Once the power supply is in place, align the screw holes and insert the screws, as shown in Figure 16-13. If necessary, support the power supply with one hand while you insert screws with the other. Many good cases have a tray that supports the power supply, while other cases simply leave the power supply hanging in mid-air, secured only by the screws. In the latter situation, you may want to get someone to volunteer a second pair of hands to hold the power supply while you insert the screws, particularly if you're working in an awkward position. We've seen at least one motherboard destroyed by a dropped power supply, which ripped the processor, heatsink/fan, and socket right out of the motherboard on its way past.

Figure 16-13. Secure the power supply with the four screws provided

The next step in assembling the system is to connect the power cables from the power supply to the motherboard. The 20-pin or 24-pin main power connector is usually located near the right front edge of the motherboard. Locate the corresponding cable coming from the power supply. The main power connector is keyed, so verify that the cable is aligned properly before you attempt to seat it.

Once everything is aligned, press down firmly until the connector seats, as shown in Figure 16-14. It may take significant pressure to seat the connector, and you should feel it snap into place. The locking tab on the side of the connector should snap into place over the corresponding nub on the socket. Make sure the connector seats fully. A partially seated main power connector may cause subtle problems that are very difficult to troubleshoot.

All recent Intel systems and many AMD systems require the ATX12V +12V power connector. On most motherboards, the +12V power connector is located near the processor socket. Orient the cable connector properly relative to the motherboard connector, and press the cable connector into place until the plastic tab locks, as shown in Figure 16-15.

Figure 16-14. Connect the Main ATX Power Connector

Figure 16-15. Connect the ATX12V Power Connector

After you connect the motherboard power connectors, connect the power cables for the following items:

- Any supplementary power connectors present, such as the supplementary Molex connector on the motherboard, the PCI Express graphics power connector, the fan or supplementary power connector on your AGP video card, and so on

- All hard drives, optical drives, tape drives, floppy drives, and so on

- Any supplemental fans that connect to the power supply rather than to the motherboard

Once you've verified that everything is installed and connected correctly, dress the cables, reconnect the main power cable, and apply power to the system.

Troubleshooting power supplies

Suspect a power supply problem if you experience any of the following symptoms, particularly in combination:

- Memory errors. Such errors may be caused by defective or poorly seated memory or by overheating, but insufficient or poorly regulated power from a failing or inadequate power supply is a likely cause. If a memory testing utility such as Memtest86 reports errors at a consistent address or range of addresses, the problem is probably the memory itself. If memory errors occur at random, nonreproducible addresses, the problem is most likely the power supply.

- Sporadic or regular boot failures. Obviously, such errors may be caused by hard drive, cable, or disk controller problems, but inadequate or poorly regulated power is also a common cause of this problem.

- Spontaneous reboots or system lockups during routine operations, especially during OS installations, that are not attributable to running a particular program. Numerous other factors can cause this problem, but one common cause is insufficient or poorly regulated power to the memory and/or processor.

- Lockups after you install a new processor, memory, drive, or expansion card. Driver issues aside, this problem commonly occurs when new components overload a marginal power supply. This problem is particularly likely to occur if you make dramatic changes to the system, such as replacing a slow processor with a fast, high-current processor or adding a high-current video card. The power supplies provided with commercial systems, particularly inexpensive ones, often have very little reserve.

In-depth power supply troubleshooting is impractical unless you have a well-equipped test bench. There are, however, a couple of things you can do to isolate the problem to the power supply:

Use the motherboard monitoring utility.

Most motherboard makers provide a monitoring utility to track system temperatures, fan speeds, and power supply voltages. (Intel, for example, provides the Intel Active Monitor, shown in Figure 16-16.) Install and enable this utility and use it to keep an eye on voltages. Most monitoring utilities allow you to set threshold values. If a voltage drops below or climbs above the acceptable range, the monitoring utility generates an alert. Some monitoring utilities allow you to log data, which can be very helpful in troubleshooting power supply problems.

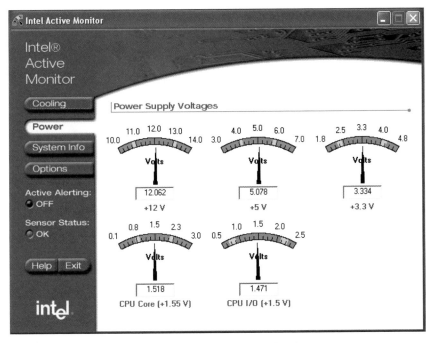

Figure 16-16. Use the motherboard monitoring utility to watch voltages

Swap the power supply for a known-good unit.

If you have a spare known-good power supply or a second system with a compatible power supply, try installing the known-good unit temporarily. If the problems stop, it's likely that the original power supply is marginal or defective.

Power Protection

Even the best power supply is helpless without a source of reliable, steady AC power. Simply plugging your system into a wall receptacle and hoping for the best is a sure road to disaster, sooner or later. Before we smartened up, we lost many hours' work to power failures, and more than one system to lightning damage. All of that was preventable, if only we'd installed proper power protection. There are two types of power protection.

Advice from Brian Bilbrey

At home, I keep a new ATX12V Antec power supply on the shelf. That power supply is equivalent to the most powerful one currently in my collection of computers, and so can be used to replace any of them. Power supplies have moving parts to keep the system cool, and also have first exposure to any input power problems, so they are the single most likely component to fail. That invariably happens on Sunday night at 9:03 PM with a presentation due on Monday morning. Spares on hand are good.

Passive power protection

> *Passive power protection* defends your system against spikes and other power anomalies that might damage the system or cause it to hang, but does nothing to protect against power failures. The most common form of passive power protection is the familiar surge suppressor outlet strip.

Active power protection

> *Active power protection* provides backup power to allow the system to continue running when utility power fails. The most common form of active power protection is a battery-backed backup power supply. Most active power protection devices also provide at least minimal passive protection.

In this section, we'll take a brief look at both types of protection.

Passive power protection

The best first step in protecting your computer from surges, spikes, and other garbage on the utility power line is to install some form of passive power protection. There is a bewildering array of passive power protection devices available, from the $5 outlet strips sold by hardware stores to $500 power conditioners sold by specialty vendors. As you might expect, the more expensive devices are superior in reliability, the level of protection they provide, and their ability to withstand damage.

You don't need to spend $500 on passive power protection, but we do recommend using high-quality surge protectors on all your systems. Stick with high-end models from APC (*http://www.apc.com*), Belkin (*http://www.belkin.com*), or Tripp Lite (*http://www.tripplite.com*), and you won't go far wrong. Plan to spend at least $40 to $50 for a high-quality surge protector with basic AC protection, and as much as $100 for one of similar quality with additional features such as video and broadband Internet ports. Figure 16-17 shows the $90 Tripp Lite HT10DBS surge protector, which is designed for home theater systems, but is equally at home protecting our computer room.

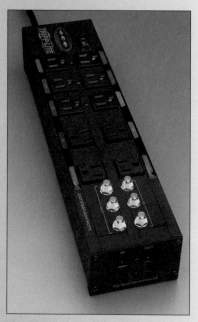

Figure 16-17. The Tripp Lite HT10DBS surge protector (image courtesy of Tripp Lite)

QUIS CUSTODIET IPSOS CUSTODES?

The ancient Romans pondered the question: Who will guard the guardians? When it comes to surge protectors, the question is: What will protect the protectors? The answer is *defense in depth*. The best first line of defense is a whole-house surge suppressor. These relatively inexpensive devices connect between the utility grid and your breaker panel, at the service entrance where electric power enters your home. A good whole-house surge suppressor safely dissipates massive overvoltages and overcurrents, such as those produced by nearby lightning strikes. A whole-house surge suppressor doesn't take the place of using individual suppressors on sensitive equipment, but it does reduce spikes and surges to a level that individual protectors can easily deal with.

In most jurisdictions, these devices must be installed by a licensed electrician. Even if that's not true where you live, we recommend paying a qualified person to do the job. Either that, or have your spouse standing by with a 2×4, defibrillator, and burn kit in case you grab the wrong wire.

Active power protection

For a corporation, active power protection can mean anything up to standby generators and alternative power grids. In a home or SOHO environment, though, active power protection means a backup power supply.

THEY SAY UPS, WE SAY BPS

There really is a difference between an *uninterruptable power supply* (*UPS*) and a *standby power supply* (*SPS*), but common usage now designates a unit properly termed an SPS as a UPS. We call a unit of either sort a *backup power supply* (*BPS*), which neatly sidesteps the terminology problem.

A BPS comprises a battery and some supporting circuitry, and is designed to supply power to your PC for a short period if the utility power fails. This temporary reprieve allows you to save your work and shut down the PC in an orderly fashion. BPSs differ in the quality of the power they supply, how much power they can supply, and for how long they can supply it. BPSs also condition the utility power to protect equipment against spikes, surges, drops, brownouts, and electrical noise.

BPS types

All BPSs have three common elements: a *battery*, which stores electrical energy against power failures; an *inverter*, which converts DC voltage supplied by the battery to the AC voltage required by the load; and *charging circuitry*, which converts AC mains power to the DC voltage required to charge the battery. IEEE recognizes three categories of BPS:

Online

An *online UPS* (often called a *true UPS* or a *dual-conversion UPS*, to differentiate it from an SPS) connects the load directly to the inverter, which converts DC voltage supplied by the battery to standard AC voltage. The charging circuitry charges the battery constantly while the UPS is operating, and the equipment always runs from battery power supplied by the inverter. Online UPSs cost more than SPSs, described shortly, but have two advantages. Because the PC runs on battery power all the time, there is no switch-over time, and no switch to fail. Also, because the PC does not connect to mains power, it is effectively isolated from AC line problems.

Don't Leave the Back Door Open

When you install power protection, make sure to protect every cable that connects to your system. It does no good to protect the AC power line if you leave a fax line, cable TV line, or cable modem line unprotected. Surges and spikes can arrive on any wire that connects to your computer, directly or indirectly.

Line-interactive

A *line-interactive UPS*, also called a *single-conversion online UPS*, differs from an online UPS in that the load normally runs primarily from utility power as long as that power is available. Rather than convert utility power to DC, use it to charge the battery, and then reconvert it to AC for the load (the "dual-conversion" part), a line-interactive UPS feeds utility power directly to the load under normal conditions. Minor variations in utility power are smoothed out by the inverter using battery power. The defining characteristics of a line-interactive UPS are that the inverter runs at all times, and that the load is always dynamically shared between inverter and utility power. During routine operation, utility power may support 99% of the load and the inverter only 1%. During a brownout, the inverter may support 10% or more of the load. Only during a blackout does the inverter assume 100% of the load. A true line-interactive UPS has no switch-over time, because the inverter and utility power dynamically share the load at all times, so a power failure simply means that the inverter instantaneously assumes 100% of the load. Although line-interactive units do not isolate the load from the AC line to the extent that an online UPS does, they are quite good at maintaining clean, steady AC to the load. Line-interactive UPSs are common in data centers, but uncommon in the PC environment.

Offline

The most common form of BPS used with PCs is an *offline power supply*, sometimes called a *standby power supply* (*SPS*). BPS marketers dislike "standby" and downright hate "offline," so offline power supplies are always described as "uninterruptable" power supplies, which they are not. The defining characteristics of an SPS are that it has a switch and that the inverter is not always running. During normal operation, the switch routes utility power directly to the load. When utility power fails, that switch quickly disconnects the load from the utility power and reconnects it to the inverter, which continues to power the equipment from battery. SPSs are less expensive than online and line-interactive units, because they can use a relatively inexpensive inverter, one rated for low duty cycle and short run time.

WAIT JUST A MOMENT, PLEASE

Most PC power supplies have sufficient "hold-up" time to continue supplying power to the system for the few milliseconds the SPS requires to switch over to battery power. That's not necessarily true for external devices that are powered by a power brick, which may not have enough "inertia" to keep powering the external device during the time required for the SPS to switch to battery power. For noncritical externally powered devices like speakers, that doesn't matter. But it may matter very much for an external hard drive, which may corrupt data if the power fails even momentarily, including failures that are too short to cause the lights to flicker.

We had never thought about this issue until one of our readers pointed it out. In retrospect, this may explain several puzzling reports we've had of external USB hard drives being corrupted without any obvious explanation.

Unlike online and line-interactive units, SPSs do not condition or regenerate incoming AC before supplying it to the load. Instead, they pass utility AC power through a passive filter similar to an ordinary surge suppressor, which means that SPSs do not provide power as clean as that provided by online and line-interactive units. In theory, SPSs have another drawback relative to online and line-interactive units. Actual switching time may be considerably longer than nominal under extended low-voltage conditions and with partially depleted batteries. Because the hold-up time of a PC power supply decreases under marginal low-voltage conditions, in theory an SPS may require longer to switch than the hold-up time of the PC power supply, resulting in a system crash. In practice, good SPSs have typical switching times of 2 to 4 ms and maximum switching times of 10 ms or less, and good PC power supplies have hold-up times of 20 ms or longer at nominal voltage and 15 ms or longer during sustained marginal under-voltage conditions, which means this is seldom a problem. Two types of SPS are common:

Standard SPS

> A *standard SPS* has only two modes—full utility power or full battery power. As long as utility power is within threshold voltage limits (which can be set on many units), the SPS simply passes utility power to the equipment. When utility power dips beneath threshold, the SPS transfers the load from using 100% utility power to using 100% battery power. Some standard SPSs also transfer to battery when utility voltage exceeds an upper threshold. That means that the SPS switches to battery every time a surge, sag, or brownout occurs, which may be quite frequently. This all-or-nothing approach cycles the battery frequently, which reduces battery life. More important, frequent alarms for minor power problems cause many people to turn off the alarm, which may delay recognition of an actual outage so long that the battery runs down and work is lost. Most entry-level SPS models are standard SPSs. The American Power Conversion (APC) Back-UPS series, for example, are standard SPSs.

Line-boost SPS

> A *line-boost SPS* adds *line-boost* mode to the two modes of the standard SPS. A line-boost SPS is sometimes advertised as a line-interactive UPS, which it is not. Unlike line-interactive units, which use battery power to raise AC output voltage to nominal, line-boost units simply have an extra transformer tap, which they use to increase output voltage by a fixed percentage (typically, 12% to 15%) when input voltage falls below threshold. For example,

Marketing-speak

Nowadays, even the best manufacturers describe their line-boost models as "line interactive" units. Although we prefer to reserve the term "line interactive" for delta-conversion online UPSs, that's probably a losing battle. There's nothing wrong with a good line-boost unit. In fact, it's the best choice for most home and SOHO applications. We use Falcon Electric line-boost units to protect several of our own systems.

when AC input falls to 100VAC, a line-interactive unit uses battery power to raise it 15V to 115VAC nominal. For 95VAC input, the line-interactive unit raises it 20V to 115VAC nominal. For 100VAC input, a line-boost unit uses the extra tap to raise output voltage by the fixed percentage (we'll assume 12%), yielding 112VAC output. For 95VAC input, the line-boost unit raises it by the same fixed percentage, in this case to 106.4VAC. That means that output voltage follows input voltage for line-boost units, with the resulting transients and current surges on the load side as the inverter kicks in and out. Most midrange and high-end PC SPS models are line-boost SPSs. The American Power Conversion (APC) Back-UPS Pro and Smart-UPS series, for example, are line-boost SPSs.

BPS characteristics

Here are the most important characteristics of a BPS:

Volt-Ampere (VA) rating

> The *VA rating* of a BPS specifies the maximum power the unit can supply, and is determined by the capacity of the inverter. VA rating is the product of nominal AC output voltage and the maximum amperage rating of the inverter. For example, a 120V 650VA unit can supply about 5.4A (650VA/120V). Connecting a load greater than the amperage rating of the inverter overloads the inverter, and soon destroys it, unless the BPS has current-limiting circuitry. Watts equal VA only for 100% resistive loads (for example, a light bulb). If the load includes capacitive or inductive components, as do PC power supplies, the draw in VA is equal to the wattage divided by the *Power Factor* (*PF*) of the load. Non-PFC PC power supplies typically have Power Factors of 0.65 to 0.7. For example, one of our SPSs is rated at 1000VA but only 670W, which means that the manufacturer assumes a PF of 0.67 when rating wattage for this unit.

Run time

> The run time of a BPS is determined by many factors, including battery type and condition, amp-hour capacity; state of charge; ambient temperature; inverter efficiency; and percentage load. Of those, percentage load is most variable. The number of amp-hours a battery can supply depends on how many amps you draw from it, which means that the relationship between load and run time is not linear. For example, a 600VA SPS may be able to supply 600VA for 5 minutes, but 300VA (half the load) for 20 minutes (four times longer). Doubling load cuts run time by much more than half; halving load extends run time by much more than twice.

VA RATING VERSUS RUN TIME

Many people believe VA rating and run time are somehow related. They're not, except that units with larger VA ratings typically also have a larger battery, which provides longer run time for a given load, both because the battery itself is larger and because the unit is supplying fewer amps than its rated maximum. It is, however, quite possible to build a BPS with a very high VA rating and a tiny battery or vice versa.

Output waveform

Utility AC voltage is nominally a pure sine waveform, which is what power supplies and other equipment are designed to use. The output waveform generated by BPSs varies. In order of increasing desirability (and price), output waveforms include: *square wave, sawtooth wave, modified square wave* (often somewhat deceptively called *near sine wave, stepped approximation to sine wave, modified sine wave,* or *stepped sine wave*—marketers are desperate to get the words "sine wave" in there, especially for units that don't deserve it). The cheapest units generate square wave output, which is essentially bipolar DC voltage with near-zero rise time and fall time, which allows it to masquerade as AC. Midrange units normally provide pseudo–sine wave output, which may be anything from a very close approximation to a sine wave to something not much better than an unmodified square wave. The output waveform is determined by the inverter. The inverter is the most expensive component of a BPS. Better inverters—those that generate a sine wave or a close approximation—are more expensive, so the quality of the output waveform generally correlates closely to unit price. Astonishingly, we once saw specifications for a no-name BPS that listed output waveform as "pure square wave," presumably intending to confound buyers with "pure" (a Good Thing) and "square wave" (a Bad Thing).

BE CAREFUL USING A SURGE SUPPRESSOR WITH AN SPS

We have heard reports of fires caused by connecting a surge suppressor between the BPS and the PC. Although we have not been able to verify the reports, it makes sense that feeding square wave power to a surge suppressor designed to accept sine wave input could cause it to overheat. On the other hand, there is nothing wrong with using a surge suppressor between the BPS and the wall receptacle. In fact, we recommend it, both to provide increased protection against spikes reaching the PC and to protect the BPS itself.

Choosing a BPS

Use the following guidelines when choosing a BPS:

Select BPS type according to your needs and budget.

Nowadays, you can buy $40 BPSs at big-box stores. They're not very good BPSs, true, but they're better than nothing. When new, a cheap BPS may give you only a minute or two of run time; as the battery ages, the run time may drop to only a few seconds. Still, the vast majority of power outages last for one second or less, so even a five-second run time provides some protection.

The next step up is a consumer-grade SPS, such as one of the APC Back-UPS or Back-UPS Pro units. These units provide much better protection and much longer run times than the low-end units. We consider these units to be the minimum for "serious" power protection, and use them on some of our secondary systems. Better still are the line-boost units, such as the APC Smart-UPS and the Falcon Electric (*http://www.falconups.com*) SMP and SUP series, which we consider the minimum acceptable for important systems. Finally, there are the true UPSs, such as the Falcon Electric SG and SSG series units, which we use on servers and primary desktop systems.

PROTECT YOUR BPS

Whether you buy a $40 cheapie or a $1,000 online UPS, don't use it by itself. Always put a surge protector between the wall receptacle and the BPS. The $40 unit doesn't provide much protection against spikes and surges, so the surge protector is needed to protect your equipment. The $1,000 UPS does a wonderful job of protecting your computer, but deserves protection of its own. If a huge spike or surge comes down the wire, it's much better to buy a new $50 surge protector than a new $1,000 UPS.

Pick a unit with adequate VA and run time.

You can calculate VA requirements by checking the maximum amperage listed on the PC power supply and on each other component the UPS will power. Total these maximum amperages and multiply by the nominal AC voltage to determine VA requirements. The problems with this method are that it is time-consuming and results in a much higher VA than you actually need. A better method is to use one of the sizing tools that most BPS makers provide on their web sites. For example, the APC UPS Selector (*http://www.apc.com/sizing/selectors.cfm*) allows you to specify your system configuration, the run time you need, and an allowance for growth. From that information, it returns a list of suitable APC models, with the estimated run times for each.

Consider buying one BPS for multiple PCs.

If you need to protect multiple PCs in close proximity, consider buying one larger unit rather than several inexpensive smaller units.

The larger unit will probably cost less for the same cumulative VA and run time, and will likely provide superior features (such as line-boost and a better waveform).

Get the best waveform you can afford.

The very cheapest units provide square wave output, which PC power supplies can use for short periods without damage. However, running a computer on square wave power for extended periods stresses the power supply and may eventually damage it. Also, square wave units are entirely unsuitable for other electronic devices, which they can quickly damage. Buy a square wave unit only if the alternative is not being able to afford a BPS at all. For general use, buy a unit that provides simulated sine wave if you expect to run the PC for 10 minutes or less on backup power before shutting it down. Buy a true sine wave unit if you expect to run the PC for extended periods on backup power, or if you also plan to power equipment that is intolerant of pseudo–sine wave power (such as some displays).

So, what do we actually use? For years, we used and recommended APC units exclusively. Then one of our APC Smart-UPS units failed prematurely. We wrote that off to bad luck. Then, a couple months later, a Back-UPS Pro failed. Then a Back-UPS. Then another Smart-UPS. These weren't battery failures, either, which we expect with any UPS. These were failures of the inverters or control circuitry, and all but one of the failed units was two years old or less.

Obviously, four failures isn't a statistical universe, even among the limited number of units we run, but it did give us pause. Then we began hearing from readers whose experiences were similar to our own. Like us, they'd used APC units for many years with no problems, and, like us, they'd recently begun experiencing a higher rate of premature failures with their newer APC units. Obviously, even that didn't prove anything, but we became very concerned.

Then one day we were talking to our friend and colleague, Jerry Pournelle, who for more than 20 years has written the *BYTE* "Chaos Manor" column. We told him of our concern with failure rates on the APC units. "Talk to Falcon Electric," said Jerry, "I've been using their UPSs for years. They're bulletproof. One of mine even got knocked over by an earthquake and never missed a beat."

We took Jerry at his word and ordered some Falcon Electric (*http:// www.falconups.com*) units. After researching and testing them, we decided Jerry was right. Falcon Electric makes the best UPSs available, so we've standardized on them. Falcon's customer list is heavily skewed towards military, industrial, telecommunications, and medical organizations, which was no small factor in our decision. Those folks need rock-solid reliable power protection, and what's good enough for NATO, Lucent, and General Atomics is good enough for us.

Robert uses the Falcon Electric 2 kVA SG-series UPS Plus shown in Figure 16-18 to protect his entire office—servers and desktop systems. These units resemble a standard mini-tower PC (including the cooling fans). The unit on the bottom—you might have already guessed—is an external battery bank that extends run time long enough to outlast about 95% of the power outages we're likely to suffer. Barbara uses a similar Falcon Electric online UPS in her office, and we run most of our secondary systems on Falcon Electric SMP and SUP series line-boost units. We've been through dozens of thunderstorms and several power outages since we converted to Falcon Electric units, and have never had the slightest glitch.

Figure 16-18. A Falcon Electric SG Series 2 kVA online UPS with external battery bank

Index

About the Authors

Robert Bruce Thompson is the author or coauthor of numerous online training courses and computer books. Robert built his first computer in 1976 from discrete chips. It had 256 *bytes* of memory, used toggle switches and LEDs for I/O, ran at less than 1 MHz, and had no operating system. Since then, he has bought, built, upgraded, and repaired hundreds of PCs for himself, employers, customers, friends, and clients. Robert reads mysteries and nonfiction for relaxation, but only on cloudy nights. He spends most clear, moonless nights outdoors with his 10" Dobsonian reflector telescope, hunting down faint fuzzies, and is currently designing a larger truss-tube Dobsonian (computerized, of course) that he plans to build.

Barbara Fritchman Thompson worked for 20 years as a librarian before starting her own home-based consulting practice, Research Solutions (*http://www.researchsolutions.net*), and is also a researcher for the law firm Womble Carlyle Sandridge & Rice, PLLC. Barbara, who has been a PC power user for more than 15 years, researched and tested much of the hardware reviewed for this book. During her leisure hours, Barbara reads, works out, plays golf, and, like Robert, is an avid amateur astronomer.

Colophon

Our look is the result of reader comments, our own experimentation, and feedback from distribution channels. Distinctive covers complement our distinctive approach to technical topics, breathing personality and life into potentially dry subjects.

The cover image is a photograph by Marcia Friedman. The text and heading fonts are Linotype Birka and Adobe Formata Condensed, and the code font is TheSans Mono Condensed from LucasFont.

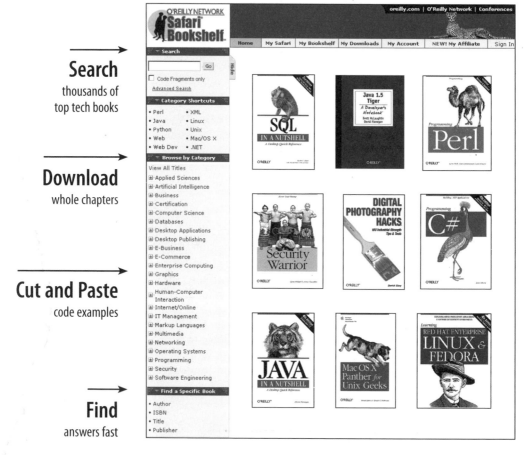